About Island Press

Since 1984, the nonprofit organization Island Press has been stimulating, shaping, and communicating ideas that are essential for solving environmental problems worldwide. With more than 1,000 titles in print and some 30 new releases each year, we are the nation's leading publisher on environmental issues. We identify innovative thinkers and emerging trends in the environmental field. We work with world-renowned experts and authors to develop cross-disciplinary solutions to environmental challenges.

Island Press designs and executes educational campaigns, in conjunction with our authors, to communicate their critical messages in print, in person, and online using the latest technologies, innovative programs, and the media. Our goal is to reach targeted audiences—scientists, policy makers, environmental advocates, urban planners, the media, and concerned citizens—with information that can be used to create the framework for long-term ecological health and human well-being.

Island Press gratefully acknowledges major support from The Bobolink Foundation, Caldera Foundation, The Curtis and Edith Munson Foundation, The Forrest C. and Frances H. Lattner Foundation, The JPB Foundation, The Kresge Foundation, The Summit Charitable Foundation, Inc., and many other generous organizations and individuals.

The opinions expressed in this book are those of the author(s) and do not necessarily reflect the views of our supporters.

Waters of the United States

Waters of the United States

POTUS, SCOTUS, WOTUS, AND THE POLITICS OF A NATIONAL RESOURCE

Royal C. Gardner

ISLANDPRESS | Washington | Covelo

Design and Typesetting by 2K/DENMARK.

Sustainable Typesetting® ID: ST49535052-24-A01
The ID number certifies that this book fulfills the standards and recommendations of Sustainable Typesetting® providing reduced CO_2 emissions.

Library of Congress Control Number: 2024935680

All Island Press books are printed on environmentally responsible materials.

Manufactured in the United States of America
10 9 8 7 6 5 4 3 2 1

Keywords: The 1948 Federal Water Pollution Control Act, *Chevron* deference doctrine (the *Chevron* rule), Clean Water Act, Clean Water Rule, Coastal Zone Management Act, commerce clause, *County of Maui v. Hawaii Wildlife Fund,* downstream effects, Federal Water Pollution Control Act, Federal Water Power Act, *Gibbons v. Ogden,* intermittent streams, interstate waters, jurisdictional waters, *National Association of Manufacturers v. Department of Defense,* National Pollutant Discharge Elimination System (NPDES) permit (402 permit), navigable waters, Navigable Waters Protection Rule, *New Hope Power Company v. U.S. Army Corps of Engineers, Pascua Yaqui Tribe v. U.S. Environmental Protection Agency,* point and nonpoint source pollution, *Rapanos v. United States,* Refuse Act, Rivers and Harbors Appropriations Acts, *Sackett v. U.S. Environmental Protection Agency, S.D. Warren Co. v. Maine Board of Environmental Protection,* Solid Waste Agency of Northern Cook County, *United States v. Riverside Bayview Homes,* US Environmental Protection Agency (EPA), water pollution, water quality, Water Quality Improvement Act of 1970, wetland restoration, wetlands, *Willson v. Black Bird Creek Marsh Company*

For Mary Celine
with love

Contents

Introduction

Ken Guckenberger grew up in St. Petersburg, Florida, long before it was known for its world-class museums and craft breweries.[1] His family lived adjacent to Coffee Pot Bayou, an inlet connected to Tampa Bay. In the mid-1970s, the water of Coffee Pot Bayou could only be described as fetid. He recalls that the daily afternoon discharges from the downtown sewage treatment plant were particularly rough on the nearshore waters. Dolphins and manatees were not to be seen.

In March 1991, when home on a school break, Ken saw something for the first time: a school of dolphins playing off his backyard dock. In subsequent years, seagrass rebounded in Tampa Bay, and manatees began to regularly appear in Coffee Pot Bayou. The roseate spoonbill, once thought extinct in Florida outside the Everglades, graced the area with its presence. In 2018, Ken and his daughter witnessed a mullet run, a frenzy that he likened to the wildebeest migration in Africa, as thousands of fish headed to their spawning ground. He had never seen that many fish concentrated in Coffee Pot Bayou.

What accounted for the improvement in water quality over five decades? It was a concerted effort on the part of concerned citizens and federal, state, and local government officials. At the heart of the improvement is the Clean Water Act, enacted by Congress over President Nixon's veto in 1972. And at the heart of the Clean Water Act is the term "waters of the United States."[2]

If a waterbody is considered "waters of the United States," then the protections of the Clean Water Act apply. If the waterbody is not "waters of the United States," then the decision of whether and to what extent to provide legal protections is largely left to the states. Tampa Bay and Coffee Pot Bayou, which are traditionally navigable waters, fall easily under the umbrella of "waters of the United States." Whether other waters, such as nonnavigable tributaries and wetlands, should be afforded similar status has been hotly debated.

Yet the need to protect streams and wetlands is uncontroversial from a scientific perspective. Ensuring water quality in larger waterbodies requires regulating pollution in smaller upstream waters. Dr. Mažeika Sulliván, director of the Belle W. Baruch Institute of Coastal Ecology and Forest Science at Clemson University, analogizes streams and wetlands to capillaries, which play critical roles in the human body.[3] Healthy people need healthy arteries, which rely in part on healthy veins and capillaries. Likewise, on the landscape, the health of rivers and bays depends on the health of streams and wetlands. The loss and degradation of streams and wetlands have a cascading effect on the larger ecosystem, with the public losing the benefits that these water resources provide.

The story of the Clean Water Act is not necessarily one of linear progress, always on an upward trajectory. For example, in 2021 the state of Florida authorized the emergency discharge of phosphate mining wastewater to Tampa Bay. Over the course of ten days, Tampa Bay received approximately 205 tons of total nitrogen, which exceeded the waterbody's typical annual nitrogen load.[4] The discharge exacerbated an outbreak of red tide, a naturally occurring harmful algal bloom, leading to fish kills totaling more than 3.5 million pounds.[5] Floating front-end loaders were used to remove tons of dead, rotting fish from Tampa Bay and Coffee Pot Bayou. But Coffee Pot Bayou is thriving again, although seagrass coverage in Tampa Bay has declined.[6] Nature is resilient, and if given a chance, the aquatic ecosystem can recover.

In May 2023, however, the US Supreme Court issued an opinion that struck at the heart of the Clean Water Act. In *Sackett v. U.S. Environmental Protection Agency*, the Court interpreted "waters of the United States" in a most restrictive manner, removing millions of miles of streams and millions of acres of wetlands from federal protection.[7] How we arrived at this juncture, where five members of the Court have effectively gutted a key provision of the Clean Water Act, and what can be done in response, is a complicated story of politics, history, and law—and acronyms.

CHAPTER 1

As Iowa Goes, So Goes the Nation

> Nothing galled [one Iowa farmer] more than a regulation Obama issued in 2015. . . . WOTUS felt like the government's hands on her throat.
>
> —*The Washington Post*, December 29, 2017

In Washington and elsewhere, *POTUS* is the well-known acronym for "President of the United States." Telegraph operators were early adopters of POTUS, using it in the 1890s.[1] POTUS was patterned after the acronym *SCOTUS*—for "Supreme Court of the United States"—which telegraph operators had been using for two decades previously.[2] Although opportunities for telegraphists waned with the advent of new technology, the use of POTUS and SCOTUS lives on in print, social media, and common parlance. The official Twitter account for the President of the United States, launched by President Obama in 2015, is @POTUS, and SCOTUSblog is an excellent source for news and analysis of the Supreme Court. The actions and decisions of POTUS and SCOTUS are often controversial, arousing passionate and partisan responses. Though more obscure, WOTUS evokes intense feelings as well.

WOTUS refers to "waters of the United States," a statutory term that is at the center of the Clean Water Act, landmark environmental legislation enacted by Congress in 1972.[3] Depending on your perspective, WOTUS includes parts of the ocean, navigable rivers and streams, lakes and ponds, nonnavigable tributaries, and wetlands—and, under some circumstances, agricultural fields. WOTUS as an acronym seemed to make its first appearance in the 2000s. A 2002 draft environmental impact statement submitted to the US Department of Transportation contained the phrase "Riverine WOTUS."[4] The first entry for WOTUS in the *Federal Register* was in a 2008 rule issued by the Surface Mining Reclamation and Enforcement Office,[5] and it was first invoked in a judicial opinion (unpublished) in 2015 by the US District Court for the Southern District of Georgia.[6] (Earlier WOTUS references unconnected to the Clean Water Act include Ron Wotus, an infielder for the Pittsburgh Pirates in the 1980s and later a coach for the San Francisco Giants, not to be confused with John Wetteland, who was a relief pitcher for the New York Yankees, Texas Rangers, and others.)

As a general matter, if a water—such as a river, stream, lake, pond, or wetland—is considered a WOTUS, then it is protected by the Clean Water Act. If a body of water is not a WOTUS, then it is not federally protected. Federal protection for a WOTUS does not mean that the water is off limits to pollution and must remain pristine and inviolable. Rather, if a water is WOTUS, then anyone who wants to discharge pollutants (broadly defined) must obtain a federal permit before doing so.[7] In fact, the federal government (and state agencies with delegated authority) issues thousands of Clean Water Act permits each year,[8] authorizing the discharge of about 200 million pounds of toxic substances directly into "protected" waters, and has approved the elimination of tens of thousands of acres of wetlands and hundreds of miles of streams through filling.[9] However, the federal permit process can be daunting, hence the farmer's strangulation metaphor.[10]

The debate over WOTUS and the Clean Water Act is about relationships, partly ecological but mostly political. From an ecological perspective, waters are interconnected, from "ridge to reef."[11] Headwater streams flow into higher-order streams, some of which are classified as rivers. Wetlands, such as marshes, swamps, and bogs, have surface and groundwater connections to these waters. Riparian and floodplain wetlands flow to and from a river network, whereas nonfloodplain wetlands have a unidirectional, lateral flow to other waters.[12] Wetlands are sometimes referred to as nature's kidneys, because they can filter out contaminants before they reach other waters. Wetlands are also viewed as "ecological supermarkets" because they support a vast array of plants and animals.[13] Many migratory bird species depend on wetland habitat, and most commercial and recreational seafood species spend some portion of their life cycle in wetland and estuarine habitats.[14] Hunters and fishers are often ardent supporters of wetland and stream conservation.[15]

What occurs upstream affects the quality of the water downstream. A single incident can have immediate and serious consequences. For example, in Florida in 2004, the dike of a phosphogypsum pond that contained the waste from a fertilizer plant breached, sending 65 million gallons of wastewater into Archie Creek, a stream that flowed into Hillsborough Bay, which is connected to Tampa Bay.[16] The spill killed or damaged 150 acres of mangroves and 22 acres of seagrass and disrupted the local fishery. The company was fined $270,000 by state and county agencies.[17] That money did not go to the commercial fishing operations, however, and they instituted their own lawsuit to recover economic damages. That litigation finally settled nearly twenty years after the spill, demonstrating that after-the-fact litigation may not be the most effective or efficient means of protecting the environment and livelihoods.

But the cumulative impact of many lesser actions can also have devastating impacts. Although nutrient-laden runoff from one agricultural field may not be a big deal, it is when multiplied a thousandfold. The fertilizer runoff from farms along the Mississippi River, from Minnesota on down, contributes to the dead zone in the Gulf of Mexico, an area where low oxygen levels preclude aquatic life.[18] Some years the dead zone is as large as New Jersey.[19] The draining of wetlands for agricultural purposes, which resulted in the loss of the pollution filtration services provided by those wetlands, only exacerbates the situation. Congress took all these connections into account when drafting the Clean Water Act, recognizing that "water moves in hydrologic cycles, and it is essential that discharge of pollutants be controlled at the source."[20]

Congress's authority is not unlimited, however. As a technical matter, when legislating Congress must rely on enumerated powers listed in the Constitution. As a practical matter, the Constitution's interstate commerce clause provides Congress a vehicle to legislate broadly, including to protect the environment. Congress relied on the interstate commerce clause when enacting the Clean Water Act.[21] Whether Congress (or the agencies) exceeded these constitutional limitations, impinging on state sovereignty, is a continuing subject of debate.

The Clean Water Act opens with a singular objective: to restore and maintain the chemical, physical, and biological integrity of the nation's waters.[22] One principal feature is that it prohibits the point source discharge of pollutants to navigable waters in the absence of a federal permit. Yet the Clean Water Act also recognizes that the states retain "primary responsibilities" to combat water pollution and to develop and use land and water resources.[23] The Clean Water Act envisions the federal government and the states collaborating together under the model of cooperative federalism. It has not always worked out that way.

No one seriously questions Congress's authority under the interstate commerce clause to regulate activities that affect navigable waters. The classic definition of *navigable waters* includes waters that are navigable in fact (currently used in interstate commerce), navigable in the past (once navigable, always navigable), and navigable in the future (susceptible for use in interstate commerce if reasonable improvements are made), as well as waters subject to the ebb and flow of the tide.[24] A river that supports (or once supported) barge traffic is a clear example of a traditional navigable water. But Congress did not use this traditional definition in the Clean Water Act. Instead, Congress intended to cover a broader expanse of the nation's waters. The Clean Water Act's legislative history indicates that its geographic scope should be asserted "to the maximum extent permissible under the Commerce Clause."[25] The statutory text is less illuminating. It rather unhelpfully defined navigable waters as "waters of the United States, including the territorial seas."[26] The precise parameters of the geographic jurisdiction of the Clean Water Act—that is, what is and what is not a WOTUS—was kicked to executive branch agencies (responsible to POTUS) and the judicial branch (with SCOTUS as the ultimate arbiter).

Over the years, the US Environmental Protection Agency (EPA) and the US Army Corps of Engineers (Corps), the two agencies responsible for administering the Clean Water Act, have issued regulations defining WOTUS, sometimes narrowly, sometimes expansively. Every revised WOTUS definition leads, almost reflexively, to legal challenges brought by environmental groups and the regulated community. *The regulated community* is a phrase that conjures up (in my mind at least) a collegial group of people, perhaps gathering for a social event to discuss matters of mutual interest. In reality, however, *the regulated community* is a polite term for polluters. The community consists of homebuilders, manufacturers, miners, foresters, ranchers, and farmers, all of whom produce necessary and useful things (including food!) that we depend on to survive and thrive, but they also produce pollution that may harm water quality. Not infrequently, a revised WOTUS regulation will draw fire from both sides, with the regulated community contending it is too broad and the environmental groups asserting it is too narrow. On occasion, Corps regulators have been known to say that they must have struck the proper balance if both sides are upset.

In 2015, during the Obama administration, the EPA and the Corps promulgated the Clean Water Rule,[27] a regulation that, depending on one's point of view, either helpfully clarified the definition of WOTUS, failed to encompass all waters that should be protected, or represented a massive federal land grab and an unconstitutional intrusion into the province of states—even a hand on the throat of property owners. The agricultural community was among the Clean Water Rule's most vocal opponents, pointing out that farm ditches could now be subject to federal oversight and creating a "Ditch the Rule" campaign.[28] The Missouri Farm Bureau's parody of "Let It Go," from the movie *Frozen*, was particularly entertaining.[29] And the farmers were not wrong: Under the Clean Water Rule some ditches could be classified as WOTUS.[30]

But one person's ditch can be another person's stream.[31] The label *ditch*, signifying a human-made channel, sometimes carries with it a value judgment. Consider the Erie Canal, which was completed in 1825, providing a waterway connecting the Atlantic Ocean to the Great Lakes. Critics of New York Governor DeWitt Clinton's project derided it as "Clinton's Big Ditch."[32] However, that ditch was used for the transport of interstate commerce and thus is a traditional navigable water, including the portions of the former uplands that were dug out.

Ditches on agricultural lands are not traditional navigable waters, of course. They are constructed primarily to drain fields (which may include wetlands) and collect runoff (which usually includes excess nutrients and pesticides). The former function results in the elimination of waters, which can affect downstream water quality; the latter also contributes to the degradation of downstream water quality. For example, Iowa, which has drained nearly 90 percent of its historic wetland base, has some of the worst water quality in the country.[33]

Nationwide, agriculture is a primary source of water pollution.[34] According to the Natural Resources Defense Council, the sector is the top contributor of water pollution in streams and rivers and number two in wetlands. It is the third greatest source of contaminants to lakes. Here's the (un)funny thing: Although the Clean Water Act regulates some agricultural operations (e.g., concentrated animal feeding operations), many farming activities are not covered. The Clean Water Act focuses on point source discharges of pollution, such as discrete conveyances from a pipe. Runoff from agricultural fields is nonpoint source pollution, which does not require a federal permit. Nonpoint source pollution is a matter left to the states.[35] The EPA and the Corps also declared, through a regulation, that "prior converted croplands"—areas that were once wetlands but that had been placed in agricultural production—did not fall under the definition of WOTUS.[36] Furthermore, Congress specifically provided that "normal" farming and ranching activities, "such as plowing, seeding, cultivating, minor drainage, [and] harvesting," do not need a Clean Water Act section 404 permit, which is required if one adds dredged or fill material to a WOTUS.[37] As professor

Dave Owen put it, "Farmers could continue farming lands that once were streams or wetlands, even if those lands continued to flood. They also could continue to discharge large amounts of pollutants into wetlands, streams, lakes, and rivers."[38]

If the Clean Water Act generally left farmers alone, what accounted for the agricultural community's visceral reaction to the Obama administration's Clean Water Rule? Although the scope of WOTUS was slightly increased (as will be discussed in more depth later), the existing exemption for prior converted croplands remained intact. The 2015 regulation did not expand coverage over agricultural runoff, nor could it affect the statutory exemption for normal farming and ranching activities.

Some of the antipathy might be explained by a concern that, if one day a farmer wanted to cease operations and sell to a developer, then the Clean Water Act might apply at that point, thus decreasing the land's value or at least slowing down the deal. Some may have objected out of a concern that the Clean Water Rule was but a first step to greater and more intrusive federal regulation. But much of the concern probably flowed from hostility toward federal regulation in general.

As a presidential candidate in 2016, Donald Trump tapped into the agricultural community's suspicion of the federal bureaucracy. His antiregulatory theme included attacks on the Obama administration's Clean Water Rule—which he called a "horrible rule," promising to jettison it in his first day in office.[39] This message resonated with farmers (and other members of the regulated community). As *The Washington Post* reported, one farmer believed that the WOTUS issue "won him [Trump] Iowa," a state that Barack Obama carried in 2008 and 2012.[40]

Did WOTUS flip Iowa and help elect Donald Trump POTUS? Obviously, there were much bigger issues at the heart of the campaign—such as the future appointments of justices to SCOTUS. But the WOTUS issue, lurking in the background, influenced some voters. The Iowa Farm Bureau Federation cheered the state of Iowa's intervention in a lawsuit challenging the Clean Water Rule,[41] and the chair of the Iowa Corn Growers Association voted for Trump in part because of the concern about the impact of WOTUS on agricultural operations.[42] And it is interesting to examine the 2016 Electoral College map with the position of states in recent major Clean Water Act rulemakings and cases (Figures 1-1 and 1-2). The alignment is striking: In general, states that have advocated a more narrow view of the Clean Water Act went for Trump, and states that backed a broader Clean Water Act favored Hillary Clinton.[43]

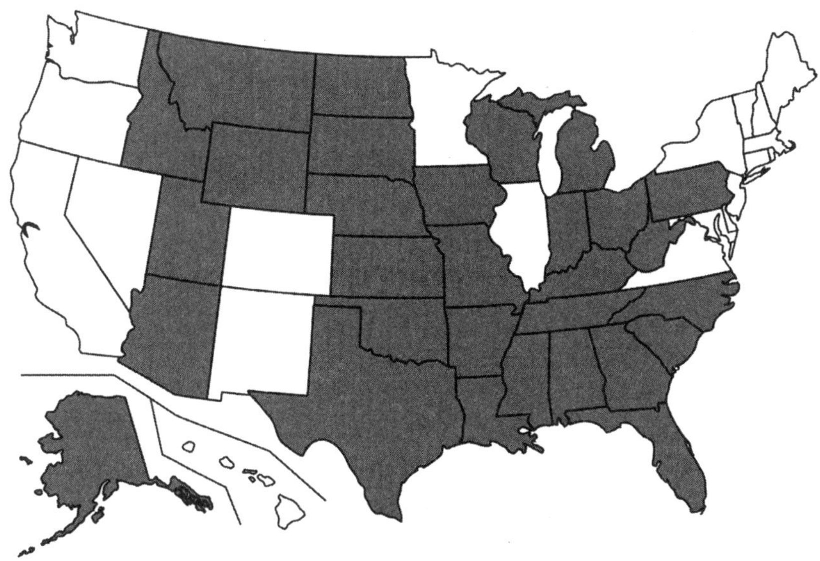

Figure 1-1. The 2016 Electoral College map, with gray indicating states won by Trump and white indicating states won by Clinton. Source: RealClearPolitics.

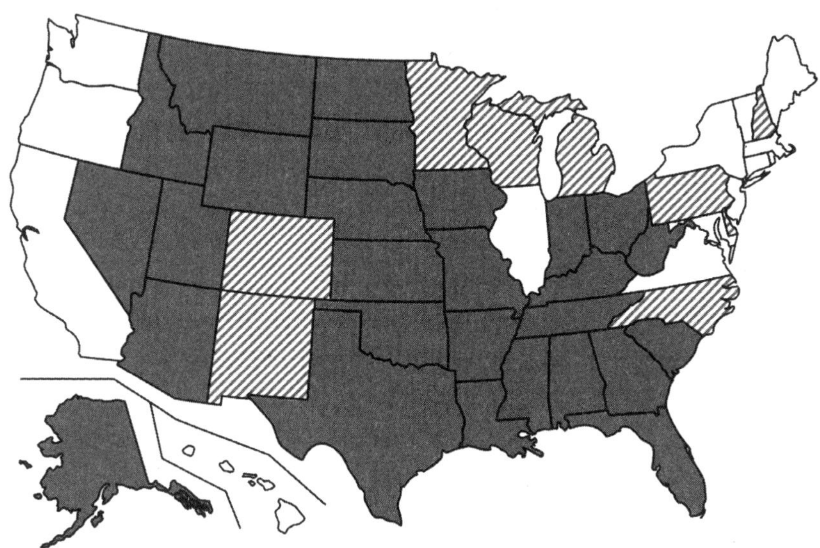

Figure 1-2. State views of the Clean Water Act, based on their positions regarding the Clean Water Rule (CWR, Obama WOTUS regulation) and the Navigable Waters Protection Rule (NWPR, Trump WOTUS regulation). Gray indicates states opposing the CWR or favoring the NWPR, and white indicates states favoring the CWR or opposing the NWPR. Gray and white stripes indicate that a state opposed both the CWR and the NWPR or took no position. See Table A-1 in the Appendix for specific details.

Five swing states that opposed the Obama administration's Clean Water Rule later argued that the Trump administration's approach went too far: Colorado, Michigan, New Mexico, North Carolina, and Wisconsin. Of those five, all went for Joe Biden in 2020, except for North Carolina.

As President Obama once observed, "Elections have consequences."[44] Just a little more than one month after he was inaugurated in 2017, President Trump signed an executive order that began the process to repeal and replace the Obama administration's Clean Water Rule.[45] Later, during a trip to Iowa, President Trump recalled the Oval Office signing ceremony:

> And I signed that, and behind me I had homebuilders and farmers mostly, and ranchers. And many of them never cried in their life, including when they born, and they were crying.... They were crying behind me.... They were crying because we gave them back their land. We took it away. It was like eminent domain. It was terrible. We gave it back.[46]

Video of the event demonstrated a lack of lachrymose attendees: No one in the crowd was crying, although the homebuilders, farmers, and ranchers were clearly happy.[47] The only tears shed over the executive order might have been the tears of anger or anguish of environmental advocates.

Proponents of a limited definition of WOTUS are quick to point out that a non-WOTUS can be protected by the states. Yet that defense tends to overlook history, current practice, and political realities. The failure of the states to protect water quality was what spurred Congress to pass the Clean Water Act in the first place. The Clean Water Act established a national baseline of protection, and states could regulate more strictly if they wanted. Most did not, and many states simply relied, at least in part, on the federal agencies to protect water quality in their jurisdictions. Moreover, on occasions when the definition of WOTUS has contracted (such as when SCOTUS ruled that isolated ponds and wetlands were not WOTUS), states did not readily fill the gap, which requires state legislative action and state appropriations—and time. It took California more than ten years to fully respond to one SCOTUS decision.[48] It also requires political will, and in the red states there is little appetite to create or expand (and fund) regulatory programs.

WOTUS was not the only front of the Trump administration's attacks on the Clean Water Act. It wanted to deregulate discharges to groundwater that flowed to surface waters. It sought to make it easier for states to assume federal responsibilities over wetlands and streams where states were prodevelopment but made it more difficult for states to deny water quality certifications to halt pipeline projects. It backed off enforcement efforts and limited the ability of the EPA to veto harmful projects. In some cases, the Trump administration was successful in its efforts, but in other cases it was stymied by environmental groups and its own inability to understand the niceties of administrative law.[49]

The Clean Water Act and WOTUS make for a fascinating case study of the relationship (and tensions) between the federal and state governments. The Clean Water Act also implicates separation-of-powers questions fundamental to our system of government: To what extent can Congress delegate lawmaking authority to executive branch agencies? Can the president rule by decree through executive orders? How may executive branch agencies properly exercise their authority? What is the role of the judiciary when reviewing the actions of Congress and executive branch agencies? Ultimately, which branch gets to say what the "law" is?

Not surprisingly, the answers are complex. But to understand the full context of the Trump administration's actions, which ultimately led to a Supreme Court decision that drastically reduced Clean Water Act protections across the country—and to craft effective responses to achieve the objective of restoring and maintaining the quality of the nation's waters—one must have a working understanding of our constitutional system.

CHAPTER 2

The (Shifting) Rules of the Game

> All legislative Powers herein granted shall be vested
> in a Congress of the United States.
> The executive Power shall be vested in a President of
> the United States of America.
> The judicial Power of the United States, shall be vested
> in one supreme Court.
>
> —US Constitution, Articles I, II, and III

Aficionados of *Schoolhouse Rock* no doubt recall fondly "I'm Just a Bill," which explained the legislative process to children. It covered how a bill is considered in congressional committees, and if voted on affirmatively by both the US House of Representatives and the US Senate, it goes to the president to sign. If the president signs the bill, it becomes law. If the president vetoes the bill, Congress has an opportunity to override the veto with a two-thirds vote in both chambers. Although *Schoolhouse Rock* is a bit vague on the details of overriding a veto, it nonetheless notes that such an outcome is "very unlikely." The lesson concludes with the bill receiving the good news: "He's signed you, Bill. Now you're a law!" Although people of a certain age can recite from memory the refrain of "I'm Just a Bill," few can recall the subject of the bill sitting on Capitol Hill. It was a federal requirement that all school buses must stop at railroad crossings.

In real life, Congress has done no such thing. Instead, the operation of school buses, including whether they need to stop at railroad crossings, is largely left to the states.[1] In creating a fictional scenario where Congress cared enough about the safety of schoolchildren to pass legislation, *Schoolhouse Rock* missed an opportunity to introduce youngsters to the concept of federalism. *Schoolhouse Rock* also (understandably) declined to explore what often happens after a bill is enacted and executive branch agencies issue regulations that interpret or fill in the gaps of the statute. Also avoided was the quagmire of judicial review of legislative and executive branch actions (Figure 2-1).

Figure 2-1. The classic explanation of the legislative process. Source: © ABC Photo Archives.

The Constitution does not provide clear answers about the scope of legislative, executive, and judicial power with respect to school buses or any other matter, including water quality. The Supreme Court, however, has developed various tests and rules and principles to resolve federal–state and interbranch disputes. During his Senate confirmation hearing to become chief justice, John Roberts famously described the judiciary's role as being limited "to call balls and strikes, and not to pitch or bat,"[2] but the Court has been known to change the strike zone, sometimes dramatically, which has affected the outcome of many cases. Let's explore some key general concepts of our system of government, which are relevant to environmental protection, and consider how they have changed over time.

The President Is Not a King

Rejection of the monarchy was one of the main points of the American Revolution. Check out the Declaration of Independence: It is a long list of grievances—"repeated injuries and usurpations"—attributable to the king of Great Britain, who is characterized as a tyrant.[3] Instead of a king who is "absolute master of his own conduct in the exercise of his office,"[4] we have a president whose powers are checked by the other branches of government. As now-Justice Ketanji Brown Jackson observed, "the primary takeaway from the past 250 years of recorded American history is that Presidents are not kings."[5] This maxim has been invoked in a variety of settings. At one level, it means that no person is above the law. The law applies to the president personally, and the office of the presidency does not provide the occupant, or former occupant, with wholesale immunity from civil and criminal liability.[6] In addition, as *Schoolhouse Rock* implies, the nonmonarchical status of presidents also means that they cannot simply rule by decree. A law requires the assent of Congress.

But what about executive orders? What is their legal status? Presidents since Washington have issued executive orders.[7] Presidents have also long been criticized for their use of these seemingly unilateral actions, which some see as an unconstitutional mechanism to bypass Congress. The legitimacy of any particular executive order depends on whether the president is acting pursuant to authority granted by the Constitution or by Congress (through a statute). When President Truman ordered the desegregation of the military in 1948, he was acting as the commander in chief of the armed forces, a role the Constitution assigns to the president.[8] Yet even that authority is not unlimited, as Truman discovered when, during the Korean War, he directed the secretary of commerce to seize and operate steel mills to ensure that a labor dispute did not disrupt production for the war effort. The Supreme Court rejected this use of an executive order, emphasizing that "the framework of our Constitution . . . refutes the idea that [the president] is to be a lawmaker."[9] Because Congress had not authorized the seizures, the president could not do it by fiat.[10]

Often an executive order tells an agency how to exercise its discretion. For example, in 1977, Jimmy Carter issued Executive Order 11990 on Protection of Wetlands.[11] It called on agencies to minimize wetland loss and degradation when carrying out their responsibilities, such as avoiding the placement of new federally financed construction projects in wetlands. Or a president might create a task force or committee to report on and develop strategies to respond to a specific problem, as President Obama did in 2009 with Executive Order 13508 on Chesapeake Bay Protection and Restoration.[12] One part of the order directed the secretary of agriculture to focus the agency's "working lands and land retirement programs within priority watersheds in counties in the Chesapeake Bay watershed . . . [and to] apply priority conservation practices that most efficiently reduce nutrient and sediment loads to the Chesapeake Bay."[13] Like most executive orders, however, Executive Order 13508 was careful to note that it was not expanding any agency's statutory authority, because that would require Congress's involvement. The executive orders also typically make clear that they do not create legally enforceable rights. The standard boilerplate for executive orders includes this disclaimer:

> This order is not intended to, and does not, create any right or benefit, substantive or procedural, enforceable at law or in equity, by any party against the United States, its departments, agencies, or entities, its officers, employees, or agents, or any other person.[14]

Accordingly, courts have uniformly rejected attempts to enforce the provisions of an executive order.[15] Although the orders are legally relevant (by informing the public about how an agency is expected to exercise its authority), they are not, by themselves, legally binding. Executive orders (in the nonmilitary context) are not "law" like statutes or regulations.

Nondelegation: The Search for Intelligible Life

The Constitution vests Congress with "all legislative Powers." Obviously, Congress exercises those powers when it approves a bill. But may Congress share that power with the executive branch? May Congress delegate this law-making authority to agencies, or would that run afoul of the Constitution's pronouncement that Congress has all the legislative powers? One concern about delegation is that Congress may be abdicating its responsibilities and that unelected bureaucrats are exercising legislative power when they issue rules that the regulated community must follow.

Congress has delegated decision-making authority to the executive branch since the founding, and the Supreme Court has generally approved, so long as Congress provided some parameters. But on rare occasions the Court has struck down a law that grants the executive branch too much discretion. It last did so in 1935, in *Schechter Poultry Corporation v. United States*, striking down a statute that gave an agency the power to prescribe "codes of fair competition" for various industries.[16] Congress cannot simply say to the executive branch, "You write the rules as you deem fit."

Over the years, this "nondelegation doctrine" has been reduced to a simple phrase: an intelligible principle.[17] That is, Congress may give an agency the authority to issue legally binding regulations if it also articulates an intelligible principle for the agency to follow. Note that "intelligible" does not mean "intelligent." Rather, the principle or parameters or guideposts must be comprehensible or able to be understood. Thus, when Congress in the Clean Air Act authorized the EPA to set air quality standards "requisite to protect the public health," the Court concluded that this limiting principle was clear and that no delegation of legislative power had occurred.[18] In the Court's view, "requisite" meant "sufficient, but not more than necessary," and this somehow sufficiently constrained EPA's discretion when it determined the acceptable level of ozone in parts per million.[19]

Do not worry if you are confused, for you are not alone. To say that the EPA is not exercising legislative power when it issues a regulation (also known as legislative rule) is a legal fiction. To maintain the façade of a strict separation of powers between the branches, the Court is pretending that Congress did not delegate *any* legislative power. It would be more intellectually honest, as Justice Stevens suggested in a concurring opinion in the Clean Air Act case, to say that Congress can delegate legislative power, so long as that power is "adequately limited by the terms of the authorizing statute."[20]

But the Court is poised to go in a different direction that could upend decades of precedent. In 2019, the Court considered the constitutionality of the Sex Offender Notification and Registration Act (SONRA), which allowed the attorney general to decide whether sex offenders who were convicted before the law's enactment needed to register with the state where they live.[21] At the time, the Court consisted of only eight justices, as Justice Kennedy had stepped down and Justice Kavanaugh had yet to be confirmed. Four justices, led by Justice Kagan, voted to uphold SONRA, finding that Congress had laid down intelligible principles for the attorney general to follow. She noted that "if SONRA's delegation is unconstitutional, then most of Government is unconstitutional."[22] Three justices, led by Justice Gorsuch, voted to strike down the law on nondelegation grounds, stating that "the Constitution promises that only the people's elected representatives may adopt new federal laws restricting liberty."[23] And in a very odd concurring opinion, Justice Alito voted in favor of the law but declared he would support an effort to reexamine the nondelegation doctrine. However, "because a majority is not willing to do that, it would be freakish to single out the provision at issue for special treatment."[24] In other words, Justice Alito did not find a sex offender to be a sufficiently attractive party to reinvigorate the nondelegation doctrine. Bring me a more sympathetic defendant (perhaps a member of the regulated community), he seemed to suggest, and I will dismantle the administrative state.

In Defense of the Administrative State

Proponents of a stronger nondelegation doctrine assert we need to return to first principles: The Framers intended that the legislative power reside with the branch that has the most political accountability.[25] In their view, the administrative state—primarily executive branch agencies—is an affront to the Constitution's separation of powers. These "headless" agencies are staffed by unelected bureaucrats who issue ukases that burden the American people (and businesses). Congress's fecklessness shifts responsibility to the agencies to make the "hard choices," thereby undermining the fundamental connection between the people and their elected representatives, ultimately threatening our liberty. Let me offer a contrary view.

Certainly, the Framers never envisioned the growth of executive branch agencies and their thousands of pages of regulations. But the Framers also did not envision the automobile, genetically modified food, or credit default swaps. Daily life is infinitely more complex than it was in the late eighteenth century, and a principal role of government is to provide for public safety. It is unrealistic to expect that individual members of Congress can make informed decisions about technical matters regarding environmental protection. Should Congress have to expressly decide how many parts per million of ozone is acceptable for human health? Should Congress have to vote on every species to be protected by the Endangered Species Act? Should Congress have to identify which individual streams and wetlands are protected by the Clean Water Act? While Congress may be passing the buck to regulatory agencies to make hard decisions, Congress is also empowering the subject matter experts to act. "Bureaucrat" is often a pejorative term, but agency staffers (especially in the environmental field) are specialists. Congress should be able to articulate general goals or principles and rely on these subject matter experts and specialists to make technical decisions informed by science.

Moreover, the agencies are not headless; they are subject to numerous political checks. Agencies are run by political appointees who are nominated by the president and confirmed by the Senate. The EPA's administrator, deputy administrator, and assistant administrators (e.g., the assistant administrator for the Office of Water) are all political appointees. They set the overall policy direction of the agency (within limits prescribed by Congress). Dick Cheney understood how government worked, and as vice president he made sure he had the lead on nominations at the deputy and assistant administrator or secretary level.[26] Thus, any time an agency issues a regulation—which may have the force of law—the regulation must be approved by the agency's political appointees.[27] In addition, all regulations are reviewed by the Office of Management and Budget (OMB) to ensure that they are consistent with the president's philosophy. And OMB is led by—you guessed it—political appointees.

Congress has also dictated the general process by which agencies may promulgate rules, through the Administrative Procedure Act.[28] A proposed regulation (after it is approved by political appointees within the agency and at OMB) is published for public notice and comment in the *Federal Register*, which is the official journal of the federal government. The notice of the proposed regulation typically contains the statutory authority for the rule, the reason for the rule, and the proposed text of the rule. The public, from the regulated community to environmental groups to literally anyone, is then usually given the opportunity to provide comments. (Bots have become a problem.[29]) Some noncontroversial proposed rules yield only a few comments, whereas others generate more than a million responses. The agency then must consider those comments when preparing the final rule. Note that the rulemaking process is not a plebiscite. The agency is not bound to follow the majority of the comments. The agency can adopt a rule that the public (at least through its comments) detests.

But doesn't this suggest that agencies are not politically accountable? No, because after the agency considers the public comments and drafts a final rule, the political appointees at the agency and OMB must sign off on the final rule. No rule of any consequence goes forward without someone appointed by the president approving it.[30]

Furthermore, Congress is another political check on the agencies. In the first instance, an agency can only exercise the authority that Congress grants it. (More on that shortly.) Congress also controls the agency's budget. An agency cannot act unless it has appropriations. And, of course, if Congress disagrees with an agency regulation, it can always enact a law that overrides the offending regulation. For example, in December 2016 during the waning days of the Obama administration, the Department of Interior issued the Stream Protection Rule (after a public notice and comment period).[31] This regulation was aimed at reducing the environmental impacts of mountaintop removal coal mining operations. "Mountaintop removal mining" is exactly what it sounds like: To get to the coal, the top of the mountain is removed. The overburden—the rock and soil that has been removed—is then deposited in the valley below. It's an efficient operation but it results in streams and wetlands in the valleys being smothered. The Stream Protection Rule required mining permits to place more emphasis on limiting impacts to surface water and groundwater.

Congress and the new Trump administration were more concerned about energy production than environmental impacts. In February 2017, Congress voted to repeal the Stream Protection Rule, and President Trump signed it into law.[32] Under the Congressional Review Act, the Department of Interior is prohibited from promulgating any new regulation that is substantially similar, unless Congress provides the agency the authority to do so.[33]

The bottom line is that the subject matter experts in the agencies are not freelancing. Any regulations that they develop are reviewed and approved by political appointees in the executive branch. Congress retains the authority to override agency regulations. And the judicial branch is also a check on agency power, as agency regulations are also subject to judicial review.

The Least Dangerous Branch?

Agency regulations breed litigation. When an agency action such as the promulgation or application of a regulation is challenged, the arguments fall into three camps: procedural (the agency failed to follow the proper process), statutory (the agency is acting beyond its authority or it has misinterpreted a statute), or constitutional (even if the agency followed the proper process and even it is acting consistent with the relevant statutes, the agency action is void because it violates the Constitution). Courts generally consider arguments in that order, ordinarily not reaching the constitutional questions unless necessary.

A key question regarding judicial review of agency actions is the proper standard of review. How deferential, if at all, should a court be to an agency's technical judgment? Due to their training, judges (like most lawyers) are probably most comfortable opining about process. (Attend any law faculty meeting and I bet you will witness at some point concerns expressed about process.) Moreover, deciding a matter on procedural grounds can allow one to avoid having to grapple with more complex, technical issues related to the merits. But sometimes cases cannot be resolved on procedural grounds, and the merits must be addressed. Questions of statutory interpretation often involve technical matters beyond a judge's expertise. For many years, in the context of judicial review of agency regulations, courts have applied what is known as the *Chevron* test, which balances a court's authority to interpret statutes and an agency's technical expertise.

In 1984 in *Chevron v. Natural Resources Defense Council*, the Supreme Court specified how a court should review an agency's interpretation of a statute that Congress authorized it to administer.[34] The case involved the meaning of *stationary source* in the Clean Air Act and whether the EPA could adopt a plantwide definition of source, thereby allowing the "bubble" concept, a form of emission trading. Under the bubble concept, a plant or factory was treated as a single source of pollution, allowing individual stacks to emit more pollution, so long as greater control was placed on other stacks, thereby not increasing overall emissions or exceeding an emissions cap. The *Chevron* test has two steps. First, a court must inquire whether "Congress has directly spoken to the precise question at issue."[35] If Congress was clear in the statute, then Congress's intent must be followed. If the statute is silent or ambiguous, then the court moves to *Chevron*'s second step and determines whether the agency's interpretation is "permissible" or reasonable.[36] In the case of the term *stationary source*, the Court concluded that Congress had not spoken directly to the bubble issue, and that EPA's interpretation was reasonable in light of the Clean Air Act's structure and objectives. The Court therefore deferred to the agency's interpretation. As Justice Scalia later explained, "statutory ambiguities, in other words, were left to reasonable resolution by the Executive."[37]

However, some justices view the *Chevron* test as an abdication of judicial responsibility, inconsistent with the Constitution's separation of powers. Rather than deferring to an agency's technical expertise (if reasonable), these justices invoke Chief Justice John Marshall's pronouncement in *Marbury v. Madison* that it is the role of the judiciary "to say what the law is."[38] For example, Justice Gorsuch, before his appointment to the Supreme Court, stated that *Chevron* allows "executive bureaucracies to swallow huge amounts of core judicial and legislative power."[39] The change in the Court's composition may lead to *Chevron* being expressly overruled. At a minimum, however, the Court is adopting new rules, such as the major questions doctrine, that hollow out *Chevron* and limit the authority of agencies to interpret statutes.

Under the major questions doctrine, Congress must "speak clearly if it wishes to assign to an agency decisions of vast economic and political significance."[40] The doctrine received the clearest imprimatur from the Court in the 2022 case of *West Virginia v. Environmental Protection Agency*, which considered the Obama administration's Clean Power Plan, a regulation developed through the notice and comment process.[41] The Clean Power

Plan required the electric generation industry to shift from coal-burning plants to natural gas and wind farms. The Court deemed this industrywide approach to dealing with carbon dioxide emissions to be a major question. Therefore, the Court stated that separation of powers principles required the EPA to "point to 'clear congressional authorization' for the power it claims."[42] Because Congress did not provide this clear authorization, the Court struck down the Clean Power Plan. (Technically, the regulation wasn't even in force, but the Court eschewed traditional principles of judicial restraint to hear the case.) In a concurring opinion, Justice Gorsuch stated that "basic questions about self-government, equality, fair notice, federalism, and the separation of powers" were at stake.[43] In dissent, Justice Kagan observed that "the Court appoints itself—instead of Congress or the expert agency—the decision-maker on climate policy. I cannot think of many things more frightening."[44]

In theory, the major questions doctrine simply reinforces the notion that Congress must be clear when delegating authority to the executive branch. But as a practical matter, it enlarges the power of the judiciary, which decides what constitutes a "major" question. Whether a particular issue is one of "vast economic and political significance" depends on the perspective of individual judges.

While Justice Kagan expressed concern that the Supreme Court was displacing elected legislators and agency experts, in actuality a single US district court judge can appoint himself or herself the decision-maker on complex policy issues. In recent years, district courts have increasingly issued nationwide injunctions in lawsuits against executive branch agencies, and the question of a district court's authority on this point is unsettled.[45] On one hand, district courts have traditionally enjoyed broad discretion to fashion equitable remedies. In cases where an agency rule is successfully challenged, district courts might vacate the rule, offering programmatic relief. One argument in support of this broad power is that it avoids duplicative litigation. But why should a single judge in Texas or California or New York be able to vacate a rule nationwide? Shouldn't the relief extend only to the plaintiffs in the lawsuit or be limited to the geographic scope of the court or the circuit in which it sits? When a single judge can invalidate an agency regulation across the country, forum shopping is encouraged. It is no coincidence that many challenges to Obama-era regulations were filed in US district courts in Texas and challenges to Trump-era regulations were filed in New York or California.[46] The Supreme

Court has yet to directly address the issue of nationwide injunctions but may do so soon.[47]

The Ebb and Flow of Congress's Commerce Powers

Under our constitutional system, individual states have a general police power. In this context, police power does not mean law enforcement; rather, it refers to a state's authority to adopt laws and regulations for the health, safety, and prosperity of its citizens. Accordingly, states enjoy broad authority to regulate activities that affect the natural environment. In contrast, Congress does not have a general police power.[48] It cannot simply legislate on any issue it desires. Instead, Congress must invoke an authority listed in the Constitution. Congress often relies on its power over interstate commerce, which is specifically enumerated in Article I.

Through a series of decisions, the Supreme Court interpreted the commerce clause broadly to permit Congress to regulate the channels of interstate commerce (e.g., rivers and highways), instrumentalities of interstate commerce (e.g., people and items transported across state borders), and intrastate activities that in the aggregate substantially affect interstate commerce.[49] Initially, however, the Court had a more limited view of Congress's powers.

At its heart, commerce is an exchange, whether commercial or of a more personal nature. (In 1828, *Webster's Dictionary* defined commerce to include "familiar intercourse between the sexes."[50]) In the constitutional context, the Court has long considered commerce to mean the buying and selling of goods. This led to decisions where the Court made distinctions between the production or manufacture of goods and the selling of those goods. If manufacturing was not "commerce," then Congress had no authority (under the commerce clause at least) to regulate the production process—no matter the health and environmental impacts. This reasoning led the Supreme Court to hold in *Hammer v. Dagenhart*, in a 5–4 decision in 1916, that Congress had no authority to regulate child labor.[51] The maximum number of hours a child could toil in a factory or a coal mine or on a farm was "purely" a state matter that was subject to the state's police power.

But, not for the first or the last time, the Court reversed itself on an issue of constitutional law after its composition changed. Twenty-five years later, the Court expressly overruled *Hammer v. Dagenhart*, upholding the Fair Labor Standards Act of 1938, which established minimum wages and maximum hours for employees producing goods that would cross state lines. The

Court stated that "while manufacture is not, of itself, interstate commerce, the shipment of manufactured goods interstate is such commerce, and the prohibition of such shipment by Congress is indubitably a regulation of the commerce."[52] Thus Congress could regulate not only the channels and instrumentalities of interstate commerce but also activities that have a substantial relation to or substantially affect interstate commerce. This last clarification proved to be the most expansive and is most pertinent to the field of environmental law.

Wheat, Weed, and Broccoli

The outermost limits of Congress's power to regulate activities that substantially affect interstate commerce are illustrated by *Wickard v. Filburn*.[53] To ensure a stable supply of wheat for consumers and a reasonable return for wheat farmers, Congress passed New Deal legislation (the Agricultural Adjustment Act of 1938) that authorized the Department of Agriculture to impose marketing quotas on wheat farms. Farmers were assigned an acreage allotment with an expected yield. Excess harvests resulted in penalties. Filburn, who had a small farm in Ohio, received an 11.9-acre wheat allotment. However, he had the audacity to sow 23 acres, which produced an excess of 239 bushels. This use of his own property resulted in a $117 fine. Filburn argued that this regulation of his wheat production—some of which was for his own consumption—was beyond Congress's power to regulate interstate commerce. In his view, this was purely a local matter and not the business of the federal government.

Yet the Supreme Court upheld the law, reasoning that even purely local activities could have a substantial effect on interstate commerce.[54] Although one farmer's consumption of home-grown wheat would have a negligible effect on the market, the cumulative impact of many farmers could disrupt wheat demand, supply, and prices. Thus the law was constitutional, despite the fact that home-grown consumption of wheat is not even commerce, at least not in the sense of an exchange between two people. Whether the price support scheme was wise or workable or fair, the Court declined to say. That judgment was left to Congress.

The aggregation principle articulated in *Wickard* underpins many federal environmental laws. For example, the filling of an individual wetland may have little impact on the species of migratory birds that use it as habitat or on the water quality of a nearby river. But the destruction of these aquatic sites in the aggregate—the cumulative impact of many minor activities—can nevertheless have a substantial negative impact on a species or on water quality and thereby on interstate commerce. Hunting, birdwatching, and fishing generate billions of dollars in economic activity.[55] Protecting waterbird and fish habitat supports this commercial activity.

Decades later, the Court had an opportunity to reexamine the holding of *Wickard v. Filburn*. This time, instead of wheat, the crop was marijuana. And in place of the farmer was a patient with cancer who wanted to consume home-grown marijuana without fear of federal prosecution. In *Gonzales v. Raich*, in a 6–3 decision, the Court found that *Wickard* controlled: Congress's interstate commerce powers reached trivial, local, noncommercial activities because in the aggregate these activities could affect a national market.[56] In this case of marijuana, Congress wanted the national market to be zero. The Court reasoned that medicinal marijuana could affect the overall demand for marijuana. The fact that state law might permit the activity was irrelevant.[57] The aggregation principle endured, and environmentalists considering the big picture breathed a sigh of relief, even if they may have been sympathetic to Angela Raich's plight.

The Supreme Court has chipped away at the edges of Congress's interstate commerce powers, however.[58] Most recently, the Court held that the Affordable Care Act's mandate that individuals must purchase health insurance was beyond Congress's commerce clause powers.[59] The Court was concerned, in part, with Congress regulating inaction (not buying health insurance) and the lack of a limiting principle. If Congress could require people to buy health insurance, could Congress require people to purchase other things, such as broccoli?[60] The Court answered no, emphasizing that "the Commerce Clause is not a general license to regulate an individual from cradle to grave, simply because he will predictably engage in particular transactions. Any police power to regulate individuals as such, as opposed to their activities, remains vested in the States."[61]

The commerce clause is not Congress's only enumerated power. Congress also has the power to tax and spend, among others. Indeed, although the Supreme Court ruled that the commerce clause did not authorize the Affordable Care Act's individual mandate, the requirement to purchase insurance was nevertheless upheld under Congress's taxing powers.[62] (Congress imposed a tax penalty on those who did not buy insurance.) This power over money gives Congress a mechanism to influence the behavior of individuals and, as we will see, states. Congress may not require you to eat broccoli, but it can offer you a carrot (or a stick).

May I See Your ID?

Have you ever wondered why the United States has a uniform drinking age of twenty-one? It wasn't always that way. Under the Twenty-First Amendment, which repealed Prohibition, states have the sole authority to set alcohol consumption rules, rather than the federal government. In the 1970s, after the Twenty-Sixth Amendment was passed, which lowered the voting age from twenty-one to eighteen, some states began to lower their drinking ages as well. This resulted in a patchwork of rules: The minimum drinking age ranged from eighteen to twenty-one, with variations for beer or wine and hard alcohol.[63]

Although one could toast the beauty of federalism, the variations in the minimum drinking age had some negative consequences. Lower drinking ages were associated with increased traffic accidents involving teenagers. A Massachusetts Institute of Technology study found that fatalities for eighteen- to twenty-year-olds in Massachusetts increased by about 40 percent after the drinking age was lowered.[64] From a federal (and parental) perspective, concerns were raised about the underaged in one state traveling to a neighboring state where they were of legal age and then traveling back. But even with this connection to a channel of interstate commerce, Congress lacked the authority to mandate a uniform national drinking age because of the Twenty-First Amendment. However, Congress could control access to federal highway funds.

In 1984, Congress enacted a law directing the Department of Transportation to withhold a portion of federal highway grants to states that did not raise their drinking age to twenty-one.[65] South Dakota resisted, allowing nineteen-year-olds to consume beer with up to 3.2 percent alcohol. When the Department of Transportation reduced federal highway funds by 5 percent, South Dakota sued, alleging that the feds had unconstitutionally infringed on a core power of the states under the Twenty-First Amendment. The Supreme Court found South Dakota's arguments about weak beer to be weak tea.

The Court held that Congress, through its spending power and conditional grants, could encourage states to adopt a uniform policy.[66] The Court noted that a main purpose of the highway funding, to increase safe interstate travel, "had been frustrated by varying drinking ages among the States" which created an incentive for young people to drink and drive.[67] As for South Dakota's claim that the withholding of federal monies amounted to compelling the state to adopt a federal policy, the Court was unconvinced.

Such a small percentage of funding did not support the state's claim of coercion, characterizing it to be "more rhetoric than fact."[68]

When more money was involved, the Supreme Court reached a different conclusion and used some rhetoric of its own. Medicaid, a program that provides health insurance to disabled and low-income people, is voluntarily administered by the states with the financial support of the federal government. The Affordable Care Act required states to expand Medicaid coverage beyond the populations traditionally served, with the federal government picking up almost all of the increased costs.[69] If a state declined to expand Medicaid, however, it risked losing *all* Medicaid funding—which on average amounted to 10 percent of a state's annual budget. In the 2012 case of *National Federation of Independent Business v. Sebelius*, the Court did not see this arrangement as presenting the states with a choice but rather as a "gun to the head."[70]

Putting aside the colorful phrase, the key takeaway is that, under our constitutional system of dual sovereignty, Congress cannot simply commandeer the states.[71] Congress may not order states to address particular problems or to require states to regulate according to federal dictates. Congress cannot do so through a direct order or even indirectly through the conditioning of funds, if the conditions amount to coercion. Where one draws the line between "encouragement" and "economic dragooning" (another colorful phrase used by the Court) is an open question.

The US Legal System in a Nutshell

New law students sometimes make the mistake of thinking that law school will teach them what the "law" is. But the law is not static; it is always changing. Even the basic rules about the separation of powers between the branches and the federal–state relationship are moving targets. So, to sum up our brief review of our complex legal system (in a general matter):

- A statute requires the approval of both houses of Congress and the president's signature. If the president vetoes a bill, Congress may override that veto, in which case the bill would become law. As a general rule, executive orders issued by the president are not "law" in this sense because they are not legally enforceable.
- Congress may (currently) delegate lawmaking authority to executive branch agencies. But the Supreme Court might adopt a new approach to the nondelegation doctrine, which would limit Congress's ability to do so.

- Acting under authority delegated from Congress, executive branch agencies may promulgate legally binding rules—regulations—so long as the agency uses the proper process, which usually requires a public notice and comment period. Often these regulations interpret an ambiguous statutory term or fill in gaps in the statutory scheme.
- Executive branch regulations are subject to approval by presidential appointees, both inside and outside the agency. The regulations may be overridden by a statute enacted by Congress. They are also subject to judicial review.
- Under the *Chevron* doctrine (at the moment), the courts will defer to an agency's regulation (and technical expertise) that is a reasonable interpretation of a statute. But a court will not defer to an agency's regulation regarding a "major question" of "vast economic and political significance," unless Congress has clearly delegated that authority to the agency. What constitutes a "major question" or something of "vast economic and political significance" or a clear delegation of authority is up to the courts.
- A single US district court can issue an injunction that invalidates an agency regulation nationwide (for now).
- Congress (currently) has vast powers under the interstate commerce clause, but they are not unlimited. States have broader authority to regulate under the police power to adopt laws and regulations regarding health, safety, and prosperity.
- Under our federal system, Congress can encourage states to regulate in a particular manner, but Congress cannot simply commandeer the states and order them to apply and enforce federal law and regulations. The states are not "mere marionettes" of the federal government.

We are now a long way from *Schoolhouse Rock*. But with this background, we are ready to navigate the meandering history of the waters of the United States.

CHAPTER 3

Navigable WOTUS

> History is a guide to navigation in perilous times.
> History is who we are and why we are the way we are.
>
> —David McCullough, 1984

At a Wesleyan University commencement ceremony in Connecticut, historian David McCullough emphasized, not surprisingly, the importance of understanding history.[1] McCullough's first book chronicled the Johnstown Flood of 1889, where humans had horribly mismanaged a river system: They "had tampered drastically with the natural order of things and had done so badly," leading to a dam bursting and more than 2,000 deaths.[2] At the commencement ceremony nearly a century later, a recent flood was on the audience's minds, albeit it on a much smaller scale. A moment of silence was observed for the people and businesses affected by the overflows from the Connecticut and Housatonic Rivers. *The New York Times* reported that people in "low-lying areas" were forced to evacuate.[3] "Low-lying areas" often refers to wetlands or former wetlands. Our nation's history has been to fill wetlands, build in floodplains, and then be surprised when devastating floods result. "Ignorance of history is not only stupid," McCullough told the graduates. "It's rude."[4]

Manners aside, not only is history a guide to navigation in perilous times, but the history of navigation can help inform us about the origins of waters of the United States.

Navigable Waters as Public Highways

Federal interest in navigable waters predated the adoption of the US Constitution. One of the few achievements of the Confederation Congress, operating under the Articles of Confederation, was the enactment of the Northwest Ordinance of 1787.[5] The Northwest Ordinance is best known for establishing a process for statehood for territories northwest of the Ohio River. It outlawed slavery and provided for religious and civil liberties (such as trial by jury) in the territory, which ultimately included Illinois, Indiana,

Michigan, parts of Minnesota, Ohio, and Wisconsin. But the subject of navigable waters was deemed so important that the ordinance declared that "the navigable waters leading into the Mississippi and St. Lawrence, and the carrying places between the same shall be common highways."[6] The use of these highways was to be "forever free" from territory or state taxes or duties. The first Congress convened under the Constitution affirmed the Northwest Ordinance—and thus the concept of navigable waters as public highways—in the Act of August 7, 1789.[7]

Subsequent sessions of Congress reemphasized the public's interest in navigable waters. For example, in the Land Act of 1796, Congress sought to raise revenue by auctioning land in what would become the state of Ohio, with a minimum price of $2 per acre.[8] In doing so, Congress was careful to ensure that the sale did not affect public rights, stating that "all navigable rivers, within the territory to be disposed of by virtue of this act, shall be deemed to be, and remain public highways."[9] However, nonnavigable waters could be subject to private ownership: In cases "where the opposite banks of any stream, not navigable, shall belong to different persons, the stream and the bed thereof shall become common to both."[10]

Not much was required for a water to be considered navigable. At this time in history, commerce in fur trading was carried out through small, manually operated watercraft such as rafts, canoes, and batteaux.[11] Technological advancements, such as steamboats, led to a conflict between federal and state authorities over their respective spheres of regulation, ultimately requiring the Supreme Court to weigh in on the matter in a classic case.

WOTUS in the SCOTUS (the Early Days)

The 1824 Supreme Court case of *Gibbons v. Ogden*[12] had it all. It involved famous Americans such as Robert Fulton, who designed the first commercially successful steamboat; Fulton's investor, Robert Livingston, who was a member of the committee that drafted the Declaration of Independence but was out of town for its signing; Daniel Webster, who argued on behalf of Gibbons (and later, in fiction, against the Devil); Webster's co-counsel, William Wirt, who unsuccessfully prosecuted Aaron Burr for treason; and Chief Justice John Marshall, credited with establishing the foundation of judicial review and thus the Supreme Court's power, who presided over oral arguments and wrote the Court's opinion. It was the feds versus the states. There were arguments about "strict construction," which were rejected, and it laid the foundation for Congress to claim vast powers under the commerce clause. And it even contained a fleeting reference to "the waters of the United States."

Commuting in the New York metropolitan area has long been a grind, expensive and time-consuming. It was worse at the end of the eighteenth century. In one sense, *Gibbons v. Ogden* is about a state government's attempt to spur technological innovation and support the development of public transportation. (Or it could be viewed as entrepreneurs attempting to corner the market with the government's imprimatur.) In 1798, the state of New York granted Fulton and Livingston a monopoly to operate steamboats on waters of the state, on the condition that they develop a vessel that could zoom up the Hudson River at the speed of 4 miles per hour.[13] In 1807 Fulton demonstrated that his efforts were no folly as the maiden voyage of his steamship traveled from New York City to Albany in a mere thirty-two hours, instead of four days by sailboat.[14] With the monopoly secured, Fulton and Livingston sold to Aaron Ogden the exclusive rights to operate steamboats between New York and New Jersey. Thomas Gibbons was Ogden's business partner. As so often happens, the partnership soured, and Gibbons went into direct competition with Ogden. Ogden then sued to protect his exclusive rights to operate steamships on New York waters, and he prevailed in the New York courts. Gibbons appealed to the US Supreme Court.

Gibbons's defense was based on the Constitution's supremacy clause. In the case of any conflict between federal and state law, the federal law prevails. Gibbons argued that a 1793 act of Congress authorized his operations, and therefore the New York law granting a steamship monopoly on New York waters and restricting his service was void. In response, Ogden contended that the power of Congress to regulate interstate commerce was limited to activities such as buying and selling and did not extend to transport on navigable waters. The case squarely presented the Court an opportunity to delineate the boundaries of federal and state powers.

Ogden asserted that any powers granted by the Constitution must be "construed strictly." But Chief Justice Marshall questioned, "What do gentlemen mean, by a strict construction?"[15] He then rejected a narrow interpretation of the Constitution, noting that to deny Congress the powers granted "would cripple the government, and render it unequal to the object for which it is declared to be instituted."[16] The extent of Congress's powers was to be interpreted based on the Constitution's language in light of its purposes.

Turning to the definition of *commerce*, which was construed to mean "commercial intercourse" or the buying and selling of goods, the Court concluded that the term readily encompassed navigation. The Court observed that "all America understands, and has uniformly understood" that to be the case because "the power over commerce, including navigation, was one of the primary objects for which the people of America adopted their government."[17] Indeed, in connection with commerce, the Constitution itself prohibits states from imposing duties on vessels traveling from one state to another.[18] Accordingly, Congress has the power to regulate navigation—with "no limitations" other than those prescribed in the Constitution.

Ogden pointed to the Tenth Amendment, which provides in part that the powers not granted to the federal government are reserved to the states, for the proposition that the states may exercise concurrent jurisdiction over navigation. Acknowledging that "State governments remain, and constitute a most important part of our system," the Court nevertheless concluded that states have no role in regulating interstate commerce.[19] To hold that the states retained their "original powers" would "explain away the constitution of our country, and leave it a magnificent structure, indeed, to look at, but totally unfit for use."[20] Ultimately, the Court decreed that, because Gibbons had a federal license granted under a statute properly adopted by Congress exercising its commerce clause powers, he had the right "to navigate the waters of the United States" for his "coasting trade."[21] The New York law granting Ogden the monopoly was declared void.

Gibbons v. Ogden is an important case for several reasons. It established that Congress's power under the interstate commerce clause is to be construed broadly and specifically held that Congress could regulate the use of navigable waters—channels of interstate commerce. Although the Court recognized that the federal government and the states could exercise concurrent jurisdiction over some matters, it reaffirmed the principle that federal law is supreme and will preempt a contrary state law. (In doing so, the opinion also laid the foundation of the "dormant commerce clause," which prohibits states from imposing excessive burdens on interstate commerce.[22]) And, although not central to the holding, the phrase "waters of the United States" made its first appearance in a Supreme Court opinion involving a dispute between federal and state powers. In this context, "waters of the United States" simply meant a traditional navigable water, that is, a waterway used to transport goods. But the Court referred to the "deep streams which penetrate our country, pass[ing] through the interior of almost every State in the Union," and the Court's decree expressly invalidated New York's attempt to prohibit vessels "from navigating the waters of the state of New York."[23]

Because Gibbons had the right to navigate the "waters of the United States," which included "waters of the state," the Supreme Court held that federal jurisdiction extended beyond coastal waters and to inland waters.

Wetlands in SCOTUS (for the First Time)

Unlike traditional navigable waters, which were valued as channels of commerce, wetlands were traditionally viewed as wastelands, mosquito-breeding nuisances that should be drained and put to higher uses (such as farming). The first US Supreme Court opinion that directly involved wetlands, *Willson v. Black Bird Creek Marsh Company*,[24] subscribed to this narrow understanding. It also recognized a larger role for states in the regulation of water resources than *Gibbons v. Ogden* had.

The official version of *Willson v. Black Bird Creek Marsh Company* sets the stage by noting that in 1822 Delaware authorized "the owners and possessors of the marsh, cripple, and low grounds" adjacent to Black Bird Creek, a tributary of Delaware Bay, to construct a dam across the creek and to drain the marsh.[25] Early volumes of US Supreme Court opinions were notorious for being incomplete and containing errors[26]—indeed, even Willson's name is probably misspelled, because lower court documents call him Wilson.[27] With respect to the word *cripple*, an unofficial version of the case published in 1903 included a footnote explaining that "there is no such word in English," at least in the context of waters.[28] Instead, the footnote suggested that *cripple* was the Dutch word *kreupel* (or the German *krüppel*), meaning "low wet land, overgrown with bushes."[29] In any event, despite the misspellings, it was clear that the case concerned, in part, marshes and other wetlands.

Willson (or Wilson) was accustomed to traversing Black Bird Creek for commercial purposes, under a federal license issued pursuant to the same 1793 federal law at issue in *Gibbons v. Ogden*. When Willson encountered the obstruction to Black Bird Creek, he ordered the crew of his sloop *The Sally* to sally forth and dismantle the dam. Although Willson was able to continue his voyage, the company sued him for $20,000 in damages, a not insignificant sum in those days.[30]

Willson defended himself by citing *Gibbons v. Ogden* for the proposition that "navigable streams are the waters of the United States."[31] He argued that a state had no authority to close a navigable water, and the Delaware law therefore unconstitutionally interfered with Congress's power over interstate commerce. The company, represented by William Wirt (who now, in contrast to his position in *Gibbons v. Ogden*, was advocating for state authority), characterized the creek as "one of those sluggish reptile streams, that do not run but creep, and which, wherever it passes, spreads its venom, and destroys the health of all who inhabit its marshes."[32] Surely, he contended, states retained the authority to construct a dam and drain the area to reduce the "pestilence" and restore people to "health and vigour."[33]

A mere three days after oral arguments at the Supreme Court, Chief Justice Marshall issued a brief opinion. The Court seemingly made a distinction between the creek and the surrounding wetlands. Because the creek was a traditional navigable water (used for commerce or subject to the ebb and flow of the tide), Congress could enact a law regulating its use, and any contrary state law would be unconstitutional.[34] Here, however, the Court concluded that because Congress did not expressly preclude Delaware from exercising control over "those small navigable creeks into which the tide flows, and which abound throughout . . . the middle and southern states," Delaware's law was a valid exercise of state power.[35] Concerning the marsh and the cripple (kreupel), the Court observed that measures designed to protect public health and safety—such as "excluding the water from the marsh"—were "undoubtably . . . reserved to the states."[36] States could authorize the draining of wetlands, so long as their laws "do not come into collision" with the powers of the federal government.[37] And of course there was no specific federal law at the time concerning the regulation of activities affecting wetlands.

In the end, the Court stated that for both the creek and the wetlands, states retained authority, but it was subject to federal law. Should a state law conflict with a federal law, the federal law would be supreme and the state law void. The difference between the creek and the wetlands was that for the navigable creek, which was akin to a public highway, Congress could invoke its powers under the commerce clause. For the wetlands, the Court left open the possibility of a federal law trumping a state law but did not identify under which power Congress might act.

Willson v. Black Bird Creek Marsh Company is an instructive case regarding the federal–state relationship. First, contrary to suggestions in *Gibbons v. Ogden*, it held that states have some role to play regarding traditional navigable waters. It also emphasized that states retained the general authority to enact health and safety measures, and this police power "undoubtably" encompassed the authority to govern activities in wetlands. However, Congress could override state laws regarding navigable waters and wetlands—so long as Congress could point to an enumerated power.

Expanding the Concept of Navigable Waters (and Congress's Commerce Powers)

Steamboats were instrumental to the economic development of the United States in the 1800s.[38] Because they allowed goods to be shipped upstream and downstream on river systems, farmers could send their produce to new markets. The ability of communities to receive and send products led to regional specialization and spurred manufacturing. A passenger trade developed as people could travel greater distances more quickly. One downside: Steamboats were dangerous and had an unfortunate propensity to explode.[39] The steamboat *Sultana*'s boiler explosions in April 1865 on the Mississippi River near Memphis killed nearly 1,200 people and was one of the greatest maritime disasters in US history, although it was obscured by other events (such as Abraham Lincoln's assassination and the end of the Civil War).[40] Concern about steamboat safety had led Congress to enact laws in 1838 and 1852 to require steamboats to be inspected and to operate with a federal license.[41]

The Supreme Court considered the constitutionality of these laws in the 1870 case of *The Daniel Ball*.[42] The steamboat was traveling on the Grand River in Michigan with goods and passengers without a federal inspection or license and was fined $500. The steamboat owners argued that under English common law, only waters that were subject to the ebb and flow of the tide were considered navigable. Because the Grand River was not subject to the ebb and flow of the tide, they contended it was not a navigable water, and Congress therefore had no authority to regulate the *Daniel Ball*.

The Supreme Court rejected the English tidal approach, instead adopting a broader definition of navigability.[43] The Court focused on "navigable capacity" and whether rivers were "navigable in fact." According to the Court, waters were navigable in fact if "they are used or are susceptible of being used in their ordinary condition as highways for commerce over which trade and travel are or may be conducted in the customary modes of trade and travel on water."[44] Under this formulation, the Court easily found that the Grand River was navigable.

But the steamboat owners also asserted that the *Daniel Ball* was merely traveling from Grand Rapids to Grand Haven, wholly within Michigan. They pointed out that *interstate* commerce implies that there is such a thing as *intrastate* commerce. The Court itself in *Gibbons v. Ogden* carefully observed that Congress's power to regulate commerce "among the several States" did not extend to commerce that is completely internal—for example, commerce that is carried on between two people in the same state.[45] But the Court found that the *Daniel Ball* was laden with goods destined for other states, thus concluding that the *Daniel Ball* was engaged in interstate commerce. Congress could then appropriately regulate the *Daniel Ball* as an "instrument" of commerce.[46] (An interesting side note: After the *Daniel Ball* was licensed, it caught fire and sank in 1876, although reportedly no passengers were harmed.[47])

At this point, the Court had interpreted Congress's commerce clause powers to cover the "channels" of interstate commerce (i.e., the waterways acting as public highways) and the "instrumentalities" of interstate commerce (i.e., the vessels transporting goods). In *The Daniel Ball* case, the Court stated that it was rendering no opinion about "the power of Congress over interstate commerce when carried on by land transportation."[48] Congress's attempts to regulate land-based activities (well beyond the transportation of goods) proved to be a subject of contention.

Early Cooperative Federalism: Fraud in Draining the Swamp

In addition to the commerce clause and other enumerated powers in Article I of the Constitution, Congress may also exercise power under the property clause, which is found in Article IV. The federal government has always been the nation's largest property owner,[49] and the property clause states that "Congress shall have Power to dispose of and make all needful Rules and Regulations respecting the Territory or other Property belonging to the United States." In essence, the property clause gives Congress a general police power over federal lands.[50] It also authorizes the federal government to dispose of—sell or otherwise transfer—federal lands. In the 1800s, a significant portion of federal landholdings were wetlands, and the federal policy toward these areas was to give them to the states to drain them.[51]

Beginning in 1849, Congress enacted a series of laws typically called the Swamp Lands Acts.[52] The laws transferred title of "these swamp and overflowed lands" that were unfit for cultivation from the federal government to the states, with the understanding that the states would drain these areas, allow settlement, and put them to a more productive use. The laws delegated authority to the secretary of interior to make "an accurate list and plats of the lands described aforesaid." The identification of the transferable lands was performed by the General Land Office, the agency within the Department of Interior responsible for surveying and selling public lands.[53] The 1849 act focused on Louisiana, and ultimately fourteen other states also benefited from the arrangement: Alabama, Arkansas, California, Florida, Illinois, Indiana, Iowa, Michigan, Minnesota, Mississippi, Missouri, Ohio, Oregon, and Wisconsin.[54] More than 64 million acres were transferred to the states—which is greater than the combined areas of Connecticut, Massachusetts, New Hampshire, New Jersey, New York, Rhode Island, and Vermont. However, this early federal–state program suffered from a significant drawback: It was rife with fraud. As one scholar observed in a 1924 treatise on public lands, "No better bait was ever thrown to speculators than the swamp lands of the various states."[55]

The fraud by the states began with the selection of lands eligible to be transferred. State agents identified huge swathes of land adjacent to creeks and rivers without regard to the surveys done by the General Land Office. Consequently, the states claimed vast expanses of nonwetland areas. As Benjamin Hibbard, an agricultural economics professor at the University of Wisconsin, reported,

> Time and again it was found on examination reported that 75 per cent of the land claimed was not in any sense swampy or subject to serious overflow. . . . The game was to get as much land as possible. Taking advantage of the great extent of actual swamp in Florida, the state agents selected as swamp land whole townships which upon investigation were found to be substantially dry land.[56]

Although selling "swampland in Florida" is now associated with land scams whereby naive northerners purchased undevelopable wetlands at inflated prices,[57] the earlier swampland fraud was just the opposite: Dry lands were being acquired under the guise that they were wet.

The lands subject to "the rapacity of state authorities" often "embraced the finest . . . agricultural land in a locality."[58] The states also transferred to railroads and mining companies "extensive areas of valuable land" that were fraudulently classified as "wet land."[59] In some cases, the lands claimed by the states (which were then sold to speculators) were already owned by settlers, which then created title disputes where the proper landowners did not fare well. Toss in some self-dealing by politicians who bought land at below-market prices, and you have an unsavory concoction of corruption. Instead of draining the swamps, the states embarked on a land grab.[60]

A Bridge over Troubled (Navigable) Waters

The states' rapacious behavior also spilled over into the use of traditional navigable waters. As the nation grew demographically and economically, states (and local governments) authorized the construction of bridges to facilitate the flow of land-based traffic. However, these bridges had the effect of cutting off upstream access by larger vessels. At the same time, wharves and piers were being constructed in a random fashion, leading to congestion on the waterways. Concerned about the impact of these activities on navigation, the US Army Corps of Engineers, beginning in 1877, sought from Congress the authority to regulate activities that could be harmful to navigation.[61] These proposals, such as the "Dolph Bill" introduced by Senator Joseph Dolph of Oregon, failed to garner sufficient congressional support in the 1880s.[62]

The need for such legislation became more apparent after the 1888 Supreme Court case of *Willamette Iron Bridge Co. v. Hatch*.[63] Ten years earlier, the Oregon legislature enacted a law permitting the construction of a bridge between Portland and East Portland on the Willamette River by the Portland Bridge Company, which had been established by Dr. James Hawthorne, "whose name served as euphemism for insanity in the popular press."[64] (Hawthorne opened the first insane asylum in the Pacific Northwest.) Hawthorne's politically connected partners included the current and a future mayor of Portland. The Portland Bridge Company soon assigned its rights to the Willamette Iron Bridge Company, which commenced construction of the project in 1880.

Yet one person's bridge, fostering connections, can be another person's barrier. Lownsdale owned a wharf and warehouse 600 feet above the bridge. The warehouse stored wheat from the Willamette Valley destined for Europe and other foreign ports, and the bridge hindered the passage of seagoing vessels. Hatch owned a steamboat that towed vessels to and from wharves on the river and was similarly aggrieved. They brought suit alleging that the bridge unlawfully impeded navigation in contravention of the act of Congress admitting Oregon to the Union, which provided "that all the navigable waters of [Oregon] shall be common highways, and forever free . . . [from] any tax, duty, impost, or toll therefor," harking back to a similar declaration in the Northwest Ordinance of 1787.[65] Hatch and Lownsdale prevailed in the lower courts, and the Willamette Iron Bridge Company sought review by the US Supreme Court.

Interestingly, Senator Dolph—proponent of failed legislation to require federal permission to obstruct navigable waters—represented Hatch and

Lowndsdale. (At the time, it was not unusual for sitting senators to argue before the Supreme Court.) Senator Dolph fared as poorly in the Supreme Court as he had with his legislative colleagues. Although the Court recognized that Congress unquestionably had the power to regulate navigation on public rivers to prevent obstructions, the Court held that it had not done so with respect to the Willamette River.[66] The Court stated that "there is no common law of the United States which prohibits obstructions and nuisances in navigable rivers," and if Congress wants to prevent such obstructions, it must enact a law.[67] The Court suggested that it was "almost superfluous to cite authorities on the subject" before reeling off more than ten cases, starting with *Willson v. Black Bird Creek Co.*[68]

There Ought to Be a Law (1888 Edition)

After this judicial loss, Senator Dolph redoubled his efforts in Congress, where he finally prevailed in the 1888 River and Harbor Appropriations Act, enacted six months after the *Willamette Iron Bridge Company* decision.[69] Section 2 made owners and operators of bridges placed in "any navigable waters of the United States" liable for damage caused to other property as a result of diverting the water's natural course (through the caving of banks, for example). Section 9 required bridge owners to remove or alter bridges "whenever the Secretary of War shall have good reason to believe that any railroad or other bridge now constructed, or . . . which may hereafter be constructed, over any of the navigable waterways of the United States is an obstruction to the free navigation of such waters." Uncooperative bridge owners were subject to a monthly fine of $500, which would be placed in a fund set aside for improving the navigation of the particular "waterway."[70] At this point, Congress appeared to use the terms *navigable waterways* and *navigable waters of the United States* interchangeably. In any event, Senator Dolph had provided relief for his warehouse- and steamboat-owning constituents (and clients) in a rare circumstance where a sitting US senator argued a case before the US Supreme Court, lost, and then successfully sponsored legislation effectively overturning the Court's decision.

Interestingly, the 1888 River and Harbor Act contained a kernel of environmental sensitivity. Much of the act was devoted to appropriating funds for public works projects in navigable waters, such as improving harbors, dredging channels, and constructing locks and dams (including $35,000 for "improving" the Housatonic River in Connecticut, which we opened the chapter with).[71] Section 11 stated that in any projects funded by the 1888 Act that were

> found to operate (whether by lock and dam or otherwise), as obstructions to the passage of fish, the Secretary of War may, in his discretion, direct and cause to be constructed practical and sufficient fish-ways, to be paid for out of the general appropriations for the streams on which such fish-ways may be constructed.[72]

This provision also applied to previously funded public works projects as well as to any such future projects undertaken by the federal government. Section 11 is significant for at least two reasons. First, Congress recognized the environmental harm that public works projects such as dams could cause, even though the term *environmental* had yet to break into the lexicon. Second, it demonstrated that Congress was not concerned about rivers only as public highways; Congress was also focused on the biological integrity of those waters (although the phrase *biological integrity* would have been foreign to members of the Fiftieth Congress). The 1888 act is an early example of where Congress indicated concern about water quality in navigable waters and provided a means (money for fish passageways) to mitigate harm caused by federal projects.

A Nascent Permit Program (1890 Edition)

Although section 9 of the 1888 act offered the federal government the means to order the removal of bridges that obstructed navigation, it did not delineate a process for the secretary of war to determine that a structure unduly obstructed navigation. The River and Harbor Act of 1890 remedied that omission by that calling on the secretary to notify the bridge owner and provide a "reasonable opportunity to be heard."[73] The secretary also needed to "specify the changes required to be made, and . . . prescribe in each case a reasonable time in which to make them."[74] Although the bridge owners now had some due process afforded to them, the penalties for noncompliance were stiffened: It became a criminal misdemeanor not to make the alterations (including bridge removal) ordered by the secretary, with a fine of up to $5,000. Moreover, the 1890 act introduced the concept of continuing violations: Every month that the offending structure remained in place was a new violation, subject to fresh penalties.[75]

The 1888 act was reactive, with the secretary of war making an after-the-fact determination that a structure had an injurious impact. In contrast, the 1890 act established a permit regime. Certain actions involving navigable waters were prohibited, unless the secretary granted permission.

As was the case in the 1888 act, in the 1890 act Congress seemingly evinced an environmental concern. Section 6 prohibited the discharge of waste without a permit. In particular, the prohibition covered

> any ballast, stone, slate, gravel, earth, rubbish, wreck, filth, slabs, edgings, sawdust, slag, cinders, ashes, refuse, or other waste of any kind, into any port, road, roadstead, harbor, haven, navigable river, or navigable waters of the United States which shall tend to impede or obstruct navigation.[76]

Although the waste could affect water quality, Congress's primary concern was whether the waste was so extensive that it interfered with commerce. (As we will see, this language was later dusted off and resurrected in the 1960s for environmental purposes.)

In addition to a prohibition on the discharge of waste, section 7 of the 1890 act prohibited the building of "any wharf, pier, dolphin, boom, dam, weir, breakwater, bulkhead, jetty, or structure of any kind" in any navigable waters of the United States, unless the secretary issued a permit.[77] Broader still, section 10 proscribed "the creation of any obstruction, not affirmatively authorized by law, to the navigable capacity of any waters, in respect of which the United States has jurisdiction."[78]

The 1890 act was a significant expansion of federal powers. Bridges and other structures could no longer simply move forward based on state or local approvals, subject to later possible federal objections. Instead, the construction of *any structure of any kind* in a navigable water of the United States was flatly prohibited without advance permission from the secretary of war. But the 1890 act asserted federal authority beyond navigable waters to include nonnavigable tributaries, if their use would affect a downstream navigable water. The 1890 act was thus watershed legislation, in every sense of the word.

The US Supreme Court affirmed consideration of the entire watershed, at least for purposes of navigation, in *United States v. Rio Grande Dam and Irrigation Co.*, decided in 1899.[79] In this case, the federal government sought to enjoin the construction of a dam in the territory of New Mexico near Hot

Springs (which was later named Truth or Consequences after the television game show[80]). Although the Rio Grande in New Mexico was found to be nonnavigable, the Court had no difficulty in concluding that the federal government could regulate activities on the nonnavigable portion in New Mexico when they would affect navigation on the navigable portion of the river in Texas. The Court observed that the 1890 act's prohibitions were not limited to obstructions only in navigable waters; rather, the prohibitions extended to "any obstruction to the navigable capacity, and *anything, wherever done or however done*, within the limits of the jurisdiction of the United States, which tends to destroy the navigable capacity of one of the navigable waters of the United States."[81] The Court simply recognized the truth that activities on nonnavigable tributaries can affect navigable waters, with the consequence being that the federal government has regulatory authority over the entire watershed.

A Still Existing Permit Program (1899 Edition)

In subsequent Rivers and Harbors Appropriations Acts, Congress continued to tinker with federal authority over navigable and nonnavigable waters. After Congress directed the secretary of war to identify all existing authorities regarding navigable waters and make recommendations for revisions that may be "in the public interest" (a responsibility that was delegated to the chief of the Corps of Engineers), Congress passed the 1899 Rivers and Harbors Appropriations Act.[82] Notably, section 9 of the 1899 act stated that congressional approval was required for the construction of any bridge, dam, or dike over or in any "navigable river or other navigable water of the United States."[83] This provision apparently was in response to a court decision that raised a nondelegation issue over the 1890 act's requirement that bridges and other structures be approved by the secretary of war; the court seemed to question whether Congress could delegate this authority to the executive branch.[84] Similarly, section 10 prohibited any obstructions to "the navigable capacity of any of the waters of the United States" without congressional authority.[85] This appears to be the first time that Congress uses the phrase "waters of the United States," and in this context it is limited to traditional navigable waters.

Section 10 also left in place the requirement for a permit from the secretary of war (based on recommendations from the Corps) for the building of any wharf, pier, jetty, or other structure in a "navigable river, or other water of the United States." Again, in this context it is clear that "water of the United

States" refers to a traditional navigable water. Significantly, in addition section 10 declared it unlawful "to excavate or fill" in "the channel of any navigable water of the United States" without federal permission. The section 10 permit program continues to be administered by the Corps today.[86]

Section 13 of the 1899 act retained the prohibition of the discharge of waste without a permit.[87] However, the law now applied this prohibition not only to any navigable water of the United States but also to "any tributary of any navigable water." The prohibition thus covers nonnavigable waters; otherwise, the entire "any tributary" clause would be redundant. So here, once again, we see Congress asserting federal authority beyond traditional navigable waters, at least to activities that could affect navigation and interstate commerce. The section 13 permit program is technically still on the books too, although as a practical matter it has been supplanted by section 402 of the Clean Water Act, as we will see.

But federal involvement in these matters did not necessarily displace state's general police power authority regarding intrastate navigable waters. As the Supreme Court stated in the 1903 case of *Cummings v. Chicago*, "Until Congress acts on the subject, the power of the state over bridges across its navigable streams is plenary. This doctrine has been recognized from the earliest period, and approved in repeated cases"—and here the Court once again invoked *Willson v. Black Bird Creek Marsh Company*.[88] In *Cummings*, the secretary of war had approved the construction of a dock by the Calumet Grain and Elevator Company on the Calumet River under the 1899 Rivers and Harbors Appropriations Act.[89] The City of Chicago's Department of Public Works objected, however, and threatened prosecution. The company argued that the feds trumped the state (and local governments acting under the authority of the state). But the Supreme Court rejected that argument, reasoning,

> The effect of that [1899] act, reasonably interpreted, is to make the erection of a structure in a navigable river, within the limits of a state, depend upon the concurrent or joint assent of both the national government and the state government. The Secretary of War, acting under the authority conferred by Congress, may assent to the erection by private parties of such a structure. Without such assent the structure cannot be erected by them. But under existing legislation they must, before proceeding under such an authority, obtain also the assent of the state acting by its constituted agencies.[90]

The Supreme Court once again affirmed that the federal and state governments could have concurrent jurisdiction over the same activities in the same waters.

Congress Finally Defines Navigable Waters

With the advent of hydropower in the 1880s, companies began to dam rivers and streams to produce electricity, which raised several concerns. Naturally, the Corps was concerned that the dams would unduly obstruct navigation. More broadly, President Theodore Roosevelt and progressives were worried about monopolies and giving away natural resources without charge. In 1903, Roosevelt vetoed a congressionally approved power station at Muscle Shoals, Alabama, expressing disquietude that access to these navigable waters was being "practically given away" without any time constraints.[91] In addition, he opposed federal taxpayers having to foot the bill to construct locks and other navigation facilities to ensure that waterborne commerce was not interrupted.

Congress responded to these concerns by passing the General Dams Act of 1906, which authorized the secretary of war and chief of engineers to impose "any condition" on the construction of hydroelectric dams deemed "necessary to protect the present and future interests of the United States."[92] Roosevelt believed this provision gave the federal government the authority to charge the power companies for the use of navigable waters. Interestingly, his secretary of war, William Taft, had a more restrictive interpretation, contending that any conditions could relate only to navigation. Taft (who soon became president) also took a dim view of the executive branch making navigability decisions; in his view, the "power to determine whether certain waters are or are not navigable is vested in the courts and in Congress and is ordinarily not a matter for executive determination."[93]

In 1920, Congress enacted the Federal Water Power Act,[94] which created the Federal Power Commission (FPC), the forerunner of the Federal Energy Regulatory Commission. The law eliminated the need for express congressional approval of each hydroelectric dam. Instead, the FPC could issue thirty- to fifty-year licenses and attach conditions. Congress also decided to specifically define the term *navigable waters* to mean

> those parts of streams or other bodies of water over which Congress has jurisdiction under its authority to regulate commerce with foreign nations and among the several States,

> and which either in their natural or improved condition, notwithstanding interruptions between the navigable parts of such streams or waters by falls, shallows or rapids compelling land carriage, are used or suitable for use for the transportation of persons or property in interstate or foreign commerce, including therein all such interrupting falls, shallows, or rapids; together with such other parts of streams as shall have been authorized by Congress for improvement by the United States, or shall have been recommended to Congress for such improvement after investigation under its authority.[95]

Accordingly, at least for purposes of the Federal Water Power Act, navigable waters included waters used in commerce—as well as those that could be used in commerce with some reasonable improvements. Perhaps more importantly for our purposes, as we delve into the parameters of waters of the United States, it is a reminder that Congress can always step in and provide a clearer or more comprehensive definition of the term.

CHAPTER 4
Handouts to the States

> It's all about the Benjamins, baby.
>
> —Puff Daddy, 1997

In his late-twentieth-century ode to accumulating wealth,[1] Puff Daddy (né Sean Combs, later P. Diddy, and then simply Diddy) extolled a certain quality of life, albeit hedonistic. The key to supporting this desired lifestyle required a sufficient amount of US currency featuring a non-POTUS individual not named Hamilton. Diddy went on to be a record producer and executive, achieving his ambitious financial goals.[2] His diversified business interests included owning and investing in AQUAhydrate, a bottled water company.[3] In a small way, clean water contributes to Diddy's cash flow.

In the early twentieth century, a major quality-of-life issue was clean water, or lack thereof, due to effluent such as sewage. At the federal level, all three branches of government were reluctant to tread into an area that was traditionally the states' responsibility. Although the states would bristle at any attempt at national regulation of water pollution, they had no such compunction about accepting federal monies or allowing municipalities to feed at the federal trough. Thus initial efforts to deal with water pollution from a national perspective involved the federal government providing funding to the states and municipalities. Because of concerns about federalism and state sovereignty, federal water pollution legislation focused largely on the Benjamins. And as we will see, this federal–state relationship was largely ineffective in dealing with the nation's growing water quality problems. To paraphrase a later Diddy ditty, more money doesn't necessarily solve your problems and may actually create new ones.

Stay in Your (Navigational) Lane

William M. Black graduated at the top of his West Point class in 1877 and was commissioned in the US Army Corps of Engineers, eventually rising to be chief of engineers.[4] In 1900, then a major, he served in Cuba as the chief engineer of the island in the aftermath of the Spanish–American War. One of his responsibilities entailed improving sanitary conditions, including repairing the sewage system, which had been intentionally clogged by the departing occupiers.[5] One of his "most visible" public works projects "was the construction of the sea wall and boulevard along the waterfront... [that] turned the La Punta section of Havana harbor, across from the Morro, from a garbage dump and sewer outlet inundated by waves, to one of the most beautiful promenades in the world."[6] In Major Black's modest estimation, "no piece of public improvement in this city has met with such universal appreciation and approval."[7]

It was perhaps this experience in Cuba that, in 1910, led Black, now a lieutenant colonel, to work with a cadre of New Yorkers to try to use the Corps' authority under the Refuse Act (section 13 of the Rivers and Harbors Act of 1899) to prevent the construction of a proposed sewer outlet to the Hudson River.[8] During this time, the *New York Times* reported that "the Hudson River is so dirty that it can barely support fish" due to sewage.[9] Black's attempt to use the Corps' authority under the Rivers and Harbors Act to respond to water pollution foundered on rocky shoals, however. The judge advocate general issued a legal opinion concluding that water pollution was a state and not a federal issue. In the top military lawyer's view, "the control of waters for drinking and sanitary purposes, and the regulation of the flow and of the deposit of sewage, are matters fully within the control of the several States as an incident of their police power."[10] Despite the plain language of the Refuse Act regarding the prohibition of waste, its use was constrained to protecting navigation, no matter the level of public health concerns.

Love in the Time of Cholera (and Yellow Fever, Smallpox, and Plague)

Rather than using any regulatory powers, the federal government was at this time content to study the problem of water pollution through the Public Health Service, the origins of which had a navigable water connection. In 1798, Congress established the Marine Hospital Service to care for sick and injured merchant marines, which led to a network of hospitals located on the coast and along inland waters.[11] The Marine Hospital Service's responsibilities eventually expanded to include ensuring that diseases such as cholera, yellow fever, smallpox, and the plague did not enter the United States through its ports. In 1902, Congress authorized a Hygienic Laboratory as part of the Marine Hospital Service to investigate these diseases more broadly, and the service was then renamed the Public Health and Marine Hospital Service in recognition of its broader responsibilities.[12] A decade later, Congress shortened the name to the Public Health Service and authorized it to study the connection between water pollution and human health, "including sanitation and sewage and the pollution either directly or indirectly of the navigable streams and lakes of the United States."[13] Although the condition of navigable waters was to be the focus of such investigations, Congress in 1912 recognized the interconnectedness of river basins by requesting that the Hygienic Laboratory consider indirect sources of pollution, which would include waste flowing from nonnavigable tributaries.

One of the early reports by the Hygienic Laboratory on water pollution examined the condition of the lower Missouri River (Figure 4-1).[14] Sampling along the river and at the mouths of its tributaries, the Hygienic Laboratory found unacceptable levels of pollution. An "undue prevalence" of typhoid fever was the result of sewage-polluted waters of the Missouri River.[15] Although the report suggested that streams could safely be used as sewers,[16] there needed to be some restrictions on the amount of effluent, depending on the use of the waterway. Given the interstate nature of the Missouri River, the report called for a federal regulatory program: "To treat the problem of pollution on these great interstate or international waterways with justice and equity to all concerned there is a necessity for Federal control."[17] The Hygienic Laboratory envisioned the federal restrictions to establish a floor of protection, "the minimum necessary for the prevention of the spread of disease in interstate traffic, leaving to the various States the right to exact more rigid requirements . . . within their own borders consistent with their own State laws."[18]

Despite the clear linkage between water pollution and health, Congress fashioned only a limited regulatory response, focusing on oil discharges. The Oil Pollution Act of 1924 prohibited oil discharges to the "coastal navigable waters of the United States," which Congress defined to be "all portions of the sea within the territorial jurisdiction of the United States, and all inland waters navigable in fact in which the tide ebbs and flows."[19] Although the geographic scope of the prohibition was narrow, Congress did make clear that it was concerned not only about the "menace" of oil pollution to navigation but about its negative impact on "health [and] sea food" as well.[20] Enforcement proved to be uneven, however.[21]

No Deal during the New Deal

Of course, a regulatory program is not the only way to improve water quality. During the multiple administrations of Franklin Delano Roosevelt, public

TREASURY DEPARTMENT

United States Public Health Service

HYGIENIC LABORATORY—BULLETIN No. 89

MAY, 1913

SEWAGE POLLUTION OF INTERSTATE AND INTERNATIONAL WATERS

WITH SPECIAL REFERENCE TO THE SPREAD OF TYPHOID FEVER

VI. THE MISSOURI RIVER FROM SIOUX CITY TO ITS MOUTH

By

ALLAN J. McLAUGHLIN

WASHINGTON

GOVERNMENT PRINTING OFFICE

1913

Figure 4-1. A call for federal control over water pollution in interstate waters.

works projects abounded. The Public Works Administration (PWA) invested more than $4 billion in projects, some of which were designed to abate water pollution.[22] For example, "more than two-thirds of all new sewage treatment plants constructed nationwide between 1933 and 1939 were PWA projects," with $325 million being devoted to sewage treatment works.[23] Roosevelt imposed some conditions on this funding, as the PWA was to deny proposals for "sewage systems which might allow untreated sewage to increase overall pollution in any lake or stream." These projects led to significant public health benefits as typhoid deaths and illnesses declined.

Yet water quality problems persisted, and less progress was made on the regulatory front. Through a 1934 executive order, Roosevelt created the National Resources Board to advise him on policy regarding the development and use of land and water, as well as the "proper division of responsibility" between federal, state, and local governments.[24] The board consisted of the heads of six agencies, including the secretary of the interior and the secretary of war, and three private individuals, including Frederic Delano, who happened to be Roosevelt's uncle.

The National Resources Board's general position on water pollution was that it was a state matter, and the federal role should be limited to conducting studies and providing the states grants and technical support. (The board also endorsed the "streams are nature's sewers"[25] view toward water pollution: dilution is the solution.) Supporters of this position included, perhaps surprisingly, the surgeon general and the head of the Public Health Service and, perhaps less surprisingly, the US Chamber of Commerce and industry groups such as the National Association of Manufacturers, the American Coal Association, and the American Mining Congress.[26] As we will see, these business and industry organizations continue today to embrace the concern for state primacy in environmental matters, which conveniently for them typically leads to less regulation.

In contrast to the "study and pay the states" approach, some in Congress also advocated for a federal regulatory program. They pointed out that the states had failed: "State laws and regulations in pollution control were nonexistent, either inadequately written or inadequately enforced in a number of states, including those with the greatest pollution."[27] Supporters of a federal regulatory approach included conservation organizations, such as the Izaak Walton League and the Audubon Society, which recognized that water pollution affected not only public health but fish, wildlife, and recreation too.[28]

In 1936, Senator Augustine Lonergan of Connecticut introduced bills, endorsed by the North American Wild Life Conference,[29] to establish federal water quality standards, enforceable through federal injunctions.[30] That bill failed. Its opponents favored the creation of a water pollution control division within the Public Health Service, with more limited powers.[31] The next year, Congressman (and later US Supreme Court Justice) Fred Vinson of Kentucky proposed H.R. 2711, which was eventually adopted by both the House and the Senate.[32] It was weak sauce: Although a new Division of Water Pollution Control would be housed within the Public Health Service, the bill lacked any enforcement provisions. Instead, the Public Health Service would provide grants and loans for the construction of pollution treatment works.

The geographic scope of H.R. 2711 is noteworthy, however. In section 2, the Division of Water Pollution Control was directed to prepare plans, in cooperation with state and local governments and relevant industries, to improve the water quality of "the navigable waters of the United States and the streams tributary thereto."[33] Planning was thus intended to cover both navigable and nonnavigable waters. This point is underscored in the bill's next sentence, which calls on the division to make joint investigations with states regarding "the condition of any waters of the United States, either navigable or otherwise."[34] The phrase "waters of the United States" is repeated in section 4, which authorized the Public Health Service to investigate and make "appropriate recommendations with regard to the control of pollution of the waters of the United States."[35] This appears to be the first instance, in a bill passed by Congress, where the term "waters of the United States" covered waters beyond traditional navigable waters.

Ultimately, however, President Roosevelt vetoed H.R. 2711.[36] The justification for the veto, charitably characterized as "obtuse,"[37] was based not on federalism and state sovereignty concerns but rather on a separation of powers issue. In his June 1938 veto message, Roosevelt expressed his support for the establishment of a Division of Water Pollution Control within the Public Health Service; however, he objected to a perceived intrusion of Congress into the workings of the executive branch.[38] Roosevelt noted that the bill allowed the surgeon general to make direct recommendations to Congress for specific grant and loan projects, "without any opportunity for review by the Chief Executive."[39] In his view, such a process "provide[d] for the legislative assumption of responsibilities of the Executive branch."[40] Accordingly, Roosevelt rejected the bill, sending the matter back to Congress to be reworked.

In January 1940, Congressman (and later Senator) Karl Mundt of South Dakota proposed the Navigable Waters Anti-Pollution Act, which would have empowered the Corps of Engineers to set and enforce water quality standards.[41] Although the bill focused on navigable waters, it authorized the Corps to "promulgate regulations governing the discharge of any matter or materials directly or indirectly into such waters," which suggested that the Corps could regulate discharges of pollutants into the nonnavigable tributaries that (indirectly) flowed into and affected navigable waters.[42] But Mundt's bill died in committee. Undaunted, Mundt prevailed on the House to amend a competing bill with a provision that prohibited the discharge of new sources of pollution into "the navigable waters of the United States and the streams tributary thereto" without a permit from the Division of Water Pollution Control.[43] Despite Roosevelt's support of the Mundt amendment, the Senate objected, and the effort stalled at the conference committee level.[44] The world war then intervened, and any serious efforts at water pollution control were placed on hold.

The 1948 Federal Water Pollution Control Act: The Surgeon General as Cheerleader and Banker

Finally, in 1948, Congress passed a water pollution bill that was acceptable to the president, who was now Harry Truman.[45] The bill was also acceptable to those, such as Senate majority leader (and soon-to-be vice president) Alben Barkley of Kentucky, who were concerned about federal intrusion into state and local matters. Consequently, to paraphrase a quote attributed to Churchill, it was a modest law with a great deal to be modest about.

The Federal Water Pollution Control Act did not grant any federal agency the authority to establish any tangible pollution limits or water quality standards. It did not establish a federal permit program. It did not contain any independent enforcement powers that could be exercised by a federal agency under the act. Furthermore, the geographic scope of the act was exceedingly narrow, covering only interstate waters, defined as "all rivers, lakes, and other waters that flow across, or form a part of, State boundaries."[46] The act did not provide for any role for the Corps of Engineers. Instead, the Public Health Service, through the surgeon general, was to exercise limited authority, confined primarily to exhortations and the approval of loans to states.[47]

The first sentence of the Federal Water Pollution Control Act conveyed its modest ambitions. Despite a nod to federal jurisdiction over the "waterways of the Nation" and the public health and welfare benefits of stream pollution abatement, the act opened by declaring it "to be the policy of Congress to recognize, preserve, and protect the primary responsibilities and rights of the States in controlling water pollution."[48] The primacy of the state role is evident throughout the act. Although the surgeon general was directed to develop programs to reduce and eliminate water pollution in interstate waters and their tributaries, it was to be done in cooperation with state agencies (and local governments and industry).[49] The surgeon general could conduct an investigation into the condition of "any waters in any State" but could do so only jointly with a state or interstate agency.[50] The surgeon general was relegated to "encourag[ing] the enactment of uniform State laws relating to water pollution [and] encourag[ing] compacts between States for the prevention and abatement of water pollution."[51]

To be sure, the Federal Water Pollution Control Act stated that "pollution of interstate waters . . . which endangers the health or welfare of persons in a State other than that in which the discharge originates" was a public nuisance.[52] Therefore, the surgeon general could initiate an enforcement action—but only after providing notice to the polluter and state of origin, and only if the state declined to take action and the condition persisted, and a public hearing was held to develop remediation recommendations.[53] If the nuisance continued, the surgeon general—with the consent of the state where the pollution originated—could then seek to convince the US attorney to bring an enforcement action. As one scholar observed, "It is difficult to imagine an enforcement procedure more poorly designed to secure prompt and meaningful action on the part of an industrial or municipal polluter, the assumed villains during this era."[54] Not surprisingly, such highly contingent enforcement "powers" were never used.[55]

A provision, at least in theory, that had more utility was the authorization of loans for the construction of wastewater treatment projects. But the amounts appropriated were small (never exceeding $3 million per year),[56] and the loans, which required the approval of the surgeon general and the relevant state, were unpopular with local governments.[57] Thus the 1948 act did little to improve the nation's water quality.

Ike's Veto: Mo' Money, Mo' Problems?

In 1956, Congress amended the Federal Water Pollution Control Act.[58] The surgeon general and the Public Health Service were now placed within the Department of Health, Education, and Welfare. The act's geographic provisions—limited to pollution of interstate waters—remained the same, but the loan program for the construction of wastewater treatment projects was replaced with a grant program.[59] Loans require repayment; grants do not. Accordingly, the grant program was much more popular with municipalities, and Congress continued to increase funding, so much so that it prompted a veto in 1960 by President Eisenhower.

The proposed 1960 amendments to the Federal Water Pollution Control Act in H.R. 3610 sought to nearly double the grant program from $50 million to $90 million annually, at a cost of $900 million over a ten-year period.[60] Although Ike considered rivers and streams to be a "priceless national asset," in this case the cost was too high.[61] He supported federal–state cooperation to combat water pollution, but emphasized that state and local governments needed to take the lead. In his view,

> Because water pollution is a uniquely local blight, primary responsibility for solving the problem lies not with the Federal Government but rather must be assumed and exercised, as it has been, by State and local governments. This being so, the defects of H.R. 3610 are apparent. By holding forth the promise of a large-scale program of long-term Federal support, it would tempt municipalities to delay essential water pollution abatement efforts while they waited for Federal funds.[62]

Of course, water pollution is not a "uniquely local blight." Indeed, an impetus for the Federal Water Pollution Control Act was the concern about pollution in one state affecting the water quality in another state. Nevertheless, Ike's concern that federal largesse would "provide excuses for inaction" on the part of state and local governments led him to reject the legislation, and Congress did not override his veto.

More than a decade later, when Richard Nixon (Ike's former vice president) was president, he expressed similar concerns about the costs of a water pollution bill. But by that time, momentum had shifted in the country and in Congress in favor of a strong federal response. Congress overrode Nixon's veto, enacting the present-day form of cooperative federalism to combat water pollution, in which the states were expected to do more than simply receive federal funds.[63]

CHAPTER 5

You Say You Want a Revolution

> The objective of this [law] is to restore and maintain the chemical, physical, and biological integrity of the Nation's waters.
>
> —Amendments to the Federal Water Pollution Control Act, 1972

The 1960s in the United States were a time of tumult—politically, racially, socially, culturally. Political assassinations from JFK to MLK to RFK scarred the nation. Federal civil rights laws were enacted but were met with fierce resistance in the states. Sexual mores evolved (or just become more open). Drug usage, especially that of marijuana, increased (or just became more open). Traditional gender roles were questioned (or defended). The changing music scene rankled older generations (as has always been the case between all generations). Seemingly impossible accomplishments occurred: Neil Armstrong walked on the moon, and the Mets won the World Series.

While some heralded the Age of Aquarius, others decried it as moral decay, bereft of institutional moorings. Federal efforts to protect water quality followed a similar track.

In the water context in the 1960s and early 1970s, revolution was afoot as well. The Rivers and Harbors Act, long consigned to merely protecting navigational interests, was surprisingly dusted off and used to protect water quality, as a result of a Supreme Court ruling. Congress tinkered with and made incremental changes to the Federal Water Pollution Control Act, ultimately leading to a complete restructuring of the law in 1972 to give us what today we call the Clean Water Act. The feds were no longer focusing on just interstate waters but rather were concerned about all the nation's waters.

A linchpin to the ambitious objective of restoring and then maintaining the integrity of the nation's waters was a broader conception of "navigable waters" as "waters of the United States." In addition, in light of the states' continued inability to combat water pollution, the Clean Water Act strengthened the federal role in a new model of cooperative federalism. Federal permits would now be required for the discharge of pollutants to nonnavigable waters. Although the states could take the lead in administering these regulatory programs if they wished, the federal government would do so if they declined. The Clean Water Act, along with other laws that are triggered when the Clean Water Act applies, was revolutionary in its resetting of the federal–state relationship. It also resulted in remarkable progress in improving the quality of the nation's waters. But the revolution and its aftermath had (and continue to have) their critics, who still yearn for the simpler times of yesteryear.

Resurrecting the Refuse Act

Hiding in plain sight, section 13 of the Rivers and Harbors Act of 1899—known as the Refuse Act—prohibited the discharge of "any refuse matter of any kind or description whatever" into navigable waters, except for runoff from streets and sewers.[1] On its face, the statute appeared to proscribe the discharge of *any* waste, as the phrases "of any kind" and "of any . . . description whatever" compel a broad reading. But the executive branch had long interpreted the Refuse Act to apply only to discharges that interfered with navigation. As a 1912 judge advocate general's legal opinion stated, concerns about water quality should be left to the states.[2] A negligent act involving aviation fuel caused the Department of Justice (DOJ) to reconsider this position.

In November 1963, Standard Oil employees cleaning and repairing a storage tank in Jacksonville, Florida, along the St. Johns River failed to close the main shutoff valve. Before the error was realized, 300 gallons of gasoline befouled the river. The trial court dismissed the misdemeanor case, reasoning that valuable gasoline could not, as a matter of law, constitute "refuse."[3] The DOJ sought review by the US Supreme Court, saying the law was clear: Congress wanted to prohibit all foreign matter from being discharged into navigable waters. Standard Oil also claimed the law was clear but asserted an opposite conclusion. Refuse was waste, something that lacked value. In its view, the government's interpretation would not provide fair notice to the regulated community. The 6–3 Supreme Court opinion sided with the government.[4] Although both Justice Douglas's majority opinion and Justice Harlan's dissent began by analyzing the plain language of the statute, each offered a contrasting method of statutory interpretation.

The majority opinion invoked legislative history, specifically the history of the previous Rivers and Harbors Acts to interpret the phrase "any refuse matter of any kind or description."[5] It noted that the 1899 act was largely a codification of these prior laws, which did not make a distinction between refuse matter that had value and refuse matter that did not. Instead, the Court concluded that Congress intended the phrase "any refuse matter" to mean any foreign substance.[6] The Court noted that Congress had identified an exception—municipal runoff from streets and sewers—which further supported a broad reading of *refuse matter*. If Congress wanted to make other exceptions, including for discharges of things of value, then it should have said so. The Court should not invent new exceptions divorced from the statutory language.[7]

The majority also interpreted the phrase *refuse matter* in light of the law's overall purposes. The Court asserted that Congress had been concerned not only about a discharge's effect on navigation but about water quality as well. Recalling that "a river is more than an amenity, it is a treasure," the Court commanded that "refuse matter" should be construed "charitably"—that is, broadly, to effectuate Congress's intent.[8]

Justice Harlan's dissent took a different tack in examining the plain language of the act. He consulted *Webster's New International Dictionary* (3rd edition), published in 1961, for the common meaning of *refuse*: "waste, rubbish, trash, debris, garbage."[9] (As we will see, which dictionary the Court should consult to divine the plain meaning of words is hotly debated. Justice Scalia was not a fan of the international edition, which apparently was too infused with the permissiveness of the 1960s.[10]) The dissent pointed out that Congress did not prohibit the discharge of "all matter" but "all refuse matter," and the Court's construction effectively excised the word *refuse* from the act.[11]

Justice Harlan also construed the statutory language in light of the act's purpose, but he emphasized that the legislative history demonstrated that Congress had been concerned about navigational obstructions, not water pollution.[12] Moreover, Justice Harlan invoked the rule of lenity, which counsels that criminal laws should be interpreted narrowly, in part to give potential offenders fair notice. In his view, the Court's overly broad reading of the law suggested that "dropping anything but pure water into a river would appear to be a federal misdemeanor."[13] His dissent stated that if Congress wanted to regulate water pollution, Congress should do so expressly. The Court should not expand the reach of federal laws into areas that were traditionally the province of state and local governments.[14]

As a result of the *Standard Oil* decision, thousands of industrial operations were suddenly in violation of the Refuse Act for discharging pollutants to navigable waters without a Corps permit. They could be subject to federal prosecution, and the Corps could seek an injunction to stop the flows. But this bombshell case had a long fuse, not exploding until a few years later after environmental advocates recognized its utility in conjunction with *qui tam* lawsuits, which allowed private citizens to sue polluters for a bounty.

Emergence of Water Quality Standards and Water Quality Certifications

Meanwhile, as the Refuse Act was being revived, Congress continued to tinker with and make incremental changes to the Federal Water Pollution Control Act. Amendments in 1961 significantly increased federal funding for state and local governments to support wastewater construction and pollution control programs.[15] At the federal level, the administrative responsibility shifted from the surgeon general to the secretary of the Department of Health, Education, and Welfare (HEW).[16] And federal enforcement powers to abate water pollution as a nuisance were expanded from the very limited "interstate waters" to include "navigable waters."[17] Although the states welcomed more money from federal coffers, the increased geographic scope was opposed by supporters of states' rights.

A more significant shift in the federal–state relationship occurred in 1965 with the passage of the Water Quality Act.[18] For the first time, states were called on to establish water quality standards for interstate waters within their respective territories and adopt an implementation plan to enforce those standards.[19] HEW, through a newly created Federal Water Pollution Control Administration, would review a state's water quality standards to determine whether they properly considered the "use and value for public water supplies, propagation of fish and wildlife, recreational purposes, and agricultural, industrial, and other legitimate uses."[20] But, as explained in Chapter 2, the states are not mere marionettes of the federal government; the feds cannot simply order the states to develop water quality standards. The 1965 law contemplated that states would not voluntarily do so and thus authorized HEW to set the standards.[21] This established a template still used today: States are given the opportunity to act, but if they decline, the federal government will step in.

The federal government was also given the authority to enforce water quality standards, whether they were promulgated by a state or HEW. If a "discharge of matter" caused the receiving interstate waters to fall below its water quality standards, the federal government could seek an injunction to abate that discharge as a nuisance—whether the pollutant was "discharged directly into such waters or reache[d] such waters after discharge into tributaries of such waters."[22] Congress again recognized that the protection of interstate waters required a watershed approach. And Congress also recognized the impact that water pollution could have on aquatic species and commerce related to those aquatic species: "Substantial economic injury result[ing] from the inability to market shellfish or shellfish products in interstate commerce because of pollution" was grounds for an injunction.[23]

In 1966, President Johnson transferred the Federal Water Pollution Control Administration and its responsibilities from HEW to the Department of Interior. Interior Secretary Stewart Udall noted that twenty-seven states had committed to establishing water quality standards.[24] On the day that the Department of Interior assumed responsibility, he reiterated President Johnson's declaration that "no one has the right to use America's rivers and America's waterways that belong to all the people as a sewer."[25] (Interior's turn at the helm was ultimately short-lived, as the EPA took over in 1970.)

While Congress encouraged states to develop and enforce water quality standards, it also gave states a role in federal permitting and licensing. The Water Quality Improvement Act of 1970 required that any applicants for a federal permit or license for an activity that "may result in any discharge into the navigable waters of the United States" obtain a certification from the state where the discharge would occur.[26] The state needed to certify that the proposed activity would not violate applicable water quality standards. If the state denied the certification, the activity could not proceed. In effect, the certification requirement gave the states a veto over any federal permit or license of an activity that could result in the discharge of pollutants to navigable waters.[27]

Although states could often exercise concurrent jurisdiction over a regulated activity, the water quality certification was a radical step in the federal–state relationship. Rather than the feds telling the states what to do, the states could now dictate to the federal agencies what permits and licenses they could grant. As we will see later, when states invoked this power to stop energy infrastructure projects for reasons related to climate change concerns, the Trump administration sought to curtail this aspect of states' rights.

Bastard Origins of EPA

In his January 1970 State of the Union address, the first issue President Nixon discussed was the raging war in Vietnam.[28] He touched on crime and welfare reform. But much of his address—about one quarter—was devoted to environmental issues. The great question of the 1970s, he suggested, was whether we would "make our peace with nature and begin to make reparations for the damage we have done to our air, to our land, and to our water."[29] In addition to proposing a $10 billion program for the construction of municipal wastewater treatment plants, he observed that "comprehensive new regulations" would be needed to protect the nation's natural resources, including water.[30] Several weeks later, President Nixon submitted to Congress comprehensive environmental legislative proposals, which called for more aggressive federal enforcement of water quality standards. He recognized that water pollution from agricultural operations was "the most troublesome to control."[31] And he proposed that "the Federal pollution control program be extended to include all navigable waters, both inter- and intra-state, [and] all interstate ground waters."[32] Congress did not immediately act on his proposals, however.

Instead, Nixon moved forward by decree. He issued a reorganization plan, which was effectively an executive order to establish the EPA.[33] Conceding that such a step was contrary to his position that "new independent agencies normally should not be created," he nevertheless recognized the need to have one agency whose overall mission focused on protecting environmental quality.[34] The plan directed that the environmental responsibilities of Interior, HEW, and other agencies be transferred to the EPA.[35]

Astute readers will recall from Chapter 2 that executive orders don't ordinarily, by themselves, have the force of law. Under our system of checks and balances, a president may not simply create agencies out of whole cloth. Such unilateral action runs counter to everything we learned from *Schoolhouse Rock*. Can the EPA legitimately come into being without Congress's approval? No; the president cannot act alone in this context.

But Nixon did not act alone. Congress, through a duly enacted statute, had previously given the president the authority to reorganize executive branch operations, within certain limits. In 1966 Congress had codified and revised laws pertaining to government operation and employees. In a chapter on executive reorganization, the law stated that the president shall determine, from time to time, whether agency functions should be consolidated to promote "better execution of the laws," as well as efficiency and cost savings.[36] Before moving these functions or creating or eliminating an agency, the president was required to submit the reorganization plan to both houses of Congress.[37] If either the House of Representatives or the Senate passed a resolution expressing disapproval, then the reorganization could not proceed.[38] In July 1970, Nixon submitted his plan to Congress. Neither house passed a resolution of disapproval, and the plan became effective in October 1970. The EPA officially opened on December 2, 1970.[39]

The "legislative veto" process—whereby a single house could override an executive action—was a common mechanism at the time.[40] It provided the executive branch flexibility to implement the law under congressional oversight. However common and useful the legislative veto might have been, there was significant question about its constitutionality. Indeed, in the 1983 case of *Immigration and Naturalization Service v. Chadha*, the Supreme Court held that use of the resolutions of disapproval to void executive actions violated the separation of powers.[41] The Court ruled that Congress could take legislative action only by passing a bill in both houses and presenting it to the president for signature or veto. The Constitution did not contemplate that one house could control the executive branch. Even a resolution of disapproval from both houses is insufficient. If Congress wanted to act legislatively, it needed to present a bill to the president. If the president vetoed it, Congress could override that veto. But the "legislative veto" process ran afoul of the constitutional requirement of presentation.

Does this mean that the EPA is unconstitutional? Perhaps to the disappointment of some in the regulated community, the answer is no. The prohibition of the legislative veto is a limitation on Congress's power. It does not affect the executive action that Congress may have disapproved of or acquiesced in. Moreover, since the EPA's inception, Congress has granted EPA regulatory authority in a host of bills that were properly presented to the president and that become law through either presidential signature or the override of a presidential veto. And Congress has passed appropriation bills to fund the EPA, all of which have also been properly presented to the president. So the existence of the EPA rests on a strong statutory basis, despite questions surrounding its birth through executive decree.

But the EPA is technically not a Cabinet department, such as the Department of the Interior or the DOJ or even the more specialized Department of Veterans Affairs. The law authorizing President Nixon to reorganize the government specifically prohibited the establishment of a new executive branch department.[42] Although there have been bills proposed to elevate EPA's status to a Cabinet department, none has passed.[43] Does this matter? Other than optics, not particularly. Whether EPA is classified as a department does not affect its statutory authorities. However, it does mean that the administrator of the EPA is not in the line of succession for the presidency, which after the vice president, speaker of the House, and president pro tempore of the Senate is limited to the heads of departments. Consequently, the EPA administrator cannot be the designated survivor and has no excuse not to attend State of the Union addresses.[44]

Bounty Hunters

To be clear, Nixon was not an environmentalist. An iconic picture of Nixon walking on the beach of San Clemente, in suit and wingtip shoes, perhaps unintentionally captures his awkward relationship with environmental matters.[45] He created the EPA mostly as a political gesture: He wanted the support of green voters. But his rhetoric on stronger environmental enforcement was not matched by his actions.

After the Refuse Act was dusted off, or reinterpreted to cover pollution affecting water quality, environmentalists noticed another neglected provision. Concerned citizens who reported Refuse Act violations were eligible for half of any fines recovered from the polluters. This economic incentive contributed to the DOJ becoming "inundated by reports of Refuse Act violations by bounty-hunting environmentalists."[46] To halt the flow, the DOJ issued guidelines in June 1970 that established enforcement priorities that can only be described as bizarre.

The 1970 guidelines sharply curtailed use of the Refuse Act for water pollution abatement purposes.[47] It provided that DOJ should focus only on "accidental or infrequent" discharges from "occasional or recalcitrant" polluters.[48] Intentional dischargers responsible for continuous or regular discharges of pollutants would not be subject to civil or criminal actions under the Refuse Act. Indeed, the guidelines specifically exempted discharges "of a continuing nature resulting from the ordinary operations of a manufacturing plant."[49] The proffered explanation for targeting reluctant polluters and accidental discharges, instead of purposeful and intentional polluters, was that the Refuse Act should be used only to protect against refuse that interfered with navigation, despite the Supreme Court's more generous view of the statute in *Standard Oil*.[50] The Court had polished up an old tool to fight water pollution and handed it to the executive branch, and the executive branch essentially responded with "no thanks, we're good."

In response to DOJ's own recalcitrance, the House Conservation and Natural Resources Subcommittee, led by Wisconsin Congressman Henry Reuss, examined whether the use of *qui tam* actions would be appropriate.[51] In some situations where the federal government declines to take an enforcement action, a private person may sue to enforce the law on behalf of the government through a *qui tam* action.[52] Monies recovered in a *qui tam* action are shared between the government and the person who filed the lawsuit. The House Committee issued a report that endorsed the use of citizen suits to enforce the Refuse Act in the absence of federal action.[53]

But Congress (as a whole, through presentment to the president) had not expressly authorized the use of citizen suits to enforce the Refuse Act, and courts expressed their own recalcitrance about permitting *qui tam* actions to proceed. Lower courts initially rejected Refuse Act citizen suits on multiple grounds, concluding that the environmental plaintiffs lacked standing or that the reporting mechanism provided the exclusive remedy for private citizens.[54] Nevertheless, the viability of such lawsuits remained an open question as the cases proceeded through the judicial system. But before the Supreme Court had the opportunity to rule on the matter, Nixon issued another executive order that rendered the question moot.

Merry Christmas!

The Refuse Act did not prohibit all discharges of waste; rather, it prohibited the discharge of waste without authorization from the Corps of Engineers. But the Corps did not have a formal permit program with respect to refuse. On December 23, 1970, Nixon signed Executive Order 11574, which established the Refuse Act Permit Program, to remedy the situation.[55] It was an early holiday gift to the regulated community.

The executive order tasked the secretary of the army (who oversees the Corps) with evaluating permit applications "to regulate the discharge of pollutants and other refuse matter into the navigable waters of the United States or their tributaries and the placing of such matter upon their banks."[56] But the Corps was not to make water quality decisions on its own. The Corps needed to consult with EPA in developing the permit program's regulations, and the Corps was required to defer to EPA's determinations regarding water quality standards. Moreover, the Corps could not issue a permit if a state denied a water quality certification. The Corps finalized its regulations in 1971, and more than 15,000 industrial dischargers applied for the permit.[57] By entering the permit process, the dischargers were effectively protected from *qui tam* actions brought by environmentalists. No court would entertain a lawsuit complaining about unpermitted discharges while the Corps was considering a permit application.[58]

The executive order also effectively ended federal enforcement of the Refuse Act. One lawyer in the US Attorney's Office for the Southern District of

New York, who had been active in pursuing both civil and criminal sanctions under the Refuse Act, reckoned that the permit program bought the regulated community "several years of virtual legal immunity while applicants wait for their permits to be processed."[59] He observed that "Nixon's permit program knocks the teeth out of water-pollution enforcement throughout the country. In effect, the permits will be veritable licenses to pollute."[60] He made these remarks shortly after being fired for suing General Motors for dumping chemical wastes directly into the Hudson River.[61]

But the Refuse Act Permit Program was short-lived. Jerome Kalur and Donald Large, two conservation-minded lawyers, filed a lawsuit with themselves as plaintiffs, as well as on behalf of other people and environmental groups who recreationally used the Grand River in northeastern Ohio, a traditional navigable water.[62] Kalur and Large attacked the Corps' regulations on both procedural and substantive grounds. They claimed that the National Environmental Policy Act (NEPA, discussed in more detail below) required the Corps to prepare environmental impact statements as part of the permit decision process.[63] The Corps countered by contending that because it was "an agency dedicated to guarding the environment," it was irrational to require it to conduct a separate analysis of water quality impacts when making permit decisions.[64] Perhaps aware that the Corps, at this stage in its history, did not have a tradition of environmental protection, the court was unpersuaded and ordered that the Corps revise its regulations to incorporate the NEPA process.[65] More substantively, Kalur and Large also claimed that the plain language of the Refuse Act authorized the Corps to grant permits only for discharges to navigable waters and that discharges to nonnavigable tributaries were flatly prohibited. The US District Court for the District of Columbia agreed:

> An examination of the statute indicates that it is divided into two parts, the first part setting forth the prohibition against the "discharge . . . of refuse matter", and the second part providing an exception for permits for such discharges by the Chief of Engineers. The first part, or prohibition applies by its terms to "any navigable water, or . . . any tributary of any navigable water. . . ." Discharges of "refuse" matter are clearly prohibited in both navigable waters and in non-navigable tributaries of navigable waters.
>
> The second part of the section, pertaining to the permits provision, is more limited in scope. The Secretary of the Army

> "may permit the deposit of any material above mentioned in navigable waters. . . ." This separate proviso makes no mention of tributaries in contrast to the specific language in the prohibition part of the section. The conclusion that is drawn from this language is that the Corps of Engineers has no authority to authorize deposits of refuse matter in non-navigable tributaries of navigable waterways.[66]

The District Court noted that there were "many clean and still unspoiled rivers, streams, and lakes that do not fall within the expanding definition of 'navigable.'"[67] The Refuse Act "absolutely" prohibited the discharge of refuse into these nonnavigable waters. Accordingly, the court held that the Corps had exceeded the congressional authority in creating a program to "shield polluters and potential polluters where Congress has specifically prohibited such activity."[68]

Congress was about to completely overhaul the Federal Water Pollution Control Act, however. In doing so, it expressly gave the Corps (and the EPA) the authority to grant permits for the discharge of pollutants to nonnavigable tributaries, thus mooting Kalur and Large's lawsuit. But Congress also expanded federal jurisdiction to cover the "waters of the United States," a term that has bedeviled the agencies, courts, regulated industries, and environmentalists ever since.

Expanding Jurisdiction: WOTUS

On October 4, 1972, Congress voted to approve amendments to the Federal Water Pollution Control Act and presented it to President Nixon.[69] Nixon vetoed the bill, citing concerns about the cost of municipal wastewater programs (similar to Ike's objections).[70] Congress then overrode Nixon's veto by a vote of 247–23 in the House and 52–12 in the Senate on October 18.[71] Remarkably, this rebuff of Nixon occurred just weeks before he was reelected in an electoral landslide, 520–17, winning every state, except for Massachusetts, and the District of Columbia.

The new law's definition of *navigable waters* departed from the term's traditional meaning. The House and Senate bills defined the term differently. House Bill 11896 repetitively defined *navigable waters* to mean "the navigable waters of the United States, including the territorial seas."[72] However, Senate Bill 2770, which passed by a vote of 86–0, defined *navigable waters* as "the waters of the United States, including the territorial seas"—dropping the modifier "navigable" before the term "waters of the United States."[73] When reconciling the bills at conference, the conferees adopted the Senate's version. The Conference Report explained that the "conferees fully intend[ed] that the term 'navigable waters' be given the broadest possible constitutional interpretation unencumbered by agency determinations which have been made or may be made for administrative purposes."[74] This view was emphasized in the subsequent debate in the House, when Representative Dingell stated that the new definition of *navigable waters* was expansive and "clearly encompasses all water bodies, including streams and their tributaries, for water quality purposes."[75]

It's been said that citing legislative history is like picking out your friends in a crowd. Often you can find some stray statement that supports your position, and courts are generally reluctant to rely solely on legislative history to ascertain the intent of Congress. Although the precise parameters of "waters of the United States" are unclear, one thing is certain: By deleting *navigable*, Congress intended to assert federal jurisdiction beyond traditional navigable waters.

From Navigable Waters to WOTUS

As we have seen, Congress's use of various terms to describe which waters are subject to federal control has evolved over the years. (Table A-2 in the Appendix traces this journey in detail.) The classic definition of *navigable waters* or *navigable waters of the United States* covers waters used in commerce, or subject to the ebb and flow of the tide—also known as traditional navigable waters. Congress provided a definition of *navigable waters* for purposes of the Federal Water Power Act to include waters that were navigable in fact or that could become navigable with reasonable improvements. *Coastal navigable waters*, used in the Oil Pollution Act of 1924, is obviously a subset of *navigable waters*. Similarly, *interstate waters*, waters that cross a state boundary, is of more limited scope.

Yet Congress has demonstrated on several occasions that it wanted to regulate activities on waters that were not navigable. Section 10 of the Rivers and Harbors Act of 1890, as interpreted by the Supreme Court, applied to activities on nonnavigable tributaries when those actions affected navigable waters. Section 13 of the Rivers and Harbors Act of 1899 expressly refers to "any tributary" of a navigable water. And the 1938 water pollution bill, vetoed by Franklin Roosevelt, sought to cover "any waters of the United States," whether navigable or not.

Depending on the context, the term *waters of the United States* can be synonymous with or broader than traditional navigable waters. When first used by Congress in the Rivers and Harbors Act of 1899, the context made clear that the term was limited to traditional navigable waters, as the prohibitions regarding waters of the United States were intended to maintain the navigational capacity of those waters. By 1938, however, Congress used the term to encompass both navigable and nonnavigable waters ("any waters of the United States, either navigable or otherwise"), albeit in a vetoed bill. In 1972, when Congress debated and deliberately dropped *navigable* from the phrase *navigable waters of the United States*, it chose a broader understanding of the waters to be afforded federal protection under the Clean Water Act.

Waters of the United States is the linchpin to the Clean Water Act. Everything flows from that term. To achieve the law's objective "to restore and maintain the chemical, physical, and biological integrity of the Nation's waters,"[76] all point source discharges of pollutants to the waters of the United States are prohibited—unless they are authorized by a federal permit.[77] If a waterbody qualifies as a "water of the United States," then it is covered by the Clean Water Act's protections and federal permits are required for many (but not all) polluting activities. If a waterbody is not a "water of the United States," then the provisions of the Clean Water Act, including the permit requirements, do not apply. Protection of those waters then falls solely to state and local governments. WOTUS is thus jurisdictional; a sharp line is drawn that determines whether polluters must apply for a federal permit or not. Let's examine the two major Clean Water Act permit programs, one that the EPA administers and the other that the Corps implements.

NPDES Supplants RAPP

One of the challenges with environmental law is the array of bewildering acronyms. The Clean Water Act is no exception, and the 1972 law introduced the NPDES permit program in section 402. *NPDES* stands for the National Pollutant Discharge Elimination System and is often pronounced "nip-dees." A NPDES permit is also called a section 402 permit. However it is referenced, the more important point is that it replaced the teetering Refuse Act Permit Program, administered by the Corps and beset by legal challenges.[78] Instead of relying on the creaky bones of a nineteenth-century law that was more concerned about navigation, Congress replaced the Refuse Act Permit Program with a comprehensive federal water pollution abatement program. And Congress chose the EPA, rather than the Corps, to oversee the NPDES program.[79]

For the first time, the federal government applied nationally uniform effluent standards to categories and classes of polluters.[80] So a factory discharging chemical wastes into a water of the United States needed a NPDES or section 402 permit from the EPA, and this permit set a limit on the amount of pollution that could be discharged. As a starting point, the limit would be based on technology-based effluent standards, known as TBELs (pronounced "tee-bells"). The TBELs are based on what is practicable for a particular industry and are developed by EPA through a notice-and-comment rulemaking process.[81]

Although it had created a new and expansive federal regulatory program, Congress was mindful that water quality issues had traditionally been within the province of state and local governments. Indeed, the 1972 law stated that Congress recognized "the primary responsibilities and rights of States to prevent, reduce, and eliminate pollution, to plan the development and use (including restoration, preservation, and enhancement) of land and water resources."[82] And, consistent with our constitutional system, Congress could not simply commandeer the states to regulate pollution, because the states are not mere marionettes of the federal government. Instead, Congress offered the states a choice: EPA could issue the NPDES permits, or the states could assume responsibility for the federal program and issue the permits on behalf of the federal government.[83]

Most states acceded to this form of cooperative federalism. Indeed, today almost every state has assumed the NPDES program (the outliers are Massachusetts, New Hampshire, and New Mexico).[84] Although the states operating a NPDES program must follow EPA rules, most states have accepted this arrangement because they want to retain control over these decisions that can have economic consequences for local businesses. This carrot has proven to be attractive.

But the states' role is not limited to making section 402 permit decisions. Congress recognized that requiring a technology-based approach might not result in waters that were fishable, drinkable, and swimmable. For example, there could be many dischargers to a river and its tributaries, and even if they all complied with their TBEL limits, the cumulative impact of the multiple sources of pollution could result in poor water quality. In addition, there are other sources of pollution, from nonpoint sources, such as runoff from lawns and agricultural fields, that are not captured by the NPDES program. The contribution of the nonpoint source pollution, combined with the regulated point source dischargers, could also result in poor water quality. Congress therefore supplemented TBELs with WQBELs, or water quality–based effluent limitations. States are requested to designate specific water uses (such as fishing and swimming) for each segment of a waterbody and to develop water quality criteria that would achieve those uses.[85] These WQBELs can then (in theory) be incorporated into section 402 permits, thus further limiting the amount of pollution authorized to be discharged.

For the first time, Congress had expressly created a federal permit program focused on abating water pollution. Even municipal wastewater treatment plants (now called publicly owned treatment works [POTWs]), long the recipients of federal largesse, were now also subject to TBELs.[86] The traditional financial carrot had given way to, or at least was being supplemented by, the regulatory stick. And, for the first time, a federal regulatory agency with a clear environmental mission was at the helm. But the Clean Water Act still maintained an important role for the Corps of Engineers.

Section 404: An Uneasy Alliance

Historically, the Corps of Engineers did not view itself as an environmental agency. It was part of the military, and its military mission was (in part) to keep waterways navigable for military purposes. Early on, however, the Corps was also tasked with the responsibility to keep waterways open for commercial purposes.

When Congress revamped the Federal Water Pollution Control Act, section 402 dealt with what might be considered conventional pollutants, such as chemical waste. But Congress also considered the question of discharging dredged or fill material, which could consist of uncontaminated sediments or earth—basically "clean" dirt. It might seem counterintuitive to classify such materials as pollutants, but when discharged into a waterbody they have environmental impacts, even beyond a sediment plume that could block sunlight and choke aquatic life. The discharge of dredged or fill material might eliminate a waterbody entirely (or partly), and the removal of that waterbody from the landscape also degrades the ecosystem services that the water previously provided.

The Corps had regulated the discharge of dredge or fill material in conjunction with structures under its Rivers and Harbors Act authorities dating back to the 1890s. But these authorities only generally applied only to traditional navigable waters. In the lead-up to the Clean Water Act, the House of Representatives wanted the Corps to maintain its authority over discharges of dredged and fill material.[87] The Corps, for its part, was amenable to accepting this responsibility because, in part, it wanted to retain permitting control over its own civil works activities, such as flood control and navigation projects.[88] More environmentally minded senators were skeptical that the Corps would willingly pivot to promoting water quality. A compromise was struck: The Corps would acquire permitting authority related to the discharge of dredged or fill material under section 404, but it would be obligated to consult with the EPA and follow EPA's regulations when making permit decisions.[89] Moreover, the EPA was granted a right to veto a Corps permit, if the EPA determined that the permitted activity "would have an unacceptable adverse impact on one or more of various resources, including fisheries, wildlife, municipal water supplies, or recreational areas."[90]

This is a unique administrative relationship, and tensions in implementation occurred. As professor Oliver Houck once trenchantly observed, "Section 404 lies like an open wound across the body of environmental law.... [It] is constructed on the backs of two beasts moving in different directions."[91] And the EPA and Corps' initial, divergent views of the reach of "waters of the United States" only underscored the concern about inconsistent missions.

Are "Navigable Waters of the United States" and "Waters of the United States" Synonymous? (No)

In January 1973, the EPA published for public comment a proposed rule regarding its new NPDES program. In defining *navigable waters* for purposes of the Clean Water Act, the proposal merely repeated the statutory definition: "the waters of the United States including the territorial seas."[92] When issuing the final rule four months later, the EPA dutifully reported that it had received written comments from interested parties, as well as "a number of verbal comments."[93] The agency also noted, with no explanation, that it had clarified the definition of *navigable waters* by "incorporating additional language."[94] The Clean Water Act (at least for the NPDES program) now covered

> (1) All navigable waters of the United States;
> (2) Tributaries of navigable waters of the United States;
> (3) Interstate waters;
> (4) Intrastate lakes, rivers, and streams which are utilized by interstate travelers for recreational or other purposes;
> (5) Intrastate lakes, rivers, and streams from which fish or shellfish are taken and sold in interstate commerce; and
> (6) Intrastate lakes, rivers, and streams which are utilized for industrial purposes by industries in interstate commerce.[95]

The EPA's definition of *navigable waters* obviously encompassed nonnavigable waters as well.

With its new permitting responsibilities under the Clean Water Act, the Corps conducted its own rulemaking to update its regulations. In the preamble to its final rule, the Corps recalled that the Clean Water Act's Conference Report called for the term to be given "the broadest possible constitutional interpretation unencumbered by agency determinations which have been made or may be made for administrative purposes."[96] A reasonable reading of that passage would be that "waters of the United States" should not be limited to previous determinations limiting federal jurisdiction to traditional navigable waters. Yet, in contrast to the EPA, the Corps opined that a navigational connection *was* the constitutional limit. Thus the Corps defined *navigable waters of the United States* (for Rivers and Harbors Act purposes) and *navigable waters* (that is, "waters of the United States" for Clean Water Act purposes) to be the same: "those waters of the United States which are subject to the ebb and flow of the tide, and/or are presently, or have been in the past, or may be in the future susceptible for use for purposes of interstate or foreign commerce."[97] In effect, the Corps concluded it was business as usual. Environmental groups promptly sued.

In March 1975, in *Natural Resources Defense Council v. Callaway*, the US District Court for the District of Columbia ruled against the Corps.[98] In a brief order, the court concluded that Congress intended for federal jurisdiction to be asserted "over the nation's waters to the maximum extent permissible under the Commerce Clause of the Constitution," beyond "the traditional tests of navigability."[99] The court ordered the Corps to revoke the offending regulation and proceed with a rulemaking that "clearly recogniz[ed] the full regulatory mandate of the [Clean] Water Act."[100] The Corps was not pleased and issued a press release expressing alarm that it would now have to regulate "the rancher who wants to enlarge his stock pond, or the farmer who wants to deepen an irrigation ditch or plow a field, or the mountaineer who wants to protect his land against stream erosion."[101]

Despite its reluctance, the Corps embarked on a series of rulemakings to comply with the court's instructions.[102] The first phase, effective in 1975, revised the regulations to cover traditional navigable waters and their adjacent wetlands.[103] The second phase, effective the following year, extended Clean Water Act jurisdiction to primary tributaries of navigable waters, lakes greater than 5 acres in area, and wetlands adjacent to those waterbodies.[104]

Finally, in the third phase, which was effective in 1977, the Corps arrived at the following regulatory definition of waters of the United States:

> (1) The territorial seas with respect to the discharge of fill material . . .;
> (2) Coastal and inland waters, lakes, rivers, and streams that are [navigable in fact], including adjacent wetlands;
> (3) Tributaries to navigable waters of the United States . . .;
> (4) Interstate waters and their tributaries, including adjacent wetlands; and
> (5) All other waters of the United States not identified in Categories 1–3, such as isolated lakes and wetlands, intermittent streams, prairie potholes, and other waters . . . the destruction of which could affect interstate commerce.[105]

The most significant expansions in jurisdiction involved adjacent wetlands and other nonnavigable waters, such as so-called isolated wetlands and intermittent streams that had some connection to interstate commerce. Environmental interests had prevailed, and now it was the regulated community's turn to attack. They first went to Congress to limit the scope of the Clean Water Act.

The 1977 Amendments: An Attempted Counterrevolution

In 1977, Congress amended portions of the Clean Water Act.[106] Some changes were significant (such as provisions dealing with toxic pollutants), and some not so much (such as changing the formal name of the law from the *Federal Water Pollution Control Act* to the *Clean Water Act*). Of particular significance was one proposed amendment that failed: an attempt to revise the definition of *waters of the United States*.

The senators from Texas led the charge. Senator Lloyd Bentsen, later the losing Democratic vice president candidate in 1988, introduced an amendment to limit the Clean Water Act's jurisdiction to traditional navigable waters and their adjacent wetlands.[107] He focused his ire on the section 404 program, claiming that it had "become a symbol to many Americans of how a well-intentioned legislative initiative can turn into a quagmire of disruption, frustration, and bureaucratic entanglement for the ranchers, farmers, foresters, and average citizens of this country."[108] His Republican counterpart, John Tower, emphasized that if Congress did not act, the result would be an "unwarranted and despotic intrusion by the Federal Government over every brook, creek, cattle tank, mud puddle, slough, or damp spot in every landowner's backyard across this Nation."[109]

In contrast, some senators did not view federal protection of "waters of the United States" as a tyrannical overreach. For example, Democratic Senator Gary Hart of Colorado asserted that the federal government's concerns about water went beyond mere navigable capacity, stating that "there is a national and Federal interest in waterways other than those on which a ship can be floated."[110] Similarly, Republican Senator John Chafee of Rhode Island opposed the Bentsen amendment because it "would leave many of our Nation's ecologically important wetlands with no protection."[111] The Senate ultimately rejected the Bentsen amendment.[112]

The regulated community fared better in the House. The bill approved by the House Committee sought to limit Clean Water Act jurisdiction to traditional navigable waters and adjacent wetlands, defining *adjacent* to mean wetlands "periodically inundated" by contiguous or adjacent navigable waters.[113] But when the House and Senate bills went to the Conference Committee, the Senate version, which made no changes to the Clean Water Act's jurisdiction, prevailed. As Republican Senator Howard Baker remarked, the 1977 act "retain[ed] the comprehensive jurisdiction over the Nation's waters exercised in the 1972 Federal Water Pollution Control Act."[114] WOTUS remained undisturbed.

But the negotiations did not end with the regulated community walking away empty-handed. First, Congress provided relief to the perceived beleaguered farmers and ranchers: Normal farming and ranching activities were expressly exempted from the section 402 and 404 programs. Activities such as "plowing, seeding, cultivating, minor drainage, harvesting for the production of food, fiber, and forest products" are not regulated by the Clean Water Act (unless toxic pollutants are involved).[115] The "construction or maintenance of farm or stock ponds or irrigation ditches, or the maintenance of drainage ditches" are exempt.[116] Furthermore, the "construction or maintenance or farm roads or forest roads" is exempt, so long as they are done in accordance with best management practices.[117] Current and ongoing farming and ranching (and silvicultural) practices thus are spared the fate of falling under the "despotic intrusion of the Federal government." However, an expansion of operations could trigger the need for a permit if it reduced or impaired flow or circulation of a water of the United States.[118] Nevertheless, even if a permit was needed, Congress authorized the Corps to grant general permits (essentially advance authorization) for minor activities,[119] and one general permit that applies nationwide authorizes the filling of up to a half acre of nontidal waters for a range of agricultural activities, "including the construction of building pads for farm buildings."[120] An acre is about the size of a football field, excluding the end zones. So a farmer can generally fill an area about the size of half a football field without much hassle.

The 1977 Clean Water Act amendments also created a process for states to assume control of the federal section 404 program.[121] States already had this option under the section 402 or NPDES program, so it was not particularly controversial in this context. As with section 402 assumption, when making section 404 permit decisions, a state would have to apply the federal rules. There are two big differences between section 402 and section 404 assumption, however. First, federal money was available to cover some of the costs of the former but not the latter. Thus, although most states have assumed the section 402 program, only three (Michigan, New Jersey, and Florida) have assumed the 404 program.[122] Second, states were limited with respect to what waters they could assume responsibility for in the section 404 program. A state could not administer the section 404 program and authorize dredged or fill material (on behalf of the feds) in traditional navigable waters, "including wetlands adjacent thereto."[123] Congress wanted the federal government to retain permitting authority over structures that could affect traditional navigable waters (as it had since the 1800s).

This section 404 state assumption provision also provides some insight into the scope of waters of the United States. By declining to allow states to assume section 404 permitting authority for wetlands adjacent to traditional navigable waters, Congress made clear that at least some wetlands were waters of the United States. But Congress did not take this opportunity to clarify what it meant by *adjacent*, leaving it to the agencies and ultimately the courts.

A State's Right to Eliminate or Reduce Water Pollution

In most cases, a state's motivation to assume federal Clean Water Act responsibilities is to maintain local control over water resources and economic decisions.[124] For example, state assumption may speed up and simplify the permitting process, which the regulated community favors. From an environmental perspective, the Clean Water Act and agency regulations set a floor, a minimum level of protection, that a state must adhere to when assuming a program. And many states seem content to simply require the minimum.

But what if a state wanted to go beyond the federal floor and regulate water pollution more strictly than the EPA or the Corps? As noted in Chapter 3, the Supreme Court has long recognized that states, through their general police powers, have concurrent jurisdiction over activities that affect waters within their jurisdictions. States are free to establish their own permit programs that can operate separately or in coordination with the feds. However, Congress has given the states an additional tool, nestled in section 401 of the Clean Water Act.

Section 401 requires an applicant for any federal license or permit for an activity that "may result in any discharge" into the waters of the United States to obtain a state water quality certification.[125] The state must certify that the activity will comply with water quality standards, and the state may impose conditions on the proposed activity. If the state refuses to issue a water quality certification, then the federal agency may not issue the license or permit. In effect, Congress has given the states a veto over federal permitting decisions.[126]

Note that this veto power goes beyond EPA section 402 permits or Corps section 404 permits. It applies to *any* federal license or permit that may involve a discharge to waters of the United States. Thus the construction of oil and gas pipelines crossing jurisdictional waters that requires a Federal Energy Regulatory Commission license or authorization will also require a state water quality certification.[127] If a state wants to protect its water resources without going through the assumption process, Congress has provided it an effective mechanism. Of course, as we will see, once states started using this tool during the Trump administration, support for "states' rights" in this context waned in some quarters.

WOTUS as a Jurisdictional Hook for Other Environmental Laws

Congress was incredibly active in enacting environmental laws in the 1970s. In addition to the Clean Water Act, Congress passed a panoply of statutes, from the Clean Air Act (which also uses a form of cooperative federalism) and the Federal Insecticide, Fungicide and Rodenticide Act (which requires farmers who purchase pesticides to register) to the Toxic Substances Control Act (which in theory contemplates the testing of chemicals before they reach the consumer market) and the Resource Conservation and Recovery Act (which governs the disposal of solid and hazardous waste). All have some connection to water quality: Air pollution such as mercury emissions from coal-fired power plants can settle in waterbodies, pesticides applied to farm fields run off into streams and wetlands, chemical manufacturing plants may discharge liquid waste to adjacent waters, and improperly disposed waste may leach into groundwater, eventually leading to surface water contamination. Effective implementation of these laws can help promote water quality, at least indirectly.

There are other laws that have a more obvious connection. In 1974, Congress approved the Safe Drinking Water Act (SDWA), which focuses on public water systems that provide drinking water.[128] The EPA sets national health-based standards, and much as in the cooperative federalism model in the Clean Water Act, states can apply to implement the SDWA to ensure adequate testing, conduct inspections, and take enforcement actions.[129] Whereas some source waters, such as rivers, lakes, and streams, are "waters of the United States," some source waters are not. Groundwater can be an SDWA source water, but groundwater has been excluded from the regulatory definition of "waters of the United States."[130] To the extent that the Clean Water Act limits pollutants to SDWA source water, it contributes to the SDWA's objectives. Similarly, to the extent that the SDWA's voluntary tools and partnerships enhance the protection of source water, they contribute to the Clean Water Act's objectives.

Two other environmental statutes play more directly into the Clean Water Act permit process: NEPA and the Endangered Species Act (ESA). NEPA is a broad stop-and-think law, requiring informed decision making on the part of federal agencies.[131] For many proposed federal actions, an agency must consider the likely environmental impacts of its preferred alternative, but it also must consider other alternatives and their consequences. Alternatives must include a "no-action" option, which could be not moving forward with a project or denying a permit.[132] For relatively minor federal actions, a brief environmental assessment (EA) suffices to inform the agency and complies with NEPA.[133] For major federal actions (a term of art), a more comprehensive environmental impact statement (EIS) is required.[134] If an agency fails to produce an appropriate EA or EIS, environmental groups may seek to challenge the proposed action in court and compel the agency to reexamine the action's environmental impacts. A decision by the EPA to issue a section 402 permit and a decision by the Corps to issue a section 404 permit are federal actions subject to NEPA. Thus, when considering permit applications, the agencies must prepare an EA or EIS, depending on the scope and impacts of the proposed activity.[135]

Similarly, if a proposed federal action may affect an ESA-listed species, the agency must first consult with the US Fish and Wildlife Service or the

National Marine Fisheries Service about the action's likely impact on the protected species.[136] Known as section 7 consultation, the process will result in the resource agency finding that the proposed action jeopardizes the continued existence of the species, or not.[137] If it's a jeopardy opinion, the action will not go forward (or if it does, civil and criminal penalties may apply if a protected species is harmed).[138] If it's a nonjeopardy opinion, the action may go forward without the fear of ESA penalties. As is the case with NEPA, both the EPA's section 402 permit decisions and the Corps' section 404 permit decisions can trigger a section 7 consultation under the ESA. Unlike NEPA, however, the ESA process may dictate an outcome.

But here's the kicker in the water context: NEPA and ESA section 7 apply only if a water of the United States is involved. If a water is considered to be non-WOTUS, then no Clean Water Act permit is required to discharge pollutants into it. It can be degraded and filled without EPA or Corps action. And if no federal permit is needed, and there's not some other federal connection, then NEPA does not apply. The ESA section 7 consultation would also fall by the wayside.[139] (And there's no requirement for a state water quality certification under Clean Water Act section 401 either.) The conclusion that a water is not covered by the Clean Water Act has a cascading effect.

Real Enforcement?

Historically, the federal government was quite shy about exercising enforcement authority to remedy water pollution violations. The 1948 Federal Water Pollution Control Act created a complex and ineffective enforcement process where the surgeon general could initiate an enforcement action only with the consent of the state where the pollution originated. When environmental groups brought Refuse Act cases to the DOJ, Nixon's attorney general issued guidelines that made clear that the administration had no interest in prosecuting polluters. But in 1972, Congress wrote some serious enforcement provisions into the Clean Water Act.

Any person (broadly defined to include companies) that discharged pollutants to a water of the United States without a permit could be subject to civil and even criminal penalties.[140] The Clean Water Act provided that civil penalties are $25,000 per day of violation; as of 2023, adjusted for inflation, the amount is over $64,000 per day of violation.[141] If a permit was issued with conditions, and the permittee failed to abide by those conditions, that violation could be subject to penalties too.[142] The federal government was authorized to bring enforcement actions against polluters without seeking state permission.[143] And the states were also authorized to bring enforcement actions.[144]

Perhaps mindful that federal agencies might be reluctant to use their enforcement hammer (as Nixon demonstrated) or that state agencies would be timid about going after major employers in a community (as history taught time and again), Congress came up with a backup plan. If the feds or the state were not "diligently" prosecuting a Clean Water Act violation, a citizen could enforce the law.[145] After providing notice to the federal and state governments and the polluter, environmental groups could sue polluters for ongoing violations under the Clean Water Act's "citizen suit" provision.[146] Although any penalties imposed would go to the US Treasury, the prevailing environmental litigant could receive attorneys' fees, a bit of a carrot for picking up the stick.[147]

The Clean Water Act was remarkable on several fronts. It set a lofty goal: to restore and maintain the chemical, physical, and biological integrity of the nation's waters. To do so, it expanded the waters subject to federal protection to the "waters of the United States," which at least some members of Congress expected to cover as many waters as constitutionally permissible and not be bound to navigational concerns. It generally prohibited unpermitted point-source discharges of pollutants to the waters of the United States. It created two federal permit programs run by the EPA and the Corps, but in the spirit of cooperative federalism, the states were encouraged to assume responsibility for the operation of those programs. And federal agencies, state agencies, and even private citizens could bring enforcement actions.

Not surprisingly, the regulated community chafed at the Clean Water Act permit requirements and potential enforcement actions. From a strategic perspective, the most effective way to gut the Clean Water Act is to strike at its jurisdictional heart, the waters of the United States. After the regulated community was unsuccessful in reducing the Clean Water Act's coverage in Congress in 1977, they turned to the courts, where they eventually found relief.

CHAPTER 6

WOTUS in SCOTUS: A Trilogy

> It's time to stand the history of wetlands destruction on its head. From this year forward, anyone who tries to drain the swamp is going to be up to his ears in alligators.
>
> —President George H.W. Bush, addressing members of Ducks Unlimited, 1989

In the 1980s, wetlands enjoyed a bit of respectability. No longer viewed as mere nuisances that ought to be drained and filled to be put to productive use, wetlands were a featured part of George H.W. Bush's 1988 presidential campaign. He asserted a "straightforward" position: "All existing wetlands, no matter how small, should be preserved."[1] The EPA and the Corps included wetlands in their definitions of "waters of the United States," affording them the protections of the Clean Water Act. If a developer wanted to fill certain wetlands, it would need a Clean Water Act section 404 permit, triggering other environmental requirements, such as an environmental assessment and a state water quality certification. A developer might well analogize wading through the regulatory thicket to dealing with alligators.

In January 1990, President Bush directed the Domestic Policy Council, a group of senior advisors, to create a wetlands task force to recommend how best to achieve the goal of "no net loss" of wetlands.[2] A critical component of meeting this goal is establishing a baseline—how many acres of wetlands remain—which naturally leads to another question: What exactly qualifies as a wetland for Clean Water Act purposes? Did President Bush really mean that the federal government could and should protect all wetlands?

In May 1990, the Domestic Policy Council visited a corn field in Louisiana.[3] The site had at one time been a wetland but had been in agricultural production for decades after being ditched and drained. Yet, under a federal wetland delineation manual produced in 1989, it was possible to still call this area a water of the United States. (At a disturbed site, a regulator could rely on the presence of relic hydric soils to make this determination.) An academic might marvel at the elasticity of the law that allows us to classify a corn field as a "navigable water," but it is quite a different matter to try to explain that to the farmer. Or to President Bush.

The regulatory community unleashed its own alligators, challenging in court the notion that wetlands and other nonnavigable waters qualify as waters of the United States. Remarkably, three times between 1985 and 2006, the US Supreme Court considered the issue. In the first case, the Court unanimously deferred to the agencies' technical expertise and found that it was reasonable for the federal government to protect wetlands adjacent to larger waterbodies. In the second case, the Court invoked federalism concerns to hold that the Clean Water Act did not reach "isolated" waters. In the final case of the trilogy, *Rapanos v. United States*, the Court splintered, with no majority opinion, thus setting the stage for greater regulatory uncertainty.

The Tail Does Not Wag the Dog

With two agencies administering the Clean Water Act, some uncertainty was built into its structure. One source of friction was whether the EPA or the Corps of Engineers had the final say on what waters were covered for section 404 permits. As the permitting agency, the Corps naturally thought it had the authority. EPA believed otherwise.

In 1979, the secretary of the army requested that Attorney General Benjamin Civiletti resolve the issue.[4] In what is known as the Civiletti Memorandum, he emphasized that "navigable waters" is "a linchpin" of the Clean Water Act.[5] The term specifies the geographic jurisdiction not only for the section 404 program but for the section 402 program, as well as for programs regulating the discharge of oil, hazardous substances, and vessel sewage.[6] Civiletti found "no support either in the statute or its legislative history for a conclusion that a waterbody would have one set of boundaries for purposes of dredged and fill permits under [section] 404 and a different set for purposes of the other pollution control measures in the Act."[7] On that point, he asserted that "there can be no serious disagreement."[8]

The question remained who then could speak definitively on what constituted waters of the United States, although it was an easy one to answer. Considering the structure of the Clean Water Act, and given that the bulk of responsibilities were assigned to the EPA, Civiletti concluded that the EPA had the ultimate authority to make the call.[9] He observed that the Corps' position was "substantially undercut" by the fact that it operated the section 404 program in accordance with EPA guidelines and that the EPA could veto the Corps' decision to issue a permit.[10]

Through rulemakings in 1980 and 1982, the EPA and Corps harmonized their competing regulatory definitions of waters of the United States.[11] Both agencies succinctly defined wetlands as

> areas that are inundated or saturated by surface or ground water at a frequency and duration sufficient to support, and that under normal circumstances do support, a prevalence of vegetation typically adapted for life in saturated soil conditions. Wetlands generally include swamps, marshes, bogs, and similar areas.[12]

And both agencies treated wetlands adjacent to a waterbody qualifying as a water of the United States as waters of the United States themselves.

Round One: *United States v. Riverside Bayview Homes*

The significant but not-so-great lake separating parts of modern-day Michigan and Ontario was known to the Mississauga as Waawiyaataan(ong), which means "(at) the whirlpool."[13] Rechristened as Lac Sainte-Claire by French explorers in 1679 in honor of Saint Clare of Assisi, the patron saint of good weather (as well as eye disease and television), the waterbody is known today to English speakers as Lake St. Clair.[14] It is sometimes called the sixth Great Lake,[15] a questionable characterization, given that it is only about 6 percent of the size of Lake Ontario. What is not open to debate is that Lake St. Clair is a WOTUS, at least on the US side.

In 1960, Riverside Bayview Homes acquired two parcels in Michigan, totaling approximately 80 acres, that were adjacent to Black Creek, a tributary of Lake St. Clair.[16] The area had previously been farmed and was platted for a residential subdivision, with fire hydrants and storm sewers already in place.[17] Unfortunately for the company, the site also contained wetlands. In November 1976 Riverside Bayview Homes applied to the Corps for a Clean Water Act section 404 permit.[18] The next month the company, apparently tired of waiting for an answer, started filling the property without a permit. The Corps obtained a court injunction ordering the developer to stop its filling of the marshes. The case bounced around in the judicial system for several years until in 1981 the US District Court held that the property was a wetland adjacent to a navigable water, thus covered by the Corps' regulation and the Clean Water Act.[19] The housing development could not proceed.

Undaunted, Riverside Bayview Homes appealed to the Sixth Circuit Court of Appeals, where it found a more sympathetic bench. The Court of Appeals expressed concern about the impact of the Corps' regulation on private property rights. If Riverside Bayview Homes could not construct homes on its property, the government's action could amount to an unconstitutional taking of private property; in the Court of Appeals' view, the regulation would have the same effect as if the government had physically seized the property.[20] To avoid this potential constitutional conflict, the Court of Appeals interpreted the regulation to require frequent overland flooding from Lake St. Clair and its tributary, Black Creek.[21] In other words, for the Corps to classify the marsh as an adjacent wetland, the area needed to have a regular hydrologic surface connection with a traditional navigable water. Because there seemed to be no such connection in this case, the court ruled that the regulation (and thus the Clean Water Act) did not cover the marsh. The problem with the court's reasoning was that the Corps' regulation said no such thing. It did not contain a requirement of frequent inundation, and thus the Court of Appeals had essentially substituted its judgment for that of the agency.

Now it was the federal government's turn to seek further judicial review, this time before the US Supreme Court. The oral argument revealed some confusion about whether the marsh had a direct surface connection to Lake St. Clair and Black Creek or whether groundwater supplied the only nexus. Indeed, the attorney for the United States admitted that "this was one of the first Section 404 cases ever tried. . . . I don't think at the time of the trial, anybody knew exactly what they were doing."[22] With a similar surprising candor, she also conceded that "for several years the exhibits in the case were lost" and that she had not fully understood the case until they were found.[23] Nevertheless, the Supreme Court had little difficulty reaching a unanimous decision in favor of the federal government and the Corps.[24]

First, the Supreme Court quickly disposed of the unconstitutional takings issue that the Court of Appeals had used to justify its reading of the regulation. The mere requirement that a property owner must apply for a permit before embarking on a development project cannot, by itself, constitute a taking of private property.[25] Why not? Because, as the Supreme Court noted (and experience has shown), the government may very well grant the permit and the property owner can proceed on its merry way. If the federal government denies a permit, then a takings claim may be ripe. But Riverside Bayview Homes failed to pursue a takings claim in the proper forum, and thus it was premature to consider its assertion that the application of the Clean Water Act to its site significantly interfered with its private property rights.[26]

With the specter of unconstitutional takings and the requirement of frequent flooding removed, the Supreme Court then examined the question of whether, as a factual matter, the 80 acres were "adjacent wetlands" under the regulation. In the Court's opinion, it was an "easy" question.[27] The regulations defined wetlands as areas "inundated or saturated by surface or ground water at a frequency and duration sufficient to support, and that under normal circumstances do support, a prevalence of vegetation typically adapted for life in saturated soil conditions." The District Court had clearly found that the site contained vegetation produced by groundwater saturation; it was irrelevant that frequent flooding did not cause this hydrophytic vegetation. Thus the site had wetlands—but were they *adjacent* wetlands?

The Corps' regulation defined *adjacent* to mean "bordering, contiguous, or neighboring."[28] At oral argument, the attorney for the government more loosely suggested that *adjacent* meant "immediately next to, abuts, adjoins, borders, whatever other adjective you might want to use."[29] Riverside Bayview Homes' attorney asserted that the wetlands were isolated, with no hydrologic connection to other waters, arguing that it was 200 feet away from a canal that led to Black Creek. When asked whether the wetlands were nevertheless "neighboring," he replied, "I would say it is not far away."[30] Ultimately, the Supreme Court stated that the wetland conditions "extended" to Black Creek, which itself was a traditional navigable water.[31] Accordingly, the marsh was an "adjacent wetland."

Still, the question remained whether it was reasonable for the Corps and EPA to interpret "navigable waters" and "waters of the United States" to include wetlands whose primary connection to larger waterbodies was through a subsurface connection. Here the Supreme Court invoked a formulation of the familiar (and deferential) *Chevron* test: "An agency's construction of a statute it is charged with enforcing is entitled to deference if it is reasonable and not in conflict with the expressed intent of Congress."[32] Assuming that congressional intent was not clearly expressed, the Court devoted its analysis to whether it was reasonable to classify "navigable waters" to include a wetland adjacent to, but not regularly flooded by, a traditional navigable water.

While acknowledging that it might be strange to define "waters" to include land, the Supreme Court noted the difficulty of making a clear demarcation.

> The Corps must necessarily choose some point at which water ends and land begins. Our common experience tells us that this

> is often no easy task: the transition from water to solid ground is not necessarily or even typically an abrupt one. Rather, between open waters and dry land may lie shallows, marshes, mudflats, swamps, bogs—in short, a huge array of areas that are not wholly aquatic but nevertheless fall far short of being dry land. Where on this continuum to find the limit of "waters" is far from obvious.[33]

Faced with such uncertainty, the Court suggested that legislative history (e.g., congressional committee or conference reports) and the goals of the Clean Water Act could provide guidance as to what is reasonable.

Improving water quality is the primary focus of the Clean Water Act, and Congress wanted to limit pollutants at their source. Recognizing that adjacent wetlands are part of a larger aquatic ecosystem, the Court observed that they "as a general matter play a key role in protecting and enhancing water quality" of traditional navigable waters.[34] An adjacent wetland may perform this water quality function regardless of whether it is flooded by a traditional navigable water. Indeed, the Court stated that "wetlands that are not flooded by adjacent waters may still tend to drain into those waters [and i]n such circumstances, the Corps has concluded that wetlands may serve to filter and purify water draining into adjacent bodies of water."[35] Moreover, the Court recalled the important flood control and habitat functions of adjacent wetlands. Thus it was reasonable for the Corps to define *navigable waters* to include adjacent wetlands, and the Court unanimously deferred to the Corps' "technical expertise" and "ecological judgment."[36] Note that the *Riverside Bayview Homes* Court's paean to wetlands is a far cry from the earlier view of wetlands as mere public nuisances.

In a footnote, however, the *Riverside Bayview Homes* Court emphasized that this opinion applied only to adjacent wetlands.[37] It specifically left unresolved the question of whether the Clean Water Act covered isolated wetlands, areas that had no hydrologic connection to other waters. In a bit of foreshadowing, the issue of isolated wetlands came up during oral argument. When asked about the constitutional authority for the Corps to regulate isolated wetlands, the attorney for the United States replied that the Corps' jurisdiction was based on the commerce clause. She said that the presence of migratory birds at an isolated wetland could provide a sufficient connection to interstate commerce. The transcript of the oral argument reports parenthetically that there was "general laughter" (twice) in response to the concept that birds created a nexus to interstate commerce.[38]

The 1986/1988 Regulations and the Migratory Bird Rule

In 1986, shortly after its victory in *Riverside Bayview Homes*, the Corps revised and reorganized its regulations. In doing so, the Corps did not modify its definition of *waters of the United States*. However, the Corps did break out and give the term its own distinct part in the regulations (part 328).[39] Figure 6-1 illustrates how the regulation would play out on the landscape.

In the preamble to the regulation, the Corps attempted to clarify what it considered jurisdictional under section 328.3(a)(3): the "isolated waters" that would be regulated if their use, degradation, or destruction could affect interstate commerce.[40] The Corps announced that it would regulate activities in isolated waters (including wetlands) that "are or would be used as habitat by other migratory birds which cross state lines."[41] This became known as the Migratory Bird Rule or, more derisively, as the "Glancing Geese Test" or "Reasonable Bird Test": Would a reasonable bird flying over an isolated wetland consider it suitable habitat?

In 1988, the EPA updated its Clean Water Act regulations. Its definition of *waters of the United States* remained unchanged, and to be consistent with the Corps it included the Migratory Bird Rule in the preamble.[42] Thus the Corps'

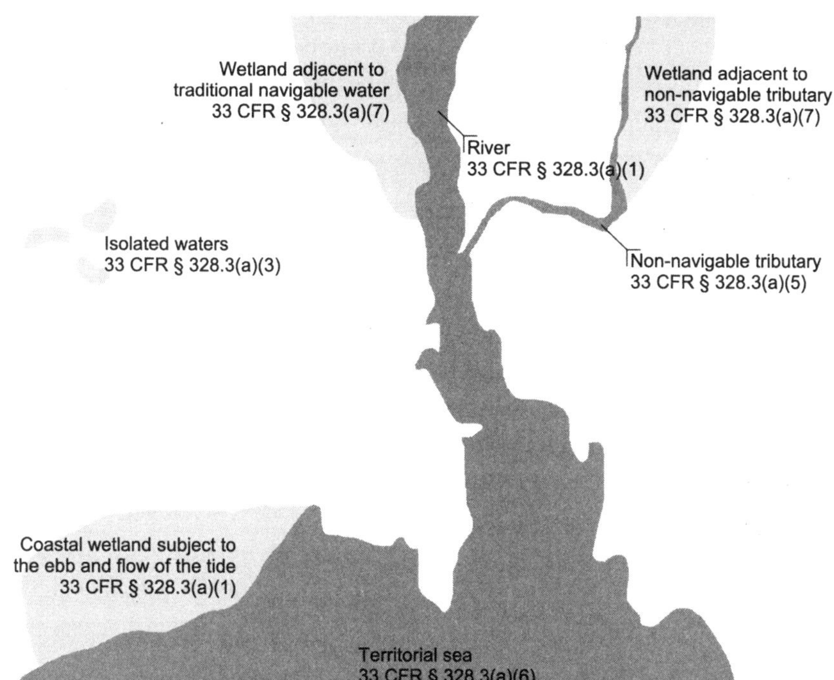

Figure 6-1. Waters of the United States, circa 1986.

1986 WOTUS definition and the EPA's 1988 WOTUS definition were aligned (and are sometimes jointly referred to as the 1986/1988 rules). Differences remained, however, in how to delineate wetland boundaries—that is, where to draw the line between wetlands and uplands, the "point at which water ends and land begins," as the Court in *Riverside Bayview Homes* characterized it.

Wetland Delineation Manuals

Several federal agencies regulate or survey wetlands for different purposes, and over the course of years, each developed its own delineation manual or approach to classifying wetlands. The Corps used a manual issued by its Environmental Laboratory at the Waterways Experiment Station in 1987, which emphasized the three-parameter approach (hydrology, vegetation, and soils). The EPA used its own manual, produced in 1988, which allowed greater reliance on vegetation. The US Fish and Wildlife Service relied on its own classification system for a national wetlands inventory, and the then-Soil Conservation Service (now Natural Resources Conservation Service) had yet another manual, which it used for wetland delineations for the Food Security Act. In a spasm of good government, the agencies decided in the late 1980s that it made common sense if all the federal agencies involved with wetlands used the same delineation manual. After a round of internal agency meetings, a joint, uniform federal wetland delineation manual was released in 1989.[43] This manual, known as the 1989 Manual, prompted all hell to break loose.

Although wetland delineation is based on science, its application is an art. Different regulators using the same methods can draw a wetland boundary line in different places. The 1989 Manual granted flexibility to regulators, allowing them in some cases to rely primarily on the presence of hydric soils to declare an area a wetland. The perceived effect of the 1989 Manual was that it could be used to classify more areas as wetlands, thereby dramatically enlarging the regulatory coverage of the Clean Water Act.[44] Property owners newly subject to federal regulatory constraints were outraged—not only at the result but by the process. And if property owners were dyspeptic, so was Congress. The agencies appeared to have expanded their jurisdiction after a series of closed meetings, and the National Law Journal discussed the controversy under the headline "Even the Deserts Are Wet."[45]

The adverse public reaction caught the agencies by surprise. In their view, this was a technical manual. It was an "interpretive rule," and such manuals had always been produced in this fashion.[46] But although the agencies may have had the legal authority to issue the 1989 Manual without a notice and comment period, it was clear in hindsight that it was not a politically astute decision to proceed without involving the public.

In 1991, the Bush administration attempted to blunt the procedural objections by initiating a public notice and comment rulemaking to codify a new manual. A proposed rule was published in the *Federal Register*,[47] but it too was met with a hail of criticism. The environmental community was appalled at the new method; it claimed that under the proposed manual, 100,000 acres of the Everglades would no longer qualify as wetlands.[48] The regulated community, though generally pleased with the more restrictive approach, were nonetheless concerned about the time and expense it would take to make such delineations. The agencies received more than 100,000 public comments.[49] While considering these comments, the Bush administration ran out of time, and the Clinton administration declined to proceed with the proposal.

This particular chapter of the delineation wars was settled when, in the end, Congress reasserted its authority—through the appropriations process. In a spending bill, Congress specifically prohibited the Corps from expending funds to implement the 1989 Manual and directed the Corps to return to the 1987 Manual (which would not cover areas such as the Louisiana corn field).[50] Of course, the 1987 Manual never went through public notice and comment either, but at least Congress's actions can be deemed to implicitly ratify the Corps manual. Since then, the Corps has developed a series of regional supplements to the 1987 Manual, all produced after an opportunity for public notice and comment.[51]

Round Two: *Solid Waste Agency of Northern Cook County v. U.S. Army Corps of Engineers*

The Solid Waste Agency of Northern Cook County (SWANCC), a consortium of twenty-three Chicago-area cities and villages, banded together in the 1980s to manage garbage on a regional basis.[52] One of its more pressing needs was to find a suitable site for a nonhazardous waste landfill. The site selected was a 533-acre parcel where sand and gravel mining operations had taken place up until about 1960. Over time, the abandoned sand and gravel pits became more than 200 permanent and seasonal ponds.[53] Unfortunately for SWANCC, 121 species of birds found the ponds wonderful habitat, and the site was host to the second largest blue heron rookery in northeastern Illinois.[54]

After more than six years of efforts, SWANCC had obtained all the necessary permits and approvals from the county, the Illinois EPA, and the Illinois Department of Conservation. The Illinois EPA had issued a water quality certification for the project. The last remaining hurdle was the US Army Corps of Engineers. Although the ponds were not technically wetlands, they were covered by the same regulation ("other waters . . . the use, degradation, or destruction of which could affect interstate commerce"), and the Corps asserted jurisdiction on the basis of the Migratory Bird Rule.[55] In 1994, the Corps denied the permit, and SWANCC filed a lawsuit challenging the legitimacy of the Migratory Bird Rule on statutory and constitutional grounds.

The statutory argument focused on whether the Migratory Bird Test was a permissible construction of the Clean Water Act. The lower courts applied the deferential *Chevron* test. The question came down once again to one of reasonableness: Was the Migratory Bird Rule a reasonable interpretation of the Clean Water Act? The Seventh Circuit rejected SWANCC's contention that the Migratory Bird Rule was an unreasonable interpretation because its focus was on wildlife, not water quality, by recalling that protecting the *biological* integrity of the nation's waters was a main purpose of the Clean Water Act.[56] Furthermore, the Seventh Circuit considered it "well established that the geographical scope of the [Clean Water] Act reaches as many waters as the Commerce Clause allows."[57] Thus, in the court's view, the reasonableness of the Migratory Bird Rule depended on whether the presence of migratory birds established a sufficient commerce connection.

Of course, birds themselves do not engage in commerce. Yet human activities related to birds are big business. The Seventh Circuit cited Census Bureau statistics reporting that more than 3 million Americans annually spent $1.3 billion to hunt migratory birds, with at least 300,000 of those hunters crossing state lines in pursuit of their pastime and prey.[58] Even more people (14.3 million) crossed state lines for the peaceable purpose of observing birds.[59] Accordingly, the Seventh Circuit quickly concluded, "There is no need to dally on this point: we find (once again) that the destruction of migratory bird habitat and the attendant decrease in the populations of these birds 'substantially affects' interstate commerce."[60]

Hunters and birders notwithstanding, SWANCC still needed someplace to put its trash. SWANCC's final judicial option was the US Supreme Court. The Supreme Court agreed to hear the case, and in a 5–4 decision it reversed the Seventh Circuit.[61] The decision was a stunning setback for the federal government's authority to regulate isolated waters, including wetlands, as waters of the United States.

The Supreme Court did not need to reach the constitutional question, grounding its decision on the statutory language of the Clean Water Act. In particular the Supreme Court returned to the term *navigable*, emphasizing that although *Riverside Bayview Homes* said that the word had "limited import," this did not mean that *navigable* had no effect.[62] As the Supreme Court explained,

> We found that Congress' concern for the protection of water quality and aquatic ecosystems indicated its intent to regulate wetlands "inseparably bound up with the 'waters' of the United States." . . . It was the *significant nexus* between the wetlands and "navigable waters" that informed our reading of the CWA in *Riverside Bayview Homes*.[63]

Although adjacent wetlands may have a "significant nexus" to navigable waters, isolated waters by definition do not. Thus the Migratory Bird Rule went beyond what was authorized in the Clean Water Act. It appeared that the Migratory Bird Rule had failed the first part of the *Chevron* test: When Congress has addressed the precise question, its intent must be followed.

Even if Congress's use of the terms *navigable* and *waters of the United States* was ambiguous (as the dissent suggested), a majority of the Supreme Court was still unwilling to grant *Chevron* deference. Traditionally, the Supreme Court has been wary of affording such deference when a regulatory agency such as the Corps interprets a statute to reach "the outer limits" of congressional power under the Constitution.[64] This is especially true, as was the case here, where "the administrative interpretation alters the federal–state framework by permitting federal encroachment upon a traditional state power," such as land use decisions.[65] This nondeferential approach permitted the Court to make decisions based on statutory grounds and to avoid constitutional questions. With the Migratory Bird Rule dispatched by its statutory analysis, the Supreme Court did not have to reach the question of whether the federal government had the constitutional authority (under the commerce clause) to regulate isolated waters.[66]

Although the *SWANCC* decision might seem academically interesting for its examination of federalism, its real-world impact was stark. The Association of State Wetland Managers estimated that 40 to 60 percent of wetlands might no longer be subject to Clean Water Act protections.[67] Some states, such as Wisconsin, and local governments responded by enacting their own wetland legislation, but other states, such as South Carolina, did not.[68]

From an environmental perspective, it could have been worse. Had the Supreme Court reached the constitutional question and ruled against the Corps, the issue for all practical purposes would be closed. (It also could have had grave implications for other environmental laws such as the Endangered Species Act.) But what could the Corps and the EPA do in response to the *SWANCC* decision? They could issue guidance, but that would be granted no deference in the courts. They could proceed with a notice and comment rulemaking and revise their regulations, but that would take years, and even then the courts might not be deferential. The cleanest fix would be to have Congress clarify its intent with respect to the geographic scope of the Clean Water Act, but with Democrats leading the Senate and a Republican majority in the House of Representatives, a bipartisan solution was unlikely at best.

After much consideration, the Corps and the EPA labored mightily and in 2003 brought forth a meek Advance Notice of Proposed Rulemaking (ANPR).[69] An ANPR informs the public that a notice and comment rulemaking is contemplated but asks the interested public for suggestions. Thus, after two years, the agencies decided only to announce that they intended to issue a proposed regulation at some point in the future, but first they needed the public's help. The agencies received thousands of comments and suggestions and ultimately abandoned the rulemaking effort.[70] Perhaps there was no agreement within the agencies (and among the political appointees) on how to proceed. Perhaps they were embarrassed by the public reaction to the leak of one purported proposal. Perhaps the status of isolated waters was just too difficult to grapple with. Or perhaps in subsequent court cases, the agencies were winning most of the battles. It appeared that the lower courts were narrowly interpreting the *SWANCC* decision to mean that only the Migratory Bird Rule was invalid. The Corps was regulating many wetlands that were far from traditional navigable waters, but the lower courts allowed this so long as there was a hydrologic connection, no matter how attenuated it seemed.

It is important to note that isolated waters is a legal concept. Wetland scientists disagree with the premise that wetlands can somehow be isolated from the larger landscape.[71] However, the law likes to put things neatly into boxes or categories. Nature is a bit messier. The next case illustrates a greater divergence of law and science.

A postscript: After the decision, the state of Illinois expressed interest in acquiring the property. In December 2001, SWANCC sold most of the site to the state for $21 million. The site is now the Heron Woods State Habitat Area and is managed by the Illinois Department of Natural Resources.[72]

Round Three: *Rapanos v. United States*

Riverside Bayview Homes and *SWANCC* set out the extremes of the continuum of Clean Water Act coverage for nonnavigable waters. At one end, *Riverside Bayview Homes* confirmed the federal government's jurisdiction over wetlands adjacent to traditional navigable waters, and *SWANCC* at the other end suggested that the federal government had no authority over isolated wetlands, at least not under the Migratory Bird Rule. But there were a lot of waters in between. What about, for example, wetlands nearby nonnavigable tributaries of traditional navigable waters?

John Rapanos (with his wife and affiliated companies) owned several sites near Midland, Michigan, where he wanted to construct a shopping center.[73] These sites contained wetlands adjacent to nonnavigable tributaries that eventually drained into traditional navigable waters 11 to 20 miles away.[74] In 1988 the Michigan Department of Natural Resources told him that he would need a permit if he wanted to fill in the wetlands as part of the project.[75] Rapanos hired an environmental consultant, Dr. Goff, to conduct a wetland delineation of the property. Dr. Goff concluded that 48 to 58 acres were wetlands.[76] Apparently displeased, Rapanos directed Dr. Goff to destroy the records, or he would "destroy" Dr. Goff.[77] Rapanos then proceeded to conduct land clearing and filling operations that destroyed 54 acres of wetlands at three sites, despite cease-and-desist orders from the Michigan Department of Natural Resources and the EPA.[78]

Discharging fill material into a water of the United States without a permit can result in administrative, civil, and in the rarest cases criminal penalties. Rapanos was one of these rare cases: a flagrant and intentional refusal to seek a permit for a large-scale development. The federal government brought civil and criminal charges against Rapanos, and after a thirteen-day trial, a US District Court found him guilty of violating the Clean Water Act.[79]

Rapanos's case eventually reached the US Supreme Court, where once again the question was whether the Corps' WOTUS interpretation was reasonable. Unlike *Riverside Bayview Homes* (9–0) and *SWANCC* (5–4), this time the justices could not agree among themselves, and there was no majority opinion. Instead, the Supreme Court was fragmented 4–1–4.

Justice Scalia, writing for three other members of the Court, opened his opinion by observing that the wetland permit process was time-consuming and expensive.[80] Citing one study, he noted that permit applicants spent more than $1.7 billion annually seeking government permission to use their property.[81] Justice Scalia referred to the Corps as an "enlightened despot" and was hardly deferential of the Corps' position.[82] Indeed, he was disparaging, characterizing it as "beyond parody."[83] To underscore the risibility of the Corps' interpretation, in a footnote he quoted from the classic movie *Casablanca*:

> Captain Renault [Claude Rains]: "What in heaven's name brought you to Casablanca?"
> Rick [Humphrey Bogart]: "My health. I came to Casablanca for the waters."
> Captain Renault: "The waters? What waters? We're in a desert."
> Rick: "I was misinformed."[84]

From the federal government's perspective, Justice Scalia's opinion only got worse from here. There would be no mention of a beautiful friendship.

Justice Scalia concluded that *Chevron* deference was not appropriate because there is only one reasonable interpretation of the Clean Water Act's terms. According to Justice Scalia and *Webster's Second*, his preferred dictionary, *navigable waters* (and thus *waters of the United States*) must refer to "only relatively permanent, standing or flowing bodies of water," such as streams, oceans, rivers, lakes, and bodies of waters that form "geographical features."[85] In his view, this interpretation inexorably flows from Congress's use of the definite article ("the") immediately preceding the term "waters of the United States."[86] Had Congress simply said "water of the United States," the agencies could regulate water in general. However, because Congress had chosen the words "the waters," the agencies were constrained to more substantial bodies of waters.

The reliance on "the" is a bit of legal sophistry. One can search the voluminous legislative history of the Clean Water Act and will be disappointed to find no debate, discussion, or stray statement about the import of the definitive article in defining the geographic scope of the Clean Water Act. Recall, however, that an earlier Congress in 1938 had passed a water quality bill that used the phrase "the waters of the United States"—covering both navigable and nonnavigable waters—which was vetoed by FDR. Congress's use of the definitive article in 1938 suggests that Justice Scalia's emphasis was misplaced.

Furthermore, Justice Scalia's choice of dictionary, *Webster's Second*, was questionable. That source specified that waters are "found in streams and bodies forming geographical features such as oceans, rivers, [and] lakes."[87] However, the dictionary that was more contemporaneous with the 1972 Act was *Webster's Third*, published in 1961. That dictionary offered a broader conception of waters: "the water occupying or flowing in a particular bed <the limpid ~s of a mountain brook>."[88] As my colleague professor Paul Boudreaux observed, "Even a wetland that occurs less than three months out of the year is 'water occupying a bed.'"[89]

But wetlands fell outside Justice Scalia's constricted view of "the waters": Wetlands generally were not "waters of the United States." To qualify for Clean Water Act protection, a wetland must be "a relatively permanent body of water connected to traditional interstate navigable waters."[90] In addition, the wetland must have a "continuous surface connection" with the traditional navigable water, "making it difficult to determine where the 'water' ends and the 'wetland' begins."[91] Note the sleight of hand from *Riverside Bayview Homes*, where the Court deferred to the Corps' ecological judgment about where a wetland ends and land begins. Similar language is used in *Rapanos*, but now the focus is on where the wetland begins. Because Rapanos's sites were far removed from a traditional navigable water, in Justice Scalia's view it was unreasonable (even ludicrous) to classify them as waters of the United States.

Although this restrictive and imaginative interpretation of the Clean Water Act might be reasonable, it is not the only reasonable construction. Indeed, it is not even consistent with the Supreme Court's unanimous decision in *Riverside Bayview Homes*, which specifically rejected a requirement that adjacent wetlands be connected to a traditional navigable water by surface waters. Perhaps this cramped reading of the statute and congressional intent, along with the dismissive view of agency expertise, is why Justice Scalia was able to persuade only three of his colleagues to join him. His opinion did not carry a majority of the Court.

In contrast, Justice Stevens thought that *Rapanos* presented a "straightforward" *Chevron* question.[92] He emphasized that the Corps

> has determined that wetlands adjacent to tributaries of traditionally navigable waters preserve the quality of our

> Nation's waters by, among other things, providing habitat for aquatic animals, keeping excessive sediment and toxic pollutants out of adjacent waters, and reducing downstream flooding by absorbing water at times of high flow.[93]

Accordingly, wetlands with even a distant hydrologic connection to a traditional navigable water can provide these functions and can be properly classified as an adjacent wetland. Justice Stevens even quoted *Webster's Second* for support, as it defined *adjacent* to mean "lying near, close, *or* contiguous; neighboring; bordering on" and stated that "objects are adjacent when they lie close to each other, but *not necessarily in actual contact.*"[94] Thus Justice Stevens considered the Corps' construction of the Clean Water Act to be "a quintessential example of the Executive's reasonable interpretation of a statutory provision."[95] Yet he too could convince only three of his colleagues to join him.

It fell to Justice Kennedy to break the tie. Like Goldilocks he found Justice Scalia's rigid approach to be too hard (his restrictions "are without support in the language and purposes of the [Clean Water] Act or in our cases interpreting it" and his tone is "unduly dismissive").[96] And he found Justice Stevens's deference too soft (his interpretation eliminates a proper tie to navigability, a "central requirement" of the Clean Water Act).[97] But a phrase nestled in the *SWANCC* opinion—*significant nexus*—was just right.

Justice Kennedy proposed that the proper test to apply was whether the waters in question had a "significant nexus" to traditional navigable waters in light of the Clean Water Act's overall goals. The objective of the Clean Water Act is to "restore and maintain the chemical, physical, and biological integrity of the Nation's waters," and he recalled that the Corps had recognized that wetlands can play a critical role in ensuring the integrity of traditional navigable waters. He therefore proposed the following test:

> Wetlands possess the requisite nexus, and thus come within the statutory phrase "navigable waters," if the wetlands, either alone or in combination with similarly situated lands in the region, significantly affect the chemical, physical, and biological integrity of other covered waters more readily understood as "navigable." When, in contrast, wetlands' effects on water quality are speculative or insubstantial, they fall outside the zone fairly encompassed by the statutory term "navigable waters."[98]

The only problem was that no other justice agreed with Justice Kennedy. He was the only one who embraced this "significant nexus" test.

Although the Supreme Court had splintered in its reasoning, it still had to decide what to do with Rapanos's wetlands. Justice Scalia and three members voted to vacate the lower court's judgment. Justice Stevens and three members voted to affirm. Because the lower court had not applied the "significant nexus" test to Rapanos's wetlands, Justice Kennedy joined Justice Scalia's plurality to vacate the judgment. Thus Rapanos's conviction was overturned and the case was sent back to the lower courts for further action. Rapanos eventually settled his dispute with the federal government but at a heavy price.[99] To resolve the civil enforcement action, he paid a $150,000 penalty and agreed to restore 54 acres of wetlands illegally filled, at an estimated cost of $750,000. In addition, Rapanos agreed to preserve another 134 acres, with the state of Michigan holding the conservation easement. To settle the criminal action, Rapanos agreed to accept the conviction (and stop all appeals) in exchange for no prison time. He also had to pay a criminal fine of $185,000.

The Problem with a Plurality

But which standard should the lower courts now apply? And, more broadly, what standard should the Corps and the EPA use to assess whether other wetlands are waters of the United States? There was no majority opinion in *Rapanos*; the Supreme Court did not issue a single controlling opinion.

Ironically, although Justice Kennedy was the only advocate of the "significant nexus" test, it was his opinion that was most influential. The agencies knew that if a wetland met this test, and a case made its way back to the Supreme Court, they would garner five votes upholding the federal government's jurisdiction (assuming no ideological change in the makeup of the Court): Justice Kennedy, along with four justices following the *Rapanos* dissenters' approach. But as we will see, the Court's composition never remains static for long.

In June 2007, the Corps and the EPA issued complicated guidance on the *Rapanos* decision.[100] They divided "the waters" into three main categories: those over which they would definitely assert jurisdiction, those over which they definitely would not, and those that they might—if those last areas had a significant nexus to a traditional navigable water. The agencies considered the following areas to be "waters of the United States" under all circumstances:

- Traditional navigable waters and their adjacent wetlands;
- Non-navigable tributaries of traditional navigable waters that are relatively permanent where the tributaries typically flow year-round or have continuous flow at least seasonally (e.g., typically three months); and
- Wetlands that directly abut these non-navigable tributaries.[101]

At the other end of the continuum, the agencies carved out a limited set of waters that they would (generally) decline jurisdiction over, which included swales and gullies with low volume or flows of short or infrequent duration, along with upland ditches with intermittent flows that drained only uplands.[102] The significant nexus test would be applied to the waters falling between the two extremes:

- Non-navigable tributaries that are not relatively permanent;
- Wetlands adjacent to non-navigable tributaries that are not relatively permanent; and
- Wetlands adjacent to but that do not directly abut a relatively permanent non-navigable tributary.[103]

Following Justice Kennedy's lead, the agencies stated that the significant nexus analysis would focus on whether the waters in question "significantly affect the chemical, physical and biological integrity of downstream traditional navigable waters."[104]

The federal guidance came out a few days before the final episode of *The Sopranos*. And, in some ways, the long-awaited federal guidance issued in response to *Rapanos* mirrors the concluding scene of the HBO drama in its ambiguity. Both are open to varying interpretations. But although David Chase's cut to black was ambiguous by design, the federal agencies' response to *Rapanos* was ambiguous out of necessity.

To say that the guidance was complex would be an understatement. It is not an easy read. But the federal agencies really had no choice; it was not possible to respond to *Rapanos* with simple, clear, crisp guidance. The bright line options were foreclosed. One bright line would have been simply to limit federal jurisdiction to traditional navigable waters. However, that approach did not garner a majority in the Supreme Court; it was rejected by Justice Kennedy and the four dissenters. Another bright line would have been to assert jurisdiction over all waters that are hydrologically connected to traditional navigable waters. Yet that approach was rejected by the *Rapanos* plurality and Justice Kennedy. So the federal agencies were left with the task of trying to interpret the plurality's and Justice Kennedy's approaches, neither of which provided bright lines. It was preordained that the guidance would be complex and confusing (and give rise to bad puns, with references to "muddying the waters" the most common). The agencies issued slightly revised guidance in 2008 after the public was given an opportunity to comment.[105]

The regulated community was displeased with this state of affairs, in which jurisdictional determinations were frequently made on case-by-case "significant nexus" analyses. It demanded more certainty. But, as is often said, you have to be careful about what you ask for. You might get it.

CHAPTER 7

Obama's Clean Water Rule

> Chaos was the law of nature; Order was the dream of man.
>
> —Henry Adams, *The Education of Henry Adams* (1918)

In his Pulitzer Prize–winning autobiography, which was not formally published until after his death, Henry Adams grappled with, in part, scientific developments that disrupted the accepted dogma of his time.[1] As one reviewer described it, "Henry Adams had learned, first of all, that modern science [discovered] . . . that there were no simple, immutable laws of nature which gave unity, consistency, and order to the universe."[2] The human desire for simplicity and certainty to explain the order and meaning of the universe resulted in scientific laws unfit for purpose.

Nature is actually ordered, however, albeit chaotically to the eyes of humans. Nature appears to be random only to us who have been unable to discern the totality and complexity of its governing laws. This lack of understanding has not unduly impeded people's attempts to impose order on nature, efforts that often release their own form of chaos, in unintended consequences.[3]

More broadly, one way humans also attempt to impose order is through law, but that too is often chaotic, in terms of both process and outcome. In 2014, the Obama administration tried to revise the regulatory definition of *waters of the United States* to be based on the best available science. A goal of the rulemaking process was to provide the regulated community and the public with certainty about which waters were and were not covered by the Clean Water Act. The final rule, dubbed the Clean Water Rule by the administration, was not warmly received. It was attacked on social media, which led the EPA to respond in a manner that may not have been entirely lawful. It was attacked in Congress, but any legislative change required President Obama's consent, which was not to be forthcoming. And, of course, it was attacked in the courts, but it wasn't entirely clear which court had jurisdiction to hear the many legal challenges. In the end, the Obama administration's attempt to impose order on the WOTUS world, consistent with the scientific record, was but a dream that gave way to, if not a nightmare, then more chaos.

Parsing the 2014 Proposed Rule

The EPA and the Corps' initial decision to issue guidance, rather than a regulation, in response to *SWANCC* and *Rapanos* was tactically reasonable. First, the guidance could be promulgated more quickly than a regulation. Second, because the guidance was not legally binding, it was more difficult to challenge legally. But mere guidance is a shaky foundation on which to assert regulatory authority. Moreover, the guidance called for many jurisdictional determinations to be made on a case-by-case basis, and the regulated community demanded more certainty. And environmental advocates also called for more certainty, albeit in a different direction, out of concern that wetlands, streams, and other waterbodies were at risk of loss and degradation. So, after consulting with a range of stakeholders, including representatives from state and local governments, the EPA and the Corps issued a proposed rule in April 2014 to coincide with Earth Day.[4]

In a video announcing the proposed rule, EPA Administrator Gina McCarthy (in a delightful Massachusetts accent) stated that the "proposal does not add to or expand the scope of the waters historically protected under the Clean Water Act."[5] Instead, she characterized the proposal as a clarification that provided certainty. The only certainty it provided at this stage, however, was the apoplectic reaction of the regulated community, which viewed the proposal as an overreach in violation of numerous laws and the US Constitution itself. Who was more accurate? Let's take a moment to examine the language of the then-current rule (1986/1988 definition) with the proposed rule to see to what extent it "clarified" the scope of the Clean Water Act.

First, a number of provisions in the proposed rule were the same or essentially the same as the 1986/1988 definition (Table 7-1). The least controversial parts—jurisdiction over traditional navigable waters, interstate waters, and the territorial sea—remained unchanged, except for renumbering and an inconsequential comma.

Further upstream, the provisions regarding impoundments and tributaries were also largely unchanged (Table 7-2). If anything, the proposed rule tightened up the jurisdictional reach a bit. Instead of including all impoundments of *any* water of the United States, the proposal limited jurisdiction to impoundments of traditional navigable waters, interstate waters, the territorial sea, and tributaries—thus excluding impoundments of adjacent wetlands. Similarly, the proposed rule's provision on tributaries excluded tributaries of certain wetlands. The provision regarding "adjacent wetlands" was rewritten to protect all adjacent waters, including wetlands.

1986/1988 RULES	**2014 PROPOSAL**
(1) All waters which are currently used, or were used in the past, or may be susceptible to use in interstate or foreign commerce, including all waters which are subject to the ebb and flow of the tide	(1) All waters which are currently used, or were used in the past, or may be susceptible to use in interstate or foreign commerce, including all waters which are subject to the ebb and flow of the tide
(2) All interstate waters including interstate wetlands	(2) All interstate waters, including interstate wetlands
(6) The territorial seas	(3) The territorial seas

Table 7-1. Comparing the definition of WOTUS in the 1986/1988 rules and 2014 proposed rule: traditional navigable waters, interstate waters, and the territorial sea.

1986/1988 RULES	**2014 PROPOSAL**
(4) All impoundments of waters otherwise defined as waters of the United States	(4) All impoundments of waters identified in paragraphs (1)–(3) and (5) [traditional navigable waters, interstate waters, the territorial sea, and tributaries]
(5) tributaries of waters identified in paragraphs (1)–(4) [traditional navigable waters, interstate waters, other waters with a commerce connection, and impoundments]	(5) All tributaries of waters identified in paragraphs (1)–(4) [traditional navigable waters, interstate waters, the territorial sea, and impoundments]
(7) Wetlands adjacent to waters (other than waters that are themselves wetlands) identified in paragraphs (1)–(6) [traditional navigable waters, interstate waters, other waters with a commerce connection, impoundments, and the territorial sea]	(6) All waters, including wetlands, adjacent to a water identified in paragraphs (1)–(5) [traditional navigable waters, interstate waters, the territorial sea, impoundments, and tributaries]

Table 7-2. Comparing the definition of WOTUS in the 1986/1988 rules and 2014 proposed rule: impoundments, tributaries, and adjacent waters.

1986/1988 RULES	2014 PROPOSAL
(3) All other waters such as intrastate lakes, rivers, streams (including intermittent streams), mudflats, sandflats, wetlands, sloughs, prairie potholes, wet meadows, playa lakes, or natural ponds, the use, degradation or destruction of which could affect interstate or foreign commerce including any such waters: a. Which are or could be used by interstate or foreign travelers for recreational or other purposes; or b. From which fish or shellfish are or could be taken and sold in interstate or foreign commerce; or c. Which are used or could be used for industrial purposes by industries in interstate commerce	(7) On a case-specific basis, other waters, including wetlands, provided that those waters alone, or in combination with other similarly situated waters, including wetlands, located in the same region, have a significant nexus to a water identified in paragraphs (1)–(3) [traditional navigable waters, interstate waters, and the territorial sea]

Table 7-3. Comparing the definition of WOTUS in the 1986/1988 rules and 2014 proposed rule: a significant shift from a commerce connection to a significant nexus test.

This clarification seemed minor, covering open waters, such as ponds, that might not be considered wetlands due to the lack of vegetation. This proposed change was hardly earth shattering. Thus far, at first glance, all the hullabaloo seemed unwarranted.

The most significant proposed change involved the replacement of the "other waters" provision with waters that have a "significant nexus" to traditional navigable waters, interstate waters, and the territorial sea (Table 7-3). This proposed change would codify into regulation Justice Kennedy's preferred approach and the agencies' post-*Rapanos* practice. Removing the explicit language about interstate commerce did not mean that the agencies were asserting authority untethered from the commerce clause, as traditional navigable waters themselves are channels of interstate commerce.[6]

The proposed rule also identified which waters would never be considered waters of the United States, including groundwater, wastewater treatment ponds and lagoons, prior converted cropland, and certain ditches (Table 7-4).[7] Thus the proposed rule created a continuum. At one end, certain waters would always be treated as jurisdictional; at the other end, certain waters would always be treated as nonjurisdictional. For waters in the middle of the continuum, the significant nexus test would be applied. If those waters contributed significantly to the chemical, physical, or biological integrity of traditional navigable waters, interstate waters, or the territorial sea, they would be covered. If not, they were not waters of the United States.

CATEGORICALLY JURISDICTIONAL	SIGNIFICANT NEXUS TEST	CATEGORICALLY NONJURISDICTIONAL
Traditional navigable waters	Other waters	Groundwater
Interstate waters		Treatment ponds and lagoons
Territorial sea		Prior converted cropland
Impoundments		Certain ditches
Tributaries		
Adjacent waters		

Table 7-4. The WOTUS and non-WOTUS categories of the proposed 2014 rule.

In explaining the proposed rule, the EPA and the Corps emphasized "that the categorical finding of jurisdiction for tributaries and adjacent waters was not based on the mere connection of a water body to downstream waters, but rather a determination that the nexus . . . is significant based on data, science, the [Clean Water Act], and caselaw."[8] The 1986/1988 rules had treated tributaries and adjacent wetlands in a similar fashion, and on the surface it seems that the proposed rule simply did the same. But digging into the proposed rule's clarification of the terms *adjacent* and *tributary* suggested otherwise.

The Devil Is in the Definitions

The 1986/1988 rules defined *adjacent* to mean "bordering, contiguous or neighboring," without elaborating on those terms. *Bordering* and *contiguous* suggest a direct connection, such as abutting or touching. In contrast, *neighboring* could mean "next to" but also "nearby" or "in the vicinity"—in the neighborhood. Like the 1986/1988 rules, the 2014 proposed rule defined adjacent to be "bordering, contiguous or neighboring," but it also offered a definition of "neighboring" that contained two parts. A water would be neighboring and therefore adjacent if it were located within the riparian area or floodplain of traditional navigable waters and their tributaries.[9] Floodplains can cover significant chunks of an area. For example, 41 percent of properties in Fort Lauderdale, Florida, are in a hundred-year floodplain.[10] Although the agencies noted that Federal Emergency Management Agency (FEMA) 100-year flood maps do not necessarily delineate a floodplain for

Clean Water Act purposes, they recognized that "the FEMA defined floodplain may often coincide with the current definition proposed in this rule."[11] The regulated community was alarmed that a water such as wetland "in the general neighborhood" of a traditional navigable water or its tributaries would now fall under the jurisdiction of the federal government. In their view, the federal agencies' proposal was a land grab and downright unneighborly.

Alternatively, a water would also be considered "neighboring" if it had a hydrologic connection to a traditional navigable water or its tributaries through shallow groundwater or confined surface water.[12] From a scientific perspective, this makes sense and takes into account the hydrologic cycle. To the regulated community, however, a reliance on a mere hydrologic connection was contrary to *Rapanos*, where even Justice Kennedy rejected such an approach. This aspect of neighboring might increase federal jurisdiction too.

The definitional section of the 2014 proposed rule also sought to provide specific meaning to the term *tributary* for the first time in regulation. It defined a tributary as a water that has a bed, banks, and an ordinary high water mark and contributes flow to a traditional navigable water, interstate water, the territorial sea, or an impoundment.[13] Furthermore, wetlands, lakes, and ponds could be tributaries if they contributed flow.[14] Notably, the proposed definition made no distinction between natural and human-altered or human-made waters, and accordingly encompassed some ditches and canals. In terms of the flow contribution, tributaries would include perennial waters (those that flowed all year), intermittent waters (those that flowed weekly to seasonally), and ephemeral waters (those that flowed more sporadically, only as a result of precipitation events). The regulated community again expressed concern, especially about ephemeral tributaries and ditches. Once again, they argued that such an assertion of jurisdiction was untethered to the Clean Water Act. The agencies had a different view of the law and offered an additional justification: They had science on their side.

Following the Science

Housed within the EPA, the Office of Research and Development conducts scientific research to inform EPA's decisions. During the first term of the Obama administration, it was tasked with the responsibility of summarizing and explaining how streams and wetlands contribute to the chemical, physical, and biological integrity of downstream waters, including traditional navigable waters. Over the course of several years, the Office of Research and Development reviewed and synthesized more than 1,200 peer-reviewed scientific publications.[15] It released a draft report in September 2013 for public comment and peer review by the Scientific Advisory Board,[16] which Congress created to provide independent scientific and technical advice to the EPA on a range of matters, including rulemakings. When publishing the proposed WOTUS rule in April 2014, the EPA and the Corps committed that the final report would inform their final decision.[17]

The final report, titled *Connectivity of Streams & Wetlands to Downstream Waters: A Review & Synthesis of the Scientific Evidence*, was released in January 2015.[18] More than 400 pages in length, the Connectivity Report comprehensively explained the central role that tributary streams and wetlands play "in maintaining the structure and function of downstream waters."[19] As an initial matter, streams—perennial, intermittent, and ephemeral—are the main water source for most rivers. First-order headwaters (streams in the upper reaches of a watershed) contribute approximately 60 percent of water volume to downstream waters.[20] The Connectivity Report emphasized and described how streams and wetlands contribute to the quality of downstream waters by removing and storing materials; for example, a primary wetland function is to retain and store pollutants, preventing or reducing these contaminants' impacts on downstream waters.[21] Furthermore, the report found that wetlands and streams act as refuges and provide habitat for fish, shellfish, and wildlife,[22] which, based on the plain language of the Clean Water Act, Congress explicitly sought to protect. The report also explained the flood control function of wetlands: By capturing and storing water, wetlands reduce or delay floods—thereby regulating navigable waters—and over time, the water can move back to a navigable water as baseflow.[23]

The Connectivity Report noted the broader contributions of streams and wetlands over time and in the context of other waters in the watershed. A single, small wetland may have little influence on downstream waters; however, the cumulative impacts of many wetlands in a watershed can have a substantial impact on downstream waters. Similarly, an individual ephemeral stream may contribute a small amount of water and organisms to downstream waters in a given year, but the aggregate contribution from that stream over time or from all of the ephemeral streams in that watershed can be significant.[24]

In summary, the Connectivity Report highlighted the many ways nonnavigable streams and wetlands are integral to all aspects of the quality of the nation's waters. Not everyone was impressed. When the Connectivity Report came out, a former Pentagon official was heard to dismissively remark on the margins of a national conference: "400 pages to say that water runs downhill."[25] But although the report's findings and conclusions did not necessarily surprise anyone, it was a necessary exercise. The agencies wanted to establish a firm scientific foundation to justify the Clean Water Rule.

Public Comments

The 2014 proposed rule was just that: a proposal. It was published in the *Federal Register* for public comments, and the public indeed responded—with over one million comments, after the comment period was extended to November 14, 2014.[26] Many were postcards or short form letters, expressing a strong view. For example, environmental organizations, such as the Denver office of Clean Water Action, sponsored a campaign to have concerned citizens submit the postcard shown in Figure 7-1.[27]

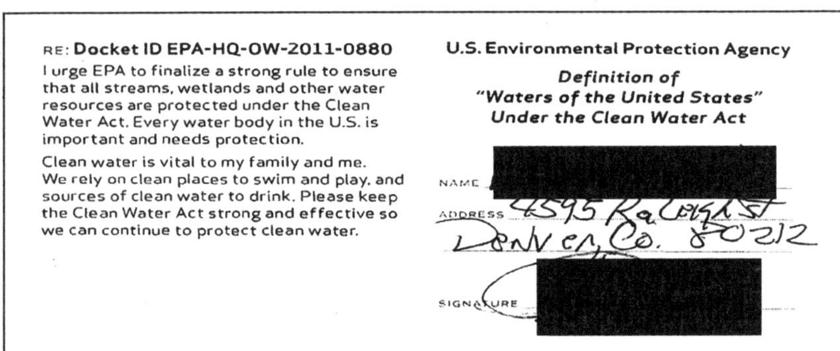
RE: **Docket ID EPA-HQ-OW-2011-0880**

I urge EPA to finalize a strong rule to ensure that all streams, wetlands and other water resources are protected under the Clean Water Act. Every water body in the U.S. is important and needs protection.

Clean water is vital to my family and me. We rely on clean places to swim and play, and sources of clean water to drink. Please keep the Clean Water Act strong and effective so we can continue to protect clean water.

U.S. Environmental Protection Agency

Definition of "Waters of the United States" Under the Clean Water Act

NAME

ADDRESS 4595 Raleigh St Denver, Co. 80212

SIGNATURE

Figure 7-1: A sample postcard from the pro–Clean Water Rule campaign.

Farm organizations and other members of the regulated community marshalled their troops through similar efforts, as the Kentucky Farm Bureau Insurance Companies did, resulting in letters with the same message (and exclamation points):

> If imposed, this would impact the way I farm, and because of the lack of clarity contained in the proposed rule it could also create a huge economic burden for me and my family. I feel this rule has the potential to expand your jurisdiction to virtually any area of my farm including ponds, ditches and occasionally wet areas, even if they are isolated and protected. This is wrong!

> Because of the confusion this proposed rule will generate, I call on EPA and the U.S. Army Corps of Engineers to withdraw this rule completely![28]

On one hand, participation in a rulemaking process by submitting public comments can serve a salutary purpose, leading to more engaged and informed stakeholders. It is a genuinely good thing for people to take an active interest in the functioning of their government. On the other hand, these types of mass comments are not particularly effective at persuading the agencies. The rulemaking process is not a plebiscite; content matters more than volume.

The most effective comment letters support their positions with specificity, such as data or concrete examples of the proposed rule's impact (for good or ill).[29] As a general rule, generalities don't generate a reaction. Effective comment letters also anticipate judicial review. The specific information provided (or issues raised) can be used later to defend—or attack—a rule.

Cognizant that the comment letters can be part of a record in a subsequent lawsuit, some commenters' submissions read almost like legal briefs. For example, Earthjustice, which describes itself as the "premier nonprofit public interest environmental law organization," provided a comment that cited scientific literature and made legal arguments, focusing on the Clean Water Act's water quality objective, explaining why the agencies' proposal was justified or why it did not go far enough.[30] Although Earthjustice was generally supportive of the proposed rule, it contended that the coverage of impoundments and tributaries was too narrow. It also objected to the proposed rule's categorical exclusion of groundwater and voiced concern about the "waste treatment system" exclusion, offering specific examples of how mining and utility companies were degrading water quality through unregulated discharges of mining tailings and coal ash.[31]

In contrast, the Waters Advocacy Coalition did not like the rule at all.[32] At first glance, this might appear surprising, given the group's name and its claim that its members were "committed to the protection and restoration of America's wetlands and waters."[33] In reality, the coalition consisted of a broad swath of the regulated community, from agricultural and oil and gas groups to homebuilder and golf course superintendent associations. Spoiler alert: Many of these organizations would be plaintiffs challenging the legality of the Clean Water Rule. Although, to be fair, that's not much of a spoiler. The legal arguments were telegraphed in the comment letter. In the coalition's view, the proposed rule was unconstitutional, beyond Congress's commerce powers. It intruded into the province of the states. It was unnecessary, unclear, and lacking in scientific justification. Even the process was asserted to be flawed. Accordingly, the coalition urged the agencies to withdraw the proposed rule,[34] a conclusion that might cause a reasonable person to question the coalition's commitment to protecting and restoring the nation's waters.

When an agency publishes a proposed rule, it sometimes solicits comments on specific issues or alternative approaches. For example, in the 2014 proposed rule, the EPA and Corps asked for comments on whether particular types of waters—such as prairie potholes, vernal pools, Delmarva and Carolina bays, pocosins, and playas—should be categorically included or excluded as waters of the United States.[35] Also, ensconced on page 23 of the eighty-eight-page notice in the *Federal Register* was a request that commenters provide "from scientific literature any suggestions for additional clarification of current explicit limits on adjacency, such as a specific distance or a specific floodplain interval."[36] Both the categorical treatment of specific types of waters and the question of precise distance requirements would be significant—and controversial—aspects of the final rule.

Ditch the Rule

Community organizer Saul Alinsky, a bête noir of conservatives (even though he has been dead since 1972), wrote in his *Rules for Radicals*, "Ridicule is man's most potent weapon. It's hard to counterattack ridicule, and it infuriates the opposition, which then reacts to your advantage."[37]

Though probably no fan of Alinsky, the Missouri Farm Bureau followed his advice when organizing against the proposed Clean Water Rule. It produced probably the funniest, most entertaining riposte in the WOTUS campaign, a parody video using a signature tune from the Disney movie *Frozen*.[38] The video featured a seventh-generation farming family with Kacey Clay belting out how ridiculous it is for the EPA and Corps to regulate farm ditches. In place of "Let It Go," she sings "That's Enough" as she cautions, "Agriculture is safe, that's what they say—it's what they always say." The video is punctuated with her three adorable children in floaties, flippers, and goggles, as well as in a canoe with their dad, Andy Clay, in a bone-dry ditch. It's really well done and effectively ridicules the perceived absurdities of the agencies.

The parody video led to the Clay family being interviewed on *Fox and Friends*, which presented an opportunity to warn a larger audience about the dangers of the proposed Clean Water Rule.[39] A Fox host introduced them as being "fed up with the EPA's proposed Clean Water Act"—mistakenly confusing the statute with the proposed rule. When asked how the Clean Water Act is affecting them, Andy noted that its impact was "huge." When gently pressed for details, he spoke about how the rule would require him to get a Clean Water Act permit to plant crops. He also suggested that the rule would prohibit people from mowing their lawns without a federal permit. Both statements are not true; they are myths. In Clean Water Act section 404(f), Congress expressly exempted normal farming activities such as planting, plowing, and cultivating from regulation, and nowhere in the proposed rule was there a hint that lawns (a nonwater) would be regulated. But the proposed Clean Water Rule would treat some ditches as waters of the United States, and "Ditch the Rule" neatly encapsulated a call to end apparent government overreach.

The Missouri Farm Bureau video garnered more than 150,000 views. It also got EPA's attention. (Indeed, I first learned of it when an amused EPA employee forwarded it to me.) The EPA crafted a multiprong social media response that included #DitchTheMyth and #CleanWaterRules campaigns (Figure 7-2).

The EPA also used Thunderclap, described as a "crowdspeaking platform" that facilitated "virtual flash-mobs"—the dissemination of similar messages across multiple platforms at the same time.[40] At an appointed date and time in September 2014, the following message was conveyed on 980 social media accounts on Facebook, Twitter, and Tumblr: "Clean water is important to me. I support EPA's efforts to protect it for my health, my family, and my community."[41] Each message contained a hyperlink leading to EPA's webpage on the proposed rule. In theory, the message reached 1.8 million people, assuming that all the followers of the 980 accounts stopped scrolling long enough to notice it.[42]

Senator James Inhofe noticed it (or, much more likely, his staff or a member of the regulated community flagged it for him). Senator Inhofe, perhaps best known for bringing a snowball onto the Senate floor to illustrate his belief that climate change is a hoax, was the chairman of the Senate Environment and Public Works Committee.[43] He wrote to the US Government Accountability Office (GAO) to request that the GAO, a congressional agency that examines how federal funds are spent, investigate whether EPA's social media campaign ran afoul of certain restrictions on the use of appropriated funds.[44] In particular, he wanted to know whether #DitchTheMyth,

Figure 7-2. A tweet into the abyss.

#CleanWaterRules, Thunderclap, and EPA's webpage with hyperlinks to groups supporting the proposed rule, such as beer brewers and surfers, amounted to covert propaganda or improper lobbying.

For an agency to act lawfully, Congress must both grant the agency the authority to act and appropriate the money necessary for the agency to act. When enacting an appropriations law, however, Congress will often place specific restrictions on how those funds may be spent. In this case, Congress had prohibited EPA from spending any money, directly or indirectly, on covert propaganda, that is, "communications that fail to disclose the agency's role as the source of information."[45] Congress also prohibited EPA from spending any money, directly or indirectly, on indirect or grassroots lobbying efforts to support or oppose any pending bills in Congress.[46]

Although the GAO found the #DitchTheMyth and #CleanWaterRules campaigns to be permissible because EPA was identified as the source, it clapped back on the use of Thunderclap. The GAO found that the Thunderclap messages were covert propaganda.[47] Although EPA was quite open about the campaign—indeed, anyone signing up to convey the Thunderclap message knew that it was drafted by EPA—the GAO was concerned that the EPA's involvement was not so readily apparent to the followers of the 980 social media accounts. As the GAO explained,

> EPA constructed a message to be shared by others that refers to EPA in the third person and advocates support of the agency's efforts. In stating "clean water is important to me" and "I support EPA's efforts," EPA deliberately disassociates itself as the writer, when the message was in fact written, and its posting solicited, by EPA.[48]

The GAO emphasized that the "covert propaganda" could have reached potentially 1.8 million recipients, an overly optimistic figure to anyone who has ever posted on social media and despaired for the lack of likes, or even any acknowledgment.

The GAO also concluded that an EPA blog trying to corral the all-important craft beer drinker and surfer dude contingents was improper lobbying.[49] EPA's communications director posted that brewers and surfers relied on clean water, although for different reasons. Brewers need clean freshwater to make a healthy and tasty product, and surfers want to ride clean waves (in all senses of the word *clean*). One can only assume that a beer-drinking surfer would doubly support the proposed Clean Water Rule.

Nevertheless, in the GAO's view, the blog went astray when it linked to external websites.[50] When clicking on the links, a viewer was taken to the Natural Resources Defense Council webpage "Brewers for Clean Water" and a Surfrider Foundation blog that explained why polluted ocean water was more of a risk to surfers than mere lay-about beachgoers. The external sites not only expressed support for the proposed rule but also urged people to contact their members of Congress. Although it's a good thing to encourage political involvement, the EPA is prohibited from encouraging people to contact Congress about pending legislation, a form of indirect or grassroots lobbying. And, at the time, there were several WOTUS bills under consideration. So the GAO determined that the EPA's blog, which linked to websites, which in turn encouraged people to contact Congress, was improper.[51] The issue could have been resolved by a simple notice, now ubiquitous, that alerts a viewer when they are leaving an agency website for an external source.

The Final Clean Water Rule Finally Emerges (June 2015)

In June 2015, after considering thousands of substantive comments, the EPA and the Corps published in the *Federal Register* the final rule, a regulation they called the Clean Water Rule.[52] The preamble to the rule, which explained the agencies' reasoning and their response to comments, took up several hundred pages. Some portions of the final rule, such as provisions regarding traditional navigable waters, interstate waters, and the territorial seas, remained the same. Slight changes were made for impoundments and tributaries. Jurisdiction over impoundments was expanded to impoundments of any water of the United States, which simply brought the Clean Water Rule back in line with the 1986/1988 approach. With respect to tributaries, the final rule dropped tributaries of impoundments. The provision of adjacent waters made it explicit that it included not just wetlands but ponds, lakes, oxbows, impoundments, and similar areas. As Table 7-5 shows, these changes did not appear to be monumental. But the agencies also clarified the definition of *neighboring* to be distance based. It also declared that five particular wetland types would be subject to the significant nexus test and added a new eighth category of waters—those within a 100-year floodplain or 4,000 feet of a high tide line or an ordinary high water mark, when those waters had a significant nexus to downstream waters. These modifications proved to be much more contentious.

Recall that the definition of *adjacent* includes *neighboring*. The proposed rule had defined *neighboring* to include waters, such as a wetland, in the riparian area or floodplain of traditional navigable waters and tributaries (as well as interstate waters, the territorial sea, and impoundments). To provide clarity, the agencies added to the final rule a specific distant component to the concept of neighboring. If the wetland was within 100 feet of the ordinary high water mark of traditional navigable waters or tributaries, it was deemed to be "neighboring," and thus "adjacent," and thus a WOTUS.[53] Waters within this distance were treated categorically; they were jurisdictional by rule.

The same categorical treatment was applied to wetlands and other waters located on a 100-year floodplain that were within 1,500 feet of the ordinary high water mark of the primary water (the one producing the flood).[54] Similarly, wetlands and other waters were also jurisdictional by rule if they were located within 1,500 feet of the ordinary high water mark of the Great Lakes.[55] The agencies were providing certainty as to what waters were covered by the Clean Water Act. If a member of the regulated community wanted to discharge a pollutant to those waters, it would first need to secure a permit. The distance-based provisions offered clear, bright lines.

In the proposed rule, a water could also be considered "neighboring" (and thus adjacent and thus a WOTUS) if it had a confined surface or shallow subsurface connection with other waters. "In order to provide the clarity and certainty that many commenters requested," the agencies deleted this provision.[56] But although such waters might not be jurisdictional by rule, they could still be picked up under the significant nexus test (categories 7 and 8). This did not provide a clear, bright line.

2014 PROPOSAL	2015 FINAL RULE
(1) All waters which are currently used, or were used in the past, or may be susceptible to use in interstate or foreign commerce, including all waters which are subject to the ebb and flow of the tide	Same
(2) All interstate waters, including interstate wetlands	Same
(3) The territorial seas	Same
(4) All impoundments of waters identified in paragraphs (1)–(3) and (5) [traditional navigable waters, interstate waters, the territorial sea, and tributaries]	(4) All impoundments of waters otherwise identified as waters of the United States
(5) All tributaries of waters identified in paragraphs (1)–(4) [traditional navigable waters, interstate waters, the territorial sea, and impoundments]	(5) All tributaries of waters identified in paragraphs (1)–(3) [traditional navigable waters, interstate waters, and the territorial sea]

Table 7-5a. Minor edits: comparing the definition of WOTUS in the 2014 proposed rule and the 2015 final rule.

2014 PROPOSAL	2015 FINAL RULE
(6) All waters, including wetlands, adjacent to a water identified in paragraphs (1)–(5) [traditional navigable waters, interstate waters, the territorial sea, impoundments, and tributaries]	(6) All waters adjacent to a water identified in paragraphs (1)–(5), including wetlands, ponds, lakes, oxbows, impoundments, and similar areas [waters are adjacent—and jurisdictional by rule—based on distance]
(7) On a case-specific basis, other waters, including wetlands, provided that those waters alone, or in combination with other similarly situated waters, including wetlands, located in the same region, have a significant nexus to a water identified in paragraphs (1)–(3) [traditional navigable waters, interstate waters, and the territorial sea]	(7) All waters listed in (i)–(v) where they are determined on a case-by-case basis to have a significant nexus to a water identified in paragraphs (1)–(3): (i) Prairie potholes (ii) Carolina bays (iii) Pocosins (iv) Western vernal pools (v) Texas coastal prairie wetlands (8) On a case-specific basis, other waters, including wetlands, provided that those waters alone, or in combination with other similarly situated waters, including wetlands, located in the same region, have a significant nexus to a water identified in paragraphs (1)–(3) [traditional navigable waters, interstate waters, and the territorial sea], if within certain distances

Table 7-5b. More substantive changes: comparing the definition of WOTUS in the 2014 proposed rule and the 2015 final rule.

Under the new rule, the significant nexus test would be applied to five specific wetland types (category 7). In a new eighth category, jurisdiction would be also asserted over all waters located within 100-year floodplains if those waters had a significant nexus to downstream waters.[57] Likewise, all waters located within 4,000 feet of the high tide line or ordinary high water mark of a primary water would be considered WOTUS if there was a significant nexus between the waters.[58] Any such waters beyond the 100-year floodplain and the 4,000-foot line would categorically be nonjurisdictional, however.[59]

Do not be alarmed if you have trouble following the details. For visual learners, the Congressional Research Service provided the helpful diagram in Figure 7-3.

With the executive branch acting, the stage was set to move the WOTUS battle over to the other branches.

Congressional Review Act: Sidestepping the Filibuster

It is important to keep in mind that regulatory agencies act under the authority granted to them by Congress. If Congress does not agree with how an agency is implementing its responsibilities, it can hold investigative hearings (or it can ask the GAO to investigate). The hearings may have a persuasive effect on agency behavior, but an agency might just accept its public beating and keep the offending rule or policy in place. Alternatively, Congress can withhold an agency's appropriations or put conditions on how an agency might spend its funds (as was the case with respect to wetland delineation

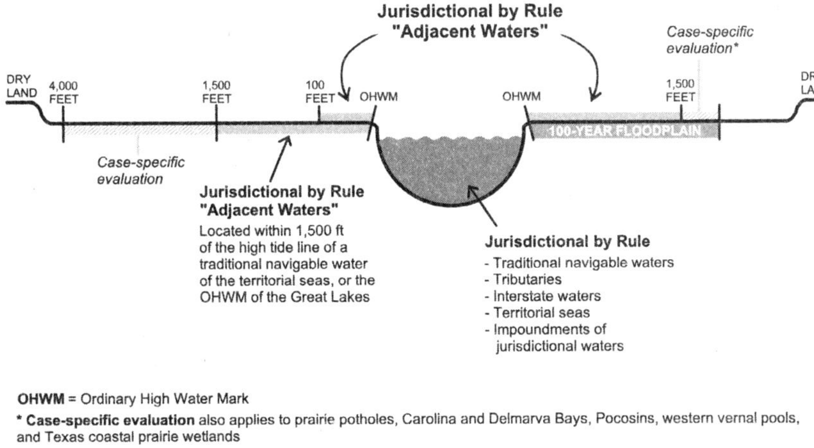

Figure 7-3. A handy jurisdiction illustration adapted from the Congressional Research Service.

manuals). Or Congress could restrict or revoke the agency's authority. Both the appropriation and authorization options require Congress to approve a bill in both chambers, however. This can be exceedingly difficult, especially in light of the Senate's filibuster rules. Although a simple majority is needed to approve a Senate bill, a three-fifths vote is required to end debate, essentially requiring a supermajority of sixty votes to pass most laws.

For many years, Congress used the legislative veto, which allowed one house of Congress to invalidate an agency action through adoption of a resolution of disapproval. As explained in Chapter 5, the Supreme Court struck down the legislative veto as unconstitutional. Congress can take legislative action only through bicameral approval of a bill, which is then presented to the president for signature or veto. In 1996, in the Congressional Review Act, Congress came up with a new mechanism, which some viewed as a revival of the legislative veto.[60] In reality, the Congressional Review Act simply simplifies the process of bicameral action.

Under the Congressional Review Act, an agency must submit rules to Congress before they can take effect.[61] Once Congress is notified and the final rule is published in the *Federal Register*, a complicated sixty-day clock starts. (The clock is based on session or legislative days.) During that time period, Congress can consider a joint resolution of disapproval. But Congress can consider a joint resolution of disapproval at any time. What makes the Congressional Review Act process different is that it eliminates the filibuster if the matter is raised during the sixty-day period. Debate is limited, and no amendments are permitted. The required text for the joint resolution is brief and straightforward: "The Congress disapproves the rule submitted by the [agency] relating to [name of the rule], and such rule shall have no force or effect." If both houses pass the joint resolution—and if the president signs it—then the rule does not go into effect (if the effective date has not yet occurred) or is treated as never having taken effect (if the effective date has passed). In addition to invalidating the rule, this process then prohibits the agency from reissuing a substantially similar rule without congressional approval.

After the EPA and the Corps submitted the Clean Water Rule to Congress and published it in the *Federal Register*, the Senate acted first. Senator Joni Ernst of Iowa introduced a joint resolution of disapproval, stating that "only in Washington do unelected bureaucrats take 300 pages to simplify and provide clarity," adding that Iowans were now "concerned that any low spot on a farmer's field—or a ditch—or a puddle after a rainstorm, may now fall under the EPA's watch."[62] She was giving voice to the farmers who felt that the Clean Water Rule was a hand on their throat. The Senate voted to disapprove the Clean Water Rule 53–44.[63] The House followed suit, by a margin of 253–166.[64] The joint resolution was then presented to President Obama.

Not surprisingly, given that his political appointees had overseen the development of the Clean Water Rule, President Obama vetoed the joint resolution. In his brief statement, President Obama asserted that the rule made clear the jurisdictional boundaries of the Clean Water Act, providing "businesses and communities the regulatory certainty and clarity."[65] Although a veto was preordained, opponents of the Clean Water Rule were pleased. As the Pacific Legal Foundation posted, "President Obama and his defenders in Congress now 'own' the WOTUS rule much more definitively than previously."[66]

Battle on the Judicial Front

The Clean Water Rule, with its distance-based rules, did indeed provide more certainty than the pre-2015 regime, which relied on the significant nexus test to a greater degree. But this was not the type of certainty that the regulated community desired. The certainty it wanted was the certainty associated with lack of regulation, that they could go about their business unimpeded by the requirement to apply for a federal permit. Even before the Clean Water Rule went into effect, the regulated community and the states sympathetic to their cause filed lawsuits challenging the legality of the new regulation.

Their public comments in the rulemaking process had already largely laid out the litigation roadmap. The lawsuits contained process, statutory, and constitutional arguments, plus a few others thrown in for good measure.

Procedural violations associated with the rulemaking process:

- Substantial changes to proposed rule without additional public comment
- Final rule that is not a "logical outgrowth" of the proposed rule
- Failure to make all information relied on available to the public
- Failure to respond appropriately to comments

Clean Water Act (statutory) violations:

- Exceeding the agencies' Clean Water Act authority
- Inconsistency with Clean Water Act's plain language

Constitutional violations:

- Commerce clause
- Tenth Amendment
- Due process clause

Other violations:

- Regulatory Flexibility Act
- Unfunded Mandates Reform Act
- National Environmental Policy Act
- Anti-Lobbying Act
- Executive orders

Although the public comments had foreshadowed the litigation strategy, one big question remained: In which court or courts should these challenges be brought? Ordinarily, cases begin with trial courts, such as a US district court, if it is a federal matter. But the Clean Water Act contains a provision for the direct review of certain EPA actions by an appellate court, a US court of appeals.[67] It was not clear where a challenge to the Clean Water Rule should be filed. To play it safe, the regulated communities and their supporting states filed in multiple US district courts (as plaintiffs) and US courts of appeals (as petitioners). Environmental groups and their allied states followed the same tactical approach and intervened in those cases or brought their own cases—sometimes to support the Clean Water Rule, but sometimes also attacking the Clean Water Rule for not being broad enough.

At one point, there were cases filed in eight different US district courts and four different US courts of appeals, all of which dealt with whether the agencies had acted lawfully in promulgating the Clean Water Rule.[68] The first issue each court had to address, however, was whether it was the proper court to hear the matter. It all became very meta: Which court had jurisdiction to consider the question of Clean Water Act jurisdiction?

E Pluribus Unum

Translated, the motto of the United States is "out of many, one." That also happened to be the strategy of the US Department of Justice (DOJ) in defending the Clean Water Rule. Rather than litigate in courts all around the country, DOJ sought to centralize or consolidate the litigation, for efficiency purposes but also because one win would ensure total victory. The regulated community preferred to have the option to attack on multiple judicial fronts, in part because it increased the likelihood of appearing before judges more amenable to their arguments. In addition, that one judge might be persuaded to issue a nationwide injunction.

Congress created a mechanism to deal with civil actions pending in multiple US district courts involving common factual questions. The US Judicial Panel on Multidistrict Litigation, known as the MDL Panel, has the authority to assign all those cases to a single judge who would then coordinate or consolidate pretrial proceedings. In the Clean Water Rule litigation, DOJ made a motion before the MDL Panel to have all the pretrial proceedings centralized in the US District Court for the District of Columbia, a forum that would probably be more hospitable to the agencies than in, say, a US district court in Texas. However, the MDL Panel denied the motion and declined to consolidate the cases.[69] One of the reasons concerned the uncertainty of the overarching question of whether US district courts or US courts of appeals had jurisdiction over the issue. Unable to resist the pun, the MDL Panel observed that "centralization thus would require the transferee judge to navigate potentially uncharted waters with respect to law of the case."[70] To the delight of the forum-shopping regulated community, the multiple cases at the US district court level would proceed independently.

The US courts of appeals also have a process to consolidate related cases that are pending in various circuits. In contrast to the MDL Panel's decision, the four Clean Water Rule cases pending before the US courts of appeals were consolidated and randomly assigned to the Sixth Circuit, which is based in Cincinnati, Ohio.[71] So the litigation challenges to the Clean Water Rule moved forward on two different tracks: in multiple US district courts and in a single US court of appeals.

First Out of the Gate: US District Court for the District of North Dakota

If you Google "What is North Dakota known for?," you will probably be told it's the Peace Garden State (not to be confused with New Jersey, also called the Garden State, although apparently the less pacifistic kind). You'll also be informed about North Dakota's badlands, which Theodore Roosevelt described as "so fantastically broken in form and so bizarre in color as to seem hardly properly to belong to this earth."[72] A website devoted to twenty fascinating things about North Dakota brags that rapper Wiz Khalifa was born in Minot.[73] You might also learn about North Dakota's importance to the nation's agriculture, as it is the leading producer of "spring wheat, durum wheat, dry edible peas, dry edible beans, honey, flaxseed and canola."[74] But although it does not jump out on a general internet search, North Dakota is also known for its prairie potholes—wetlands that are incredibly important as nesting and breeding grounds for migratory waterfowl.[75] Many North Dakotans, especially farmers and ranchers, are particularly sensitive about any federal regulation over prairie potholes.[76] Accordingly, North Dakota was among the first states to challenge the Clean Water Rule.

Eleven other states joined North Dakota in the case that was filed in Fargo.[77] The states requested that Judge Ralph Erickson issue a preliminary injunction to keep the Clean Water Rule from entering into force. When deciding whether to issue an injunction, a court typically considers the likelihood of success on the merits, the risk of irreparable harm to the parties, and the public interest. On August 27, 2015, the day before the Clean Water Act was to become effective, Judge Erickson granted the plaintiffs' motion for preliminary injunction, ordering the agencies not to implement the new rule.[78]

Judge Erickson concluded that states were likely to prevail on several claims. He found the categorical distance-based approach unsupported by the scientific record.[79] From a process perspective, he also held that the possibility of a distance-based approach was not properly highlighted in the proposed rule; thus, the final rule was not a logical outgrowth of the proposal, and the public was improperly deprived of an opportunity to comment on geographic distance as a bright jurisdictional line.[80] Furthermore, he found it likely that the EPA and the Corps had exceeded the authority that Congress had granted, as interpreted by the Supreme Court. He noted that the Eighth Circuit had held that the agencies could regulate waters that met either Justice Kennedy's or Justice Scalia's approach in *Rapanos*. In Judge Erickson's view, the Clean Water Rule went further than both, as even the EPA estimated a 2.84–4.65 percent increase in positive jurisdictional determinations.[81] Such an expansion of federal authority, limited as it might be, was deemed to be an invasion of state sovereignty, impeding the states' traditional role over land use decisions. Although Judge Erickson acknowledged that the Clean Water Rule's distance-based provisions provided some certainty to the regulated community, he nonetheless decided that the public interest weighed in favor of ensuring that federal agencies did not exceed their congressional mandates.[82]

There was some initial confusion about the scope of the injunction. The EPA interpreted it as applying only to the thirteen states that were parties

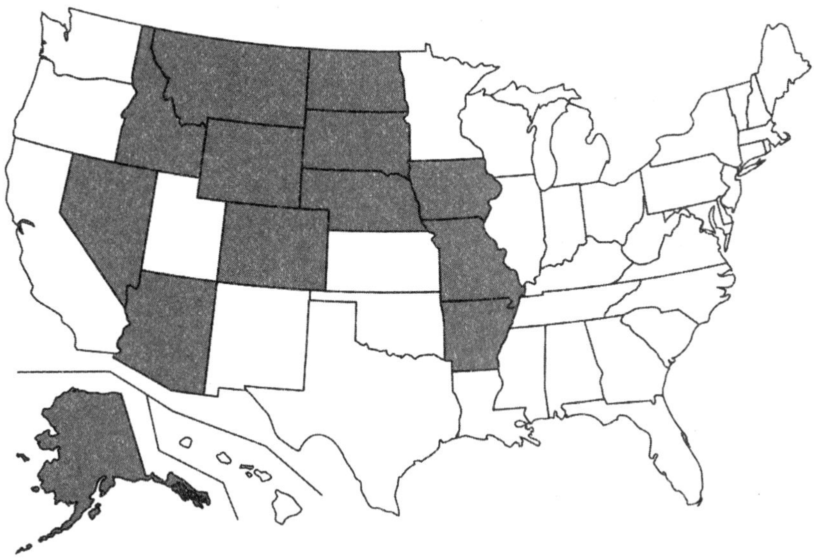

Figure 7-4. The state of play in August 2017. White indicates states where the Clean Water Rule was in effect (albeit briefly). Gray indicates states where the Clean Water Rule was enjoined and where the pre-2015 regime was in effect.

to the case (Iowa had joined late), whereas the states sought a nationwide injunction. The EPA emphasized the general principle that an injunction should not burden a defendant more than is necessary to provide a plaintiff complete relief. Similar cases were being considered throughout the country. Some states, such as New York, supported the Clean Water Rule and would find it to be unfair to apply the injunction in their jurisdiction. After briefing on the issue, Judge Erickson clarified that the injunction applied only to the states before him.[83] Accordingly, the WOTUS map appeared as shown in Figure 7-4.

A postscript for Judge Erickson: In 2017, President Trump gave him a promotion, appointing him to serve on the Court of Appeals for the Eighth Circuit.[84]

The Sixth Circuit Puts the Cart before the Horse

Federal courts are courts of limited jurisdiction. Before a court issues a decision, it typically is satisfied that it has the authority to rule. Indeed, even if no party raises the issue of jurisdiction, the court may do so *sua sponte*—on its own accord. However, the Court of Appeals for the Sixth Circuit decided to reach the issue of injunctive relief (i.e., whether to issue a national stay halting the Clean Water Rule's implementation) before deciding whether it even had jurisdiction to consider the case. What made this even stranger was that the petitioners, eighteen states challenging the Clean Water Rule, asked the court to dismiss the case for lack of standing. Given the success at the district court level in North Dakota, the regulated community and the states opposed to the Clean Water Rule figured the lower courts presented a more hospitable battleground. So, in effect, they were telling the Sixth Circuit, "never mind." But the federal government and eight states that had intervened in support of the Clean Water Rule contended that the Sixth Circuit was the proper forum. They favored this approach because if the Sixth Circuit had jurisdiction, then whatever it decided about the Clean Water Rule would control. If it upheld the regulation, then any injunctions issued by the US district courts, including out of the District of North Dakota, would be overridden.

In an opinion issued in October 2015, the Sixth Circuit acknowledged that the petitioners wanted to dismiss the case.[85] But two judges were chomping at the bit to strike down, at least temporarily, the Clean Water Rule. And they did so, over the dissent of one judge, who pointed out the impropriety of the court using its discretionary powers before deciding whether the court even had jurisdiction.

In granting a national stay, the two judges focused on the Clean Water Rule's distance-based requirements.[86] They thought that the challenging states had made a persuasive argument that when the agencies proposed the rule, they had failed to sufficiently alert the public to the possibility of such a categorical approach. The Clean Water Rule would therefore not be a logical outgrowth from the proposal. Moreover, the two judges were troubled by the perceived lack of scientific support to make these bright-line determinations. In their view, the lack of scientific support indicated a failure to engage in a reasoned decision-making process, thus rendering the agencies' actions arbitrary and capricious.

The two judges did downplay the states' sovereignty concerns, noting that there was "no compelling showing that any of the petitioners will suffer immediate irreparable harm—in the form of interference with state sovereignty."[87] Despite this lack of imminent injury, the two judges voted in favor of a national stay because it "silences the whirlwind of confusion that springs from uncertainty about the requirements of the [Clean Water Rule] and whether they will survive legal testing."[88] They wrote that a national stay would "restore uniformity of regulation under the familiar, if imperfect,

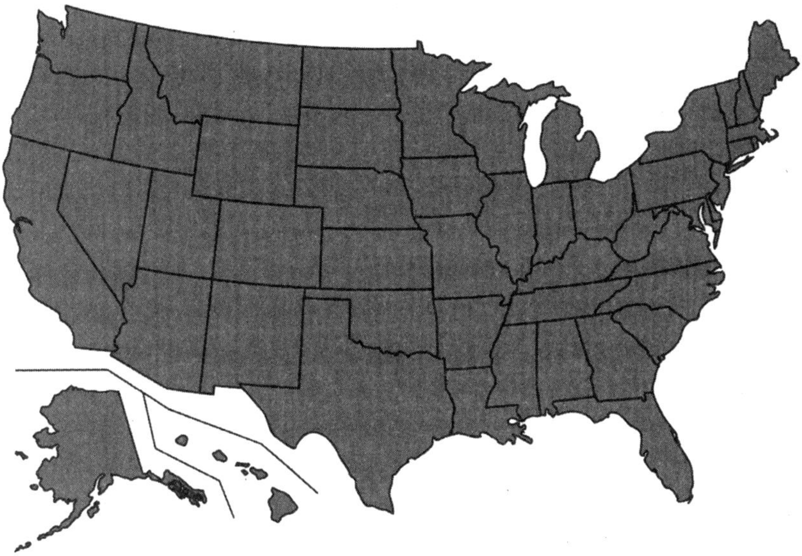

Figure 7-5. Result of the Sixth Circuit's national stay: The Clean Water Rule is not in effect and the pre-2015 regime applies throughout the land.

pre-[Clean Water] Rule regime, pending judicial review."[89] At least for the moment, the Clean Water Rule was dead nationwide.

Several months later, in February 2016, the Sixth Circuit finally got around to deciding whether it had jurisdiction. Although two of three judges thought the court did not have jurisdiction, the court nevertheless issued a fractured opinion concluding that it did.[90] Judge McKeague reasoned that although a strict reading of the judicial review provision would suggest no jurisdiction, he noted that many courts, including the Sixth Circuit, had "gradually expanded" "the scope of direct circuit court review"—yet "Congress ha[d] not moved to amend the provision or otherwise taken 'corrective' action."[91] Judge Keith strictly construed the statutory provisions and concluded the court lacked jurisdiction.[92] Challenges to WOTUS rules, in his view, must be brought first in US district courts. Although Judge Griffin agreed with Judge Keith's interpretation of the statute, he believed the court was bound by the precedent of a prior Sixth Circuit case.[93] Accordingly, he voted with Judge McKeague, and a nationwide stay remained in place (Figure 7-5). The Clean Water Rule remained in a judicially induced coma for the time being.

Two subsequent developments would upset this uniformity and order. On January 13, 2017, the US Supreme Court agreed to review the Sixth Circuit's decision that it had jurisdiction.[94] WOTUS was again before SCOTUS, but with a meta-twist: The Supreme Court would decide the question about which court had (original) jurisdiction about (Clean Water Act) jurisdiction.

And on January 20, 2017, Donald J. Trump was sworn in as the forty-fifth president of the United States.

CHAPTER 8

Zombie WOTUS

> The President should be applauded for making EPA and the Corps reconsider this debacle. Ultimately, this rule should be taken out behind the barn and put out of its misery.
>
> —National Cattlemen's Beef Association, February 2017

The debacle to which the National Cattlemen's Beef Association referred was the Clean Water Rule. The trade organization for farmers and ranchers seemed to suggest that the Obama administration regulation should be dispatched quickly with a figurative shot to the head,[1] although perhaps a more humane method (stunning and sticking) was envisioned. The cause for accolades was President Trump's executive order that called on the EPA and the Corps to repeal the Clean Water Rule and replace it with one in line with Justice Scalia's *Rapanos* plurality opinion. Before the Trump administration could complete the rulemaking process, however, the US Supreme Court entered the picture, issuing an opinion that resurrected the Clean Water Rule, a result that the regulated community likened to a horror movie. The Trump administration then tried to kill the reemergent regulation through a regulatory sleight of hand by changing its "applicability date." But the Trump administration soon learned that it's hard to kill a zombie and that procedural niceties matter.

POTUS on WOTUS

In one of his first acts in office, President Trump nominated Scott Pruitt, Oklahoma's attorney general, to serve as administrator of the EPA. Ordinarily, the person running the EPA is committed to protecting the environment. In contrast, Pruitt was known as a climate change denier, evincing more than a passing interest in assisting the regulated community, as the campaign contributions he received from the oil and gas industry illustrated.[2] (Ultimately his tenure at EPA was cut short in part by multiple ethics scandals, including using an EPA staffer to contact the CEO of Chick-fil-A to try to secure a franchise for his wife.[3]) As Oklahoma attorney general, he sued to invalidate fourteen EPA rules, including the Clean Water Rule.[4] He took office on February 17, 2017. Less than two weeks later, President Trump issued Executive Order 13778, titled "Restoring the Rule of Law, Federalism, and Economic Growth by Reviewing the 'Waters of the United States' Rule."

The executive order opened with a statement of policy declaring that although it is in the national interest to keep navigable waters free from pollution, such concerns must be balanced with the need to "promot[e] economic growth, minimiz[e] regulatory uncertainty, and [show] due regard for the roles of the Congress and the States under the Constitution."[5] The EPA and the Corps were directed to review the Clean Water Rule in light of this policy and then, if appropriate, rescind or revise the rule. In doing so, the agencies were to "consider interpreting the term 'navigable waters' . . . in a manner consistent with the opinion of Justice Antonin Scalia in *Rapanos v. United States*."[6]

Reminiscent of the battle cry over Obamacare, President Trump called for the agencies to "repeal and replace" the Clean Water Rule. Note that the executive order carefully framed its concern about pollution only in terms of "navigable waters," as opposed to the nation's waters or waters of the United States. The emphasis on navigable waters appeared throughout the order. In essence, Trump was saying, "Make WOTUS Navigable Waters Again!"

By their nature, formal documents such as executive orders are fairly dry. The signing ceremony, which was attended by farmers, developers, and county commissioners, gave Trump an opportunity to be more expansive. He asserted that "the EPA so-called Waters of the United States rule is one of the worst examples of federal regulation, and it has truly run amok, and is one of the rules most strongly opposed by farmers, ranchers and agricultural workers all across our land. It's prohibiting them from being allowed to do what they're supposed to be doing. It's been a disaster."[7] Although Trump correctly gauged the agricultural community's antipathy toward the Clean Water Rule, he was of course mistaken about its impact. It didn't prohibit farmers from farming, and it couldn't have been a disaster because judicial challenges precluded it from even being applied. Nevertheless, Trump told his assembled supporters, "With today's executive order I'm directing the EPA to take action paving the way for the elimination of this very destructive and horrible rule."[8] The use of the word "paving" was probably more Freudian than pun.

Scott Pruitt's EPA quickly tweeted out the good news to the regulated community (Figure 8-1).

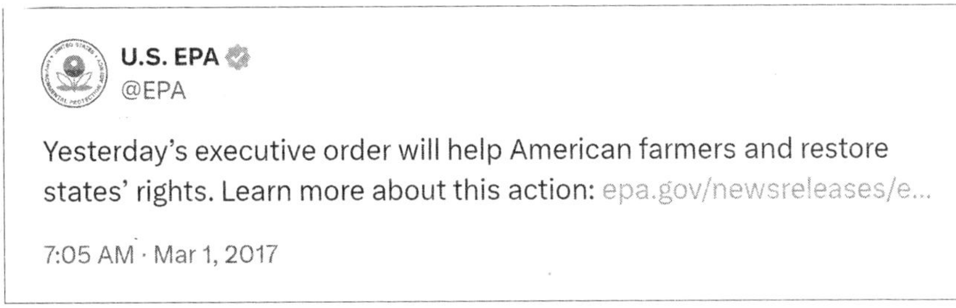

Figure 8-1. Scott Pruitt's EPA celebrating the announcement to roll back Clean Water Act protections.

But as we learned in Chapter 2, the president is not a king, and the president cannot, as a general matter, unilaterally issue agency regulations that have the force of law. Congress has set forth a process for the development of agency regulations. One key point is that, under the Administrative Procedure Act, amending or repealing a rule is itself "rulemaking," thus requiring the agencies to go through a public notice and comment process before doing so.[9]

Accordingly, in July 2017, the EPA and the Corps announced a two-step rulemaking process.[10] Step 1 would be formally rescinding the Clean Water Rule and putting back in place the pre-2015 regime, which was the 1986/1988 rules and post-*Rapanos* guidance. Step 2 would be the replacement rule, a definition of *waters of the United States* that was faithful to Justice Scalia's vision. While step 1 was proceeding, the EPA would conduct stakeholder meetings (mostly with the regulated community and states) to develop the replacement rule.

Step 1 opened with the *Federal Register* publication of the proposal to rescind the Clean Water Rule and codify the pre-2015 regime.[11] The agencies received more than 600,000 comments. The public input broke out how one would expect: Farmers and others in the regulated community were in favor of the repeal; environmentalists and advocates for clean water were not. Initially, there was no rush to finalize the proposal and formally rescind the Clean Water Rule, as the Obama-era rule was subject to the Sixth Circuit's national stay. But a Supreme Court decision brought a new sense of urgency.

SCOTUS on WOTUS: Themeless Pudding

In *National Association of Manufacturers v. Department of Defense*,[12] the usual WOTUS lineup was scrambled a bit. On one side, the federal government and two major environmental groups, the Natural Resources Defense Council and the National Wildlife Federation, argued that challenges to a WOTUS rule must be brought in a court of appeals. On the other side, the National Association of Manufacturers, farming and ranching organizations, electric utility associations, and thirty states—plus an array of environmental groups such as the Center for Biological Diversity and a slew of waterkeeper organizations represented by Earthjustice—advocated that challenges to a WOTUS rule must begin in a US district court. The division among the environmental community may have stemmed simply from differing interpretations of a complex statute, or they may have had differing strategic objectives in mind: If jurisdiction vested in the court of appeals, there would be fewer opportunities for the regulated community to forum shop and seek out judges likely to be favorably inclined toward less federal regulation, but if jurisdiction vested in the district courts, then the Clean Water Rule would spring back to life (and environmental groups also would have the opportunity to forum shop when challenging Trump administration WOTUS rules).

Ordinarily, a lawsuit seeking judicial review of an agency action would be filed in a district court (pursuant to the Administrative Procedure Act). But Congress made clear, in the text of the Clean Water Act, that lawsuits challenging EPA actions in seven categories must be brought in a court of appeals.[13] What was unclear, however, was Congress's rationale. During oral argument, Justice Kagan asked the attorney for the National Association of Manufacturers what Congress's theory was for the seven categories. The attorney replied that "to be honest, I do not—I cannot explain that and I have never heard anyone explain that to me."[14] He suggested that these (judicial) jurisdictional provisions that Congress adopted were "just not very carefully thought out."[15] Justice Kagan pressed on:

> So your basic view is, look, you should just resign yourself to thinking of this as having no particular rationale.
>
> Congress said what it said.
>
> Nobody can figure out what the reasons are that Congress included those things and not other things.
>
> It's all a themeless pudding and that's just what it is?[16]

The attorney agreed and stated that "if someone can come up with an explanation of this that makes sense, I'm very happy to hear it."[17]

Chief Justice Roberts worried about the plight of the unsuspecting Midwestern farmer who was charged with violating the Clean Water Act. If the court of appeals had jurisdiction, any action challenging the WOTUS rule would need to be made within 120 days of its promulgation. Chief Justice Roberts posed the following hypothetical scenario to the federal government:

> He's a farmer in Kansas.
> And all of a sudden, you come in and you're telling him that he can't, you know, discharge whatever into the lake.
> And—and he says, well, I don't think that's the right definition.
> And you say, well, you should have come to Washington four years ago.[18]

Although the attorney for the federal government tried to suggest that the farmer may have some due process remedies, the exchange highlighted two larger points. First, the Court was concerned about the rights of farmers and the impact of the Clean Water Act on their ability to make decisions about how best to use their property. Second, the Court did not understand that the Clean Water Act does not prevent farmers from farming. Consider the hypothetical Chief Justice Roberts proffered: What exactly would be the agricultural purpose of discharging "whatever" into a lake? Also, if a lake is involved, even Justice Scalia's dictionary recognized that type of waterbody as a "water," and thus notice concerns seem to be unwarranted. Nevertheless, the regulated community had won the narrative—the Clean Water Act and WOTUS were dangers to the agricultural community.

The regulated community also won the case. In a unanimous opinion authored by Justice Sotomayor, the Court held that all challenges to a WOTUS rule must be brought in a US district court.[19] The Court's decision was grounded in the plain language of the statute. Contrary to what the federal government argued, the Clean Water Rule did not fall under the category of "effluent limitations," a term defined as "any restriction . . . on quantities, rates, and concentrations" of certain pollutants "which are discharged from point sources into navigable waters."[20] Noting that the Clean Water Rule did not, by itself, impose any such restriction, the Court pointed out that the agencies, when issuing the rule, stated that the regulatory definition "imposes no enforceable duty" on the "private sector."[21] The federal government also argued that the Court of Appeals was the proper forum because the Clean Water Rule was akin to a section 402 permit decision. But the Court rejected this too, as permits authorize the discharge of pollutants and the WOTUS definition did no such thing. "Rather than confront [the] statutory text," the Court observed, the feds were asking the Court "to ignore it altogether" and focus on policy issues.[22] These arguments fared poorly as well.

The Court did acknowledge that vesting jurisdiction in the courts of appeals had some benefits. It could lead to a quicker and more orderly resolution of the matter, rather than having the issue hashed out in district courts around the country. Direct review in the courts of appeals also promoted a better shot at national uniformity. But the Court was unpersuaded that these policy concerns should override clear statutory text. The Court stated that "efficiency was not Congress's only consideration," and, for whatever reason, Congress chose not to embrace a path that would be more likely to lead to national uniformity.[23] You will eat your themeless pudding and like it.

In its opinion, the Court was careful not to suggest any judgment about the merits of the challenges to the Clean Water Rule. Indeed, the Court noted that it would refer to the rule neutrally as the "WOTUS rule"[24] instead of the more value-laden moniker the Obama administration had pinned on it. The Court was merely deciding whether a challenge to any WOTUS rule should start in a US district court or a court of appeals. And the text that Congress had adopted controlled.

So the National Association of Manufacturers and its allies won. But, in another sense, they and the broader regulated community also lost. Because the Sixth Circuit did not have jurisdiction to consider the challenge to the Clean Water Rule, its national stay was improper. The patchwork result was that the Clean Water Rule would be back in effect—except in the thirteen states covered by the injunction issued by the US District Court for the District of North Dakota.

The Trump administration was particularly displeased, because it did not want to see the Clean Water Rule resuscitated. Anticipating the Supreme Court's decision, EPA Administrator Scott Pruitt and his colleagues attempted to come up with an administrative workaround. Rather than formally rescind the Clean Water Rule (because the agencies were still reviewing the hundreds of thousands of comments received for that proposal), the agencies would simply suspend the Clean Water Rule by amending its applicability date. Predictably, this led to further chaos.

Wait, What's an Applicability Date?

The Office of the Federal Register is an agency nestled within the National Archives and Records Administration. The National Archives and Records Administration is rarely in the news, unless a former POTUS is reluctant about parting with national security documents after leaving office.[25] In contrast, the Office of the Federal Register is constantly in the news, or at least it is publishing notices about presidential pronouncements or agency actions that are newsworthy. It publishes (or posts) the *Federal Register*, the official journal of the US government. As we know, an agency must publish its proposed and final rules in the *Federal Register*.

To assist agencies with the technicalities of submitting rules to be published, the Office of the Federal Register has produced a helpful guide, the *Document Drafting Handbook*. The *Handbook* makes a distinction between an effective date (the date when the rule is placed in the Code of Federal Regulations) and an applicability or compliance date (the date when the rule applies to a regulated entity or the date by which compliance is required).[26] Although there is a technical difference, an applicability date can operate as an effective date.

When the Trump administration took over, it wanted to reverse the Obama administration's rules as quickly as possible. A public notice and comment rulemaking on the substance of rules can be lengthy because the agency must consider and respond to substantive comments. Instead, the Trump administration tried a shortcut for a number of rules; rather than formally rescinding, revising, or replacing them, agencies would merely add an applicability date, which would have the effect of suspending the rule for a specified period of time. The advantage of such an approach was speed: Obama-era rules could be suspended immediately. The downside of that hasty approach was that it was vulnerable to legal challenge. Indeed, attempts by the Trump administration to postpone rules ranging from motor vehicle emissions to mineral revenue collection from federal and tribal lands had been struck down for failure to provide an appropriate opportunity for public notice and comment.[27]

Despite these judicial setbacks, about a month after Supreme Court oral arguments in *National Association of Manufacturers* were held, the EPA and the Corps tried again, proposing a rule to add an applicability date to the Clean Water Rule, which would suspend it for two years.[28] The comment period was a mere twenty-one days, which included the Thanksgiving holiday. About 4,600 commenters weighed in. The regulated community welcomed the national uniformity and the certainty that would be provided. Environmental groups complained that the environmental impacts were being ignored and that the suspension was tantamount to a stealth repeal.

The Supreme Court issued its decision in *National Association of Manufacturers* on January 22, 2018. As a technical matter, the case needed to be remanded back to the Sixth Circuit for it to issue an order lifting the national stay of the Clean Water Rule, which it did on February 28, 2018. In the interim, the agencies finalized the proposed rule to add an applicability date. The notice of the final rule was published in the *Federal Register* on February 6, 2018, and was made effective immediately.[29]

The agencies explained that suspending the Clean Water Rule would bring clarity, consistency, and certainty to the administration of the Clean Water Act. This was not exactly true. In fact, it was the Clean Water Rule, with its categorical and distance-based rules, that provided clarity to the scope of waters protected by the Clean Water Act, although this clarity was not welcomed by the regulated community. With respect to consistency, the Supreme Court had just explained in *National Association of Manufacturers* that uniformity was not a high priority of Congress. And, as for certainty, the only thing about which there was no doubt was that the suspension rule would be challenged in court—but at least now we knew the proper forum would be US district courts across the land.

What's Good for the Goose

States supporting the Clean Water Rule and environmental groups wasted no time in filing lawsuits to seek to invalidate the suspension rule. New York, California, and eight other states, plus the District of Columbia, went to the US District Court for the Southern District of New York,[30] where, not coincidentally, all the judges had been appointed by Democratic presidents. The Natural Resources Defense Council and the National Wildlife Federation brought a parallel lawsuit there.[31] The regulated community intervened in both New York cases and with the Trump administration made motions to transfer them to a US district court in Texas, where, not coincidentally, all the judges had been appointed by Republican presidents.

Judge Oetken, the judge in the Southern District of New York, neatly summarized the confusing state of play:

> The 2015 definition of WOTUS has never been implemented and remains enjoined in thirteen states. The Sixth Circuit's nationwide stay has been dissolved. The plaintiffs in Texas seek a nationwide injunction against the 2015 definition. The Suspension Rule is also in effect, meaning that the 2015

> definition would not be in effect at least until 2020 even if there were no injunction against it. The 1980s definition still reigns.[32]

The regulated community and the Trump administration argued that it would be more efficient for the court in Texas, which was already familiar with the Clean Water Rule, to handle the challenge to the suspension rule. Judge Oetken disagreed, pointing out that

> the efficiency gains of transfer are offset by the loss of inter-court dialogue that would result from having one court, and one circuit, decide a matter of national importance. It is a bedrock principle of our federal court system that the adjudication of novel and difficult issues of law is best served by letting questions percolate among the lower federal courts, even at the cost of short-term disuniformity.[33]

In denying the motions to transfer, Judge Oetken also noted that there was an identical case proceeding in the US District Court for the District of South Carolina and that court had already declined to transfer the matter to Texas. Thus, even if Judge Oetken transferred the case to a federal court in Texas, there would be an ongoing parallel case in a different district court.

The case in South Carolina had been brought by the South Carolina Coastal Conservation League and other environmental groups.[34] It was assigned to Judge David Norton, a George H.W. Bush appointee. But political pedigree does not necessarily predict outcomes.

Judge Norton found that, when promulgating the suspension rule, the agencies had denied the public a meaningful opportunity to comment.[35] The agencies had refused to consider any comments related to the substance of the Clean Water Rule, contending that the addition of an applicability date did not implicate the merits of that rule. The agencies boldly stated that they were under no obligation to consider comments about the scientific record supporting the Clean Water Rule, the inadequacies of the pre-2015 regime, or "why a desire for certainty outweighs the [Clean Water Act's] objectives."[36] Judge Norton held that this refusal "to engage in a substantive reevaluation of the definition of the waters of the United States" provided the public an "illusory opportunity to comment."[37]

Judge Norton recognized that with a new presidential administration, an agency may change its views. When doing so, however, the agency must provide an explanation. Here, he concluded that by refusing to consider the merits of the Clean Water Rule and the pre-2015 regime, the agencies had failed to offer the required reasoned analysis.[38] To allow such "administrative evasiveness" would permit the federal government "to become a matter of the whim and caprice of the bureaucracy."[39] He therefore ruled that the suspension rule was invalid.

The only question remaining for Judge Norton was the scope of the injunction: Should the invalidation of the rule be limited to South Carolina or apply nationwide? He noted that the environmental plaintiffs had members throughout the United States and that the suspension rule affected "a vast array of wetlands across the United States."[40] He also pointed out the irony (or hypocrisy) of the Trump administration arguing *against* a nationwide injunction, recalling that

> under the Obama administration, such injunctions stymied many of the President's policies, with five nationwide injunctions issued by Texas district courts in just over a year[.] At that time, then-Senator and now-Attorney General Sessions characterized the upholding of one such nationwide preliminary injunction as "a victory for the American people and for the rule of law." Press Release, Sen. Jeff Sessions III, June 23, 2016. Now, many who advocated for broad injunctions in those Obama-era cases are opposing them.[41]

Although Judge Norton acknowledged that nationwide injunctions should be used only rarely, he stated that this was one such appropriate circumstance: "Just because the political shoe is on the other foot does not mean that nationwide injunctions are no longer appropriate. What is good for the goose is good for the gander."[42]

They Just Can't Kill the Beast

Under the Trump administration, the EPA and the Corps had initially embarked on a two-step approach to deal with the Clean Water: rescind and replace. The suspension rule was a sidestep, which complicated the administrative dance, leading to tangled feet and a stumble. The immediate result of Judge Norton's decision was that the Clean Water Rule was back—or at least it was in force in some parts of the country. While the litigation over the suspension rule was ongoing, district courts in addition to the

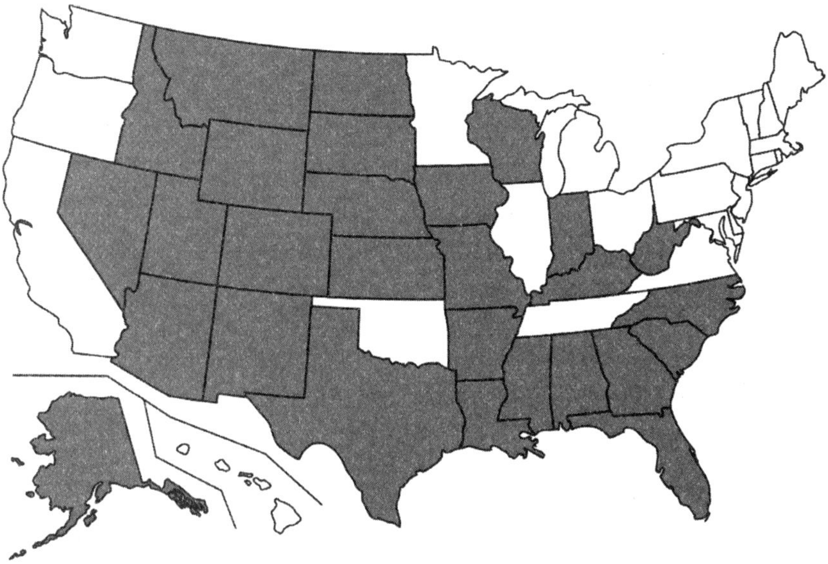

Figure 8-2. Status of WOTUS as of September 2018, with white indicating where the Clean Water Rule was in effect and gray indicating where the pre-2015 regime was in effect.

District of North Dakota had enjoined the Clean Water Rule, doubling the number of states affected to twenty-four. The WOTUS rule map now looked like Figure 8-2.

The chief environmental counsel for the National Cattlemen's Beef Association decried the Clean Water Rule's revival and, in a brief Halloween video, explained that the association was working in the courts, Congress, and the EPA "to put Zombie WOTUS back in the grave."[43] He then slayed a zombie lurking behind him with the knob of a baseball bat. (The Missouri Farm Bureau's video had much higher production value.)

The National Cattlemen's Beef Association and other members of the regulated community urged the EPA and the Corps to quickly finalize the proposed rule rescinding the Clean Water Rule. At this point, I suspect that some readers have lost the administrative plot, as multiple rulemakings were proceeding in parallel. Figure 8-3, which maps out the various rulemaking strands, may be helpful in depicting the multiverse of WOTUS rulemaking.

It took another year for the agencies to finalize the repeal rule. The replacement rule soon followed, and then it was the environmental community's turn to feel like it was in a horror movie. The call was coming from inside the (EPA's) house.

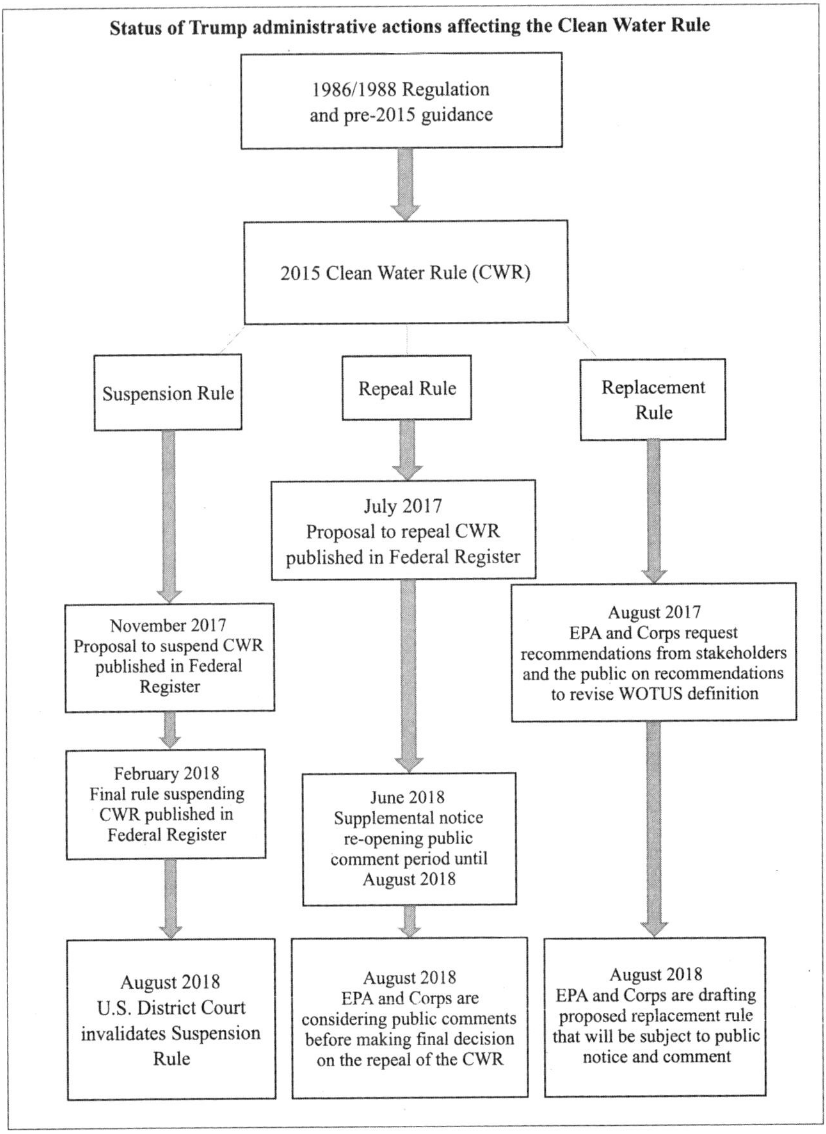

Figure 8-3. WOTUS rulemaking multiverse. Source: Royal C. Gardner and Erin Okuno, "The Shifting Boundaries of Clean Water Act Jurisdiction," Wetland Science and Practice 35 (2018): 317.

CHAPTER 9

Back to the Future

WOTUS is dead.

—POLITICO, Weekly Agriculture, September 13, 2019

POLITICO describes itself as a "news operation and information service" that is "the global authority on the intersection of politics, policy, and power."[1] As part of its service, it publishes a weekly feature devoted to agricultural politics and policy. In mid-September 2019, POLITICO led with the news that the Trump administration had formally rescinded the detested Obama administration's Clean Water Rule, declaring that WOTUS was no more.[2] Like news of Mark Twain's death, however, reports of WOTUS's demise were exaggerated, or at least premature. Although the Clean Water Rule had been killed, WOTUS itself survived. Only Congress could amend the Clean Water Act to eliminate the statutory term *waters of the United States*. The immediate effect of the Clean Water Rule's repeal was to reinstitute the pre-2015 regime. But the next step—the replacement rule, which the Trump administration called the Navigable Waters Protection Rule—would in fact threaten to hollow out WOTUS and undermine the Clean Water Act itself.

Reversing Course

Once EPA Administrator Andrew Wheeler (who had replaced the ethically casual Scott Pruitt) signed off on repealing the Clean Water Rule on September 12, 2019, the final rule went to the Office of the Federal Register to be published in the *Federal Register*. The queue was a bit long, and the notice did not appear until October 22.[3] The new rule was given an effective date of December 23, as a welcome Christmas present to the regulated community.

The *Federal Register* notice explained the EPA and the Corps' rationale for ditching the Clean Water Rule. Upon further review (and a change in political leadership), the agencies concluded that they had been mistaken in 2015.[4] Now they believed that the Clean Water Rule went too far in its interpretation of Justice Kennedy's "significant nexus" standard in *Rapanos*. The definition of "tributaries" and "adjacent" wetlands and the distance-based limitations were deemed to be beyond the agencies' statutory authority. Concern was also expressed about how the Clean Water Rule "improperly altered the balance of authorities between the Federal and State governments," contrary to Clean Water Act section 101(b).[5]

When repealing the Clean Water Rule, the agencies returned to the familiar 1986/1988 regulations, supplemented by guidance, particularly the 2008 guidance issued after *Rapanos*.[6]

The agencies noted that they were already applying this approach in the states where the Clean Water Rule had been enjoined. Moreover, the agencies emphasized the benefits of certainty and uniformity: Let's just go back to the old way of doing things, they said, while we work on a more substantive change.

Environmental groups reflexively sued.[7] They were uniformly unsuccessful, however. It's important to note that there is nothing inherently wrong with an agency changing its position. Indeed, that is a consequence of elections. A president gets to appoint the leaders of executive branch agencies, and a new administration may interpret a statutory provision differently than its predecessor. When doing so, the agency does need to follow the proper process, which typically entails a meaningful opportunity for public notice and comment. The agency must provide a reasoned explanation for its decision that takes into account all relevant factors. And the interpretation must ultimately be reasonable, considering the plain language, structure, and objectives of the statute. When repealing the Clean Water Rule, the EPA and the Corps provided interested parties several months to comment and explained why they wanted to revert back to the pre-2015 regime. It was difficult for environmental groups to argue that returning to the status quo ante, applying a rule that had been in place for more than three decades, was an unreasonable interpretation of the Clean Water Act.

With step 1 finally completed, the agencies could devote their full attention to step 2: crafting a rule in line with Justice Scalia's vision in *Rapanos*. Here, the environmental groups would have much stronger arguments.

Proposed Navigable Waters Protection Rule: A Valentine for the Regulated Community

On February 14, 2019, the Trump administration delivered the regulatory equivalent of candy and flowers to farmers, ranchers, developers, and other industries that believed themselves to be oppressed by the Clean Water Act. The EPA and the Corps published in the *Federal Register* a proposed

"Navigable Waters Protection Rule,"[8] known informally in some circles as the "N-Whopper." The preamble to the proposed rule emphasized the states' role in Clean Water Act implementation, and as the name suggested, it would focus federal efforts back on protecting traditional navigable waters.

The proposed definition of WOTUS led with the traditional navigable waters as the first category of covered waters: "waters which are currently used, or were used in the past, or may be susceptible to use in interstate or foreign commerce, including the territorial seas and waters which are subject to the ebb and flow of the tide."[9] Tributaries would be included, but only to the extent that they contributed perennial or intermittent surface flow to a traditional navigable water. Thus any ephemeral tributary would not be covered, and the notice also sought input on whether intermittent tributaries should be excluded as well.[10] Interstate waters—which had been covered by federal water quality laws since the 1948 Federal Water Pollution Control Act—were to be eliminated from the WOTUS definition.[11]

Significantly, the proposed rule also dropped the significant nexus test. Adjacent wetlands would be waters of the United States only when they abutted or had a direct, perennial, or intermittent hydrologic surface connection to other covered waters.[12] Here too the agencies sought public comment on whether only adjacent wetlands with a perennial hydrologic surface connection to a traditional navigable water should qualify.[13] In addition, the proposed rule made clear what had always been implicit: If a category of water was not listed as a WOTUS, then it was excluded.

At a press conference announcing the proposed rule, the EPA administrator claimed that "our proposal would ensure that America's water protections . . . will remain strong while giving states and tribes the certainty to manage their waterways in ways that best protect their natural resources and economies."[14] Exactly how the reduction of federal jurisdiction resulted in maintaining strong protections was unclear. Wheeler's assertion was particularly bold as the agencies professed ignorance about how many streams and wetlands would no longer be considered waters of the United States and thus fall outside the umbrella of the Clean Water Act's protections. They claimed they lacked the data to quantify the proposed rule's impact.

E&E News, an indispensable resource for anyone following WOTUS developments, pushed back with a story titled "EPA falsely claims 'no data' on waters in WOTUS rule."[15] Through a Freedom of Information Act request, E&E had obtained a PowerPoint presentation that agency staff had prepared that quantified the scope of reductions. Based on an analysis of the US Geological

Survey's National Hydrography Dataset and the US Fish and Wildlife Service's National Wetlands Inventory, EPA staff found that removing ephemeral streams from the WOTUS definition would result in excluding 18 percent of all streams.[16] If intermittent streams were not covered (an issue on which the agencies sought input), then the figure jumped to 70 percent; more than two thirds of the nation's streams would not be covered by the Clean Water Act.[17] Wetlands fared poorly as well, as EPA staff determined that more than 51 percent of the nation's wetlands would be unprotected by the feds.[18]

Not surprisingly, the regulated community commended the agencies for the proposed rule. But like a team with a big lead, they sought to keep the pressure on the agencies by asking for even further rollbacks. For example, the American Farm Bureau Federation and other agricultural organizations called for the agencies to even reconsider the scope of traditional navigable waters, recommending that waters used "in interstate commerce" was too broad and that federal jurisdiction should be limited to waters used to transport goods in interstate commerce, citing the 1870 case of *The Daniel Ball*.[19]

While farmers were generally pleased, the environmental community was appalled, dubbing the proposal the Dirty Water Rule.[20] They demanded that the agencies withdraw the proposal, arguing that it was contrary to the scientific record and the Clean Water Act's objective. As Earthjustice stated,

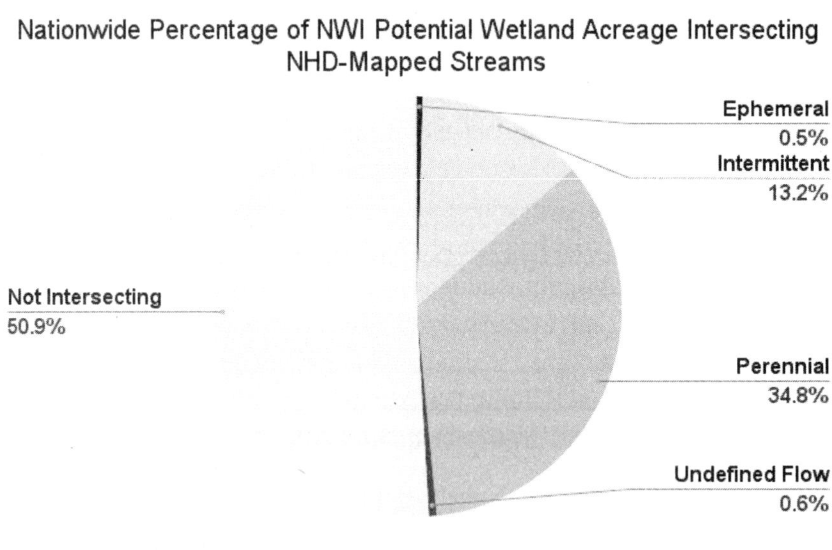

Figure 9-1. Estimated impact of the proposed Navigable Waters Protection Rule on wetlands. NHD, National Hydrography Dataset; NWI, National Wetlands Inventory. Source: US Environmental Protection Agency, via E&E News (2018).

"It is highly irresponsible and arbitrary and capricious to propose a policy reversal with sweeping impacts for the health of our waters without even bothering to assess the impacts of the change."[21] The proposed rule was seen as an abdication of the agencies' Clean Water Act responsibilities.[22] However, the political leaders of the EPA and the Corps viewed the proposed rule as resetting the proper boundaries between the federal government and the states.

"Primary" Responsibility

When the Obama administration issued the Clean Water Rule, it invoked Clean Water Act section 101(a), which announced Congress's translucently clear objective: to restore and maintain the chemical, physical, and biological integrity of the nation's waters. When the Trump administration proposed the Navigable Waters Protection Rule, it sought refuge in Clean Water Act section 101(b), which recognized that states had "the primary responsibilities and rights . . . to prevent, reduce, and eliminate pollution." In that subsection, Congress also declared that the states had the primary responsibility and right "to plan the development and use (including restoration, preservation, and enhancement) of land and water resources." Rather than explain how the proposed rule would contribute to achieving the goals of the Clean Water Act, the agencies instead pointed to the word *primary*. However, their argument overlooks the primary definition of *primary*.

When seeking to divine the meaning of a statutory term, textualists often consult dictionaries for the plain meaning of words. The two dictionaries that the US Supreme Court has relied on in interpreting the words enacted by Congress in 1972 are *Webster's Third New International Dictionary* (1961) (*Webster's Third*) and *Webster's New International Dictionary* (2nd ed., 1954) (*Webster's Second*), the latter of which was favored by Justice Scalia. Regardless of which dictionary one consults, the first entries for the definition of *primary* are consistent. In *Webster's Third*, the first entry defines *primary* as "initial": "first in order of time or development."[23] In *Webster's Second*, the first entry also defines *primary* as "initial": "first in order of time or development or intention."[24] This primary meaning of *primary* is logical in light of the overall framework of the Clean Water Act.

Congress structured the Clean Water Act to serve as a model of cooperative federalism. The federal government, chiefly through the EPA, sets certain minimum standards, including what waters are to be accorded federal protection. States have the "primary" responsibility—that is, the initial responsibility—to protect these aquatic resources. However, when the states fail to adequately protect these waters (or decline to assume the responsibilities), the federal government must step in. Thus, when properly understood, the states' "primary" responsibilities to prevent, reduce, and eliminate water pollution do not displace or limit the federal government's Clean Water Act authorities.

Yet in the Trump administration's proposed rule to revise the definition of "waters of the United States," the agencies seem to have assumed that a secondary definition of *primary* applies. The second entry in *Webster's Third* defines *primary* as "chief" or "principal": "first in rank or importance."[25] Similarly, the second entry in *Webster's Second* defines *primary* as "chief; principal": "first in dignity or importance."[26] The agencies did not explain why they decided to leapfrog over the primary (initial) definition of *primary* when considering the states' responsibilities to prevent, reduce, and eliminate water pollution. Relying on this secondary definition made little sense in light of the fact that Congress enacted the Clean Water Act precisely because the states had largely failed in these responsibilities.

Happy Earth Day (2020 Edition)!

Celebrations for the fiftieth anniversary of Earth Day in 2020 were muted. Events moved online as the world was in the early stages of the COVID-19 global pandemic, which underscored the links between zoonotic diseases and disruption of biodiversity.[27] Clean water advocates in the United States had an additional reason to be glum. The long anticipated and feared Trump administration's Navigable Waters Protection Rule was finally published in the *Federal Register* on April 21, on the eve of Earth Day.[28]

The new regulation delivered on Trump's campaign pledge to the regulated community. The revised WOTUS definition certainly provided certainty: It listed only four types of jurisdictional waters:

> (1) The territorial seas, and waters which are currently used, or were used in the past, or may be susceptible to use in interstate or foreign commerce, including waters which are subject to the ebb and flow of the tide;
> (2) Tributaries;
> (3) Lakes and ponds, and impoundments of jurisdictional waters; and
> (4) Adjacent wetlands.[29]

The significant nexus test was jettisoned. There would no longer be a need to conduct a case-by-case analysis to determine a water's contribution to the quality of traditional navigable waters. Similarly, all ephemeral waters, including ephemeral tributaries, were out. Interstate waters were also tossed overboard. And adjacent wetlands were defined very narrowly. To be protected under the Clean Water Act, a wetland needed to abut or touch a jurisdictional water or be inundated by surface floodwaters from a jurisdictional water. A groundwater connection between a wetland and a traditional navigable water would establish jurisdiction only in limited circumstances. Although wetlands that were physically separated from a jurisdictional water only by a natural feature such as a bank or dune were covered, wetlands separated by an artificial feature, such as a road, were protected only if there was a direct hydrologic surface connection between the wetlands and the other water, such as through a culvert or flood gate. Justice Scalia (who died on a hunting trip in 2016) would have been, if not proud, at least satisfied that the federal–state boundaries had been recalibrated.

The regulated community and its political allies were jubilant. When releasing the Navigable Waters Protection Rule, EPA headquarters posted a news release, quoting more than fifty politicians, from cabinet officers to US senators and House members to state officials.[30] All were uniformly positive. Senator Joni Ernst of Iowa, for example, said that "for years, Iowans have told me what an egregious overreach Obama's WOTUS rule was, giving the federal government authority to regulate *97 percent* of the land in Iowa. That's absurd, and it's why I've worked hard to get rid of it."[31] The 97 percent figure was absurd, but not for the reason suggested by Senator Ernst. It was simply not true. Iowa's remaining wetlands cover only 1.2 percent of the state's area.[32] Perhaps she was referring to Iowa's historic wetland base, more than 90 percent of which had been drained.[33] But those prior converted croplands (which could make up no more than 11 percent of the state) were expressly exempted from regulation under the Clean Water Rule.

The EPA's news release also contained praise from more than a dozen representatives of organizations representing regulated entities, from homebuilders and mining companies to manufacturers and agriculture. The statement from Zippy Duvall, president of the American Farm Bureau Federation, was illustrative. He opened by asserting that farmers and ranchers supported the new regulation because they "care about clean water and preserving the land, which are essential to producing healthy food and fiber and ensuring future generations can do the same" and ended with the pithy slogan of "clean water, clear rules."[34] Yet nowhere in the press release or in the preamble to the Navigable Waters Protection Rule did the EPA and the Corps discuss or explain how reducing Clean Water Act coverage would result in improved water quality.

In the EPA's statement trumpeting the Navigable Waters Protection Rule, the agency described the quoted representatives of the regulated community as "stakeholders." It was a rather selective sampling of the universe of stakeholders. Stakeholders who were concerned about water quality had a dramatically different view of the Navigable Waters Protection Rule. Clean Water Action, which organizes grassroots groups to promote environmental issues and candidates, pointed out that the public, including hunters and anglers, supported clean water protections. It claimed that the new rule would eliminate protection for millions of stream miles and at least half of the nation's wetlands,[35] which was consistent with EPA's internal analysis.

Playing off President Trump's "Make America Great Again" campaign, former Obama EPA chief Gina McCarthy, now president of the Natural Resources Defense Council, retorted, "You don't make America great by polluting our drinking water supplies, making our beaches unfit for swimming, and increasing flood risk."[36] She and many others were appalled that the new rule ignored the findings of the EPA Science Advisory Board.

The Science Advisory Board expressed concern that the Navigable Waters Protection Rule lacked "a scientific justification, while potentially introducing new risks to human and environmental health."[37] As a preliminary (and fundamental) matter, the agencies failed to identify how many jurisdictional waters would no longer be protected by the Clean Water Act as a result of the Navigable Waters Protection Rule. The EPA and the Corps did acknowledge that some previously protected waters would no longer be protected under the Navigable Waters Protection Rule, but they repeatedly claimed that they were not able to assess the extent to which the Clean Water Act would no longer safeguard waters protected under the pre-2015 regime or that were previously protected by the 2015 Clean Water Rule. A sample of the professed inability to quantify impacts in a meaningful way included seven categories of waters:

- "The agencies lack sufficient data to quantify the difference" of [1] jurisdictional interstate waters under the [pre-2015 regime] and the final rule.[38]
- The agencies are "unable to quantify the change in jurisdiction for [2] tributaries."[39]

- The agencies are "unable to approximate what percentage of [3] currently jurisdictional non-relatively permanent waters are ephemeral that will no longer be jurisdictional under the revised definition of 'waters of the United States.'"[40]
- The agencies are "unable to quantify" how many [4] lakes and [5] ponds will no longer be protected.[41]
- The agencies "cannot quantify" the change in jurisdiction of [6] impoundments compared to the baseline.[42]
- The agencies are "unable to quantify" how many [7] wetlands will no longer be protected.[43]

Quantifying the reduction in Clean Water Act coverage was just too hard, the agencies seemed to shrug. But reliable scientific tools and data were available to estimate the extent to which certain waters would lose protection under the Navigable Waters Protection Rule.

A Model Scientific Model

Scientific models have long been used to explain and predict outcomes, and agencies and courts regularly rely on scientific models in Clean Water Act matters.[44] To determine the magnitude of the reduction of Clean Water Act jurisdiction, the EPA and the Corps could have used a widely publicized geographic information system (GIS)-based model developed in 2019 by GeoSpatial Services of Saint Mary's University of Minnesota, called the CWA Jurisdictional Scenario Model, which compared the extent of Clean Water Act protection for aquatic ecosystems under different regulatory scenarios.[45] The CWA Jurisdictional Scenario Model uses nationally available GIS datasets, including the National Hydrography Dataset, National Wetlands Inventory, and Soil Survey Geographic Database, and allows users to compare potential jurisdiction of aquatic ecosystems for various regulatory scenarios. At least sixteen comment letters, representing a range of organizations and states, referenced or attached the CWA Jurisdictional Scenario Model in response to the proposed Navigable Waters Protection Rule.[46]

After the Navigable Waters Protection Rule was finalized, Saint Mary's updated the CWA Jurisdictional Scenario Model and modeled three scenarios, which provided a comparison of the jurisdictional reach under the Navigable Waters Protection Rule, the Clean Water Rule, and the pre-2015 regime. Several watersheds were analyzed, and model results found that under the Navigable Waters Protection Rule, stream protection would be reduced between 45 and 95 percent, and wetland coverage would shrink between 12 and 72 percent.[47] The most significant negative impacts would occur in the more arid regions of the western United States, where there are high proportions of ephemeral streams, as illustrated in the model results from the Rio Pensasco watershed in New Mexico.

The agencies' excuse for not relying on such models was that they were not sufficiently precise. For example, they pointed out that the US Fish and Wildlife Service's National Wetlands Inventory, which the Saint Mary's model relied on, was not designed to provide delineations of individual wetlands. But the point of the model was not to make jurisdictional determinations of individual plots; rather, it was to offer a broad-scale evaluation of the environmental impact of the Navigable Waters Protection Rule, and it demonstrated the magnitude of the reduction of Clean Water Act protections under the Trump administration. Whether the agencies' reluctance to consider and disclose these impacts invalidated the Navigable Waters Protection Rule would be a subject of litigation. Could they ignore science? In the initial round of litigation, the answer appeared to be yes.

First Best Shot

With its publication in the *Federal Register*, the Navigable Waters Protection Rule was slated to become effective sixty days later, on June 22, 2020. Seventeen states and the District of Columbia, led by California and New York, rushed to court to seek a preliminary injunction to keep that from happening. They filed in the US District Court for the District of Northern California, where they were more likely to draw a judge amenable to their arguments than perhaps in North Dakota or Texas. Indeed, the case was assigned to Judge Richard Seeborg, an Obama appointee who had issued a nationwide injunction prohibiting the Trump administration from adding a citizenship question to the 2020 census.[48] Twenty-three states supporting the Navigable Waters Protection Rule intervened. Thus, with forty states involved, the case represented the best opportunity to secure a ruling that applied nationwide. On June 18, the day of oral argument, POLITICO's *Morning Energy Newsletter* lead story was "Trump Water Rule Faces Its First Test," noting that "a coalition of blue states . . . backed by water groups like the Society of Wetland Scientists and the Society for Freshwater Science" were facing off with the Trump administration, which had the support of twenty-three Republican state attorneys general, "along with a pair of Idaho landowners represented by the Pacific Legal Foundation, and business groups including the American Farm Bureau Federation, the National Association of Homebuilders and the Chamber of Commerce."[49]

The preliminary injunction hearing was held over Zoom. At this early point in the pandemic, everyone was still getting acquainted with the technology. Attorneys for the plaintiff states cut each other off ("I seldom have two people on the same side interrupting each other. Most of the time it's the other problem," the judge wryly observed[50]), and the attorney for the US Department of Justice defending the rule inadvertently displayed his notes for all to see when sharing his screen. But no one mistakenly used a kitten filter and appeared as a cat (as infamously occurred in a proceeding in Texas[51]), and Zoom allowed interested stakeholders from around the country to observe the oral arguments.

California, New York, and their allies had two main arguments, one procedural and one substantive. As a procedural matter, agencies must explain the rationale for their rules, and in doing so they cannot disregard evidence that has been presented to them (under the requirements of the *State Farm* case). And as a substantive matter, the agencies' interpretation of a statute must be reasonable (under the *Chevron* doctrine). The plaintiff states contended that the EPA and the Corps had ignored the science to produce an unreasonable rule in light of the Clean Water Act's overall objective. Judge Seeborg was unpersuaded by either argument.

Judge Seeborg asked the Department of Justice attorney whether the EPA and the Corps needed to consider the magnitude of the reduction in Clean Water Act jurisdiction:

> THE COURT: Does part of that process require the agencies to do some assessment of what—what waters would have been protected under the existing regime and what will be lost under 2020? Do they have—is that part of their process, or are they not required to do that? * * *
> THE COURT: Okay. So I take it your answer is they're not required to do it as part of their—
> MR. BRIGHTBILL: They're not required to do it, Your Honor.[52]

The agencies' position was contrary to a bedrock tenet of administrative law: When engaging in rulemaking, an agency must examine relevant data and provide a reasoned explanation for its decision. Yet, in an opinion issued the next day, Judge Seeborg characterized the dispute over the science as a mere policy disagreement. In his view,

> the real difference in opinion is whether the statute clearly compels the Agencies to extend federal regulation to the broadest permissible extent under the Commerce Clause, in the name of providing *all* of the benefits for water quality the science suggests might be achievable. Because the Agencies may reasonably conclude they have no such statutory duty, discounting evidence of possible benefits is not plainly arbitrary or capricious.[53]

This seemed to conflate the procedural and substantive arguments, however.

In any event, Judge Seeborg also rejected the argument that it was unreasonable for the Trump administration to adopt a rule based on Justice Scalia's plurality opinion in *Rapanos*.[54] The states challenging the rule reasoned that because a majority of justices had rejected the plurality opinion (Justice Kennedy and the four dissenters), such an approach could not be adopted by the agencies. But that position was problematic to Judge Seeborg for several reasons. Although Justice Kennedy and the dissenters stated that the agencies could assert jurisdiction more broadly than the plurality would allow, they did not say that the agencies were *required* to do so. Thus the agencies were not required to assert jurisdiction based on a significant nexus approach or distant hydrologic connections to a traditional navigable water. In this reading of *Rapanos*, four justices (led by Justice Scalia) proclaimed that WOTUS must be interpreted in only one way; in contrast, five justices (Justice Kennedy and the dissenters) would allow the agencies more flexibility in defining the scope of WOTUS.

That flexibility—or deference to the agencies—did not mean that Justice Kennedy's significant nexus approach must be adopted by the agencies. This would be an odd result, as the significant nexus test had the support of only one justice, and the plurality opinion garnered four votes.

The plaintiff states also offered a reliance argument. States such as Massachusetts and New Mexico did not have their own Clean Water Act section 402 permit programs and instead relied on EPA. Similarly, many states do not have their own section 404 programs, relying on the Corps to review and issue (or deny) permits to fill streams and wetlands. But Judge Seeborg correctly observed that nothing in the Clean Water Act or the Navigable Waters

Protection Rule precluded these states from creating their own regulatory programs.[55] Furthermore, states had been on notice for more than two years that federal jurisdiction might recede.

Because, at this stage, Judge Seeborg determined that the plaintiff states were unlikely to succeed on the merits (and that they had failed to demonstrate any imminent harm), he declined to issue a preliminary injunction.[56] The Navigable Waters Protection Rule went into effect on June 22, 2020. Except in Colorado.

Rocky Mountain High

Colorado was one of a few states that decided not to join the litigation in the Northern District of California. Instead, the Centennial State elected to bring its own case challenging the Navigable Waters Protection Rule in the US District Court for the District of Colorado under what might be charitably called an imaginative theory.[57] Under Colorado state law, the filling of any wetland was prohibited unless authorized by a Clean Water Act section 404 permit. In essence, Colorado relied on the feds to permit filling activities. Colorado argued that if the Navigable Waters Protection Rule narrowed the waterbodies under Clean Water Act jurisdiction, there would be no mechanism to authorize activities that resulted in filling now nonjurisdictional wetlands. Development projects would be unable to proceed because the state had no independent permitting scheme to authorize the filling of waters. Because of this "permitting gap," Colorado claimed that the forgone development projects would consequently cause Colorado to suffer economic harm.[58] Alternatively, Colorado complained that it would be forced to expend resources to set up its own regulatory program.[59]

District Court Judge William Martinez, an Obama appointee, rightly rejected this argument: Any injury to Colorado was self-inflicted and the result of Colorado's own state law.[60] Colorado could choose to amend the flat prohibition on filling without a federal permit, or it could establish its own program. However, Judge Martinez was more sympathetic to another line of argument, where Colorado stated that it would have to spend more resources to police activities in waters that were no longer subject to federal jurisdiction. In Judge Martinez's view, this constituted sufficient injury for Colorado to challenge the rule.[61] And, in contrast to Judge Seeborg in California, Judge Martinez decided that Colorado was likely to prevail on the merits. He concluded that it was unreasonable for the Trump administration to adopt a rule in line with the *Rapanos* plurality opinion, reasoning that five justices (Justice Kennedy and the four dissenters) interpreted WOTUS more broadly than the Navigable Waters Protection Rule.[62] He therefore issued a preliminary injunction that prevented the Navigable Waters Protection Rule from going into effect in Colorado.[63]

Judge Martinez's rulings on both injury and the likelihood of success were questionable at best. Indeed, the injunction was later reversed by the Tenth Circuit Court of Appeals, which determined that Colorado's professed injury was too speculative to justify standing.[64] For a brief shining moment, then, the Navigable Waters Protection Rule applied throughout the country. Let's now turn to the implications of defining WOTUS so narrowly.

CHAPTER 10

Downstream Effects

> The scientific literature unequivocally demonstrates that streams, individually or cumulatively, exert a strong influence on the integrity of downstream waters.
>
> —US Environmental Protection Agency Office of Research and Development, *Connectivity of Streams and Wetlands to Downstream Waters: A Review and Synthesis of the Scientific Evidence* (January 2015)

The EPA's Connectivity Report discussed in detail the many ways that non-navigable streams contribute to downstream waters, including traditionally navigable waters. Tributary streams are the principal source of water in most rivers. They also convey pollutants such as nutrients and chemical contaminants to these downstream waters. The report explained how wetlands contribute to the water quality of traditionally navigable waters by, among other things, filtering pollutants. Importantly, the report recognized that "incremental effects of individual streams and wetlands are cumulative across entire watersheds."[1] It logically follows (and the scientific literature showed) that allowing more pollutants in tributaries degrades the water quality of traditionally navigable waters. Similarly, if you remove pollutant-removing wetlands from the landscape, the water quality of traditionally navigable waters will suffer. It's science, but not exactly rocket science.

The Navigable Waters Protection Rule left many upstream waters unprotected. An immediate consequence of the rule was that the regulated community would no longer need a Clean Water Act permit to discharge pollutants into now nonjurisdictional waters, which of course would result in an increase in pollutants in traditionally navigable waters. But the adoption of a restrictive definition of waters of the United States also would have multiple, cascading downstream legal effects. The Trump administration sought to shift the responsibility to protect these waters to the states. However, many states pegged their regulatory program to federal parameters; as federal jurisdiction contracted, so would state jurisdiction. For states that relied on Clean Water Act section 401 water quality certifications to protect their waters, they would find their authorities constrained as a result of the new definition. Similarly, if an activity did not require a federal permit, then the provisions of the National Environmental Protection Act would be inapplicable. And whereas most businesses might cheer the regulatory retreat, environmental restoration professionals in the wetland and stream mitigation industry were poised to take a hit. If permits were not required, there would be no need for their services. The cumulative impact of the Navigable Waters Protection Rule would have a strong influence on the integrity of the regulatory regime beyond just Clean Water Act permits.

Permits? We Don't Need No Stinking (Federal) Permits

One of the most dramatic consequences of the Navigable Waters Protection Rule was the evaporation of federal jurisdiction over waters in the West. Most streams in the arid and semiarid West are ephemeral,[2] which were categorically excluded from jurisdiction. Indeed, in a nine-month period after the promulgation of the Navigable Waters Protection Rule, the Los Angeles District of the Corps of Engineers determined that more than 99 percent of the 1,284 streams it reviewed in Arizona were not protected by the Clean Water Act.[3] Similarly, the Albuquerque District concluded that not one of the 258 streams it reviewed in New Mexico was jurisdictional.[4] Projects that were once subject to the Clean Water Act were reevaluated. For example, in March 2021 the Corps announced that the controversial Rosemont open-pit copper mine proposed in the Santa Rita Mountains of southern Arizona no longer needed a Clean Water Act section 404 permit.[5]

The jurisdictional retreat played out in a similar fashion elsewhere in the country. Twin Peaks Minerals had applied for a section 404 permit to conduct mining operations near the Okefenokee National Wildlife Refuge in southern Georgia, globally recognized as a Wetland of International Importance under the Ramsar Convention.[6] Environmental groups and scientists expressed concern that the mining would endanger water levels and water quality within the refuge.[7] After the Navigable Waters Protection Rule was issued, however, the Corps' Savannah District disclaimed jurisdiction over 550 acres of wetlands, because they lacked a continuous surface connection to a traditionally navigable water and thus no longer qualified as adjacent waters.[8] A Clean Water Act permit was not required under the Trump rule.

Mining companies were not alone in rejoicing at the regulatory relief. As David Groves chronicled in the *Environmental Law Reporter*, homebuilders in Daytona Beach and Orlando, Florida, found that their projects could now proceed largely unimpeded by federal oversight.[9] Developers in the Houston area seeking to construct communities in floodplains were no longer constrained by the Clean Water Act,[10] the historic flooding of 2017 apparently a distant memory.[11] (And despite the fact that Harris County, where Houston is located, has the distinction of receiving "more flood insurance funds ... than in any other National Flood Insurance Program-participating community."[12]) A chemical company building an industrial facility along the Texas–Louisiana border anticipated that it would need to mitigate the destruction of 4.5 miles of streams; a fresh jurisdictional determination under the new regime found that 88 percent of the streams did not qualify as waters of the United States.[13] It was uncertain whether the company's cost savings would be passed along to the consumers.

Under the Corps' rules, its jurisdictional determinations are valid for five years.[14] The regulated community raced to lock in their winnings, and the Corps saw a big increase in requests for jurisdictional determinations and endeavored to act expeditiously.[15] In cases where the feds were out of the picture, it was up to the states to protect—or not protect—those streams and wetlands.

Will the States Quickly Step In to Be Primarily Responsible? (Spoiler Alert: Unlikely)

Expecting the states to take action brings to mind Samuel Johnson's bon mot about a second marriage being the triumph of hope over experience. The experience in this case, of course, is the history leading up to the Clean Water Act's enactment: Despite prodding and financial incentives, the states had failed to protect the quality of the waters within their borders, necessitating federal action. And the experience since 1972 only confirmed that the states remained largely not up to the task. The Clean Water Act assigns the states the responsibility to deal with nonpoint source pollution,[16] such as runoff from agricultural fields, and the states have failed miserably in this regard. Consider Florida, for example, which has suffered regular episodes of harmful algal blooms, fueled by nonpoint source pollution.[17] Agricultural runoff flows into Lake Okeechobee, making the state's largest lake a breeding ground for blue-green algae, also known as cyanobacteria (Figure 10-1).

The algal blooms are not confined to Lake Okeechobee, however. When water levels reach a certain height, the Corps of Engineers is obliged to send the polluted water east through the St. Lucie River and west via the

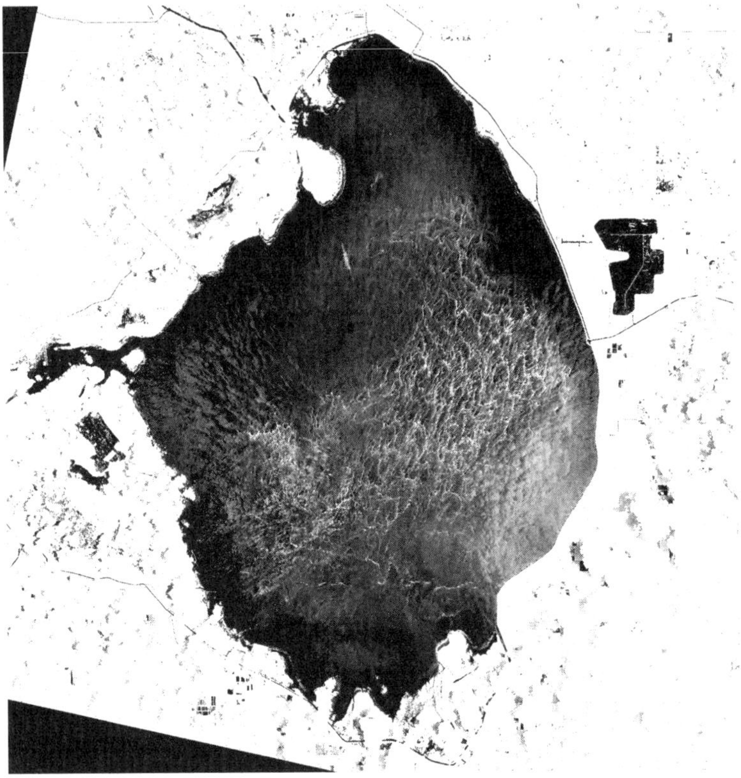

Figure 10-1. July 2, 2016, US Geological Survey Landsat 8 image of an algal bloom on Lake Okeechobee. Source: USGS via Todd Thurlow (eyeonlakeo.com).

Caloosahatchee, resulting in a trail of foul-smelling green slime that is harmful to humans and wildlife—and the state's tourist-based economy.[18] The state has established a task force to deal with harmful algal blooms, but its recommendations have been almost entirely ignored[19] as the governor and state legislature focus more on culture war issues. Although some attention has been paid to septic tanks' contribution to harmful algal outbreaks,[20] the biggest source of phosphorus and nitrogen has received a pass. The regulation of agriculture is the third rail of Florida politics. Everyone knows what the primary source of nonpoint source pollution is, but no elected official wants to address it. Instead, farmers are asked politely to adopt best management practices to reduce runoff.[21] These voluntary measures have led to predictable results and continued harmful algal bloom outbreaks. And Florida is not alone in its failure to deal with nonpoint source pollution. As Figure 10-2 illustrates, the US Geological Survey reported that chronic harmful algal blooms and their "cyanotoxins have been implicated in human and animal illness and death in at least 43 States."[22] The EPA even publishes a monthly newsletter that highlights harmful algal blooms throughout the country.[23]

Experience also demonstrated that one would be unduly optimistic to expect that most states would fill the gaps once the Navigable Waters Protection Rule came into effect. State action, or inaction, after the Supreme Court's decision in *Solid Waste Agency of Northern Cook County* (*SWANCC*) is instructive. Recall that, in that case, the Court ruled that the Clean Water Act did not cover certain geographically isolated waters (specifically that it was unreasonable for the Corps to assert jurisdiction over waters based on the presence of migratory birds). At the time, more than half the states did not regulate isolated waters, and these states did not exactly rush to adopt new rules to now protect these "state-only" waters.[24] To be sure, some did, including Indiana, North Carolina, Ohio, Washington, and Wisconsin.[25] North Carolina, for example, acted quickly, as its Environmental Management Commission quickly issued regulations in 2001 to require state permits for discharges to isolated waters.[26] Ordinarily, however, even if there is political

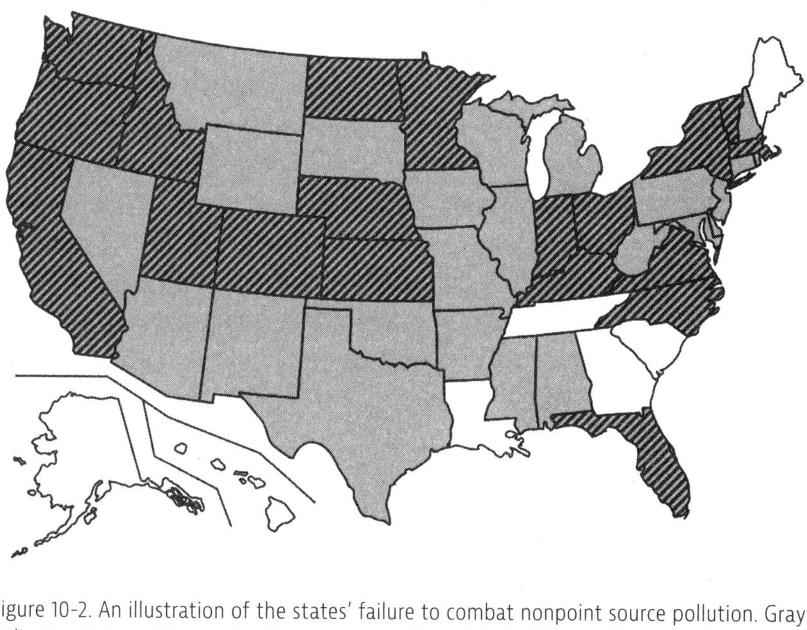

Figure 10-2. An illustration of the states' failure to combat nonpoint source pollution. Gray indicates states with reports of cyanobacterial harmful algal bloom (CyanoHAB) poisonings; gray and black stripes indicate states with reports of CyanoHABs, beach closures, and health advisories in 2016; and white indicates no reports of CyanoHAB poisonings. Source: US Environmental Protection Agency.

will, revising a regulatory regime takes more time. Indeed, it took California a decade to fully respond to the *SWANCC* decision.[27]

But more often, political will swung in the other direction. Some states tether their state regulatory programs to the federal Clean Water Act program; that is, state agencies are prohibited by state statute from regulating more strictly than the feds. Accordingly, as federal jurisdiction over waters receded as a result of the Navigable Waters Protection Rule, so would any state jurisdiction. The Environmental Law Institute conducted a study and found that in 2013, more than half the states (twenty-eight) had "stringency" prohibitions that limited a state agency from regulating more rigorously than the EPA or the Corps.[28] For instance, South Dakota's provision was straightforward, dictating that no state rule with respect to water pollution "may be more stringent than any corresponding federal law, rule, or regulation governing an essentially similar subject or issue."[29] In these states, the federal floor of protection for aquatic resources was essentially also the state ceiling. Accordingly, when the Trump rule came into force, the stringency prohibitions were an obstacle to these states protecting the waters no longer jurisdictional under the Clean Water Act.

When issuing the Navigable Waters Protection Rule, the EPA and the Corps also produced a Resource and Programmatic Assessment, in which they discussed possible state reactions to the retraction of federal jurisdiction.[30] While recognizing that "some states may adjust their current practices in light of the revised definition of 'waters of the United States,'" the agencies conceded that they "are not able to predict with any precision what changes might result in state law as a result of the final rule" and declined to speculate.[31] The lack of imagination bordered on willful ignorance. Anyone familiar with the history of the Clean Water Act knew what would probably happen: States with already weak water quality programs would not fill the gaps. In fact, the new rule prompted Ohio, which had decided to regulate isolated wetlands post-*SWANCC*, to enact legislation to specifically exempt ephemeral streams from water quality permitting requirements.[32] About half the states did not have permitting programs that encompassed non-WOTUS waters before the Navigable Waters Protection Rule, and the situation remained the same after its promulgation.[33] Instead, these states chose to rely on their authority under Clean Water Act section 401, which was also affected by the Navigable Waters Protection Rule. And the Trump administration was also working very hard on a separate EPA rulemaking that sought to limit the ability of states to use their section 401 powers.

Clean Water Act Section 401: States' Rights or "State-Level Abuse"?

The Clean Water Act has long been hailed as a model of cooperative federalism. The states can assume responsibility for issuing (or denying) federal Clean Water Act section 402 and section 404 permits. Furthermore, section 401 grants states an effective veto over activities that require a federal license or permit that may result in any discharge to a water of the United States. Before a federal agency can grant such permission, the state must be given an opportunity to review the proposed activity. Under section 401, the federal license or permit can be granted only if the affected state issues (or waives) a water quality certification that confirms that the proposed activity will not violate state water quality standards.[34] Section 401 also allows states to impose conditions when issuing a water quality certification. WOTUS is the jurisdictional hook, however: If the discharge is to a non-WOTUS water, then there is no need for a state water quality certification. Thus, to the extent that the Navigable Waters Protection Rule contracted the definition of waters of the United States, it also reduced the scope of states' section 401 programs.

The requirement for state review and approval of federal licenses and permits actually predates the 1972 act. The Water Quality Improvement Act of 1970 introduced the concept of state water quality certifications,[35] and the EPA issued regulations that governed the section 401 process in 1971.[36] Congress then incorporated state water quality certifications when overhauling the Federal Water Pollution Control Act in 1972. The US Supreme Court affirmed broad state authority under section 401 in two cases. In 1994, in *PUD No. 1 of Jefferson County v. Washington Department of Ecology*, the Court considered Washington's water quality certification in connection with a Federal Energy Regulatory Commission license for hydroelectric facilities.[37] The utility had objected to a state-imposed condition that it maintain a minimum stream flow below the dam to reduce impacts on fish. The utility argued that such a condition was unrelated to the discharge (the construction of the hydroelectric facility itself) and was trying to regulate the operation of the dam. In a 7–2 decision, the Supreme Court ruled that a minimum stream flow requirement is a permissible condition in a state water quality certification, concluding that section 401 "is most reasonably read as authorizing additional conditions and limitations on the activity as a whole."[38] The Court thought that its views were consistent with EPA's interpretation and cited *Chevron*. However, the Court did not make it clear whether it was invoking *Chevron* step 1 (in which congressional intent is clear and must be followed) or *Chevron* step 2 (in which the Court would defer to a reasonable agency interpretation).

Justice Stevens offered a one-paragraph concurrence, in an attempt to clarify:

> For judges who find it unnecessary to go behind the statutory text to discern the intent of Congress, this is (or should be) an easy case. Not a single sentence, phrase, or word in the Clean Water Act purports to place any constraint on a State's power to regulate the quality of its own waters more stringently than federal law might require. In fact, the Act explicitly recognizes States' ability to impose stricter standards.[39]

The concurrence suggested that *Chevron* step 1 was in play and that Congress clearly intended that states could regulate water quality impacts based on the activity as a whole rather than just the impacts from the discharge itself.

More than a decade later, in *S.D. Warren Co. v. Maine Board of Environmental Protection*, the Court confirmed Congress's intent to grant states wide latitude in protecting waters under their jurisdiction.[40] In this case, the Court observed that "Section 401 recast pre-existing law and was meant to 'continu[e] the authority of the State . . . to act to deny a permit and thereby prevent a Federal license or permit from issuing to a discharge source with such State,'" quoting a 1971 Senate report.[41] Thus the executive branch (through EPA regulations) and the judiciary (through two Supreme Court decisions) recognized Congress's intent to allow states to weigh in on—and even scuttle—proposed activities requiring a federal permit or license.

One might think that the Trump administration would have been copacetic with state primacy in this regard, but one would be mistaken. The Trump administration was in favor of states' rights, except when it was not. And it most certainly was not when states exercised their authority under Clean Water Act section 401 to impede energy infrastructure projects. In 2016, New York denied a water quality certification related to a Federal Energy Regulatory Commission license for the Constitution natural gas pipeline project that was envisioned to bisect New York for about 120 miles.[42] In New York, the pipeline would have negatively affected eighty-five trout streams as well as 85 acres of wetlands, but the underlying reason for the denial appeared to be more related to climate change concerns rather than immediate water quality impacts. Similarly, in 2017 Washington denied a water quality certification for the construction of the Millennium Bulk Terminals Project, which would have facilitated the export of coal from the Powder River Basin in Wyoming and Montana to Asia for coal-fired power plants.[43] Among other things, Washington objected to expected water quality impacts from filling 32 acres of wetlands, but climate change concerns were a factor too. And in 2019, Oregon denied a water quality certification for the Jordan Cove Energy Project's proposed liquified natural gas export facility, which required Clean Water Act section 404 and Rivers and Harbors Act section 10 permits.[44] The state expressed concern that it did not have reasonable assurances that the construction and operation of the facility would comply with state water quality standards. The section 401 water quality certification process was again being used as a tool on the climate change front, as the Jordan Cove project was slated to become Oregon's top emitter of greenhouse gases. Such actions were consistent with the holdings of *PUD No. 1 of Jefferson County* and *S.D. Warren Co.* However, President Trump labeled these actions "state level abuse."[45]

In April 2019, President Trump issued an executive order titled Promoting Energy Infrastructure and Economic Growth. To "promote efficient permitting processes and reduce regulatory uncertainties that currently make energy infrastructure projects expensive and that discourage new investment," President Trump directed the EPA to review and update its section 401 regulations.[46] The resulting regulations (issued after a public notice and comment process) limited state water certification conditions and limitations to the discharge and not the activity as a whole—which effectively excised climate change considerations from the process.[47] In response to commenters who queried how such a restriction on state authority was consistent with the Supreme Court's holding in *PUD No. 1 of Jefferson County*, the EPA argued that the Court had not acted under *Chevron* step 1, and thus the agency had the discretion to reinterpret the statutory provisions, so long as the result was reasonable.[48] Combined with shrinking WOTUS jurisdiction from the Navigable Waters Protection Rule, the new section 401 regulation further constrained state section 401 programs, limiting the states' scope of review, ability to request additional information, and time to make a decision.[49]

NEPA and the Federal Handle Problem

The Navigable Waters Protection Rule also had ripple effects on other federal environmental laws. The National Environmental Policy Act (NEPA), enacted during the Nixon administration, ensures that federal decisionmakers consider environmental impacts when taking actions.[50] Thus, when an agency is reviewing a permit application, it generally must prepare an assessment of the environmental impacts of (and alternatives to) the proposed activity.[51] The public is also given an opportunity to weigh in on the proposed activity. Most often, an agency will satisfy its NEPA obligations by preparing an environmental assessment (EA). Major projects require a more comprehensive study called an environmental impact statement (EIS). The decision by the Corps to grant or deny a Clean Water Act section 404 is a federal action that implicates NEPA, and thus the Corps must prepare the proper environmental documentation to inform its decision. If it does not—say, for example, that the Corps prepares an abbreviated EA when it should have completed a broader EIS—environmental groups or others may sue to prevent the action from going forward until the proper environmental study is conducted.[52] However, if a wetland or stream is no longer a water of the United States, then a federal permit is not needed to fill it. And if there is no other federal connection to the proposed activity, then NEPA would not apply. In many cases, then, if there is no WOTUS, there is no NEPA.

Of course, that is a result that the regulated community would welcome. In the regulated community's view, NEPA was not being used as a tool to inform federal agencies but instead was being wielded as a weapon to delay projects. And the data bore this out: In 1981, most EISs were completed within one year; three decades later, the average time was 4.5 years, with the median at 3.5 years.[53] Ironically, NEPA not only is invoked to halt projects deemed to be environmentally harmful (such as the Dakota Access Pipeline), but it has been used by industry groups to fight environmentally beneficial actions. For example, sugar companies in Florida have long relied on NEPA to try to delay Everglades restoration efforts to protect their access to water.[54] As Sun Tzu long ago observed in *The Art of War*, "victory may be produced . . . out of the enemy's own tactics."[55]

The Trump administration also sought victory over what it viewed as unnecessary paperwork hampering infrastructure projects by revising NEPA regulations. The White House Council on Environmental Quality (CEQ), which was established with the enactment of NEPA, is responsible for issuing general rules and guidance for NEPA compliance. (Most agencies, including the EPA and the Corps, also have their own specific NEPA rules.[56]) The CEQ's NEPA regulations had not been updated since 1978. In July 2020, after a public notice and comment period, CEQ issued new regulations that reduced the scope of analysis for environmental documentation.[57] In particular, a project's indirect or cumulative impacts no longer needed to be considered. The practical result was to essentially eliminate a requirement (under NEPA) to study the extent to which a proposed project might contribute to climate change. The regulated community was thrilled. The American Petroleum Institute declared that "NEPA modernization will help America streamline permitting to move job-creating infrastructure projects off the drawing board and into development."[58] The Competitiveness Enterprise Institute echoed a recurring Trump theme and suggested further reform: The new regulation "will not drain NEPA's regulatory swamp completely (only Congress can do that), but it should significantly lower the water level."[59] Even the agricultural community was happy, claiming that the previous NEPA rules interfered with farmers and ranchers' responsible management of land—even though a search of the *Federal Register* database since 1994 yields no example of where a farmer or rancher needed to prepare an EIS.[60] Still, although the impact on ongoing agricultural operations might be minimal, the Navigable Waters Protection Rule and the revised NEPA regulations promised a streamlined permitting process, if a federal permit was even required.

ESA: Be Careful What You Wish For

Although the regulated community, as a general matter, prefers to be exempt from regulation, one law it cannot escape from is the law of unintended consequences. No doubt the Navigable Waters Protection Rule, by eliminating Clean Water Act jurisdiction over a host of waters, removed one impediment to many development projects. But the rule also inadvertently made it harder for one particular type of project to proceed. Approvals for any proposed project that may affect an endangered species would probably now take longer under certain circumstances.

Like NEPA, the Endangered Species Act (ESA) is a procedural statute. Unlike NEPA, however, the ESA can operate as a roadblock. The ESA requires informed decision making, but it also imposes harsh penalties for those who "take" any protected species.[61] "Take" in this context is defined broadly to include any harm to a species, including destruction of its habitat.[62] A farmer or developer who "takes" a protected species without federal permission is risking civil and even criminal liability. For example, in 1994, a farmer in Kern County, California, was charged with killing five Tipton kangaroo rats when he cleared desert scrublands to raise bamboo and Chinese vegetables.[63] Despite its name, the kangaroo rat is not related to rats; it's more of a gopher.

Nevertheless, the farmer faced possible three years imprisonment. After the case became a cause célèbre for the regulated community, the Department of Justice dismissed the case.[64]

Federal permission to "take" a protected species comes in two forms. If there is a federal action in play (e.g., a Clean Water Act section 404 permit), then ESA section 7 consultation applies.[65] The federal agency (e.g., the Corps) must consult with the ESA experts—the US Fish and Wildlife Service (FWS) for terrestrial species and the National Oceanic and Atmospheric Administration (NOAA Fisheries) for marine species—to determine whether the proposed action is likely to jeopardize the continued existence of the species. The section 7 consultation process takes place within certain statutory timeframes, and it results in the FWS or NOAA Fisheries issuing its opinion on the impact of the proposed action on the protected species. If the FWS or NOAA Fisheries issues a "jeopardy opinion" concluding that the proposed action is likely to jeopardize the continued existence of the species, then the project will not go forward. In most cases, however, the consultation process concludes with the FWS or NOAA Fisheries finding that although some individuals of a species might be taken (killed), the overall effect of the proposed project will not wipe the species out. Here, the FWS or NOAA Fisheries would issue an Incidental Take Statement that authorizes the taking of the species, within limits. If the limit is exceeded, then section 7 consultation must begin again.

A different process occurs if the proposed action is entirely private, with no federal nexus. The ESA prohibition on taking a species remains in force (along with the potential penalties), and thus a developer still needs permission to take a species. Instead of section 7 consultation process, however, the developer must negotiate directly with the FWS or NOAA Fisheries to obtain a section 10 Incidental Take Permit, which may require the development of a Habitat Conservation Plan.[66] A section 10 Incidental Take Permit is the equivalent of a section 7 Incidental Take Statement: It grants permission to take (kill) a certain number of individuals. But unlike the section 7 consultation process with its timelines, the section 10 process is open-ended. There is no deadline.

Given a choice, developers prefer timeframes and the certainty that comes with them. Accordingly, developers prefer proceeding under section 7 rather than section 10, as was borne out when the *SWANCC* decision reduced Clean Water Act jurisdiction. As discussed in Chapter 6, the Supreme Court in *SWANCC* ruled that waters of the United States did not cover isolated waters.

After *SWANCC*, some developers who sought to fill isolated wetlands and whose projects may affect protected species asked the Corps to assert jurisdiction over these now nonjurisdictional waters.[67] The developers wanted to apply for a Clean Water Act section 404 because then ESA section 7 and its timelines would apply. If no Clean Water Act permit was needed, then there would be no deadlines. The Corps declined to do so, and the developers had to proceed down the longer section 10 path.

This anecdote is not to suggest that homebuilders were unhappy with the Navigable Waters Protection Rule—far from it. But at least in some individual cases, where federally protected species were on the project site, life could be more difficult.[68]

The Restoration Economy Takes a Hit

Reduced Clean Water Act protections were not good for every business. Some industries, such as craft brewers, had tried to make the case that they depend on clean water and advocated for a broader conception of waters of the United States.[69] Another group of entrepreneurs was more directly affected: mitigation bankers.[70]

The EPA and the Corps have long had a goal of no net loss of wetlands and other aquatic resources under the Clean Water Act.[71] When the Corps issues an individual section 404 permit to allow the filling of wetlands and streams, it often includes a condition that the permittee offset the environmental impacts of its project, preferably through restoration. So if a homebuilder is authorized to fill in 25 acres of wetlands for a housing development, it may be required to restore a functionally equivalent amount elsewhere in the watershed. In theory, this permittee-responsible mitigation would compensate for the lost functions of the filled wetlands. In practice, permittee-responsible mitigation frequently failed: Sometimes the permittee never started the restoration project; sometimes it started but did not complete the restoration; if the restoration project was completed, it may not have turned out as expected, resulting in a pond rather than a marsh; and even if the project turned out to be a fully functioning wetland, questions about long-term sustainability of the site remained.[72]

Confronted with the poor record of permittee-responsible mitigation, the agencies tried a different approach: encouraging entrepreneurial mitigation banking.[73] Private restoration companies would restore wetlands and streams, thus generating wetland and stream credits. The restoration companies, known as mitigation bankers, would then sell the credits to developers, which used them to satisfy their compensatory mitigation conditions. (The "banking" refers to the creation of credits, which may be "banked" for future use; it has nothing to do with financial institutions.) When the restoration companies (mitigation bankers) sold ecological credits, they were really selling a release of liability, because when the permittee purchased a credit (with the Corps' permission), responsibility for the success and stewardship of the restoration site transferred to the mitigation banker.

Mitigation banking offered a number of advantages over traditional, permittee-responsible mitigation projects.[74] Mitigation bank projects were more likely to be ecologically successful. In contrast to permittee-responsible mitigation, which is based on a promise to conduct restoration projects in conjunction with or after the filling activity, mitigation bank credits are largely performance based. Credits are released based on achieving performance standards, such as successful removal of invasives and survival of planted wetland vegetation. Rather than small, unconnected mitigation sites commonly associated with permittee-responsible mitigation, mitigation bank projects are larger. Mitigation banking also consolidates expertise and financial resources. It is in the restoration companies' interest to do a good job with the restoration projects—it's their business and they have a continuing relationship with the regulatory agencies. And once completed, a mitigation bank site should have a long-term steward in place that is responsible for ensuring the long-term maintenance of the area. Accordingly, the EPA and Corps encouraged the use of mitigation banking to offset impacts related to section 404 permit impacts—first through 1995 guidance[75] and then, after being prompted by Congress, in regulations finalized in 2008.[76] Congress also endorsed the concept of mitigation banking as early as 1998 in a transportation bill that established a preference that mitigation banks provide offsets for wetland and stream impacts from federally funded transportation projects.[77]

The "restoration economy," activities related to environmental restoration and mitigation, became a multi-billion-dollar sector. One analysis found that the ecological restoration sector employed more than 125,000 workers and generated a yearly economic output of $9.5 billion, about $4 billion of which was tied directly to mitigation projects.[78] But the mitigation market had an unusual feature in our nominally free market society: The government controlled both the demand and supply sides of the equation, by deciding how much mitigation was needed when issuing permits and by overseeing and approving the generation of mitigation credits. The mitigation banking industry depends on government regulation for its existence.

As one mitigation banker observed, the Navigable Waters Protection Rule was "big trouble" for the mitigation banking industry.[79] If the Clean Water Act no longer covered wetlands with only a subsurface connection to traditional navigable waters, then a section 404 permit would not be needed to fill those wetlands. And if a permit was not needed, then there would be no requirement to offset those impacts and thus no reason to purchase mitigation bank credits. Many banks, as one expert aptly noted, would be "dead in the water."[80]

The impact of reduced federal jurisdiction on individual mitigation bank projects ultimately depends on whether the mitigation bank is located in a state with its own wetland protection laws. If so, and if the state requires offsets to wetland impacts, then the mitigation banker may be unaffected and conceivably benefit if the removal of federal requirements results in quicker project approvals—that is, the state may be speedier in issuing fill permits than the Corps was. But if the mitigation bank was relying solely on the existence of federal regulations, then its credits would be worthless.

The Navigable Waters Protection Rule and the rulemaking on section 401 state water quality certifications were not the Trump administration's only effort to limit the protections of the Clean Water Act. As we'll see in the next chapter, the administration also sought to exempt from the Clean Water Act discharges of pollutants to groundwater that contaminated surface waters. All of these agency actions were subject to litigation challenges, of course. And whether or not these regulatory changes endured depended on the result of those court cases—as well as the 2020 election.

CHAPTER 11

Following the Science, to a Point

> The brief of the scientists really convinced me they're geniuses and they can trace all kinds of things.
>
> —Justice Stephen Breyer, commenting on an *amicus* brief filed on behalf of aquatic scientists and scientific societies during oral arguments in *County of Maui v. Hawaii Wildlife Fund* (2019) (cleaned up)

Although Justice Breyer appreciated the acumen of hydrogeologists, the Trump administration did not. Its position in *County of Maui v. Hawaii Wildlife Fund* ignored basic scientific principles. The case involved whether wastewater injected into groundwater that migrated to the Pacific Ocean (which everyone agreed was a water of the United States, at least in US territorial seas) was covered by the Clean Water Act. The Trump administration's position drew a bright line between surface waters and groundwaters. Under this approach, pollutants discharged into surface waters might require a Clean Water Act permit, if the water was a water of the United States, whereas pollutants discharged into groundwater categorically did not. From a scientific perspective it was a line that was none too bright, ignoring the obvious connections between ground and surface waters. When the Supreme Court issued its decision in *County of Maui*, Justice Breyer was able to carry five of his colleagues and wrote the majority opinion.[1] Surprisingly to many, the Court had adopted a scientifically sound approach to the issue. The decision was handed down in the early days of the COVID pandemic and appeared to be "following the science," consistent with the emerging catchphrase of the moment.[2]

In November 2020, Joe Biden, who campaigned on the promise to follow the science (in the COVID and other contexts), was elected president, much to the relief of the scientific community. (Even the journal *Nature*, in an unprecedented move, had endorsed Biden in light of Trump's hostility toward science.[3]) For a brief time, it seemed that science was in ascendancy in WOTUS world. Two US district courts invalidated the Navigable Waters Protection

Rule, based in part of the Trump administration's refusal to consider the scientific record during the rulemaking process. President Biden tasked his political appointees at the EPA and the Corps to craft a new "waters of the United States" rule that properly took science into account.

However, the Biden rule soon met the same judicial fate as Obama's Clean Water Rule and Trump's Navigable Waters Protection Rule. Ultimately, in the view of the courts, the input of scientists was relevant but not dispositive. Science, it appeared, did not provide all the answers to the political and legal question of what constitutes a water of the United States.

Poop in the Pacific

The County of Maui had a problem. It needed to dispose of bodily waste produced by the humans living in and visiting Maui. Before the Clean Water Act, the sewage was piped directly into the Pacific Ocean, with only solids removed.[4] After the Clean Water Act's enactment, the county constructed the Lahaina Wastewater Reclamation Facility, a wastewater treatment plant, which removed the solids and also treated it for pathogens.[5] Approximately 3–5 million gallons of nutrient-laden wastewater were then disposed of through well injection each day.[6] This effluent did not remain underground, however; it migrated through groundwater and emerged near the coast in the Pacific Ocean.[7] Although the county was no longer directly discharging sewage into the ocean, it was doing so indirectly, albeit at a lesser scale. Nevertheless, the indirect discharges of the treated sewage through groundwater increased nutrient pollution, contributed to algal blooms, and reduced coral coverage.[8]

The EPA and the state took no action other than studying the matter.[9] Concerned conservation groups availed themselves of the Clean Water Act's citizen suit provisions and sued the county in US District Court, claiming that it needed a Clean Water Act section 402 permit to discharge the effluent to the Pacific Ocean. The trial court agreed, concluding that the Clean Water Act regulated indirect discharges to waters of the United States where groundwater acted as a conduit.[10] The trial court also suggested that, contrary to every administration's interpretation of the term, waters of the United States could include some underground aquifers, and thus a discharge of pollutants to groundwater could trigger the need for a section 402 permit.[11] On appeal, the Ninth Circuit Court of Appeals declined to address the "groundwaters as waters of the United States" rationale but nevertheless affirmed, holding that the county had violated the Clean Water Act on the indirect discharge theory.[12] The Court of Appeals invoked Justice Scalia's plurality opinion in *Rapanos*, where he observed that Congress prohibited the discharge of pollutants *to* the waters of the United States, not *directly* to the waters of the United States. The Court of Appeals quoted Justice Scalia for the proposition that lower courts had long held that the point source discharge of "any pollutant that naturally washes downstream likely violates [the Clean Water Act], even if the pollutants discharged from a point source do not emit 'directly into' covered waters, but pass 'through conveyances' in between."[13] In the Ninth Circuit's view, because the coastal effluent was "fairly traceable" to the Lahaina Wastewater Reclamation Facility, the county was engaged in "the functional equivalent" of a direct discharge to the Pacific Ocean.[14]

The county sought review by the US Supreme Court, which granted the writ of certiorari. Note that up until then, the federal government had not been involved in the litigation, beyond EPA and the US Army Engineer Research and Development Center conducting a tracer dye study that linked the injection wells to the degraded coral reefs. The parties were the conservation groups and the county. But because any ruling by the Supreme Court would have broader ramifications for Clean Water Act implementation, the Court requested the Department of Justice's views on the matter.

For many years, the EPA's position was that the Clean Water Act permit requirements may apply to pollutants discharged from point sources that reach a water of the United States via a groundwater connection. For example, in a 2001 proposed rulemaking concerning concentrated animal feeding operations, the EPA stated,

> The determination of whether a particular discharge to surface waters via ground water which has a direct hydrological connection which is prohibited without an NPDES permit is a factual inquiry, like all point source determinations. The time and distance by which a point source discharge is connected to surface waters via hydrologically connected surface waters will be affected by many site specific factors, such as geology, flow, and slope.[15]

After the Ninth Circuit's decision in *County of Maui*, however, the Trump administration decided to seek public comment on whether EPA should revise its interpretation of the Clean Water Act.[16] After considering more than 50,000 comments, the EPA issued an interpretive statement that declared that the best reading of the Clean Water Act excluded "all releases of pollutants from a point source to groundwater, . . . regardless of a hydrologic connection between the groundwater and jurisdictional surface water."[17] In the Trump administration's view, groundwater was an issue left primarily to the states.[18]

Wait a Minute: Maybe We Can Settle This Thing

At some point, it dawned on the Maui County Council, who were Democrats, that they were aligned with the Trump administration in a case that threatened to create a huge loophole in the Clean Water Act. (There was also a change in the council's composition that made it more amenable to a voluntary resolution.) Efforts to settle had occurred over the course of the litigation, and after the Supreme Court agreed to hear the case, the County Council reconsidered the possibility of voluntarily ending the case. With the Supreme Court oral arguments set for early November 2019 and deadlines for briefing looming, the council held meetings in May to discuss the settlement. An initial vote, which was live streamed, deadlocked at 4–4.[19] Briefs were filed. But in September, the council voted to authorize the settlement.[20] The agreement required the county to seek and comply with a Clean Water Act section 402 permit for the injection wells, provide at least $2.5 million in funding for reusing treated wastewater, pay a $100,000 penalty to the US Treasury, and cover the other side's litigation costs at the trial and appellate (but not the Supreme Court) level.

The council chair called on the county's corporation counsel to sign the settlement and resolve the case. The corporation counsel balked, however, because it believed that the county mayor also had to consent to the agreement, and Mayor Michael Victorino declined to do so. The father of former major league baseball player Shane (The Flyin' Hawaiian) Victorino, the mayor likened the situation to being down one run in the last inning and ordering the batter to drop his bat.[21] He also expressed concern that under the Ninth Circuit's reasoning, individual property owners with septic tanks and cesspools might be required to obtain Clean Water Act permits. A Supreme Court decision would provide "clarity" for all.

Clarity was lacking with respect to whether the case would proceed, however. On October 3, 2019, with just a little over a month until oral arguments, the attorney for Earthjustice, which represented the conservation groups, notified the Supreme Court about the council's direction to the corporation to settle and the question of the mayor's authority.[22] The next day, the attorney representing the county before the Supreme Court confirmed that the mayor did not agree to any settlement.[23] On October 9, the County Council chair wrote to the Supreme Court, requesting that the case be dismissed or oral arguments be postponed while the settlement issue was being resolved.[24] That same day the county's corporation counsel, Moana Lutey, apologized to the court for the chair's request. Lutey noted that she was the county's chief legal advisor and had the authority to represent the county in all legal proceedings.[25] Lutey (re)confirmed that the county was not requesting a dismissal or delay. The case would proceed.

Oral Arguments: Spiked Punch Bowls and Septic Tanks

There are several ways for members of the public to attend a Supreme Court oral argument, and different rules apply to each. Some seats are reserved for attorneys who are members of the Supreme Court bar.[26] It's first come, first served for these lawyers. In the old days, partners from the big law firms would send their underlings to wait in line and hold their spots. However, the Court, which can make rules governing the conduct of attorneys within its jurisdiction, cracked down on such a practice, prohibiting "line standers." There is a separate line for the general public. Here the Court declines to assert any authority it might have, and thus free market rules apply. Semiprofessional "line standers" assemble, sometimes days in advance of particularly high-profile cases, to secure an entry ticket, which they then sell.[27] Once inside, an attendee can stay for the entirety of the proceedings. Another line for the general public, which was not immediately reinstituted when the Court reopened after the COVID pandemic, allowed many people to observe the arguments, but from the back and for only three minutes. Then another group would shuffle in. Access was easier in this line, but time was a limiting principle for the entrants.

In *County of Maui v. Hawaii Wildlife Fund*, the Court was confronted with a different problem involving limiting principles and lines: Where to draw one? In its brief and at oral argument, the county offered a nice bright line through a means-of-delivery test: For a Clean Water Act permit to be required, the pollutant must be delivered to the water of the United States from a point source, such as a pipe.[28] If the pollutant was delivered to the water of the United States through any other means, including through groundwater, then a Clean Water Act permit was not required. The county contended that groundwater pollutants were covered by the Clean Water Act's "nonpoint source program." Indeed, in the second sentence of his oral argument, Elbert Lin, the county's attorney, asserted that discharges from the Lahaina Wastewater Reclamation Facility were "already regulated" by this "nonpoint source program."[29] That statement was a bit misleading, however: The only Clean Water Act "program" dealing with nonpoint source pollution is found in section 319, which deals with education and grants. The Clean Water Act encourages states to regulate nonpoint source pollution, but it does not (and as a constitutional matter could not) command that the states do so. Although, contrary to counsel's suggestion, a Clean Water Act nonpoint source regulatory program does not exist, the Court seemed to accept this characterization.

What troubled the Court more, however, was that the "means-of-delivery" test appeared to provide a roadmap for polluters to evade the Clean Water Act. Justices Breyer and Kagan asked about a scenario where a polluter, rather than discharging its waste directly into a river through a pipe, ran the pipe into the ground 5 feet from the shore, so that groundwater brought the waste to the river.[30] "Not covered by the Clean Water Act" was the answer. The county's attorney focused on the preposition "from," arguing that the requirement for a permit for "any addition from a point source to a navigable water" covers only direct discharges. Justice Sotomayor pointed out that this interpretation would render the word "to" to mean "into."[31]

When the Department of Justice's turn at the podium came, counsel offered a simple, homespun analogy.[32] Suppose, he said, while at home he poured whiskey from a bottle (a discrete conveyance and thus a point source) into a flask and then brought the flask to a party at another location, where he poured the whiskey from the flask (also another point source) into a punch bowl. In his view, in such a scenario, the whiskey was not added to the punch from the bottle. The original point source was not covered by the Clean Water Act. Once the justices began asking questions, the party was over. Chief Justice Roberts queried whether "any little bit of groundwater is enough to break the chain." Yes, he replied. Even "two inches?," the Chief Justice asked with some incredulity.[33] Again, counsel affirmed that, in the executive branch's view, any distance that the pollutant traveled through groundwater was sufficient to remove it from the Clean Water Act's ambit.

The attorney for the conservation groups, David Henkin, faced the opposite problem. Instead of being concerned about how close to shore a pipe might be cut to avoid liability, now the Court was concerned about how far upstream liability flowed. Was there any limiting principle? Justice Alito posited the specter of "an ordinary family out in the country that has a septic tank," the leachate of which eventually reaches waters of the United States in ten years: Would the homeowners be subject to Clean Water Act liability?[34] The answer should be yes; if your fecal matter is polluting the waters of the United States, you need to remedy the situation, subject to some limitation. The Court was not warmly embracing Henkin's proffered logical stopping points, however. Chief Justice Roberts batted away the concept of proximate cause (remoteness) as a limiting principle, deeming it too abstract,[35] despite the fact that it is used on a regular basis in nearly every negligence action in the country. Henkin also relied on the Ninth Circuit's traceability standard: If the pollutant is fairly traceable to the point source, then the Clean Water Act applies. But here Justice Breyer raised the *amicus* brief of the aquatic scientists and posed another hypothetical:

> The miner gets up and every morning he throws his shaving water outside the house at Pikes Peak, okay? Now there's a very good chance that that will end up in a river, and the brief of the scientists really convinced me they're geniuses and they can trace all kinds of things. So the problem that I [see] with the traceability test is [that] it puts all kinds of people in the position of having to get a permit.[36]

Indeed, the aquatic scientists' brief explained how pollutants can be tracked through physical measurements, chemical tracers, and groundwater modeling.[37] But this may have proven too much, and Justice Breyer worried about the "500 million people . . . suddenly discovering" that they needed a Clean Water Act permit.[38] (Note that the US population was a mere 329 million at the time.) Dissatisfied with proximate cause and traceability, he offered the "functional equivalent of a direct discharge" as the standard. "But what does 'functional equivalent' mean?," Chief Justice Roberts plaintively and pointedly asked, evoking laughter in the courtroom.[39]

"Hydrologists Should Be Happy"

The day before Earth Day in 2020, the Navigable Waters Protection Rule was published in the *Federal Register*, spreading gloom in the environmental world. The day after Earth Day in 2020, the US Supreme Court issued its decision in *County of Maui v. Hawaii Wildlife Fund*, providing a ray of sunshine.[40] The Court reversed the Ninth Circuit and remanded for further proceedings, so technically the county prevailed. But the opinion was not a victory for the county; instead, clean water advocates hailed the decision.

Justice Breyer wrote the majority opinion for the Court on behalf of five of his colleagues, including the more conservative Chief Justice Roberts and Justice Kavanaugh. As foreshadowed by the oral arguments, the Court rejected the tests proposed by the conservation groups (the Ninth Circuit's traceability standard, limited by proximate causation), the county (the means-of-delivery test), and the Trump administration's EPA (supporting Maui at least with respect to groundwater).[41] The Court concluded that the traceability approach went too far and encroached on the states' authority over nonpoint source and groundwater pollution.[42] The county and the EPA's tests were flawed because the bright line would have opened up "a large and obvious loophole" that Congress could not have intended.[43] Their tests were also inconsistent with the fact that Congress specifically included "well" in the definition of point source, and wells could discharge only to groundwater. Why would Congress have included wells as point sources if it did not mean to regulate discharges from wells that reached surface waters? This "absolutist" approach promised ease of administration but was contrary to the Clean Water Act's text, structure, and purpose.

Dissatisfied with these offerings, the Court crafted its own test, which again the oral arguments presaged: the "functional equivalent of a direct discharge" standard.[44] The Court grounded its approach in the overall purpose of the Clean Water Act and in science. Under its rule, a Clean Water Act permit is required for "a discharge (from a point source) of pollutants that reach[es] navigable waters after traveling through groundwater if that discharge is the functional equivalent of a direct discharge from the point source into navigable waters."[45] The Court articulated a number of factors that could be relevant in determining whether the discharge of a pollutant qualified as a functional equivalent of a direct discharge, with transit time and distance traveled being the most important. Another factor focused on the nature of the material through which the pollutant travels, which depends on the geology and topology of an area. Additional factors included the nature of the pollutant itself: Did it maintain its properties as it was in transit? To what extent was the pollutant chemically changed by the time it emerged to surface waters? And what was the relative amount of the pollutant that eventually reached the surface waters?

The functional equivalency test resolved the loophole concern. A polluter would not be able to cut off a pipe inches or a few feet from the shore, diverting the discharge into groundwater, to claim that the Clean Water Act did not apply. The transit time would be too brief and the distance too short.

And, at the other extreme, the miner tossing his shaving water at Pike's Peak need not worry if it eventually reached a river. As for the 20 million septic tank owners, the Court was unconcerned. It observed that EPA had "applied the permitting provision to some (but not to all) discharges through groundwater for over 30 years" and there was "no evidence of unmanageable expansion."[46] The Court also noted that, if many minor activities were swept up under the "functional equivalency" test, EPA and the states could mitigate the impact by issuing general permits. Although the Court did not mention it, another response to perceived overbreadth would be to turn to the legislative branch. Indeed, in 2008, after the Ninth Circuit held that the EPA needed to regulate discharges from recreational vessels, Congress acted within one week to pass the Clean Boating Act, which made clear that discharges incidental to the normal operation of recreational vessels did not need a Clean Water Act section 402 permit.[47] Although the *Maui* Court recognized that there was ambiguity about the application of its new "functional equivalency" rule, it did not anticipate that it would result in dramatically altering the status quo (nor did it).

But it did create some uncertainty for the regulated community. To properly evaluate these factors for a particular discharge activity, one would need some knowledge of groundwater science. The transit time of the pollutant is related to groundwater flow speed and residence time distribution. Contaminant fate and transport models, which can be calibrated and validated from measured data, can provide information about how much of a pollutant may reach a surface water and how much it may be altered. A *Science* news article summarized the result with the headline "Hydrologists Should Be Happy: Big Supreme Court Ruling Bolsters Groundwater Science."[48] One of the scientists who worked on the *amicus* brief of the aquatic scientists said that if the justices were in his transport class, he'd have to give them an A+.[49]

The three dissenting justices no doubt would have assigned the majority a failing grade. Justice Thomas (joined by Justice Gorsuch) conducted a textual analysis to arrive at the conclusion that Congress intended that the Clean Water Act would cover only direct discharges to navigable waters.[50] His textual analysis, however, failed to grapple with Congress's inclusion of "well" as an example of a point source. In addition, he ignored (as did all the other justices, to be fair) the fact that Congress also included a "discrete fissure" as a type of point source. A "fissure" is a geologic term meaning a "surface of fracture or a crack in a rock along which there is a distinct separation."[51]

As the Arizona Geological Survey noted, "fissures are a direct path to the groundwater table, so pollutants and contaminants could potentially flush down the fissure into a groundwater aquifer."[52] It makes little sense for Congress to have included terms like well and discrete fissure if it did not intend for the Clean Water Act to regulate discharges from those point sources that migrated to navigable surface waters through groundwater.

Justice Alito penned a separate dissent, expressing concern that the majority's functional equivalency rule would lead to unnecessary uncertainty for the regulated community.[53] He also harked back to *Solid Waste Agency of Northern Cook County* for the proposition that the Court requires clear congressional authorization when an agency's interpretive rule is "a significant impingement of the States' traditional and primary power over land and water use," contending that "the same rules should apply here where what is at issue is a new theory propounded by private plaintiffs."[54] Relatedly, he invoked (although not expressly by name) the major questions doctrine: "Congress must speak clearly if it wishes to assign to an agency decisions of vast economic and political significance."[55] The possible federal regulation of septic tanks apparently passed the vast significance threshold. Quoting EPA's Interpretive Statement, he noted that the Ninth Circuit's traceability test could lead to Clean Water Act regulation of "commonplace and ubiquitous activities such as releases from homeowners' backyard septic systems."[56] Justice Alito "struggled" with distinguishing the Ninth Circuit's test from the majority's "functional equivalent" formulation and therefore criticized the latter for broadening the Clean Water Act's coverage in the absence of clear congressional direction.

Justice Alito had a point: There does not seem to be a significant difference between the Ninth Circuit's test, informed by proximate cause considerations, and the "functional equivalent" test. Proximate cause is a limiting principle that takes multiple factors, including time, distance, and relative contribution, into account. And the Ninth Circuit even characterized the Lahaina Wastewater Reclamation Facility wells as "the functional equivalent" of a direct discharge to the Pacific Ocean. It's not too far off to say that the Supreme Court's functional equivalency test was the functional equivalent of the Ninth Circuit's test. But, in any event, because the Court rejected the Ninth Circuit's reasoning, it vacated the lower court's opinion. The case was sent back to the lower courts to apply the new standard. So the County of Maui had technically won the battle, but it would soon lose the war.

Functional Equivalency Applied

On remand, the US District Court for the District of Hawaii faithfully applied each of the seven factors the Supreme Court had listed.[57] Transit time (in as little as eighty-four days, with peak concentration within nine to ten months) and distance (a half mile as the nene flies, or no more than 1.5 miles as the groundwater meanders) militated in favor of the need for a Clean Water Act permit, but the nature of the material it traveled through (porous volcanic rock and groundwater), which resulted in dilution and chemical changes (denitrification), did not. The District Court also noted that almost all the wastewater eventually reached the Pacific Ocean, although the precise mechanism was unclear. The District Court also observed that the Supreme Court's factors were nonexclusive, and it therefore added one more to the mix: the volume of wastewater reaching the ocean. Here the sheer immensity of the flow weighed in favor of requiring the county to obtain a Clean Water Act permit. The District Court ruled in favor of the conservation groups, ordering the county to seek a permit and to pay $1 million in attorneys' fees and costs.[58]

The ramifications of the Supreme Court's decision were not limited to Hawaii. Across the country in Massachusetts, the decision prompted the settlement of a similar dispute concerning wastewater treatment operations. In that case, the Conservation Law Foundation had sued the Wychmere Beach Club, claiming that its twenty-two leaching pits, which were only 100 to 500 feet from the shore, were discharging nitrogen into Wychmere Harbour through a groundwater conduit.[59] (Recognizing the potential impact of the *County of Maui* case, the Wychmere Beach Club filed an *amicus* brief in the Supreme Court.) Before *County of Maui*, the district court judge had held that because there was no direct discharge to the harbor, no National Pollutant Discharge Elimination System permit under section 402 was necessary. A little over a month after *County of Maui* was handed down, however, the beach club decided to settle.[60] The limited transit time and distance would clearly lead to a finding that the wastewater from leaching pits were the functional equivalent of a direct discharge. The beach club agreed to truck its wastewater offsite until it upgraded its operations. (It also agreed to pay $135,000 in attorneys' fees.)

A similar result occurred in South Carolina, where conservation groups brought a Clean Water Act citizens' suit against Kinder Morgan Energy Partners after its pipeline ruptured, leading to several hundred thousand gallons of gasoline seeping into the tributaries of the Savannah River and other waterways.[61] In 2018, the Fourth Circuit Court of Appeals held that such an indirect discharge was a Clean Water Act violation. Kinder Morgan sought Supreme Court review, which was pending at the time that *County of Maui* was decided. (Both Kinder Morgan and the conservation groups filed *amicus* briefs in *County of Maui*.) Two weeks after *County of Maui*, the Supreme Court granted certiorari but immediately vacated the lower court's judgment and remanded the matter for further considerations in light of the new functional equivalency test.[62] Kinder Morgan agreed to settle the lawsuit by creating a $1.5 million fund, administered by an organization formed by the conservation groups, to promote water quality in Anderson County, where the spill had occurred. The first grants were awarded to the Anderson Soil and Water Conservation District to teach students and residents how to monitor the quality of their drinking water.[63]

Beyond wastewater treatment facilities and pipeline leaks, the functional equivalency test has direct relevance to litigation involving coal ash ponds.[64] Among the waste products that coal-fired power plants produce is coal ash, which contains heavy metals such as arsenic, mercury, and lead. The coal ash is often disposed of in onsite ash ponds. Because coal-fired power plants need a reliable source of water (for cooling), they are typically located near rivers and other waterways. As a consequence, the coal ash ponds are located near these waters. The ash ponds themselves, more than 90 percent of which are unlined,[65] are not waters of the United States; the EPA and the Corps have excluded waste treatment lagoons or other waste treatment systems from the WOTUS regulatory definition.[66] But the Clean Water Act is implicated when the coal ash ponds transmit their waste through groundwater to nearby rivers and streams and other waters that do qualify as a water of the United States. Whether such a connection amounts to a functional equivalent of a direct discharge now depends on the application of the *County of Maui* factors.

The *County of Maui* decision certainly closed a Clean Water Act loophole—or at least didn't allow one to be created. Earthjustice, which represented the conservation groups in the case, declared it to be the "Clean Water Act Case of the Century."[67] But the century was young.

Changing of the Guard (SCOTUS Edition): From RBG to ACB

On September 18, 2020, US Supreme Court Justice Ruth Bader Ginsburg died of complications related to pancreatic cancer. With elections looming, President Trump and the Republican-led Senate wasted no time in securing a replacement. On September 26, President Trump announced that Judge Amy Coney Barrett of the Seventh Circuit Court of Appeals was his choice to succeed the Notorious RBG. The Senate expeditiously held a confirmation hearing and quickly confirmed Judge Barrett along party lines, with all Republicans voting in favor (except for Senator Susan Collins of Maine) and all Democrats voting no. The Glorious ACB, as some on the right tried to brand her,[68] was sworn in an associate justice on October 27.

In Clean Water Act cases, Ruth Bader Ginsburg was a reliable vote for deference to agency expertise and a broad conception of waters of the United States. She dissented in both *Solid Waste Agency of Northern Cook County* and *Rapanos*. In contrast, Amy Coney Barrett had less of a track record. Her only WOTUS case was *Orchard Hill Building Company v. U.S. Army Corps of Engineers*, which involved 13 acres of wetlands on former agricultural land in Illinois about 11 miles from the Little Calumet River, which was a navigable-in-fact water.[69] At the time, Seventh Circuit precedent had interpreted the fractured *Rapanos* decision to mean that Justice Kennedy's concurring opinion, and its significant nexus standard, applied in such cases.[70] The Corps claimed that the wetlands, which were hydrologically connected to the Little Calumet River through a series of constructed ditches, sewer pipes, open water basins, and Midlothian Creek, significantly affected the integrity of the river. The Seventh Circuit was unpersuaded. In an opinion (joined but not written by then–Judge Barrett), the Court explained,

> According to the [Corps], wetlands are "nature's kidneys," able to filter out pollutants that would otherwise reach downstream waters. Northeastern Illinois waters are known to suffer relatively high rates of nitrogen, and the Warmke wetlands have a "discrete and confined intermittent flow" to the Midlothian Creek. From this connection, the Corps concluded that the Warmke wetlands have the "ability" to pass pollutants along. But such a "speculative" finding cannot support a significant nexus.[71]

In the view of then–Judge Barrett and her Seventh Circuit colleagues, the Corps failed to provide sufficient evidence that the wetlands had a significant nexus to the Little Calumet River.

Of course, during the time of her confirmation hearing, most of the focus was on other issues, such as how Justice Barrett might vote regarding a woman's right to an abortion. Justice Barrett ultimately played a pivotal role in reversing *Roe v. Wade*, providing the decisive fifth vote for the majority in *Dobbs v. Jackson Women's Health Organization*. She later played a similar role in the most consequential Clean Water Act case ever decided by the Supreme Court.

Changing of the Guard (POTUS Edition): From Trump to Biden

Despite attempts by his predecessor and others to disrupt the peaceful transfer of power, Joseph R. Biden was sworn in as president shortly before noon on January 20, 2021. Talk about "American carnage" was replaced with a call for unity. And unlike his predecessor's remarks four years before, President Biden's address contained a reference to environmental challenges, noting that "[a] cry for survival comes from the planet itself. A cry that can't be any more desperate or any more clear."[72] His tone and priorities could not have been more different from Trump's. To borrow a phrase from Joe Biden's comments on an earlier legislative triumph, his 2020 electoral victory was a big effing deal.[73]

One of President Biden's first actions was to issue an Executive Order 13990, titled "Protecting Public Health and the Environment and Restoring Science to Tackle the Climate Crisis," which revoked many of President Trump's executive orders, including his order that led to the promulgation of the Navigable Waters Protection Rule.[74] But although a president may undo a predecessor's prior executive orders with immediate effect, it takes longer to undo a regulation. Revoking or amending an agency regulation typically requires the agency to follow a public notice and comment process. Biden's executive order called on executive branch agencies "to take action to address" the issuance of Trump-era regulations that lacked a science-based foundation, to "improve public health and protect our environment; [and] to ensure access to clean air and water."[75] On June 9, 2021, after the EPA and the Corps reviewed the record for the Navigable Waters Protection Rule, EPA Administrator Michael Regan (appointed by President Biden) and acting Assistant Secretary of the Army for Civil Works Jaime A. Pinkham (also a Biden political appointee) announced that the agencies yet again intended to revise or replace the regulatory definition of "waters of the United States."[76]

Under the new regime, the agencies found that, not surprisingly, the Navigable Waters Protection Rule had resulted in reduced clean water protection. The agencies noted that, under the Navigable Waters Protection Rule, at least 333 projects were found to be no longer regulated under the Clean Water Act.[77] The agencies highlighted the rule's impact in the arid west: In

New Mexico and Arizona, "nearly every one of over 1,500 streams assessed has been found to be non-jurisdictional."[78] Although the EPA and the Corps had announced that they intended to embark on a new round of rulemaking, the Navigable Waters Protection Rule would remain in effect during that process. For the moment.

The NWPR Proves to Be Ephemeral

Like every WOTUS rule before it, the Navigable Waters Protection Rule was subjected to judicial challenges. The Trump administration had prevailed in the first big case, brought by California, New York, and other blue states in the US District Court for the Northern District of California, where the court had declined to issue a preliminary injunction, thereby allowing the new rule to enter into force.[79] But the Navigable Waters Protection Rule was still under attack from environmental groups and tribes in other US district courts across the country, in Arizona, Massachusetts, New Mexico, and South Carolina. The forums were chosen with care; each was a court with a high proportion of judges appointed by Democratic presidents, a court that had previously ruled favorably from the environmental perspective, or a court in a state most significantly affected by the Navigable Waters Protection Rule. Ultimately, it was the challenges by tribes in Arizona and New Mexico cases that brought down the Navigable Waters Protection Rule.

In *Pascua Yaqui Tribe v. U.S. Environmental Protection Agency*, filed in US District Court for the District of Arizona, the complaint explained the cultural and spiritual importance of waters to the tribes and their members. For example, for the Pascua Yaqui Tribe, water has always been intrinsic to its identity, as "their ancestors built villages along the ephemeral and intermittent streams in the mountains surrounding Tucson."[80] The Navigable Waters Protection Rule removed protection of ephemeral waters, including streams where tribal members "visit to gather traditional materials and offer prayers for their ancestors."[81] Without Clean Water Act protection of these waters, the tribes were concerned that "ephemeral streams in the Santa Rita Mountains that would be destroyed by the proposed Rosemont open-pit copper mine, causing significant impacts to water quality and aquatic resources in the mountains and downstream."[82] As explained in the last chapter, they were right to be concerned.

After the EPA and the Corps had announced the new rulemaking, the agencies requested that the Navigable Waters Protection Rule be voluntarily remanded to the agency, with the case dismissed. A voluntary remand allows an agency to reconsider its initial decision, and courts typically grant such requests, partially out of respect for executive branch processes and partially for reasons of judicial economy. A court does not want to spend time reviewing a rule that an agency is poised to dispense with. In this case, the tribes and the regulated community (an amalgamation of business interests that had intervened) did not oppose the remand. The more difficult question was whether the Court should issue a remand with a vacatur. A vacatur would have the effect of invalidating the Navigable Waters Protection Rule. The tribes wanted a vacatur, the agencies took no official position, and the business intervenors were adamantly opposed.[83]

On August 30, 2021, Judge Rosemary Márquez (an Obama appointee) issued an order to remand and vacate the Navigable Waters Protection Rule.[84] A principal reason was that, when promulgating the rule, the agencies had disregarded the scientific record and failed to fully consider the impact of reducing Clean Water Act jurisdiction. Even the agencies conceded that they were concerned that the prior rulemaking "did not look closely enough at the effect ephemeral waters have on traditional navigable waters."[85] Judge Márquez concluded that the agencies had committed a serious error, warranting vacatur, in a rather conclusory fashion. The order lacked any detailed reasoning. Based on the agencies' expression of concern, Judge Márquez apparently felt no need to inquire further or to attempt to distinguish the decision by Judge Seeborg in the North District of California. Regardless of the brevity of the reasoning, vacatur meant the rule was dead. As Earthjustice's headline proclaimed, "Judge Ditches Trump's Dirty Water Rule," with a subtitle of "Victory—Navigable Waters Protection Rule, repudiated for gutting water protections, is no longer the law of the land."[86]

Less than a month later, in *Navajo Nation v. Regan*, the US District Court for the District of New Mexico issued a similar opinion, along with an order to remand and vacate.[87] Here Judge Martha Vázquez (a Bill Clinton appointee) cited *Pascua Yaqui Tribe v. U.S. Environmental Protection Agency* and, like Judge Márquez, noted that the agencies now "call into significant question whether the agencies' consideration of science and water quality impacts in developing the rule was consistent with" the Clean Water Act's objective to restore and maintain the chemical, physical, and biological integrity of the nation's waters.[88] She concluded that it was not, although the opinion was similarly brief on this issue.

There was some question about the scope of the district courts' vacatur orders: Did they apply nationwide? Was the Navigable Waters Protection Rule dead throughout the country or only in the jurisdictions where the plaintiffs resided? Although the Biden administration had not requested vacatur, it did not try too hard to prevent it and was happy to acquiesce. The EPA and the Corps halted implementation of the Navigable Waters Protection Rule nationwide.[89] In its place, the pre-2015 regulatory regime sprung back to life.

The Biden WOTUS Rule: Everything Old Is New Again

The Biden administration ensured that all interested stakeholders had the opportunity to provide input into the new regulatory definition. Before developing the proposed rule, it held a series of meetings with state associations, environmental groups, and industry organizations, including from the farming sector. The EPA and Corps also asked for preproposal recommendations, which resulted in 32,000 public comments.[90] When the agencies published their proposed rule in the *Federal Register* on December 7, 2021,[91] eighty years after the day that would live in infamy, no one could accuse the EPA and the Corps of a surprise attack. This did not mean that all constituencies would be pleased with the outcome, however.

The proposal essentially recodified the pre-2015 regime, which meant the usual complaints and concerns. While considering it a vast improvement over the Trump rule, environmental groups thought the Biden rule was still insufficiently protective, excluding wastewater treatment systems, for example. The regulated community, still disappointed over the vacatur of the Navigable Waters Protection Rule, was ill disposed to a rule that would, in its view, impede necessary development. Interested parties provided the agencies about 114,000 public comments to wade through.[92] The task would take about a year, and on the eve of New Year's Eve 2022, the agencies announced that they had finalized revisions to the definition of waters of the United States, emphasizing that unlike the Navigable Waters Protection Rule, this revision was based on the scientific record.[93]

For the most part, the final rule was a call back to the pre-2015 regime, albeit slightly reordered. No new concept was introduced. It identified five categories of waters that were jurisdictional and thus protected by the Clean Water Act:

- traditional navigable waters, the territorial seas, and interstate waters (so-called (a)(1) waters);
- impoundments of "waters of the United States";
- tributaries to traditional navigable waters, the territorial seas, interstate waters, or impoundments;

- wetlands adjacent to (a)(1) waters; wetlands adjacent to and with a continuous surface connection to jurisdictional impoundments and tributaries; and wetland adjacent to jurisdictional impoundments and tributaries that met the significant nexus standard; and
- intrastate lakes and ponds, streams, or wetlands not previously covered that either had a continuous surface connection with an (a)(1) water or tributary or met the significant nexus standard.[94]

To meet the significant nexus standard, a water, either alone or in combination with similarly situated waters, would need to have "a material influence on the chemical, physical, or biological integrity" of (a)(1) waters.[95] The final rule also contained eight largely long-held exclusions, such as waste treatment systems, prior converted cropland, and certain ditches.[96]

The final rule was published in the *Federal Register* on January 18, 2023, with a planned effective date of March 20, 2023. Like the Obama and Trump rules, the Biden rule would have a choppy rollout. The National Association of Home Builders hyperbolically claimed that Biden's "new WOTUS rule radically extends the areas in which home builders are required to get federal permits."[97] That would be true only if the Navigable Waters Protection Rule was the baseline, but it had been sidelined by the time the Biden rule came out. The Biden rule could hardly be a radical extension of the pre-2015 regime; it was instead a confirmation of the status quo.

The agricultural community was similarly hacked off. For example, the agriculture commissioner for North Dakota reflexively expressed concern that the uncertainty associated with the new rule "would cause a significant reduction in the amount of land available in North Dakota for crop production and grazing."[98] It is hard to see how this might be the case when the Clean Water Act amendments of 1977 expressly exempted normal farming activities from regulation under Clean Water Act section 404. And the runoff from agricultural fields is generally not regulated under Clean Water Act section 402, as nonpoint pollution is left to the states. He also criticized how the new rule dealt with the prior converted cropland exclusion. On this issue, he may have had a valid point.

Abandoning the Prior Converted Cropland Exclusion?

Ever since the controversy concerning the 1989 wetland delineation manual, which could have been construed to allow drained agricultural fields to be classified as wetlands based on the presence of hydric soils, the Corps had made clear that certain croplands were, as a categorical matter, not considered to be waters of the United States. In a 1990 regulatory guidance document, the Corps clarified that "prior converted cropland"—that is, cropland that had been converted to agricultural production before December 1985—and lands that were inundated for no more than fourteen consecutive days during the growing season were excluded from Clean Water Act coverage.[99] In contrast, "farmed wetlands," such as prairie potholes and playa lakes, could be viewed as wetlands for purposes of the Clean Water Act. The guidance also noted that if the prior converted cropland were "abandoned," and wetland hydrology and plants returned, then the site could qualify as a water of the United States. In accordance with the US Department of Agriculture's Food Security Act Manual, the Corps would consider an area abandoned if the farmer ceased cropping, management, or maintenance activities for five consecutive years.[100]

Guidance is not legally binding, of course. To provide the agricultural community with more certainty, the Corps and EPA sought to codify the guidance through a 1993 rulemaking. The regulation itself flatly stated that "navigable waters do not include prior converted cropland."[101] The preamble in the *Federal Register* explained that the "PC cropland" exclusion would apply to qualifying lands, so long as the area had been used to produce an agricultural commodity at least once every five years.[102] Agricultural commodities include corn, soybeans, and wheat, as well as cattle, hogs, and eggs.[103] If this activity stopped, and wetland characteristics returned, then the area might be recaptured for purposes of Clean Water Act jurisdiction. As a practical matter, this meant that if a farmer abandoned the agricultural use of an area, by for example, selling it to a developer, the Clean Water Act would pose no obstacle for five years.

This arrangement changed significantly during, somewhat surprisingly, the George W. Bush administration. In 2005, the Corps and US Department of Agriculture (through the Natural Resources Conservation Service) issued joint guidance that announced that if a farm was changed to a nonagricultural use (say, producing condos rather than corn), then the PC cropland label would immediately not apply, and "a new wetland determination [would be] required for CWA purposes."[104] The five-year exclusion was gone. Although this significant policy shift did not interfere with a farmer's ability to farm the land, it did potentially complicate the farmer's ability to sell the land. A developer might not be willing to pay as much if the site contained waters of the United States.

In 2010, in *New Hope Power Company v. U.S. Army Corps of Engineers*, the US District Court for the Southern District of Florida ruled that any such change in the abandonment policy would need to go through public notice and comment, which the Corps and Department of Agriculture did not do.[105] The court did not issue a nationwide injunction, however, and the agencies continued to assert the new abandonment rule outside that court's jurisdiction.[106] When the Obama administration issued the Clean Water Rule, it left the exclusion for prior converted cropland undisturbed, and it did not address the abandonment rule in the regulatory language or preamble. The Trump administration's Navigable Waters Protection Rule "bigly" modified the prior converted cropland exclusion, much to the delight of the agricultural community.

First, the exclusion applied to areas used for any "agricultural product," which is broader than "agricultural commodity."[107] Second, with respect to the abandonment issue, the five-year term was reinstated: An area was abandoned only if it was not used for "agricultural purposes" at least once in a five-year period.[108] The Trump administration had returned to the Corps' original policy, and a farmer essentially had a five-year window to sell property unencumbered by Clean Water Act regulation.

The Biden rule closed the window. It returned to an abandonment policy whereby an area immediately would lose its exclusion once the agricultural activity ceased.[109] If a farmer sold a parcel to a developer, then the Clean Water Act might apply; the area would still need to exhibit wetland characteristics to potentially fall under Clean Water Act jurisdiction. The agricultural community went ballistic, claiming that now 97 percent of Iowa was under the control of the federal government, for example. Of course, that was not remotely true.[110] And nothing in the Clean Water Act or the Biden rule prevented farmers from engaging in normal farming practices on the lands that still contained wetlands. Nevertheless, the agricultural community was affected by the Biden rule, just not in the way it was portrayed to the public. A complaint about potential interference with being able to sell to developers did not square with the rhetoric that the Biden rule was at war with the family farmer.

Nevertheless, the complaint about the Biden rule's impact on family farmers resonated with members of Congress, who invoked the Congressional Review Act to disapprove the new (old) WOTUS rules. In early March 2023, the House voted 227–198 to overturn the regulation.[111] David Rouzer, the North Carolina Republican serving as chairman of the House Water

Resources and Environment Subcommittee, ratcheted up the already overheated rhetoric: "President Biden's new WOTUS rule is a nuclear warhead aimed squarely at our farm families, small businesses, homebuilders, every property owner, and entire communities because of its overreaching definition."[112] The resolution of disapproval, co-sponsored by all forty-nine Republican senators, also passed, with some Democratic backing, by a vote of 53–43.[113] As expected, President Biden vetoed the attempt to undo the work of his administration.[114] But the battle lines were drawn once again, and the action moved to the courts.

A Nation Divided

Just as environmental groups and blue states had carefully chosen in which courts to challenge the Trump rule, the regulated community and the red states identified friendly territory in which to file their lawsuits attacking the Biden rule. Texas and Idaho, as well as eighteen business associations, filed in the Southern District of Texas, and twenty-four states filed in the District of North Dakota, a forum that had proven hostile to the Obama rule (also with business groups intervening). They were not disappointed with their selected venues.

Judge Jeffrey Brown (a Trump appointee) in Texas was out of the box first on March 19, 2023, the day before the Biden rule was to go into effect, issuing a preliminary injunction prohibiting the agencies from applying the revised rule.[115] Texas and Idaho and the business associations asserted that the agencies had acted unlawfully on various statutory and constitutional grounds, including that the rule violated the commerce clause, the Tenth Amendment, and the nondelegation principle. In determining whether to issue a preliminary injunction, Judge Brown put aside the constitutional questions and focused on whether the agencies had exceeded their statutory mandates, although this inquiry touched on some constitutional matters.

His analysis opened, appropriately enough, on whether *Chevron* deference should apply to the agencies' interpretation of the Clean Water Act. In his view, the agencies deserved no deference for at least two reasons. First, he noted that the Clean Water Act contains criminal penalties. He invoked the "rule of lenity," a principle of statutory construction that calls for criminal statutes to be construed in the light most favorable to the defendant.[116] Judge Brown concluded that, in line with Fifth Circuit precedent, the rule of lenity must trump *Chevron* deference. This rather curious conclusion fails to grapple with the fact that the statute involved in *Chevron* was the Clean Air Act, which, like the Clean Water Act, has a mix of administrative, civil, and criminal penalties. Judge Brown was on firmer ground with his second justification for jettisoning *Chevron*, however. Here he relied on the Supreme Court's decision in *Solid Waste Agency of Northern Cook County*, which provided that an agency is owed no deference when its interpretation raises federalism concerns "by permitting federal encroachment upon a traditional state power."[117] Because, in Judge Brown's opinion, the Biden rule encroached on states' rights, the EPA and Corps were not entitled to any deference.

Judge Brown found that the challengers were likely to prevail on two issues: the breadth of interstate waters and the significant nexus test. With respect to interstate waters, he was troubled that the Biden rule applied to all interstate waters, not just interstate waters that were navigable in fact, suggesting that the agencies had written the concept of navigability out of the Clean Water Act. But the phrase "interstate waters, including wetlands" had been part of the WOTUS regulatory landscape since the Reagan administration. Moreover, as the agencies pointed out, Congress had regulated interstate waters—regardless of their navigability—in numerous laws predating the Clean Water Act. It beggars belief that Congress in 1972 chose to expand all aspects of federal water quality efforts, including the scope of jurisdiction, but for some reason decided to exclude a class of waters over which it had previously asserted control.

Judge Brown also found fault with the agencies' articulation of the significant nexus test. He quoted the Biden rule's preamble to explain which waters would be jurisdictional under the significant nexus test: "waters that, either alone or in combination with similarly situated waters in the region, significantly affect the chemical, physical, or biological integrity of traditional navigable waters, the territorial seas, or interstate waters." The fatal flaw, apparently, was the linkage to interstate waters, which may not be navigable in fact. According to Judge Brown, this went beyond Justice Kennedy's concurrence, which suggested that "significant nexus" waters must contribute to the integrity of "other covered waters more readily understood as 'navigable.'" Since no *Chevron* deference was owed, Judge Brown could substitute his judgment for that of the agencies, and he enjoined the rule. He declined to issue a nationwide injunction, however, and the scope of his order was limited to Texas and Idaho.[118]

Two weeks later, Judge Daniel Hovland (a George W. Bush appointee) in North Dakota weighed in on the Biden rule, also issuing a preliminary injunction, on behalf of twenty-four other states.[119] After recounting the rulemaking history of the various WOTUS definitions, he stated,

> Suffice it to say the Clean Water Act, and the varied and different definitions of "waters of the United States," have created nothing but confusion, uncertainty, unpredictability, and endless litigation throughout this country to date.[120]

Suffice it to say that Judge Hovland would not be acknowledging the improvements in national water quality since the Clean Water Act's passage. Instead, he largely parroted the concerns expressed by Judge Brown in Texas. In his view, the coverage of all interstate waters exceeded the agencies' statutory authority. For good measure, and in a cursory fashion, he also broached some of the constitutional claims, principally that the Biden rule ran afoul of the commerce clause and violated the Tenth Amendment.[121] Other than quoting extensively from the states' submission, though, Judge Hovland offered little in independent analysis of the issue. He did cite *New York v. United States*, but that case stands for the proposition that the federal government may not commandeer state governments, which the EPA and the Corps did not do. The multifactored significant nexus test also raised due process concerns for him. Finally, he invoked the major questions doctrine from *West Virginia v. EPA*, asserting that "federal agencies are not permitted to exercise regulatory power 'over a significant portion of the American economy' or 'make a radical or fundamental change to a statutory scheme' through rulemaking without clear authorization by Congress."[122] Judge Hovland found that, based on the plaintiffs' potpourri of claims, they were likely to prevail on the merits and issued an injunction applicable in those twenty-four states.

Other courts also issued injunctions, bringing the total number of states where the Biden rule was inapplicable to twenty-seven, all red states. But here's the silly thing: With the Biden rule sidelined, the rule in place in those twenty-seven states was the pre-2015 regulatory regime, which was the 1986/88 regulations plus the post-*Rapanos* significant nexus guidance.[123] Although perhaps there were some differences on the margins (and certainly with respect to prior converted cropland), there was not a huge difference between the Biden rule and the pre-2015 regime. In any event, as the dust cleared, the WOTUS map looked suspiciously similar to the 2020 electoral map, with a few swing states flipping (Figure 11-1).

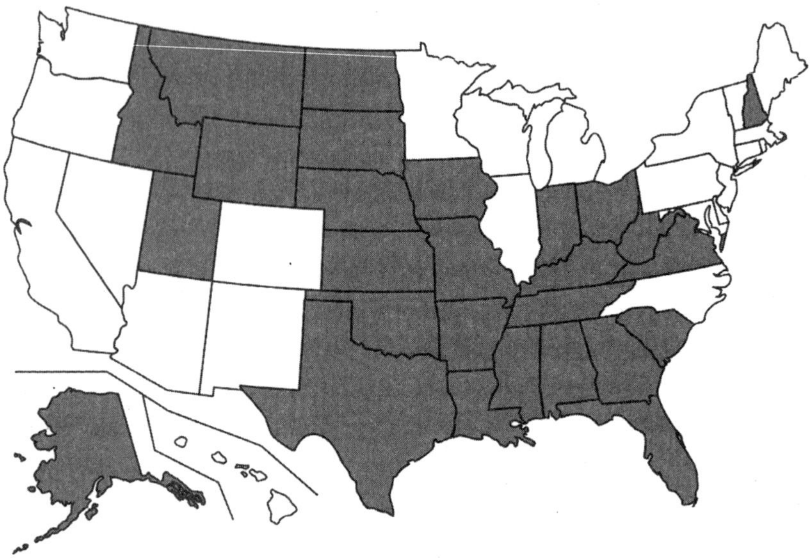

Figure 11-1. Status of WOTUS as of April 2023, with white indicating states where the Biden rule was in effect and gray indicating states where the pre-2015 regime was in effect.

A preliminary injunction is just that—preliminary. A court will still hold a hearing on the merits to consider the issues more in depth before issuing a final decision. But the US district courts had little incentive to quickly move forward, because lurking in the background was *Sackett v. U.S. Environmental Protection Agency*, a case pending before the US Supreme Court. SCOTUS would address WOTUS one more time.

CHAPTER 12

Back to the Past

> For more than a half century, the agencies responsible for enforcing the Act have wrestled with the problem and adopted varying interpretations. On three prior occasions, this Court has tried to clarify the meaning of "the waters of the United States." But the problem persists. . . . Today, we return to the problem and attempt to identify with greater clarity what the Act means by "the waters of the United States."
>
> —Justice Alito, writing for the majority in *Sackett v. U.S. Environmental Protection Agency* (2023)

The problem, according to Justice Alito and his four colleagues, was not the continuing challenge of restoring and maintaining the integrity of the nation's waters. The problem was not the states' continuing failure to regulate nonpoint source discharges and the increasing frequency of harmful algal blooms. Instead, the problem was WOTUS itself: the lack of definitional clarity of which waters were protected by the Clean Water Act. From Justice Alito's perspective, the problem was the lack of certainty provided to the regulated community—that is, polluters. The *Sackett* case provided the Supreme Court the opportunity to go once more unto the breach to try to resolve the geographic scope of the Clean Water Act.

This was not the Sacketts' first Supreme Court case. More than a decade earlier, they had prevailed on a procedural matter. The Sacketts had secured a unanimous opinion that allowed them to challenge a Clean Water Act jurisdictional determination without applying for a permit and before the agencies brought a formal enforcement action. They were victorious in their second trip to the Court as well, but this decision had substantive impacts. In *Sackett II*, the Supreme Court adopted Justice Scalia's *Rapanos* plurality opinion. In doing so, the Court disregarded its own precedent, overlooked parts of the Clean Water Act, and ignored science. The Court rejected the significant nexus approach and, in its place, declared a definitive definition that was more restrictive in coverage than every presidential administration's interpretation, from Ford to Biden. Even the Trump administration's Navigable Waters Protection Rule encompassed too many waters under the Court's ruling in *Sackett*. Because the Court was rendering a statutory interpretation, Congress can step in and reverse or blunt the ruling's impact. As a practical matter, however, *Sackett* shifted the responsibility to protect wetlands and many nonnavigable streams back to state and local governments, as had been the case before the Clean Water Act.

Sackett I: Challenging a Hobson's Choice

Michael and Chantell Sackett owned a 0.63-acre lot approximately 300 feet north of Priest Lake in the Idaho panhandle.[1] Depending on your news source, they are either sympathetic, beleaguered "mom-and-pop" property owners deserving of the Medal of Freedom[2] or knowledgeable construction industry developers (with Michael later having to register as a sex offender after he pled guilty to coercion and enticement of a minor[3]). By most accounts, Priest Lake, known as Idaho's crown jewel,[4] qualifies as a traditional navigable water.[5] The Sacketts' property contained wetlands, remnants of the Kalispell Bay Fen complex, which had drained directly to the lake; the Sacketts' wetlands were separated from Priest Lake by a road and housing development but had a hydrologic connection with Priest Lake through "shallow subsurface flow."[6] In May 2007, the Sacketts began to fill the site with sand and gravel to prepare it for the construction of a home. After neighbors complained to the EPA, the agency investigated and determined that the Sacketts had discharged pollutants (rock and dirt) into a water of the United States (a wetland adjacent to a navigable water) without a permit. The EPA issued the Sacketts an administrative compliance order, which informed them that the illegal filling could subject them to massive fines—up to $75,000 per day.[7] The Sacketts were advised they needed to remove the fill and restore the site or be subject to an enforcement action.

The Sacketts wanted to contest the agency's assertion that their property was a water of the United States and thus subject to Clean Water Act jurisdiction. But as a general matter, one can challenge in court only an agency's "final" action.[8] The judiciary does not want to get enmeshed in agency deliberations before the agency has settled on a definitive course of action. To do so is disrespectful to a coequal branch of government. It also might be a waste of judicial resources because the agency's final decision could satisfy the prospective plaintiff, thereby rendering any lawsuit moot. Accordingly, an agency's action is "ripe" for judicial review when it constitutes "final" agency action.

From the EPA's perspective, an administrative order, which is akin to a cease-and-desist order, is not final agency action. The agency has not yet made a final decision on whether to bring an enforcement action. It might or it might not. From the Sacketts' point of view, however, the order presented them with a stark choice: Restore the site or be subject to potentially millions of dollars in penalties, which is not a real choice. Although in practice wetland enforcement actions never result in maximum penalties being levied, it must have been disturbing, if not terrifying, to receive such a letter from the government.

So the Sacketts sued for the right to bring a pre-enforcement challenge—that is, the ability to contest Clean Water Act jurisdiction in court before applying for a permit or before the agency brought an enforcement action. They lost in the lower courts, but the Supreme Court agreed to hear the matter. In 2012, in a unanimous opinion written by Justice Scalia, the Court ruled for the Sacketts.

Justice Scalia noted that "final" agency action was a decision that determined rights or obligations from which legal consequences flowed.[9] Here the EPA had determined that the Sacketts needed to restore the wetlands or face significant penalties. To be final, an agency action also must be the "consummation" of the agency process. Because the compliance order was not subject to any further agency review, it was the end of the process and thus final.[10] The Sacketts had won their right to have a day in court, at their timing.

In a concurring opinion, Justice Alito emphasized that "the reach of the Clean Water Act is notoriously unclear."[11] He worried that "any piece of land that is wet at least part of the year is in danger of being classified by EPA employees as wetlands covered by the Act," putting property owners in a vulnerable position "at the agency's mercy."[12] He suggested that the Court's decision offered property owners "a modest measure of relief" but that Congress should act to clarify the scope of the Clean Water Act to provide "real relief."[13] Criticizing Congress for doing "nothing to resolve this critical ambiguity," he called for "clarification of the reach of the Clean Water Act" to "rectify the underlying problem"[14]—the underlying problem being interference with private property rights. And, as we will see, if Congress was not prepared to act, Justice Alito and the Court would.

Sackett on Remand

The Sacketts' victory allowed them to challenge the EPA's determination that the site contained a water of the United States, before the EPA brought a formal enforcement action. In the US District Court for the District of Idaho, the trial judge decided that the property did in fact contain a wetland adjacent to a traditional navigable water.[15] The Sacketts appealed once again to the Ninth Circuit. They filed their brief in a timely manner, and the EPA asked for additional time to file its brief, which the court granted. Then the EPA asked for some more time, which the court also granted. In March 2020, with the twice-extended deadline to file rapidly approaching, the EPA sent the Sacketts a brief letter informing them that it was withdrawing the compliance order and that "several years ago" the EPA had decided not to proceed with a formal enforcement action.[16] The EPA letter declared that the EPA "does not intend to issue a similar order to [the Sacketts] in the future for this Site."[17] Subsequently, the EPA asked the Ninth Circuit to dismiss the case as moot.

The Ninth Circuit was not amused. It observed that the EPA's "intention" not to enforce was not binding and that the "EPA could potentially change positions under new leadership."[18] Moreover, the court was concerned that the EPA still appeared to assert regulatory authority over the wetland, emphasizing that, during oral argument, EPA's attorney, "after more than a decade of litigation, could not answer questions about whether the Sacketts could develop their land."[19] The court criticized the EPA's actions, noting,

> If we are to take EPA's letter at face value, the agency caused the Sacketts to litigate cross-motions for summary judgment in the district court, participate in mediation, and then pursue this appeal *after* the agency had already concluded it would never enforce the challenged compliance order. Forcing the Sacketts to engage in years of litigation, under threat of tens of thousands of dollars in daily fines, only to assert at the eleventh hour that the dispute has actually been moot for a long time, is not a litigation strategy we wish to encourage.[20]

Accordingly, the Ninth Circuit decided that the Sacketts could continue their litigation quest for a ruling placing their property beyond the reach of the Clean Water Act.

But the Sacketts were not as successful when the Ninth Circuit turned to the merits—whether their wetland was a water of the United States. The appellate court determined that Justice Kennedy's significant nexus approach was the correct test to apply, and the court held that the EPA correctly concluded "that the wetlands on the Sacketts' property are adjacent to a jurisdictional tributary and that, together with the similarly situated Kalispell Bay Fen, they have a significant nexus to Priest Lake, a traditional navigable water."[21] Although a road separated the wetland from the unnamed tributary, the court noted that "a shallow subsurface flow is occurring beneath the road, connecting the Sacketts' lot to the tributary and the Kalispell Bay Fen wetland system to the north."[22] The court deferred to the EPA's scientific judgment that the wetland on the Sacketts' property, in combination with other wetlands in the system, significantly affected the integrity of Priest Lake and was "especially important in maintaining the high quality of Priest Lake's water, fish, and wildlife."[23] The Sacketts had lost the battle, but at least they had assurances from the EPA that it would not take enforcement action against them. Indeed, one imagines that EPA staff in Washington would have been quite pleased if this case had just ended here.

But having prevailed once before at the Supreme Court, the Sacketts soldiered on, asking the Court to wade into the WOTUS swamp once more. Specifically, the Sacketts requested that *Rapanos* be revisited and that the Court adopt Justice Scalia's test for wetland jurisdiction under the Clean Water Act. The Court granted the Sacketts' petition but rephrased the question presented to be "whether the Ninth Circuit set forth the proper test for determining whether wetlands are 'waters of the United States' under the Clean Water Act."[24] In any event, the Court was revisiting the scope of the Clean Water Act—which waters are protected and which are not—and any decision would have ramifications well beyond the Idaho panhandle. Therefore, a spectrum of stakeholders wanted to weigh in through *amicus* briefs.

The Many Friends of the Court

More than forty *amicus* briefs were filed on behalf of groups representing business interests, state and local governments, members of Congress, former EPA administrators, scientific societies, tribes, and environmental organizations.[25] The regulated community was almost unified in its plea for certainty: In its view, the lack of clarity concerning WOTUS was responsible for delays to vital infrastructure projects, a decline in housing stock, disruption to mining activities, and frustration within the agricultural industry. When one reads these briefs, it hard to imagine how the US economy could even function in light of such obstacles. All advocated for the Court to jettison the significant nexus test and adopt some form of Justice Scalia's *Rapanos* plurality opinion.

Although many of the *amicus* briefs supporting the Sacketts made similar arguments about statutory interpretation, a few offered additional constitutional rationales for limiting the scope of waters of the United States. For example, West Virginia and twenty-five other states focused on federalism principles and asserted that Congress's powers under the commerce clause did not extend to wetlands not continuously connected to traditional navigable waters.[26] Similarly, the Claremont Institute, represented by John Eastman (later indicted for conspiring with Donald Trump to overturn the results of the 2020 presidential election in Georgia[27]), claimed that the federal government was attempting to assert a general police power, which was reserved to the states.[28] In their view, Congress was acting beyond its enumerated powers.

Other briefs contended that, even if Congress had the authority to regulate some waters beyond traditional navigable waters, it had impermissibly delegated its lawmaking function to the EPA and the Corps. The Liberty for Justice Center, a public interest firm that litigates to promote economic liberty and private property rights, argued that "the Clean Water Act, in defining its grant of jurisdiction as the 'waters of the United States,' does not provide a sufficiently intelligible principle to guide—and, what is most important, constrain—agency action."[29] Recalling Justice Gorsuch's dissent in *Gundy* (the sex offender registry case discussed in Chapter 2), the brief concluded that the phrase is not "sufficiently definite and precise to enable Congress, the courts, and the public to ascertain whether Congress's guidance has been followed."[30] The brief warned that the merging of lawmaking authority with executive branch enforcement powers leads to tyranny.

Other *amicus* briefs were ostensibly less concerned about the specter of tyranny but asserted that states were best equipped to deal with water quality issues. Farm bureaus (representing an industry that has exemptions from the Clean Water Act) from twenty states claimed that the states already have "robust protections" in place.[31] Their brief devoted two pages extolling Iowa's "broad water quality protections," including "hundreds of pages of regulations relating to environmental protection requirements for animal feeding operations."[32] Oddly, the farm bureaus' brief neglected to mention that agriculture remains the primary source of the nation's water pollution and that Iowa's water quality is among the worst in the country.[33] Members of the Congressional Western Caucus suggested that states are "best suited to advance environmental protection."[34] To support the fanciful notion that state control "often generates better outcomes," their brief cited a law review article rather than any actual water quality data.[35]

On the other side, the *amicus* briefs supporting the EPA emphasized Congress's overall objective in enacting the Clean Water Act: to restore and maintain the integrity of the nation's waters. Several briefs focused on the magnitude of the waters that would no longer be protected under the Clean Water Act should Justice Scalia's *Rapanos* plurality opinion be adopted. The brief on behalf of twelve scientific societies pointed out that scientific models showed that more than 50 percent of wetlands in some watersheds would no longer have Clean Water Act protections if a "continuous surface-water connection" to a traditional navigable water were required.[36] The brief also noted the potential impact on nonnavigable streams, if such a requirement were applied to them: By definition, ephemeral and intermittent streams do not have a continuous surface connection to larger waterbodies and thus would not be jurisdictional waters. In the arid West, more than 90 percent of stream length in some watersheds would no longer be protected by the Clean Water Act.[37] The brief further emphasized that Justice Scalia's plurality test in *Rapanos* contained an additional demand: For a wetland to be jurisdictional, the wetland and the other water (which must be a water of the United States in its own right) must be so "inseparably bound" that it is difficult to tell where the wetland ends and the other water begins. The scientific societies noted that determining the demarcation between a wetland and open water is generally straightforward, demonstrated by the limit of the wetland vegetation, which is driven by water depth.[38] The brief raised the alarm that "because the boundaries of a wetland can be delineated in nearly every case, the 'difficult-to-tell' requirement would effectively eliminate Clean Water Act jurisdiction over almost all wetlands."[39]

Other *amicus* briefs supporting the EPA discussed in detail the impact that would occur as a result of diminished Clean Water Act coverage. Seventeen states (and the District of Columbia) expressed concern about water quality impacts downstream of states with weak regulatory programs.[40] Similarly, seventeen tribes filed a brief to underscore their cultural and spiritual connections to their waters and convey their worries about cross-border pollution,[41] perhaps in an effort to attract the vote of Justice Gorsuch, who had been sympathetic to tribal rights. A coalition of businesses banded together to try to make the economic case for maintaining federal regulation of wetlands.[42] The group included the Ecological Restoration Business Association, whose members included entrepreneurial mitigation bankers, private restoration companies that sell wetland and stream credits to section 404 permittees. It also included craft brewers, who noted that "quality beer requires clean water,"[43] perhaps to try to persuade Justice Kavanaugh, who spoke emotionally of his appreciation of the product during his contentious confirmation hearing. The briefs on the federal government's side uniformly warned that if the Court adopted Justice Scalia's *Rapanos* plurality opinion, such a constrained view of "waters of the United States" would frustrate the goals of the Clean Water Act.

The First Monday in October

The Supreme Court traditionally hears its first oral arguments of a new term on the first Monday in October. The opening session in Fall 2022 was particularly noteworthy. It was the first time the public could attend arguments since the start of the COVID-19 pandemic, when the Court shifted to arguments by phone.[44] It also was the first oral argument for Justice Ketanji Brown Jackson, whom President Biden had appointed to replace the retiring Justice Breyer. And *Sackett v. U.S. Environmental Protection Agency* was first on the docket.

Damien Schiff of the Pacific Legal Foundation, who had appeared on behalf of the Sackets in their first foray in the Supreme Court in 2012, once again took the lectern. He urged the Court to reject the significant nexus test, proffered by now-retired Justice Kennedy, who was in the courtroom but not on the bench with his former colleagues. Mr. Schiff instead advocated for a two-part test. First, to qualify as a water of the United States, an area must be a "water"—a site that is a hydrogeographic feature such as a stream, creek, river, or lake.[45] Second, the water must be navigable in fact.[46] Under this formulation, wetlands failed the initial step; they were not "waters" and thus were not worthy of Clean Water Act protection.

But a majority of the justices seemed to accept that Congress wanted some wetlands covered by the Clean Water Act. Much of the discussion focused on section 404(g)(1), which was added in the 1977 amendments. In that section, Congress explained in detail how a state could assume responsibility for the section 404 permit program but provided that the federal government would retain jurisdiction over certain waters. States could not take jurisdiction over traditional navigable waters, "including wetlands adjacent thereto."[47] Mr. Schiff argued that *adjacent* meant "abutting"—that the wetland must physically touch the other water.[48] The "touching" also needed to be on the surface (not through groundwater) and continuous (not intermittent), so much so that the wetlands were visually indistinguishable from the other water. When Justice Jackson asked whether this test would lead to debates in every future case about whether a wetland was visually indistinguishable, Mr. Schiff assured her that this would not be the result ("Absolutely not, your

Honor") and suggested that any such disputes would be minimal compared with what the significant nexus test had produced.[49]

Brian Fletcher of the Department of Justice's Office of the Solicitor General represented the agencies, and he opened by emphasizing that "everyone agrees that the waters protected by the Clean Water Act include some adjacent wetlands."[50] He characterized the agencies' use of the significant nexus test as "a limiting construction that ensures that the Act reaches only those wetlands" where "the federal interest is indisputable."[51] In response to Justice Kagan asking for the source of the significant nexus test, Mr. Fletcher pointed to the Court's own opinions in *Riverside Bayview Homes* and *Solid Waste Agency of Northern Cook County* (*SWANCC*), which contemplated jurisdiction over nonnavigable waters based on their effects on traditionally navigable waters. Some of the justices were clearly unconvinced. Justice Alito batted away the importance of the retained waters provision of section 404(g), saying that the Court was not interpreting that section but rather "that cryptic phrase, a strange phrase, 'waters of the United States.'"[52] Justice Gorsuch pushed for some bright line on adjacency: If the federal government doesn't know, he asked, how would the property owner, who could face criminal penalties for a Clean Water Act violation?[53] Justice Barrett also showed some sympathy for the beleaguered regulatory community, expressing concern about the cost of the Clean Water Act permitting process.[54]

At the conclusion of the oral arguments, it was unclear how the Court might rule. There appeared to be four votes for a narrow interpretation of the Clean Water Act (Alito, Thomas, Gorsuch, and Barrett) and four votes for a broader interpretation (Kagan, Sotomayor, Jackson, and, somewhat surprisingly, Kavanaugh, who exhibited the most familiarity with the regulatory history of waters of the United States[55]). That made Chief Justice Roberts the potential deciding vote. On one hand, he questioned the Sacketts' narrow interpretation of "adjacent," observing that a train station may be adjacent to train tracks without touching them.[56] On the other hand, he was skeptical of any test that might allow jurisdiction to be established by any hydrologic connection (although he phrased it as a "biological" or "ecological" connection[57]). Keep in mind, however, that the Chief Justice had joined Justice Scalia's plurality opinion in *Rapanos*, which suggested he would go along with Alito et al.

During oral argument, the agencies' attorney noted that the Biden administration was in the process of finalizing its WOTUS rulemaking. There was hope in some quarters that, if the Court was looking at another fractured opinion like *Rapanos*, the new rule might provide an excuse to dismiss *Sackett* as improvidently granted. The EPA and Corps issued the Biden rule at the end of 2022 and notified the Court of this development. When the Biden rule was subsequently enjoined in about half the states, the Court was similarly apprised of the situation. In the end, however, the Biden rule had no effect on the Court's decision but rather would be one of its casualties.

Sackett II: The Reckoning

Although *Sackett* was argued in October 2022, the Court did not render a decision until the end of May 2023, the longest delay between the opening argument of a term and the issuance of an opinion for at least the past twenty years.[58] The Court jettisoned the significant nexus test, but in doing so it also rejected the interpretations of eight administrations, disregarded its own precedents, and ignored basic science. News headlines noted that the Court was unanimous in striking down the significant nexus test,[59] but the details were more complex. In reality, it was a 5–4 decision. The majority, in an opinion written by Justice Alito and joined by Chief Justice Roberts and Justices Thomas, Gorsuch, and Barrett, adopted the *Rapanos* plurality's approach. Justice Thomas, with Justice Gorsuch, would have gone even further and penned a separate concurrence that advocated a more restrictive construction of the federal government's authority to regulate water pollution. Justice Kagan, joined by Justices Sotomayor and Jackson, filed an opinion that concurred in the judgment (i.e., agreed that the significant nexus test was not supported by the Clean Water Act's text) but opposed the adoption of the *Rapanos* plurality's approach. These three justices also signed on to Justice Kavanaugh's opinion concurring in the judgment, which was troubled by the majority's dismissal of forty-five years of administrative practice. Let's delve into each of the opinions.

Justice Alito's Majority Opinion: Mission Accomplished!

Justice Alito opened by acknowledging that the Clean Water Act has been a "great success" and that "many formerly fetid bodies of water" can now be safely used and enjoyed.[60] Before 1972, he noted that "existing federal legislation had proved to be inadequate."[61] However, he failed to acknowledge here that, before 1972, it was largely the responsibility of states to ensure water quality in the nation's waters. Left unsaid was that it was the failure of the states to adequately regulate polluters that resulted in the fetid waters. Instead, he quickly shifted to "an unfortunate footnote" to the Clean Water

Act's "success story": the definition of "waters of the United States."[62] Rather than recognizing that WOTUS is at the heart of the Clean Water Act—it is of course the waters that are deemed worthy of federal protection—he minimized it as a nagging concern, a mere footnote, a problem that needed to be resolved to provide clarity.

In Section I, Justice Alito again skipped over the failure of the states to regulate water pollution. He did note that "for most of this Nation's history," it was "almost entirely" the responsibility of the states and local governments to deal with water quality.[63] He recalled that, as the country's industry and population grew, so did water pollution, and the states responded with regulatory programs. The lack of effectiveness of these state efforts went unmentioned, however. Turning to the federal government and citing the Rivers and Harbors Act of 1899, he observed that early federal regulation was "largely limited to ensuring that 'traditional navigable waters'" were unimpeded.[64] (Here, he described traditional navigable waters as "interstate waters that were either navigable in fact and used in commerce or readily susceptible of being used in this way,"[65] leaving out waters that were once navigable, waters that would be navigable with reasonable improvements, and waters subject to the ebb and flow of the tide.) While minimizing the states' weak response to water pollution, he (correctly) characterized the Federal Water Pollution Control Act as "tepid." After the 1948 act (and amendments) resulted in few enforcement actions, Congress, in Justice Alito's words, "eventually replaced this scheme in 1972 with the CWA."[66]

Nowhere did Justice Alito explain *why* Congress overwhelmingly enacted the Clean Water Act—over a presidential veto. Nowhere does Justice Alito recount the nation's concern about environmental issues and water contamination that led Congress to totally restructure the Federal Water Pollution Control Act. Any concern about water quality or recognition of the success of the Clean Water Act was shunted off to the side, replaced with a concern about the breadth of the act. Justice Alito focused on the "capacious definition of 'pollutant'" and the "severe criminal penalties" that might be (but rarely are) imposed on Clean Water Act violators.[67] As an example of the broad reach of the law, he seemed to question why Congress included "mundane materials" such as rock and sand and cellar dirt as "pollutants."[68] Rock and sand discharged into waterbodies can affect water quality in a number of ways, including by causing sedimentation and, if used as fill, eliminating the waterbody entirely. Cellar dirt, if Justice Alito and his colleagues had bothered to look it up, refers to excavation and construction debris, such as broken concrete.[69] But such details were irrelevant as Justice Alito executed a rhetorical shift from the Clean Water Act as a success story to the Clean Water Act as a potent weapon wielded against regulated parties. And, at the center of this "persistent problem" was the definition of *waters of the United States.*

In Justice Alito's telling of the tale, private property rights were at risk because of federal overreach. Entities engaging in activities that degraded water quality were not called polluters; rather, they were lauded as "landowners." Of course, a landowner can be a polluter, but Justice Alito's attention was squarely on a landowner's ability to use its property as it wanted. "What are landowners to do if they want to build on their property?," he plaintively asked.[70] He bemoaned the fact that landowners often received "adverse jurisdictional determinations"—that is, a determination that the water in question was subject to the Clean Water Act. But that is not a death sentence for private property rights. A jurisdictional determination does not mean the landowner cannot proceed with its proposed project and must allow the property to remain idle. Indeed, to the dismay of the environmental community, most Clean Water Act section 404 applications are granted. Indeed, in *Riverside Bayview Homes*, the Court unanimously rejected the notion that the mere classification of a water as a water of the United States constituted a taking of private property for which just compensation was due under the Fifth Amendment.[71] Why not? The *Riverside Bayview Homes* Court suggested the reasons were "obvious"—requiring "that a person obtain a permit before engaging in a certain use of his or her property does not, itself, 'take' the property in any sense: after all, the very existence of a permit system implies that permission may be granted, leaving the landowner free to use the property as desired."[72] In Justice Alito's world, however, instead of seeking a permit to discharge pollutants, "many landowners . . . would simply choose to build nothing."[73] Justice Alito provided no citation to support this claim.

To ascertain the meaning of *waters of the United States*, Justice Alito began with the text of the Clean Water Act. He complained that Congress's use of the term was a "frustrating drafting choice" that was "not a well-known term of art."[74] (Recall, however, that Congress did previously use the phrase "any waters of the United States, either navigable or otherwise" in the 1938 Water Pollution Act, which FDR vetoed.) Like the plurality in *Rapanos*, he analyzed the term by looking at individual parts, starting with "waters." "Waters" does not mean all water—instead, it includes "only those relatively permanent, standing or continuously flowing bodies of water forming geographical features that are described in ordinary parlance as streams, oceans, rivers, and lakes."[75] Notably absent from this definition of "waters" are wetlands.

Justice Alito's source for this definition of "waters" was dictionaries. But like litigants who forum shop and file in specific courts likely to yield a sympathetic judge, Justice Alito engaged in "dictionary shopping," searching for a dictionary that would support his policy preference of excluding wetlands and other waters. As the *Rapanos* plurality had done, he chose *Webster's Second*, published in 1954, to provide the desired meaning. A later edition, *Webster's Third*, published in 1961, offered a more expansive definition of waters. This inconvenient source was just ignored, however. Instead, Justice Alito also invoked a 1979 edition of *Black's Law Dictionary* and a 1987 edition of *Random House Dictionary*.[76] Perhaps these dictionaries were readily available on the Justice's bookshelf, but they shed little or no light on the meaning of a term used by the Congress that enacted the Clean Water Act in 1972.

Justice Alito then turned to the concept of navigability. Grudgingly conceding that the Clean Water Act "extends to more than traditional navigable waters," he noted that the Court in *SWANCC* had "refused to read 'navigable' out of the statute."[77] Accordingly, Justice Alito stated that Congress's use of *navigable* indicated that WOTUS "principally refers to bodies of navigable water like rivers, lakes, and oceans."[78] Note that streams had been dropped from the list of traditional navigable waters.

Justice Alito claimed that his emphasis on traditional navigable waters was consistent with how Congress used the term *waters* elsewhere in the Clean Water Act, and the first citation to support this conclusion was a reference to "the waters of the Chesapeake Bay."[79] This provision, which was added as part of the Estuaries and Clean Waters Act of 2000,[80] does not directly inform about the term's meaning in 1972. Regardless, Justice Alito neglected to offer any context. In the 2000 law, Congress requested the EPA to conduct a study of the Chesapeake Bay ecosystem to recommend management responses to improve water quality. Congress defined the "Chesapeake Bay ecosystem" as "the ecosystem of the Chesapeake Bay and its watershed" and referenced the "Chesapeake Bay Agreement," which had as its goal "restoring and protecting the Chesapeake Bay ecosystem."[81] The Chesapeake Bay Agreement, which was signed by the District of Columbia; the states of Maryland, Pennsylvania, and Virginia; and the federal government (with EPA Administrator Carol Browner's signature), four months before Congress amended the Clean Water Act, had an entire section devoted to wetlands.[82] The district, states, and the federal government pledged to "achieve a no-net loss of existing wetlands acreage and function in the signatories' regulatory programs."[83] Thus Congress clearly considered protection of wetlands to be an intrinsic part of the overall objective of the Clean Water Act. The "waters of the Chesapeake Bay" reference did not support Justice Alito's cramped interpretation of "waters." If anything, it contradicted him: Congress (in 2000) was concerned about the broader Chesapeake Bay ecosystem, which expressly included nonnavigable wetlands.

The biggest hurdle for Justice Alito for reading wetlands out of the Clean Water Act was Clean Water Act section 404(g), which Congress had added in 1977. The amendment allowed states to assume responsibility for permitting the discharge of dredged or fill material into waters of the United States, but the states could not take over with respect to traditional navigable waters and adjacent wetlands. The federal government would retain jurisdiction over

> those waters which are presently used, or are susceptible to use in their natural condition or by reasonable improvement as a means to transport interstate or foreign commerce shoreward to their ordinary high water mark, including all waters which are subject to the ebb and flow of the tide shoreward to their mean high water mark, or mean higher high water mark on the west coast, *including wetlands adjacent thereto*.[84]

Thus, Congress expressly, in the words of the statute, stated that at least some wetlands were protected by the Clean Water Act. And the responsibility for section 404 permitting for some wetlands could not be delegated to the states, which could suggest that the states may take over permitting for nonadjacent wetlands.

To interpret this provision, Justice Alito resorted to a mathematical equation (or perhaps a Venn diagram).[85] Under his approach, WOTUS was category A. Category B was traditional navigable waters, a subset of category A. And category C was adjacent wetlands, a subset of category B. Expressed in an equation, the waters that states could assume is A minus B. C is irrelevant because it is part of B. Expressed visually, the interpretation might appear as in Figure 12-1.

Justice Kavanaugh politely referred to this interpretation as "unorthodox."[86] Justice Kagan suggested that "the majority could use every letter of the alphabet, and graduate to quadratic equations, and still not solve its

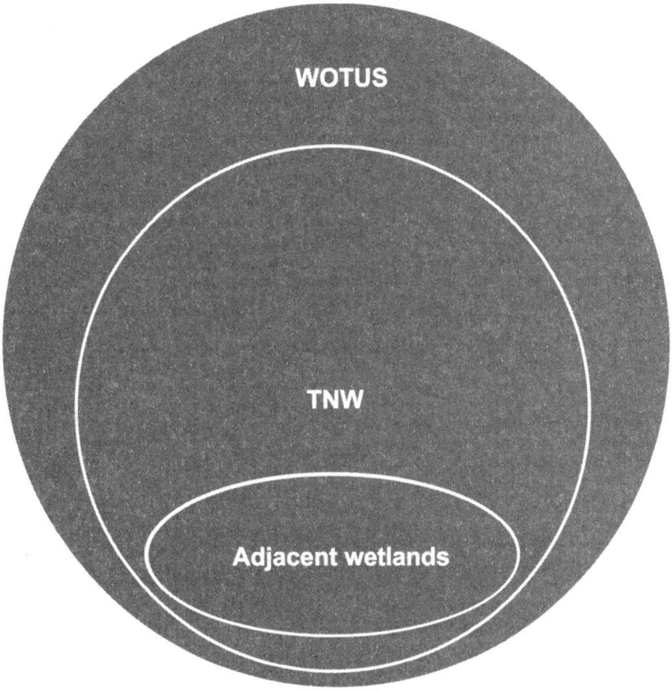

Figure 12-1. The Court's higher math: "A minus B, which includes C," where A is WOTUS, B is traditional navigable waters (TNW), and C is adjacent wetlands.

essential problem."[87] What did adjacent mean? What wetlands (and other waters) did Congress want to protect under the Clean Water Act?

Justice Alito noted that *adjacent* could mean "contiguous" or "near," citing three dictionaries.[88] He concluded that the use of the term *adjacent* was a mere reflection of "Congress's assumption that certain 'adjacent' wetlands are *part of* 'waters of the United States.'" To be part of a WOTUS, a wetland needed to touch or physically abut that larger waterbody.

In the end, Justice Alito simply fell back on the *Rapanos* plurality opinion. Wetlands were not streams, rivers, lakes, or oceans and thus were not waters. Consequently, a wetland could be considered a "water of the United States" only when it has "a continuous surface connection to bodies that are 'waters of the United States' in their own right, so that there is no clear demarcation between 'waters' and wetlands."[89] Wetlands with a continuous surface connection are protected by the Clean Water Act only if they are "as a practical matter indistinguishable from waters of the United States," such that it is "difficult to determine where the 'water' ends and the 'wetland' begins."[90]

As a practical matter, *Sackett* ends the federal regulation of nontidal wetlands, at least for the moment. As the *amicus* brief for the scientific societies explained, the continuous surface connection requirement removed about half of all wetlands from Clean Water Act coverage.[91] The "difficult to determine" test, however, was the coup de grâce. Because the boundary between most wetlands and another body of water can be delineated, it is almost never too difficult to tell where the wetland ends and the other water begins.[92] States and local governments would not only have "primary" responsibility for protecting these waters, they would be solely responsible. But no worries. Justice Alito assured us that "States can and will continue to exercise their primary authority to combat water pollution by regulating land and water use."[93] He unironically cited the *amicus* brief for the 20 farm bureaus for this proposition.

Justice Thomas's Concurrence: A Selective History Lesson

Whereas Justice Alito identified the "problem" in *Sackett* as uncertainty for polluters, Justice Thomas had larger concerns. Although he fully joined Justice Alito's majority opinion, he wrote a separate concurrence to rail against the Court's New Deal commerce clause jurisprudence and questioned whether, as a constitutional matter, the federal government could have an expansive role in environmental protection. Justice Gorsuch joined this concurrence.

Justice Thomas recounted that, at least since *Gibbons v. Ogden*, all had understood that Congress could regulate navigable waters under its commerce clause powers.[94] However, Justice Thomas viewed Congress's power to be limited in two important respects. First, Congress could regulate the nation's rivers, which served as highways for interstate commerce, only because they were channels of interstate commerce. He rejected the Court's later interpretation of the commerce clause to allow Congress (and the agencies) to regulate activities that individually or cumulatively affected interstate commerce (such as growing your own wheat or medical marijuana).[95] Second, he boldly asserted that in exercising its authority over navigable waters as channels of interstate commerce, "Congress could regulate such waters only for purposes of their navigability—by, for example, regulating obstructions hindering navigable capacity."[96] This suggested that Congress could not regulate water pollution, except perhaps to the extent that it interfered with navigation.

Justice Thomas ignored that Congress had long regulated activities on navigable waters that had no direct connection to keeping the rivers free of obstructions. Recall that concerns about steamboat safety led to federal laws in 1838 and 1852 that required steamboats on navigable waters of the United States to be inspected and operate with a federal license. One assumes that Congress passed such safety laws not because it was merely concerned that the wreckage and body count from exploding steamboats would unduly interfere with the transport of goods. The Supreme Court upheld the constitutionality of these safety laws in the 1870 case of *The Daniel Ball*, finding that the Grand River was navigable.[97]

Yet Justice Thomas invoked *Daniel Ball* as a limitation on Congress's commerce clause powers. In *Daniel Ball*, the Court concluded that waters are navigable in fact if they are, were, are susceptible to being used "as highways for commerce." According to Justice Thomas, this pronouncement was the extent of Congress's authority, and Congress legislated against this backdrop and limitation.[98] Whether Congress used the term *navigable waters* or *navigable waters of the United States* or *waters of the United States*, it all meant the same thing to Justice Thomas: "shorthand for waters subject to Congress's authority under the *Daniel Ball* test."[99] But Justice Thomas did acknowledge in a footnote that Congress departed from this traditional meaning a number of times: in the 1920 Federal Power Act, the 1948 Federal Water Pollution Control Act, and the Water Quality Act of 1965.[100] (He did not mention the 1938 Water Pollution Act passed by Congress.) If *Daniel Ball* was truly a limitation on legislative action, Congress did not seem to be aware of it.

Conflating "waters of the United States" with *Daniel Ball* waters was a neat trick. It allowed Justice Thomas to ignore the House and Senate's competing definitions of "navigable waters" in the bill that would become the Clean Water Act. There was then no need for him to grapple with the 1972 Conference Report that explained that the "conferees fully intend[ed] that the term 'navigable waters' be given the broadest possible constitutional interpretation unencumbered by agency determinations which have been made or may be made for administrative purposes." If the Clean Water Act's use of the term *waters of the United States* was simply a reflection of *Daniel Ball* waters, why did Congress bother to debate the issue and discuss it in the Conference Report?

Ultimately, Justice Thomas takes issue with the administrative state, which he views as beyond constitutional bounds. The Clean Water Act is just a symptom "of deeper problems with the Court's Commerce Clause jurisprudence."[101] Citing his dissent in *Gonzales v. Raich*, the medical marijuana case, he posited that the original meaning of commerce is "selling, buying, and bartering, as well as transporting for these purposes."[102] The acts of farming, mining, and manufacturing in and of themselves thus do not fall under the definition of commerce. If these views ever commanded a majority of the Court, nearly all federal environmental laws that regulated polluters would be rendered unconstitutional.

Justice Kagan: The Dissent That Wasn't

Justice Kagan, joined by Justices Sotomayor and Jackson, criticized the Court for rewriting Congress's landmark legislation. She emphasized that the 1972 Congress was responding to a "crisis" and that Congress's complete rewriting of the Federal Water Pollution Control Act had been effective. She pointedly noted,

> If you've lately swum in a lake, happily drunk a glass of water straight from the tap, or sat down to a good fish dinner, you can appreciate what the law has accomplished.[103]

Justice Kagan recognized that wetlands contribute to water quality, citing *Riverside Bayview Homes* and explained that wetlands do not need a continuous surface connection with larger waterbodies to perform this and other functions.[104]

She closed her opinion by referencing her dissent from *West Virginia v. Environmental Protection Agency* the previous term:

> So I'll conclude, sadly, by repeating what I wrote last year, with the replacement of only a single word. "[T]he Court substitutes its own ideas about policymaking for Congress's. The Court will not allow the Clean [Water] Act to work as Congress instructed. The Court, rather than Congress, will decide how much regulation is too much."[105]

Her *Sackett* opinion reads like a vigorous dissent, yet Justice Kagan awkwardly concurred in the judgment of the Court. A concurrence in the judgment means that the justice agreed with the outcome (in this case, reversal of the Ninth Circuit) but not the reasoning (adoption of the *Rapanos* plurality's test). Although Justice Kagan explained why she found the majority's reasoning unsound, she did not offer her own test or interpretation that ought to be applied. Moreover, since Justice Kagan dissented in *West Virginia* (and invoked it), why did she not also dissent in *Sackett*? A possible explanation is that she (and Justices Sotomayor and Jackson) wanted to support Justice Kavanaugh, who wrote a separate concurrence.[106] If they had formally dissented, they would not have been able to join Justice Kavanaugh's opinion.

Justice Kavanaugh: Adjacent versus Adjoining

Justice Kavanaugh agreed with Justice Alito and the majority that the significant nexus test should not be used to determine whether a wetland qualifies as a water of the United States.[107] And he agreed that the Sacketts should be able to build on their property unencumbered by the Clean Water Act. But he sharply disagreed with the majority's interpretation of the statutory term *adjacent*.

In Justice Kavanaugh's view, the majority's continuous surface connection requirement had improperly conflated *adjoining* and *adjacent*.[108] Citing multiple dictionaries, including a 1968 edition of *Black Law's Dictionary* and *Webster's Third*, he noted that *adjoining* means "touching," whereas *adjacent* is broader and can mean "near (but not necessarily touching)".[109] *Adjoining* is actually a subset of *adjacent*. Thus, he explained that, in the Clean Water Act context, *adjoining* and *adjacent* have separate meanings:

> Adjoining wetlands are contiguous to or bordering a covered water, whereas adjacent wetlands include both (i) those wetlands contiguous to or bordering a covered water, and (ii) wetlands separated from a covered water only by a man-made dike or barrier, natural river berm, beach dune, or the like.[110]

Justice Kavanaugh emphasized that the majority's view of *adjacent* to mean *adjoining* or *abutting* was inconsistent with forty-five years of executive branch interpretations, spanning eight administrations, from Carter to Biden.[111] All these administrations—even the Trump administration—had interpreted *adjacent wetlands* to include wetlands that did not have a continuous surface connection with a covered water. Now, however, the Court had declared such an approach to be contrary to the Clean Water Act itself.

The bottom line: All nine justices agreed on jettisoning the significant nexus test. It was rejected in Alito's majority opinion, which was joined by Roberts, Thomas, Gorsuch, and Barrett, and in Kavanaugh's concurring opinion, which was joined by Kagan, Sotomayor, and Jackson. The majority made it clear that it is the Court that decides the meaning of *waters of the United States*. There is no deference to the executive branch agencies that Congress charged with implementing the Clean Water Act and nary a mention of *Chevron*. In the majority's view, waters of the United States are only the relatively permanent, standing, or continuously flowing bodies of water forming geographic features, such as streams, oceans, rivers, and lakes. Wetlands qualify only if they have a continuous surface connection to the stream, ocean, river, or lake, such that it is difficult to determine where the water ends and the wetland begins. The majority did not see fit to cite the overall objective of the Clean Water Act contained in section 101(a): to restore and maintain the chemical, physical, and biological integrity of the nation's waters.

The Impact of *Sackett*

Brenda Mallory, chair of the White House Council on Environmental Quality under the Biden administration, called *Sackett* "one of the largest judicial rollbacks of environmental protections in U.S. history."[112] In contrast, Zippy Duvall, president of the American Farm Bureau Federation, viewed it as "a massive win for farmers, ranchers, and property owners all across the country."[113] They were both right, although the victory for farmers, ranchers, and property owners will be short-term to the extent that reduced water quality and flood protection affect them.

The EPA estimates that "117 million people, over one third of the total U.S. population, get some or all of their drinking water from public drinking water systems that rely at least in part on intermittent, ephemeral, or headwater streams."[114] Indeed, 58 percent of streams that contribute to public water drinking systems are intermittent, ephemeral, or headwater streams.[115] Although *Sackett* was a wetland case, it has serious implications for other waters such as streams. The Court's declaration that "waters," for purposes of the Clean Water Act, must be relatively permanent, standing, or continuously flowing eliminates protections for ephemeral streams. By definition, ephemeral streams do not continuously flow; they are driven by precipitation events.[116] Ephemeral streams, which make up about 18 percent of all streams in the United States, are no longer protected by the Clean Water Act.[117]

Sackett also calls into question whether, and to what extent, the EPA and the Corps may protect intermittent streams. By definition, intermittent streams, which make up about half of all streams in the United States, also do not continuously flow.[118] Although the *Rapanos* plurality expressly discussed intermittent streams, the *Sackett* majority did not. In a footnote in *Rapanos*, Justice Scalia wrote that the "relatively permanent" test did "necessarily exclude *seasonal* rivers, which contain continuous flow during some months of the year but no flow during dry months."[119] He did not see the need to provide clarity on that point, other than observing that "channels containing permanent flow are plainly within the definition, and that . . . 'intermittent' . . . streams, . . . that is, streams whose flow is 'coming and going at intervals . . . broken, fitful,' . . . are not."[120] Justice Scalia relied on his trusty *Webster's Second* for the definition of *intermittent*.

In *Sackett*, the Court did not directly address the issue of intermittent waters. It made no mention of "seasonal rivers" and did not attempt to define *intermittent*. However, the coverage of intermittent streams will no doubt be fleshed out by the agencies and litigated in the courts, as members of the regulated community seek greater freedom from regulation—that is, the freedom to pollute unimpeded by federal agencies.

On the matter of wetlands, the *Sackett* Court was much clearer: A continuous surface connection between the wetland and a water of the United States is required. In his concurrence, Justice Kavanaugh pointed out that this mandate would eliminate protection over wetlands adjacent to, but separated by levees from, the Mississippi River, "even though the adjacent wetlands are often an important part of the flood-control project."[121] He also noted that "federal protection of the Chesapeake Bay might be less effective if fill can be dumped into wetlands that are adjacent to (but not adjoining) the bay and its covered tributaries."[122] The EPA announced that, as a result of *Sackett*, up to 63 percent of the nation's wetlands would no longer be covered by the Clean Water Act.[123]

But it's much worse than that. Most of the post-*Sackett* analysis of its impact on wetland jurisdiction focused solely on the continuous surface requirement and neglected to consider the "indistinguishable" requirement: Wetlands are covered only if they are "as a practical matter indistinguishable from waters of the United States," such that it is "difficult to determine where the 'water' ends and the 'wetland' begins." The "indistinguishable" requirement is not mere rhetorical flourish; it is referenced twice as part of the Court's holding.[124] When that part of the test is factored in, *Sackett* is extinction-level event for federal protection of most wetlands.

To be sure, tidal wetlands should still be under the Clean Water Act's umbrella. But it is difficult to see how most other wetlands could qualify as a water of the United States. Justice Kavanaugh suggested that the Court's holding would lead to further uncertainty, asking whether "a continuous surface connection [could] be established by a ditch, swale, pipe, or culvert?"[125] The answer is no. The wetland might have a hydrologic connection to the larger waterbody, but if it is on the other side of the ditch, swale, pipe, or culvert, it should be rather easy to distinguish between the wetland and the other water. And, if so, then the wetland is not a water of the United States.

Council on Environmental Quality chair Brenda Mallory stated that the first key "to winning the fight for clean water in this country, in the wake of the *Sackett* decision" is "to be honest, clear, vocal, and visual about the impact of the Supreme Court's ruling."[126] An honest appraisal of *Sackett* means taking the Supreme Court at its word and applying the "indistinguishable" requirement. Several groups are doing so, and the results are bracing. An initial analysis by Wisconsin's Green Fire found that 88 percent of the state's wetlands (5.6 million out of 6.4 million acres) are not waters of the United States.[127] Five million of those acres support fish and wildlife habitat, 4.4 million acres perform a flood control function, and 3.7 million acres help filter pollutants.[128] Similarly, St. Mary's University found that 88.4 percent of New Mexico's wetlands are not jurisdictional under *Sackett*, as well as more than 95 percent of its streams and rivers.[129] A study of south Florida watersheds determined that nearly 98 percent of nontidal, freshwater wetlands are potentially not protected by the Clean Water Act (Figures 12-2 and 12-3).[130]

Some commentators have suggested that the concern about *Sackett* is exaggerated and that wetlands can still be protected under the Supreme Court's decision in *County of Maui v. Hawaii Wildlife Fund*.[131] However, that conclusion is a misreading of *County of Maui*. Under *County of Maui*, if a person discharges a pollutant to a wetland and the pollutant reaches a traditional navigable water, a Clean Water Act permit is required, if the discharge is a functional equivalent of a direct discharge to that traditional navigable water. Wetlands themselves are not protected. The wetland is relevant only as a conduit of a pollutant. But the most common pollutant discharged into wetlands is fill material, most of which remains in place, which is the purpose of fill material. Consequently, the filling of wetlands typically does not result in the functional equivalent of a direct discharge. Wetlands are filled and lost without triggering the Clean Water Act.

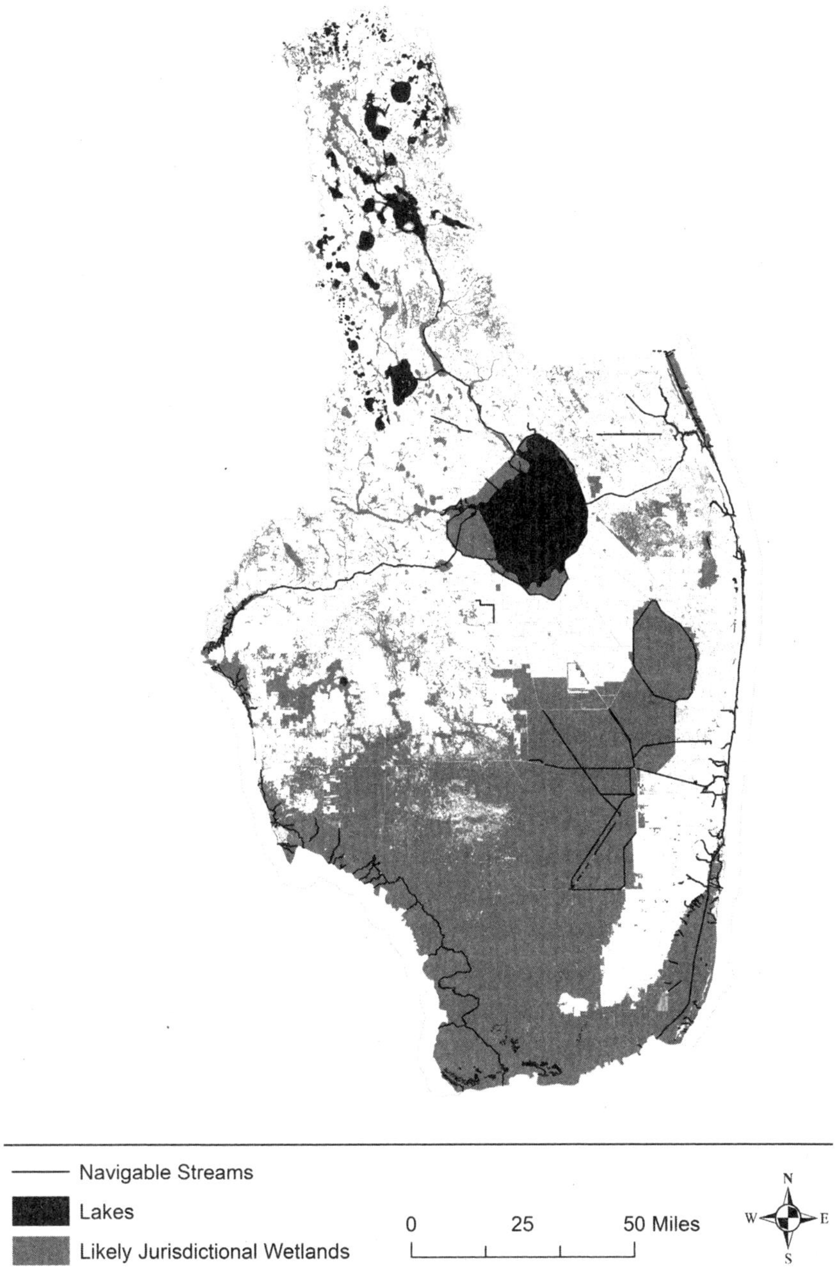

Figure 12-2. Jurisdictional wetlands in the Greater Everglades watershed under the pre-2015 regime, pre-Sackett (wetland polygons within the National Wetlands Inventory showing a "significant nexus" to navigable channels, lakes, and marine waters). Source: Analysis and cartography by Olusola Adetoro and Jason Evans, Stetson University.

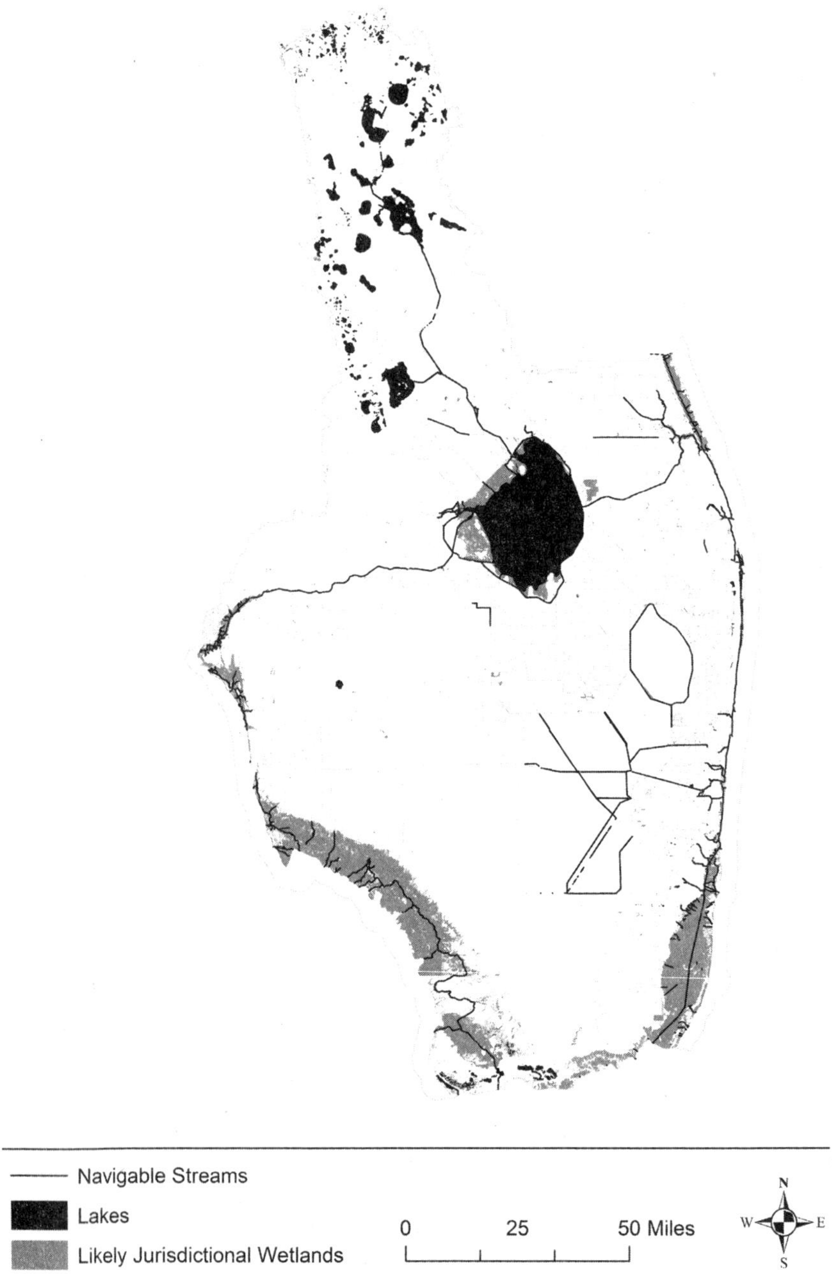

Figure 12-3. Jurisdictional wetlands in the Greater Everglades watershed, post-Sackett (wetland polygons within the National Wetlands Inventory that show "continuous" surface connection to navigable channels, lakes, and marine waters). Source: Analysis and cartography by Olusola Adetoro and Jason Evans, Stetson University.

Playing the Hand They Were Dealt

Although the Biden administration's WOTUS rule was not directly challenged in *Sackett*, it was a casualty of the decision. The Biden rule relied in part on the significant nexus test, which the Court specifically rejected. Accordingly, the EPA and the Corps stated that it would amend the Biden rule to make it consistent with *Sackett*.

The agencies announced the conforming rule on August 29, 2023.[132] The new rule renounced all references to the significant nexus test with respect to tributaries, wetlands, and other waters. It jettisoned interstate wetlands from the interstate waters provision. And it revised the definition of *adjacent* to mean a continuous surface connection. However, the agencies provided no details about the meaning of a continuous surface connection.

The new rule was published on September 8, 2023, and became effective the same day—all without the opportunity for the public to provide any input.[133] To avoid the Administrative Procedure Act's notice and comment requirements, the agencies cited the act's good cause exception. The agencies explained that they were merely doing what the Supreme Court had commanded, and public comment was therefore unnecessary.[134] The agencies had no choice or flexibility—they were merely playing the hand they were dealt.

However, the agencies chose not to deal with the "indistinguishable" requirement. Perhaps they thought that if they addressed this issue they would need to open up the process for public comment, which would take time. Or perhaps they hoped that the "indistinguishable" requirement was just rhetoric that could be safely ignored. But the lower courts, which are bound by Supreme Court precedent, and the regulated community, which will forever seek to limit federal oversight, will embrace it. Not surprisingly, in December 2023, in *Lewis v. United States*, the Fifth Circuit Court of Appeals invoked the requirement, concluding that "it is not difficult to determine where the 'water' ends and any 'wetlands' on Lewis's property begin," relying in part on photographs.[135] At some point, the agencies will be forced to reckon more directly with the Court's unscientific pronouncement about the aquatic environment.

Thus ends our journey examining the flow and ebb of federal efforts to protect the waters of the United States. It began with protecting navigable waters as arteries of interstate commerce. The federal government's initial focus was on promoting navigation, while the states were responsible for maintaining water quality. Despite prodding and financial assistance from the federal government, the states failed to regulate water pollution. (Even Justice Alito acknowledged the "fetid water" during this era.) In 1972, Congress responded by enacting landmark legislation that restructured federal and state responsibilities for protecting the nation's waters. The Clean Water Act opens with a singular objective: to restore and maintain the integrity of the nation's waters. To meet this goal, it prohibits the unpermitted discharge of pollutants to navigable waters, defined as "waters of the United States." States could assume permitting responsibility, but if they chose not to, then the feds would step in. The EPA and the Corps of Engineers, through a series of rulemakings, defined "waters of the United States" consistent with the philosophy of the president in office, with jurisdiction reaching its apex under the Obama administration's Clean Water Rule and receding under the Trump administration's Navigable Waters Protection Rule.

In *Sackett*, the Supreme Court reset the playing field, kicking the federal government out of the game, at least for certain types of waters, such as ephemeral streams and almost all freshwater wetlands. The five-justice majority emphasized that the federal government's role in protecting waters beyond traditional navigable waters is extremely limited, at least under the Clean Water Act as currently written. What options are left for clean water advocates? They will have to play both offense and defense, at multiple levels of government, as discussed in the next chapter.

CHAPTER 13

Navigating the Legal Shoals

> The vote is a power, a weapon of offense and defense, a prayer.
>
> —Carrie Chapman Catt (1920)

With a 5–4 vote, SCOTUS scuttled WOTUS. Millions of acres of wetlands and millions of miles of streams have been stripped of federal protection. The Clean Water Act's objective to restore and maintain the integrity of the nation's waters is now less a goal and more an unanswered prayer. The Supreme Court will not reverse itself. Congress has the ability to remedy the matter but currently lacks the will. Executive branch agencies find themselves constrained by judicial decisions.

Nevertheless, some federal tools remain available—in both regulatory and nonregulatory settings. To a large extent, however, efforts to protect water quality need to be focused at the state and local level. Clean water advocates must play both offense and defense, trying to strengthen water protections while being mindful of attempts to further erode them.

Ultimately, it comes down to whom we elect for federal, state, and local offices. Suffragist Carrie Chapman Catt, founder of the League of Women Voters, recognized the importance of voting. Her statement made on the occasion of the ratification of the Nineteenth Amendment is no less true today. The most effective way to ensure clean water for our current and future generations is to elect leaders who share that value.

Playing Offense (at the Federal Level)

Occasionally, when the composition of the Supreme Court changes, it will overrule its prior decisions when they involve a constitutional matter. For example, as noted in Chapter 2, the Court reversed itself with respect to whether the commerce clause gives Congress the authority to regulate child labor. Initially the Court held no, but then it said yes. More recently, we have seen the Court overrule *Roe v. Wade*, kicking the issue of abortion rights to the states. In *Sackett*, however, the Court was interpreting a statute, not the Constitution. Accordingly, even if the Court's composition changes, it will not revisit the *Sackett* decision. It is up to Congress to correct the Court's erroneous statutory interpretations.

But *Sackett* also placed some constraints on Congress when it legislates in a manner that affects the balance between the federal government and the states or when it affects private property rights. The Court emphasized that Congress must use "exceedingly clear language" when doing so. This suggests that the Court is wary of Congress simply giving the agencies wide discretion to regulate to achieve broad goals and is consistent with the Court's evolving thinking on the nondelegation principle. An even more significant threat to Congress's authorities is Justice Thomas's fever dream of revisiting the definition of *commerce*, although at present this view has garnered only one other vote.

The Court has also limited what the executive branch agencies can do. In *Sackett*, there was no hint of deference to the EPA's judgment. Instead of acknowledging the agency's "technical expertise," as the Court had done unanimously in *Riverside Bayview Homes*, the *Sackett* Court referred to the agency biologists as "field agents," evoking images of overly aggressive law enforcement personnel. The notion of *Chevron* deference, upholding an agency's reasonable interpretation of ambiguous statutory terms, was conspicuous by its absence, and the Court is poised to overrule or substantially limit *Chevron*. The Court is asserting its authority to say what the law is.

But there are still actions that Congress and the agencies can take to protect the quality of the nation's waters. Let's consider affirmative steps that are still available at the federal level.

- **Congress can amend the Clean Water Act and clarify the parameters of "waters of the United States."** Congress has previously spoken clearly when defining the scope of federal jurisdiction over waters. Recall, for example, the lengthy definition of navigable waters in the Federal Water Power Act (noted in Chapter 3). A bill to essentially overrule *Sackett* has been introduced, but of course this Congress, which voted to disapprove the Biden WOTUS rule, will not be receptive.
- **Congress could assert its authority to protect traditional navigable waters from nonpoint source pollution.** A more ambitious step for Congress would be to rewrite the Clean Water Act to assert the federal interest in combatting nonpoint source pollution. The responsibility for nonpoint source pollution currently lies with the states. Frequent outbreaks of harmful algal blooms in traditionally navigable waters and the dead zone in the Gulf of Mexico demonstrate the states'

failure in this regard. At some point, the harmful algal blooms may be a clarion call, similar to the fires on the Cuyahoga River that were an impetus for the Clean Water Act in 1972. Because any such congressional action would be tied to protecting traditional navigable waters, it should pass constitutional muster. Still, the agricultural lobby and the regulated community would fight this effort to the death.

- **The EPA and the Corps can aggressively protect intermittent streams.** Under *Sackett*, the Clean Water Act covers only waters that are "relatively permanent, standing or continuously flowing." Perennial nonnavigable tributaries of traditional navigable waters are still protected, but ephemeral streams are clearly not. What about intermittent tributaries? The pre-2015 regime, the Obama Clean Water Rule, the initial Biden WOTUS rule, and even the Trump Navigable Waters Protection Rule all covered intermittent tributaries. The rule issued to conform with *Sackett* leaves it an open question, however. (Neither the conforming rule nor its preamble mentions intermittent tributaries.) Yet more than a century ago, in *United States v. Rio Grande Dam & Irrigation Company* (discussed in Chapter 3), the Supreme Court held that Congress's authority to protect traditional navigable waters extended to activities taking place on nonnavigable tributaries. The agencies should conduct a notice and comment rulemaking to clarify that they intend to regulate discharges of pollutants to intermittent streams. In the meantime, they should assert jurisdiction on a case-by-case basis, as the EPA did (preliminarily) in November 2023 regarding stormwater discharges from Los Alamos National Laboratory and Los Alamos County that reached the Rio Grande.[1]
- **The EPA should lean heavily into *County of Maui*'s functional equivalency test.** In *County of Maui* (discussed in Chapter 11), the Court held that, under certain circumstances, the point source discharge of a pollutant to a non-WOTUS (groundwater in that case) requires a Clean Water Act permit if the pollutant reaches a WOTUS (the Pacific Ocean). Whether a permit is needed depends on whether the discharge of the pollutant is the functional equivalent of a direct discharge to a WOTUS, which is largely but not exclusively a function of transit time and distance. Note, however, that *County of Maui* is not a complete gap filler. As an initial matter, the functional equivalent test will probably be applied after the fact—that is, after the pollutant has reached and damaged a traditional navigable water.

Moreover, the non-WOTUS that initially received the pollutant is not being protected for its contributions to maintaining the integrity of the nation's waters; rather, its relevance is that is a mere conduit to a larger body of water. Finally, most wetlands can be filled without implicating *County of Maui*. If done properly, the fill should remain in place, eliminating the wetland, without resulting in the functional equivalent of a direct discharge to other waters.

- **Federal agencies should rely on statutes other than the Clean Water Act to protect water quality.** Some of these statutory authorities have a direct connection to water quality, such as the Safe Drinking Water Act. As federal protections under the Clean Water Act recede, these statutes will become even more important. The Safe Drinking Water Act contemplates protecting source waters, including streams and other waters that may not qualify as WOTUS, through cooperative efforts by the EPA, states, local utilities, tribal authorities, and other stakeholders. Other statutes may not have a direct water focus but nevertheless can be used to protect waters as, for example, wildlife habitat. More rigorous enforcement of the Endangered Species Act and the Migratory Bird Treaty Act regarding aquatic and wetland-dependent species can lead to greater protection of aquatic ecosystems.
- **Congress and the federal agencies should explore constitutional authorities, besides the authority to regulate interstate commerce, to protect water quality, including powers related to spending, public lands, and treaties.** Although Congress invoked the commerce clause as the basis to enact the Clean Water Act, other constitutional provisions can be used to promote water quality.[2] Through the spending clause, for example, Congress could condition the receipt of federal funds or federal projects (such as beach renourishment) to commitments from state and local governments to regulate water pollution and to protect waters that no longer qualify as WOTUS. In a similar vein, the Department of Housing and Urban Development has proposed a rule to limit its assistance for new construction that directly or indirectly damages wetlands.[3] The authority to protect public lands is another possible fruitful mechanism. Indeed, a lawsuit brought on behalf of the National Park Service against the state of Florida for its failure to regulate water quality entering Everglades National Park eventually led to the development of the Comprehensive Everglades Restoration Plan.[4] The treaty power

can also be a basis for congressional and agency action, with migratory bird treaties and the Ramsar Convention offering a means to promote the protection of wetlands.[5]

- **The federal government should continue to maintain and increase financial incentives for stream and wetland restoration.** Nonregulatory programs such as the Agricultural Conservation Easement Program,[6] where farmers are compensated to implement conservation measures, including restoring wetlands and protecting streams, have shown that the carrot is sometimes more effective than the stick. Congress should continue to fully fund these efforts, but the US Department of Agriculture should do a better job of monitoring and ensuring that the taxpayers and the public are receiving the benefits for which they are paying.[7]
- **Congress and the federal agencies should eliminate subsidies that support activities harmful to water quality.** For many years, the federal government encouraged and subsidized farmers to drain wetlands to put those areas into agricultural production. Beginning in 1985, however, through legislation known as Swampbuster, a dramatic shift occurred: Farmers would be penalized if they converted wetlands.[8] They would be ineligible for federal loans, subsidized insurance, and price and income supports. As a result of Swampbuster (and the Wetland Reserve Program and related efforts), wetland losses due to agriculture declined significantly. Some harmful agricultural subsidies continue, however. For example, ethanol subsidies encourage farmers to remove land in conservation programs to plant corn.[9] These taxpayer-funded payments should be phased out and eliminated. (Perhaps eliminating the primacy of the Iowa caucuses in the presidential nominating process will lessen the agricultural lobby's oversized influence.) Of course, farmers are not alone in accepting federal largesse. There is no good reason for the federal government to be subsidizing flood insurance that encourages development in floodplains, for example.[10]

Playing Offense (at the State, Tribal, and Local Levels)

The Supreme Court's decision in *Sackett* dealt only with the authority of the federal government under the Clean Water Act. It did not prevent state, tribal, and local authorities from regulating activities affecting waters within their jurisdictions. States continue to have the general police power to regulate conduct within their borders. Tribes generally have the same authority, and local governments may as well.

- **State laws or regulations should be amended to cover a greater extent of waters, where needed.** About half the states lack a wetland or stream regulatory program independent of the Clean Water Act, and action is needed to fill the gaps post-*Sackett.* James McElfish identifies those states as Alabama, Alaska, Arkansas, Colorado, Delaware, Georgia, Hawaii, Idaho, Iowa, Kansas, Kentucky, Louisiana, Mississippi, Missouri, Montana, Nebraska, Nevada, New Mexico, North Dakota, Oklahoma, South Carolina, South Dakota, Texas, and Utah.[11] There is a sense of urgency in some states on the list. For example, in New Mexico, a coalition of conservation organizations, including Amigos Bravos, is spearheading an effort for the state legislature to adopt legislation to protect New Mexico's largely ephemeral waters.[12] In Colorado, the Department of Public Health and Environment issued a temporary policy requiring notice of discharges into state waters until the state legislature takes steps to develop a state permitting process.[13] Even some states with existing regulatory programs can expand their coverage, as New York did, in reaction to the Navigable Waters Protection Rule and in anticipation of *Sackett.*[14]
- **State laws or regulations should be enacted or promulgated to more directly address the problem of nonpoint source discharges.** As the Supreme Court recognized in *County of Maui v. Hawaii Wildlife Fund*, the Clean Water Act assigns states the responsibility to deal with nonpoint source pollution. Regardless of the scope of federal waters, combatting nonpoint source pollution is an area where states need to improve, as harmful algal blooms proliferate across the country. Jason Totoiu and Jaclyn Lopez offer a suite of recommendations—Florida specific, but nationally applicable—on how to confront harmful algal blooms, from establishing drinking water standards for cyanobacteria to revising and enforcing agricultural best management practices.[15]
- **Eligible states should use (and expand) their authority under the Coastal Zone Management Act (CZMA) to protect coastal waters and adjacent shorelands.** As discussed in Chapters 5 and 10, under section 401 of the Clean Water Act, a state may condition or even effectively veto federal permits and licenses that authorize discharges to waters of the United States. As WOTUS contracts, however, so will a

state's 401 water quality certification authority. Nevertheless, a similar authority—which is not tethered to the definition of WOTUS—exists under the Coastal Zone Management Act (CZMA).[16] This law, also passed in 1972, requires proposed projects within a state's designated coastal zone to be consistent with the state's coastal zone management plan. Thirty-five states and territories (which include the Great Lakes states) have established coastal zones for CZMA purposes through a variety of approaches.[17] Many states rely on counties as the boundaries, and the counties do not necessarily border the coast. Georgia, for example, includes five inland counties that "have economies that are closely tied to coastal resources."[18] Rhode Island has designated the entire state as a coastal zone for major polluters such as power plants, petroleum and chemical facilities, mining activities, and wastewater disposal operations.[19] Because the CZMA defines "adjacent shorelands" to include all waters ("the waters therein and thereunder") without qualification, the law offers a potent tool for coastal states that want to protect their waters, at least when the project has a federal connection.

- **Tribes have an important role to play in protecting waters.** Under the Clean Water Act, tribes can be treated as states.[20] Tribal governments are thus eligible to establish water quality standards for waters within their jurisdiction and can assume federal permitting authority. But if a water is no longer a WOTUS, then Clean Water Act water quality standards no longer apply. And the reduction in Clean Water Act jurisdiction as a result of *Sackett* may render assumption of federal permitting a useless exercise. (There are now few waters to assume.) Yet in many cases, tribes have their own police powers and may regulate activities to protect all waters within their jurisdiction.
- **Local governments, where they have the power, should act to protect waters.** In 2006, Jon Kusler of the Association of State Wetland Managers (now called the National Association of Wetland Managers) estimated that "4,000 to 6,000 local governments have adopted local wetland protection regulations," ranging from wetland-specific ordinances to zoning and floodplain rules.[21] As the understanding and appreciation of wetlands have grown in the past two decades (with the notable exception of within the Supreme Court), one expects that those numbers have increased. The EPA has highlighted several local efforts, including King County in Washington and Lake County in Illinois, as models.[22]

- **States (and local governments) should fund programs to purchase land and conservation easements to protect waters.** Opportunities for bipartisan collaboration to protect waters exist even in these politically divisive times, as the 2021 Florida Wildlife Corridor Act demonstrates. Although the law's title emphasizes wildlife habitat connectivity and the act itself invokes the need for habitat protections for the state's iconic panther, its purpose also expressly includes promoting water quality. It calls for "protecting the headwaters of major watersheds," as well as "preserving and protecting land and waters that are not only vital to wildlife but are critical to this state's groundwater recharge," which supports drinking water sources.[23] The program contemplates spending hundreds of millions of dollars for land acquisition and conservation easements.[24] More broadly, in 2025, states are due to update their wildlife action plans, strategies developed under the Conservation and Reinvestment Act of 2000.[25] The update process is an opportunity to highlight conservation actions that provide benefits not only to wildlife but to the aquatic ecosystems on which they (and we) depend.
- **Where state legislatures do not act, voters should take direct action to pass constitutional amendments or other referenda, where permitted.** In more than half the states, the voters can bypass recalcitrant legislatures through citizen-initiated ballot measures and approve statutes or state constitutional amendments.[26] For example, since 1998, more than thirty states—red and blue—have legalized some form of use of marijuana through ballot initiatives.[27] It can be challenging to get a proposal on the ballot, but it remains an option for clean water advocates in some jurisdictions.
- **Rights-of-nature initiatives are more a symptom than a remedy.** In some parts of the world, waterbodies such as rivers and wetlands have been recognized to have legal rights through constitutions, legislative acts, and court decisions.[28] The rights-of-nature movement has gained some momentum in the United States as well, often through citizen-led efforts. For example, voters in Toledo, Ohio, frustrated with algal blooms, poor water quality, and lack of legislative and regulatory responses, approved the Lake Erie Bill of Rights as part of the city charter.[29] A court subsequently struck it down as beyond the city's authority.[30] Similarly, voters in Orange County, Florida, approved by almost 90 percent an amendment to the county charter to recognize

the rights of wetlands, lakes, and streams, expanding the set of people who could sue on their behalf.[31] However, the Florida legislature preempted the provision by prohibiting local governments or their voters from enacting any rights-of-nature laws.[32] Nevertheless, perhaps prodded in part by the referendum, the county updated its wetland protection ordinance to require 100-foot buffers.[33] Although rights-of-nature campaigns in the United States may be useful to educate people about the importance of protecting and respecting nature (and waters), such quixotic efforts are largely more a symptom than a remedy. Enforcement of the rights of nature to protect waters in a judicial setting raises a host of operational challenges.[34] But the fact that the rights-of-nature concept is being considered underscores the dissatisfaction of voters with the status quo.

Playing Defense

While trying to respond to *Sackett*, clean water advocates must be aware of the need to play defense too. Although the regulated community was successful in reducing clean water protections at the federal level, they will also seek to further reduce state and local protections, both directly and indirectly.

- **Fight the rollback of state and local clean water laws and regulations.** In *Sackett*, the Court emphasized Clean Water Act section 101(b), which recognizes the states' "primary" responsibility to prevent, reduce, and eliminate water pollution. But what if a state abjures its responsibility? Before *Sackett*, some states had laws declaring that they would not regulate waters more strictly than the federal government. Thus, as WOTUS receded, so did state jurisdiction and protections. In 2023 in North Carolina, after *Sackett*, the legislature enacted—over the governor's veto—a law that shrunk North Carolina's regulatory authority to coincide with that of the EPA and the Corps.[35] The North Carolina Department of Environmental Quality estimated that 2.5 million acres of wetlands would no longer have federal or state protection.[36] That figure represents about half of the state's wetlands and probably does not take into account the impact of the "indistinguishable" requirement. Local ordinances are also vulnerable. In Manatee County, Florida, the county commission decided to reduce the protective buffers around wetlands, despite widespread local opposition to the move.[37] Although proponents of stronger water quality laws were unsuccessful in these rounds, the battles will continue.

- **Tie federal funding to continued state enforcement of water quality standards.** If state or local legislators are not persuaded by voters, perhaps the withdrawal of a carrot can be a stick to prevent backsliding. For example, Florida currently has set water quality standards for phosphorus in water entering the Everglades at 10 parts per billion (ppb).[38] Because this limit serves as a water quality–based effluent limitation for purposes of the Clean Water Act, the Miccosukee Tribe and Friends of Everglades were able to seek enforcement of the 10 ppb standard in federal court.[39] But the Clean Water Act calls for water quality standards only for waters that are WOTUS. With much of the Everglades no longer qualifying as a WOTUS, the continued viability of those water quality standards under the Clean Water Act is an open question. To be sure, the 10 ppb standard is enshrined in state law. But with the underpinning of WOTUS removed, the state could conceivably amend or eliminate that standard, at the behest of agricultural interests. Meanwhile, the federal government is investing billions of dollars to restore the Everglades in a decades-long project.[40] If Florida starts watering down its water quality standards, the feds should consider withholding its share of the funding for the restoration work.
- **Watch for attempts to preempt or restrict local governments' ability to protect water quality.** One indirect threat to water quality efforts is preemption of the authority of local governments by their state legislatures. A state legislature might seek to eliminate county regulatory bodies entirely (arguing that they are duplicative), or it might target a local government's specific action. In Florida, some counties ban the sale or use of fertilizer during the rainy season to reduce nitrogen pollution entering waterways. In response, the state legislature has proposed a ban on the fertilizer bans.[41] An even more draconian bill was introduced in Florida in 2023 that would have broadly prohibited "counties and municipalities from adopting laws, regulations, rules, or policies relating to water quality or quantity, pollution control, pollutant discharge prevention or removal, and wetlands."[42] One wonders whether such a law would prevent counties from notifying the public about harmful algal blooms and bacteria in beach waters. Fortunately, this attack on home rule and water quality failed, but one can expect similar sallies in the future.

A Prayer

For matters of water quality and WOTUS, it matters who is president; POTUS sets the agenda for the executive branch and appoints the heads of agencies, as well as members of the Supreme Court, when openings arise. It matters who is in Congress because that body provides the agencies the authorization (and funding) to act, subject to the constraints of the Constitution, as interpreted by SCOTUS. But it also matters who is governor of a state, as well as who sits in the state legislature. And it matters who runs county and municipal governments. Each level of government has a role to play in protecting our waters, although their respective spheres of influence have ebbed and flowed over time.

Carrie Chapman Catt understood the power of the vote, yet she also called it a prayer. In the legal context, a prayer is a request. US Senator Raphael Warnock suggested that "[a] vote is a kind of prayer for the kind of world we desire for ourselves and for our children, and I think our prayers are stronger when we pray together."[43] Ultimately, the integrity of the nation's waters depends on informed, engaged citizens who vote—and vote in every election, from municipal to county to state to federal.

And consider running for office—just as the farmer from Iowa, whose quote opened the book, did.

Acknowledgments

Writing is generally a solo activity, but crafting a book is a team endeavor. And I have been most fortunate to have been supported by a wonderful assembly of friends, colleagues, and family in this project.

I appreciate the assistance of Stetson University College of Law, which provided me a sabbatical, allowing me time to write. Stetson has a kind and collaborative community that I have benefited from for more than thirty years. Many thanks to Erin Okuno, who helped me wrestle with WOTUS issues, first as a student research assistant and then as a colleague. Foreman Biodiversity Fellow Katherine Pratt (also a former research assistant) contributed greatly, and my current research assistant Jennifer Hollander was instrumental in bringing this across the finish line. Professors Paul Boudreaux and Jaclyn Lopez gave helpful comments, and Jamie Fox, Becky Morgan, and Jason Bent, in addition to offering encouragement, ensured that I had copious amounts of caffeine.

The Office of Faculty Support at Stetson Law has no peer, and our reference librarians enthusiastically fielded my odd requests, such as trying to ferret out when a footnote discussing *kreupel* and *krüppel* was added to a Supreme Court opinion decided in 1829. And Jason Evans and Olusola Adetoro, my Stetson colleagues on our main campus across the state, collaborated on quantifying the impact of Supreme Court decisions.

I am grateful for the outstanding legal team I worked with on *amicus* briefs we submitted in Clean Water Act cases on behalf of scientific societies and aquatic scientists: Steph Tai, Erin Okuno, Christopher Greer, and my sister Kathleen Gardner. I am indebted to the many scientists who educated me in this process, in particular Siobhan Fennessy, David Kaplan, Bill Mitsch, Mark Rains, Andy Robertson, Mažeika Sulliván, Gene Turner, Kirsten Work, and Joy Zedler. The members of the Public Policy and Regulation Section of the Society of Wetland Scientists bear special mention in this regard too.

I remain inspired by clean water advocates and environmental experts with whom I have had the honor to be associated over the years, from Friends of the Everglades at the state level to the Environmental Law Institute and the National Parks Conservation Association at the national level and my Ramsar Convention friends at the international level. Thank you for all that you do to protect water resources.

I would like to thank editor Emily Turner, Sharis Simonian, and the staff at Island Press for their always insightful yet gentle advice and suggestions. It was a pleasure to once again work with them.

Finally, I would like to express my love and gratitude to my wife Mary Fahy and our family, Jake, Colin, and Jeannette. All contributed in different ways, from creating maps to reading text and providing input on potential titles (even though "WOTUS: One Man's Obsession with a Statutory Term" was ultimately not adopted). I am incredibly thankful for their love, encouragement, and good humor on this journey.

Appendix

Table A-1. State views of the Clean Water Act, based on their litigation positions regarding the Obama administration's Clean Water Rule (CWR), *County of Maui v. Hawaii Wildlife Fund (County of Maui)*, the Trump administration's Navigable Waters Protection Rule (NWPR), and *Sackett v. U.S. Environmental Protection Agency (Sackett)*. Shaded boxes indicate a position opposing broader Clean Water Act jurisdiction.

STATE (INCLUDING DC)	**CWR**	**COUNTY OF MAUI**	**NWPR**	**SACKETT**
Alabama	Petitioner opposing CWR in *In re EPA* (6th Cir.)	*Amicus curiae* in support of County of Maui	State intervenor in support of NWPR in *California v. Wheeler* (N.D. Cal.)	*Amicus curiae* in support of Sackett
Alaska	Plaintiff opposing CWR in *North Dakota v. EPA* (D.N.D.)	*Amicus curiae* in support of County of Maui	State intervenor in support of NWPR in *California v. Wheeler* (N.D. Cal.)	
Arizona	Plaintiff opposing CWR in *North Dakota v. EPA* (D.N.D.)			*Amicus curiae* in support of Sackett
Arkansas	Plaintiff opposing CWR in *North Dakota v. EPA* (D.N.D.)	*Amicus curiae* in support of County of Maui	State intervenor in support of NWPR in *California v. Wheeler* (N.D. Cal.)	*Amicus curiae* in support of Sackett
California		*Amicus curiae* in support of Hawaii Wildlife Fund	Plaintiff opposing NWPR in *California v. Wheeler* (N.D. Cal.)	*Amicus curiae* in support of EPA

STATE (INCLUDING DC)	CWR	COUNTY OF MAUI	NWPR	SACKETT
Colorado	Plaintiff opposing CWR in *North Dakota v. EPA* (D.N.D.)	*Amicus curiae* in support of County of Maui (petition for certiorari)	Plaintiff opposing NWPR in *Colorado v. Wheeler* (D. Colo.)	*Amicus curiae* in support of EPA
Connecticut	Respondent intervenor in support of CWR in *In re EPA* (6th Cir.)	*Amicus curiae* in support of Hawaii Wildlife Fund	Plaintiff opposing NWPR in *California v. Wheeler* (N.D. Cal.)	*Amicus curiae* in support of EPA
Delaware				*Amicus curiae* in support of EPA
District of Columbia	Respondent intervenor in support of CWR in *In re EPA* (6th Cir.)	*Amicus curiae* in support of Hawaii Wildlife Fund	Plaintiff opposing NWPR in *California v. Wheeler* (N.D. Cal.)	*Amicus curiae* in support of EPA
Florida	Petitioner opposing CWR in *In re EPA* (6th Cir.)	*Amicus curiae* in support of County of Maui		*Amicus curiae* in support of Sackett
Georgia	Petitioner opposing CWR in *In re EPA* (6th Cir.)	*Amicus curiae* in support of County of Maui	State intervenor in support of NWPR in *California v. Wheeler* (N.D. Cal.)	*Amicus curiae* in support of Sackett
Hawaii	Respondent intervenor in support of CWR in *In re EPA* (6th Cir.)			*Amicus curiae* in support of EPA
Idaho	Plaintiff opposing CWR in *North Dakota v. EPA* (D.N.D.)	*Amicus curiae* in support of County of Maui	State intervenor in support of NWPR in *California v. Wheeler* (N.D. Cal.)	*Amicus curiae* in support of Sackett
Idaho	Plaintiff opposing CWR in *North Dakota v. EPA* (D.N.D.)	*Amicus curiae* in support of County of Maui	State intervenor in support of NWPR in *California v. Wheeler* (N.D. Cal.)	*Amicus curiae* in support of Sackett

STATE (INCLUDING DC)	CWR	COUNTY OF MAUI	NWPR	SACKETT
Illinois		*Amicus curiae* in support of Hawaii Wildlife Fund	Plaintiff opposing NWPR in *California v. Wheeler* (N.D. Cal.)	*Amicus curiae* in support of EPA
Indiana	Petitioner opposing CWR in *In re EPA* (6th Cir.)	*Amicus curiae* in support of County of Maui	State intervenor in support of NWPR in *California v. Wheeler* (N.D. Cal.)	*Amicus curiae* in support of Sackett
Iowa	State intervenor opposing CWR in *North Dakota v. EPA* (D.N.D.)			
Kansas	Petitioner opposing CWR in *In re EPA* (6th Cir.)	*Amicus curiae* in support of County of Maui	State intervenor in support of NWPR in *California v. Wheeler* (N.D. Cal.)	*Amicus curiae* in support of Sackett
Kentucky	Petitioner opposing CWR in *In re EPA* (6th Cir.)	*Amicus curiae* in support of County of Maui	State intervenor in support of NWPR in *California v. Wheeler* (N.D. Cal.)	*Amicus curiae* in support of Sackett
Louisiana	Petitioner opposing CWR in *In re EPA* (6th Cir.)	*Amicus curiae* in support of County of Maui	State intervenor in support of NWPR in *California v. Wheeler* (N.D. Cal.)	*Amicus curiae* in support of Sackett
Maine		*Amicus curiae* in support of Hawaii Wildlife Fund	Plaintiff opposing NWPR in *California v. Wheeler* (N.D. Cal.)	*Amicus curiae* in support of EPA
Maryland		*Amicus curiae* in support of Hawaii Wildlife Fund	Plaintiff opposing NWPR in *California v. Wheeler* (N.D. Cal.)	*Amicus curiae* in support of EPA
Massachusetts	Respondent intervenor in support of CWR in *In re EPA* (6th Cir.)	*Amicus curiae* in support of Hawaii Wildlife Fund	Plaintiff opposing NWPR in *California v. Wheeler* (N.D. Cal.)	*Amicus curiae* in support of EPA

STATE (INCLUDING DC)	CWR	COUNTY OF MAUI	NWPR	SACKETT
Michigan	Petitioner opposing CWR in *In re EPA* (6th Cir.)	*Amicus curiae* in support of Hawaii Wildlife Fund	Plaintiff opposing NWPR in *California v. Wheeler* (N.D. Cal.)	*Amicus curiae* in support of EPA
Minnesota				*Amicus curiae* in support of EPA
Mississippi	Petitioner opposing CWR in *In re EPA* (6th Cir.)	*Amicus curiae* in support of County of Maui	State intervenor in support of NWPR in *California v. Wheeler* (N.D. Cal.)	*Amicus curiae* in support of Sackett
Missouri	Plaintiff opposing CWR in *North Dakota v. EPA* (D.N.D.)	*Amicus curiae* in support of County of Maui	State intervenor in support of NWPR in *California v. Wheeler* (N.D. Cal.)	*Amicus curiae* in support of Sackett
Montana	Plaintiff opposing CWR in *North Dakota v. EPA* (D.N.D.)	*Amicus curiae* in support of County of Maui	State intervenor in support of NWPR in *California v. Wheeler* (N.D. Cal.)	*Amicus curiae* in support of Sackett
Nebraska	Plaintiff opposing CWR in *North Dakota v. EPA* (D.N.D.)	*Amicus curiae* in support of County of Maui	State intervenor in support of NWPR in *California v. Wheeler* (N.D. Cal.)	*Amicus curiae* in support of Sackett
Nevada	Plaintiff opposing CWR in *North Dakota v. EPA* (D.N.D.)	*Amicus curiae* in support of County of Maui (petition for certiorari)		
New Hampshire				*Amicus curiae* in support of Sackett
New Jersey		*Amicus curiae* in support of Hawaii Wildlife Fund	Plaintiff opposing NWPR in *California v. Wheeler* (N.D. Cal.)	*Amicus curiae* in support of EPA
New Mexico	Plaintiff opposing CWR in *North Dakota v. EPA* (D.N.D.)	*Amicus curiae* in support of Hawaii Wildlife Fund	Plaintiff opposing NWPR in *California v. Wheeler* (N.D. Cal.)	*Amicus curiae* in support of EPA

STATE (INCLUDING DC)	CWR	COUNTY OF MAUI	NWPR	SACKETT
New York	Respondent intervenor in support of CWR in *In re EPA* (6th Cir.)		Plaintiff opposing NWPR in *California v. Wheeler* (N.D. Cal.)	*Amicus curiae* in support of EPA
North Carolina	Petitioner opposing CWR in *In re EPA* (6th Cir.)		Plaintiff opposing NWPR in *California v. Wheeler* (N.D. Cal.)	*Amicus curiae* in support of EPA
North Dakota	Plaintiff opposing CWR in *North Dakota v. EPA* (D.N.D.)		State intervenor in support of NWPR in *California v. Wheeler* (N.D. Cal.)	*Amicus curiae* in support of Sackett
Ohio	Petitioner opposing CWR in *In re EPA* (6th Cir.)	*Amicus curiae* in support of County of Maui	State intervenor in support of NWPR in *California v. Wheeler* (N.D. Cal.)	*Amicus curiae* in support of Sackett
Oklahoma	Petitioner opposing CWR in *In re EPA* (6th Cir.)	*Amicus curiae* in support of County of Maui		*Amicus curiae* in support of Sackett
Oregon	Respondent intervenor in support of CWR in *In re EPA* (6th Cir.)	*Amicus curiae* in support of Hawaii Wildlife Fund	Plaintiff opposing NWPR in *California v. Wheeler* (N.D. Cal.)	*Amicus curiae* in support of EPA
Pennsylvania	—	—	—	—
Rhode Island		*Amicus curiae* in support of Hawaii Wildlife Fund	Plaintiff opposing NWPR in *California v. Wheeler* (N.D. Cal.)	
South Carolina	Petitioner opposing CWR in *In re EPA* (6th Cir.)	*Amicus curiae* in support of County of Maui	State intervenor in support of NWPR in *California v. Wheeler* (N.D. Cal.)	*Amicus curiae* in support of Sackett
South Dakota	Plaintiff opposing CWR in *North Dakota v. EPA* (D.N.D.)		State intervenor in support of NWPR in *California v. Wheeler* (N.D. Cal.)	*Amicus curiae* in support of Sackett

STATE (INCLUDING DC)	CWR	COUNTY OF MAUI	NWPR	SACKETT
Tennessee	Petitioner opposing CWR in *In re EPA* (6th Cir.)		State intervenor in support of NWPR in *California v. Wheeler* (N.D. Cal.)	*Amicus curiae* in support of Sackett
Texas	Petitioner opposing CWR in *In re EPA* (6th Cir.)	*Amicus curiae* in support of County of Maui	State intervenor in support of NWPR in *California v. Wheeler* (N.D. Cal.)	*Amicus curiae* in support of Sackett
Utah	Petitioner opposing CWR in *In re EPA* (6th Cir.)	*Amicus curiae* in support of County of Maui	State intervenor in support of NWPR in *California v. Wheeler* (N.D. Cal.)	*Amicus curiae* in support of Sackett
Vermont	Respondent intervenor in support of CWR in *In re EPA* (6th Cir.)	*Amicus curiae* in support of Hawaii Wildlife Fund	Plaintiff opposing NWPR in *California v. Wheeler* (N.D. Cal.)	*Amicus curiae* in support of EPA
Virginia			Plaintiff opposing NWPR in *California v. Wheeler* (N.D. Cal.)	*Amicus curiae* in support of Sackett
Washington	Respondent intervenor in support of CWR in *In re EPA* (6th Cir.)	*Amicus curiae* in support of Hawaii Wildlife Fund	Plaintiff opposing NWPR in *California v. Wheeler* (N.D. Cal.)	*Amicus curiae* in support of EPA
West Virginia	Petitioner opposing CWR in *In re EPA* (6th Cir.)	*Amicus curiae* in support of County of Maui		*Amicus curiae* in support of Sackett
Wisconsin	Petitioner opposing CWR in *In re EPA* (6th Cir.)		Plaintiff opposing NWPR in *California v. Wheeler* (N.D. Cal.)	*Amicus curiae* in support of EPA
Wyoming	Plaintiff opposing CWR in *North Dakota v. EPA* (D.N.D.)	*Amicus curiae* in support of County of Maui	State intervenor in support of NWPR in *California v. Wheeler* (N.D. Cal.)	*Amicus curiae* in support of Sackett

Table A-2. Evolution of "navigable waters" to "waters of the United States" through congressional action.

CONGRESSIONAL ACTION	GEOGRAPHIC SCOPE	SUBJECT MATTER
Northwest Ordinance of 1787	Navigable waters	Use of the waters is to be free from taxes or duties
Land Act of 1796	Navigable rivers	All navigable rivers are deemed public highways
Swamp Land Acts of 1849, 1850, and 1860	Swamp and overflowed lands	Transfer ownership from federal government to states
Rivers and Harbors Act of 1890	Section 6: navigable river, or navigable waters of the United States	Prohibiting discharge of refuse or waste that obstructs navigation
	Section 10: any waters, in respect of which the United States has jurisdiction	Prohibiting unauthorized obstructions to the navigable capacity of such waters (Note: In *Rio Grande*, SCOTUS found federal jurisdiction extended to nonnavigable tributaries if action affected navigable waters)
Rivers and Harbors Act of 1899	Section 10: waters of the United States, navigable river, or other water of the United States	Prohibiting obstructions to the navigable capacity to any of the waters of the United States without Corps of Engineers approval
	Section 10: any navigable water of the United States	Prohibiting excavation or fill without Corps of Engineers approval
	Section 13: any navigable water of the United States, or any tributary of any navigable water	Prohibiting the discharge of refuse without Corps of Engineers approval
General Dam Act of 1906	Navigable waters of the United States	Congressionally authorized dams may be constructed across navigable waters only with Corps of Engineers approval
Act of August 14, 1912 (Public Health Service Act)	Navigable streams and lakes of the United States	Public Health Service (PHS) may study and investigate the diseases spread through pollution either directly or indirectly

CONGRESSIONAL ACTION	GEOGRAPHIC SCOPE	SUBJECT MATTER
Federal Water Power Act	*Navigable waters* defined to include waters used in commerce and waters that could be used in commerce with reasonable improvements, even if navigable parts are interrupted by falls, shallows, or rapids	Prohibiting issuance of a license for a dam or other structure affecting navigable capacity without Federal Power Commission approval
Oil Pollution Act, 1924	*Coastal navigable waters of the United States* defined as "all portions of the sea within the territorial jurisdiction of the United States, and all inland waters navigable in fact in which the tide ebbs and flows"	Generally prohibiting discharge of oil from a vessel
HR 2711 (1937), Water Pollution Act (vetoed by FDR)	Section 2: navigable waters of the United States and streams tributary thereto	PHS, in cooperation with state agencies, municipalities, and industries to prepare comprehensive plans to eliminate and reduce pollution and improve the sanitary condition of navigable waters and tributaries
	Section 4: Any waters of the United States, either navigable or otherwise	PHS may jointly investigate conditions and discharges of sewage, industrial wastes, or substance that may deleteriously affect such waters
Federal Water Pollution Control Act of 1948	Interstate waters and tributaries thereof, surface and underground waters	Surgeon General, in cooperation with other federal and state agencies, municipalities, and industries, to prepare comprehensive programs to eliminate and reduce pollution and improve the sanitary condition of surface and underground waters
	Any waters in any state or states	Surgeon General may jointly investigate water quality conditions and discharges of sewage, industrial wastes, or substances that may deleteriously affect such waters

CONGRESSIONAL ACTION	GEOGRAPHIC SCOPE	SUBJECT MATTER
Federal Water Pollution Control Act Amendments of 1961	Interstate or navigable waters and a tributary of such waters	Pollution of interstate or navigable waters—even indirectly through a tributary—is subject to abatement action if effect of pollution on the legitimate uses of the waters is sufficiently significant to warrant exercise of federal jurisdiction
Water Quality Act of 1965	Interstate waters and tributaries of such waters	Calls on states to develop water quality standards; discharges, including indirectly through tributaries, that violate water quality standards are subject to abatement action
Water Quality Improvement Act of 1970	Navigable waters of the United States	Requires state water quality certification for federal licenses and permits authorizing activities that may result in a discharge
1972 Amendments to the Federal Water Pollution Control Act, now known as the Clean Water Act	*Navigable waters* defined as "waters of the United States, including the territorial seas"	Comprehensive water pollution law prohibiting all point source discharges of pollutants without a permit

Notes

Introduction

1. "52 Places to Go in 2014," *New York Times*, accessed February 23, 2024, https://www.nytimes.com/interactive/2014/01/10/travel/2014-places-to-go.html.
2. 33 U.S.C. § 1362(7) (2024).
3. S. Mažeika Patricio Sulliván, Mark C. Rains, Amanda D. Rodewald, William W. Buzbee, and Amy D. Rosemond, "Distorting Science, Putting Water at Risk," *Science*, 369 (August 14, 2020): 767.
4. Marcus W. Beck et al., "Initial Estuarine Response to Inorganic Nutrient Inputs from a Legacy Mining Facility Adjacent to Tampa Bay, Florida," *Marine Pollution Bulletin*, 178 (2022): 113599.
5. Ibid., 113604.
6. "Seagrass Monitoring in Tampa Bay," *Tampa Bay Water Atlas* and *Tampa Bay Estuary Program*, accessed February 23, 2024, https://tampabay.wateratlas.usf.edu/seagrass-monitoring/.
7. Sackett v. U.S. Environmental Protection Agency, 598 U.S. 651, 658 (2023).

Chapter 1

1. "POTUS," *Merriam-Webster*, accessed November 26, 2023, https://www.merriam-webster.com/dictionary/POTUS.
2. Ibid.
3. Federal Water Pollution Control Act Amendments of 1972, Pub. L. 92-500, 86 Stat. 816-903 (1972).
4. A 2002 draft environmental impact statement submitted to the US Department of Transportation contained the phrase "Riverine WOTUS." Riverside County Integrated Project Consultant Team, *Route Location and Right-of-Way Preservation for a New Multi-Modal Transportation Facility in the Hemet to Corona/Lake Elsinore Corridor in the County of Riverside: Environmental Impact Statement, Volume 1* (July 2002), S-13.
5. Surface Mining Reclamation and Enforcement Office, Rule, "Excess Spoil, Coal Mine Waste, and Buffers for Perennial and Intermittent Streams," 73 Fed. Reg. 75814 (December 12, 2008).
6. State v. McCarthy, No. CV 215-79, 2015 WL 5092568 (S.D. Ga. August 27, 2015).
7. Section 301 declares discharges of any pollutant unlawful, except in accordance with a permit, such as a section 402 permit, issued by the US Environmental Protection Agency (EPA) or a state with an EPA-approved

program, or a section 404 permit, issued by the US Army Corps of Engineers (Corps) or a state with an EPA-approved program. Clean Water Act, 33 U.S.C. § 1311 (2024).

8. For example, according to the Corps, between 2012 and 2015 "the agency authorized an average of 63,000 activities per year; 97% were authorized by nationwide and other general permits." Congressional Research Service, "The Army Corps of Engineers' Nationwide Permits Program: Issues and Regulatory Developments," by [name redacted], Report No. 97-223 (January 12, 2017), 2, https://www.everycrsreport.com/files/20170112_97-223_271c5b-98b058e7b84bab465be90e05777cf735ea.pdf.
9. "Wasting Our Waterways," Environment America, accessed December 4, 2023, https://environmentamerica.org/center/resources/wasting-our-waterways/. On the plus side, each year the Clean Water Act prevents more than 700 million pounds of pollutants from entering the waters of the United States. "Freshwater Quality," Centers for Disease Control and Prevention, accessed December 4, 2023, https://www.cdc.gov/healthywater/other/industrial/freshwater_quality.html.
10. Mary Jordan and Kevin Sullivan, "'Smothered' and 'Shoved Aside' in Rural America," *Washington Post*, December 29, 2017, https://www.washingtonpost.com/graphics/2017/national/iowa-farm-waters-trump/. The story noted that the farmer, Annette Sweeney, served in the Iowa legislature.
11. J. D. Stock et al., *From Ridge to Reef—Linking Erosion and Changing Watersheds to Impacts on the Coral Reef Ecosystems of Hawai'i and the Pacific Ocean*, 2011 (U.S. Geological Survey Fact Sheet).
12. US Environmental Protection Agency, *Connectivity of Streams and Wetlands to Downstream Waters: A Review and Synthesis of the Scientific Evidence (Final Report)*, 2015, 2–7.
13. William J. Mitsch and James G. Gosselink, *Wetlands*, 4th ed. (New York: John Wiley & Sons, 2007), 4.
14. K. A. Lellis-Dibble, K. E. McGlynn, and T. E. Bigford, *Estuarine Fish and Shellfish Species in U.S. Commercial and Recreational Fisheries: Economic Value as an Incentive to Protect and Restore Estuarine Habitat*, NOAA Technical Memorandum NMFS-F/SPO-90, Nov. 2008, https://spo.nmfs.noaa.gov/sites/default/files/TM90.pdf.
15. For example, Ducks Unlimited has long promoted wetland restoration and protection. Gildo M. Tori, Scott McLeod, Keith McKnight, Thomas Moorman, and Frederic A. Reid, "Wetland Conservation and Ducks Unlimited: Real World Approaches to Multispecies Management," *Waterbirds* 25, Special Publication 2 (2002): 115–16. At the international level, European bird hunters were part of the coalition advocating for a global wetland conservation treaty. David A. Stroud, Nick C. Davidson, C. Max Finlayson, and Royal C. Gardner, "Development of the Text of the Ramsar Convention: 1965–1971," *Marine and Freshwater Research* 73 (2022): 1109.
16. Craig Pittman, "Factory Owner Fined for '04 Spill," *St. Petersburg Times*, July 2, 2005, https://www.tampabay.com/archive/2005/07/02/factory-owner-fined-for-04-spill/.

17. Ibid.
18. Lillian Young, "Midwest Fertilizer Runoff Adds to Low-Oxygen Zone in Gulf of Mexico," *Capital News Service*, January 8, 2021, https://news.jrn.msu.edu/2021/01/midwest-fertilizer-runoff-adds-to-low-oxygen-zone-in-gulf-of-mexico/.
19. Casey Smith, "New Jersey-Size 'Dead Zone' Is Largest Ever in Gulf of Mexico," *National Geographic*, August 2, 2017, https://www.nationalgeographic.com/science/article/gulf-mexico-hypoxia-water-quality-dead-zone.
20. United States v. Riverside Bayview Homes, Inc., 474 U.S. 121, 134 (1985).
21. Environmental Law Institute, "Anchoring the Clean Water Act: Congress's Constitutional Sources of Power to Protect the Nation's Waters" (July 2007), https://www.eli.org/sites/default/files/eli-pubs/d17_07.pdf.
22. Clean Water Act, 33 U.S.C. § 1251(a).
23. Ibid., § 1251(b).
24. William W. Sapp, Tracy L. Starr, and M. Allison Burdette, "From the Fields of Runnymede to the Waters of the United States: A Historical Review of the Clean Water Act and the Term 'Navigable Waters,'" *Environmental Law Reporter* 36 (March 2006): 10191.
25. Natural Resources Defense Council, Inc. v. Callaway, 392 F. Supp. 685, 686 (D.D.C. 1975).
26. Clean Water Act, 33 U.S.C. § 1362(7).
27. US Army Corps of Engineers and Environmental Protection Agency, Rule, "Clean Water Rule: Definition of Waters of the United States," 80 Fed. Reg. 37053 (June 29, 2015).
28. Minnesota Farm Bureau Association, "Minnesota Farm Bureau Opposes Final Waters of the United States Rule," *Voice of Agriculture*, 34, no. 4 (July 2015). https://issuu.com/minnesotafarmbureau/docs/mnvoa_july_2015.
29. Brandon Blue, "Farm Bureau's 'Frozen' Parody Is the Best Thing You'll See Today," *Iowa Agribusiness Radio Network*, May 28, 2014, https://www.iowaagribusinessradionetwork.com/farm-bureau-parody-frozen-disney-let-it-go-best-thing-today/.
30. US Army Corps of Engineers and Environmental Protection Agency, 80 Fed. Reg. at 37508.
31. "Rivers, Streams, Brooks, and Drainage Ditches," Manchester-by-the-Sea Massachusetts, accessed November 27, 2023, https://www.manchester.ma.us/365/Rivers-Streams-Brooks-Drainage-Ditches.
32. Roy G. Finch, *The Story of the New York State Canals* (New York State Canal Corporation, 1925), 7, https://www.canals.ny.gov/history/finch_history.pdf.
33. Thomas E. Dahl, *Wetlands Losses in the United States 1780's to 1980's* (Washington, DC: U.S. Fish and Wildlife Service, 1990), 7. For a trenchant discussion of the current state of Iowa's water quality, see Chris Jones, *The Swine Republic: Struggles with the Truth about Agriculture and Water Quality* (North Liberty, IA: Ice Cube Press, 2023).
34. Melissa Denchak, "Water Pollution: Everything You Need to Know," *NRDC*, January 11, 2023, https://www.nrdc.org/stories/water-pollution-everything-you-need-know.

35. See County of Maui v. Hawaii Wildlife Fund, 140 S. Ct. 1462, 1471 (2020).
36. US Army Corps of Engineers and Environmental Protection Agency, 58 Fed. Reg. 45008, 45031 (August 25, 1993).
37. Clean Water Act, 33 U.S.C. § 1344(f).
38. Dave Owen, "What Do Farmers Actually Get from the New WOTUS Rule?" *Law Professors Blog Network*, January 23, 2020, https://lawprofessors.typepad.com/environmental_law/2020/01/what-do-farmers-actually-get-from-the-new-wotus-rule.html#.
39. Julia Eilperin and Abby Phillip, "Trump Directs Rollback of Obama-era Water Rule He Calls 'Destructive and Horrible,'" *Washington Post*, February 28, 2017, https://www.washingtonpost.com/news/energy-environment/wp/2017/02/27/trump-to-direct-rollback-of-obama-era-water-rule-tuesday/.
40. Jordan and Sullivan, "'Smothered' and 'Shoved Aside.'"
41. Dirck Steimel, "IFBF Backs Branstad Move to Stop WOTUS Implementation," November 23, 2015, https://www.iowafarmbureau.com/Article/IFBF-backs-Branstad-move-to-stop-WOTUS-implementation.
42. Alison Gowans, "Trump Voters in Iowa Satisfied with How He's Done So Far, Frustrated by Divided Country," *The Gazette*, June 20, 2017, https://www.thegazette.com/government-politics/trump-voters-in-iowa-satisfied-with-how-hes-done-so-far-frustrated-by-divided-country/.
43. It is also consistent with a Pew survey finding that "those living in states with relatively high per capita incomes, as well as those living in states that voted for Barack Obama in 2012, are more likely to support stricter environmental regulations [such as a broad interpretation of the definition of WOTUS] than those living in states with lower per-capita incomes and with Republican voting patterns." Kristen Bialik, "Most Americans Favor Stricter Environmental Laws and Regulations," *Pew Research Center*, December 14, 2016, https://www.pewresearch.org/short-reads/2016/12/14/most-americans-favor-stricter-environmental-laws-and-regulations/.
44. Chuck McCutcheon and David Mark, "'Elections Have Consequences': Does Obama Regret Saying That Now?," *Christian Science Monitor*, November 21, 2014, https://www.csmonitor.com/USA/Politics/Politics-Voices/2014/1121/Elections-have-consequences-Does-Obama-regret-saying-that-now.
45. Exec. Order No. 13778, 82 Fed. Reg. 12497 (March 3, 2017).
46. Michael Brice-Saddler, "Trump Claims Farmers Wept behind Him When He Signed an Executive Order. Video Shows Otherwise," *Washington Post*, June 13, 2019, https://www.washingtonpost.com/politics/2019/06/14/trump-claims-farmers-wept-behind-him-when-he-signed-an-executive-order-video-shows-otherwise/.
47. Ibid.
48. Ariel Wittenberg, "Calif. Clinches New Regs Just in Time for Federal Rollback," *E&E News*, February 4, 2019, https://www.eenews.net/articles/calif-clinches-new-regs-just-in-time-for-federal-rollback/#:~:text=If%20all%20goes%20to%20schedule%2C%20California%E2%80%99s%20rules%20could,have%20relatively%20permanent%20surface%20water%20connections%20to%20streams.

49. For one tally of the Trump administration's efforts, see Nadja Popovich, Livia Albeck-Ripka, and Kendra Pierre-Louis, "The Trump Administration Rolled Back More Than 100 Environmental Rules. Here's the Full List," *New York Times*, last updated January 20, 2021, https://www.nytimes.com/interactive/2020/climate/trump-environment-rollbacks-list.html.

Chapter 2

1. See US Department of Transportation, Federal Motor Carrier Safety Administration (FMCSA), *Information for School Bus Operators: Overview of Federal Safety Regulations*, accessed November 28, 2023, https://www.fmcsa.dot.gov/sites/fmcsa.dot.gov/files/2020-09/School%20Bus%20Brochure_508.pdf (explaining that school bus transportation to and from home and school is not subject to FMCSA regulations).
2. "Chief Justice Roberts Statement—Nomination Process," US Courts, accessed November 28, 2023, https://www.uscourts.gov/educational-resources/educational-activities/chief-justice-roberts-statement-nomination-process.
3. The one tangentially water-related grievance was number 24: "He has plundered our seas, ravaged our coasts, burnt our towns, and destroyed the lives of our people."
4. Alexander Hamilton, "Federalist No. 70," *The Federalist Papers*, March 18, 1788, http://avalon.law.yale.edu/18th_century/fed70.asp.
5. Comm. on the Judiciary v. McGahn, 415 F. Supp. 3d 148, 164 (D.D.C. 2019).
6. Clinton v. Jones, 520 U.S. 681 (1997) (no civil immunity for an incumbent president for acts unrelated to the office); Saikrishna Bangalore Prakash, "Prosecuting and Punishing Our Presidents," *Texas Law Review* 100 (2022): 113 ("Although presidents are exceptional actors on the constitutional stage and in the life of the nation, they do not have truly exceptional, if tacit, criminal shields. Great powers do not always come with great immunities.").
7. See the table with number of executive orders each president has issued. "Executive Orders," *The American Presidency Project*, accessed November 28, 2023, https://www.presidency.ucsb.edu/statistics/data/executive-orders.
8. Harry S. Truman, "Executive Order 9981: Desegregation of the Armed Forces," July 26, 1948, https://www.archives.gov/milestone-documents/executive-order-9981.
9. Youngstown Sheet & Tube Co. v. Sawyer, 343 U.S. 579, 587 (1952).
10. The Court observed that "the Constitution is neither silent nor equivocal about who shall make laws," and it is Congress, not the president. Ibid. Thus, if an executive order is to be given legal effect, the president needs to point to a constitutional provision or statute that gives the president the authority to act. In the case of the steel mills, the Court found that the powers of commander in chief did not extend to "tak[ing] possession of private property in order to keep labor disputes from stopping production." Ibid. Instead, the Court noted, "this is a job for the Nation's lawmakers, not for its military authorities." Ibid.
11. Exec. Order No. 11990, 42 Fed. Reg. 26961 (May 24, 1977).

12. Exec. Order No. 13508, 74 Fed. Reg. 23099 (May 12, 2009).
13. Ibid., 23102.
14. Even President Trump's executive order on WOTUS contained this disclaimer. Exec. Order No. 13778, 82 Fed. Reg. 12497, 12498 (March 3, 2017).
15. In the Clean Water Act context, for example, a challenge to an EPA–Corps memorandum of agreement announcing the goal of "no net loss" of wetlands could not be based on its failure to comply with executive orders on takings and regulatory impacts. Municipality of Anchorage v. United States, 980 F.2d 1320, 1326–27 (9th Cir. 1992).
16. A. L. A. Schechter Poultry Corp. v. United States, 295 U.S. 495 (1935).
17. Mistretta v. United States, 488 U.S. 361, 371–74 (1989) (discussing nondelegation doctrine in context of federal sentencing guidelines).
18. Whitman v. Am. Trucking Ass'ns, 531 U.S. 457 (2001).
19. Ibid., 473.
20. Ibid., 488 (Stevens, J., concurring).
21. Gundy v. United States, 139 S. Ct. 2116, 2121–22 (2019).
22. Ibid., 2130.
23. Ibid., 2131 (Gorsuch, J., dissenting).
24. Ibid. (Alito, J., concurring in the judgment).
25. Jack M. Beermann, "The Turn Toward Congress in Administrative Law," *Boston University Law Review* 89 (2009): 756–57. See also Jack Beermann, "The Never-Ending Assault on the Administrative State," *Notre Dame Law Review* 93 (2018): 1599.
26. Barton Gellman, *Angler: The Cheney Vice Presidency* (New York: Penguin Press, 2008).
27. Royal C. Gardner, *Lawyers, Swamps, and Money: U.S. Wetland Law, Policy, and Politics* (Washington, DC: Island Press, 2011): 23–25.
28. Administrative Procedure Act, 5 U.S.C. § 553 (2024); "Document Drafting Handbook," *Office of the Federal Register* (August 2018 edition), https://www.archives.gov/files/federal-register/write/handbook/ddh.pdf.
29. Computer programs can generate and submit thousands of repetitive comments that can appear to be from different individuals. US Senate, Committee on Homeland Security and Government Affairs, "Abuses of the Federal Notice and Comment Rulemaking Process," 2019, 6, https://www.hsgac.senate.gov/wp-content/uploads/imo/media/doc/2019-10-24%20PSI%20Staff%20Report%20-%20Abuses%20of%20the%20Federal%20Notice-and-Comment%20Rulemaking%20Process.pdf.
30. Gardner, *Lawyers*, 24.
31. Surface Mining Reclamation and Enforcement Office, Rule, "Stream Protection Rule," 81 Fed. Reg. 93066 (Dec. 20, 2016).
32. Joint Resolution, Public Law No. 155-5, 131 Stat. 10 (2017).
33. 5 U.S.C. § 801(b)(2) (2024).
34. Chevron, U.S.A., Inc. v. Natural Resources Defense Council, 467 U.S. 837, 842–43 (1984).
35. Ibid., 842.
36. Ibid., 843.

37. United States v. Mead Corporation, 533 U.S. 218, 243 (2001) (Scalia, J., dissenting).
38. Marbury v. Madison, 5 U.S. (1 Cranch) 137, 177 (1803).
39. Gutierrez-Brizuela v. Lynch, 834 F.3d 1142, 1149 (10th Cir. 2016) (Gorsuch, J., concurring).
40. West Virginia v. Environmental Protection Agency, 142 S. Ct. 2587, 2605 (2022) (internal quotation marks omitted).
41. Ibid.
42. Ibid., 2609.
43. Ibid., 2620 (Gorsuch, J., concurring).
44. Ibid., 2644 (Kagan, J., dissenting).
45. "In April 2017, then-Attorney General Jeff Sessions famously declared himself 'amazed' that a single 'judge sitting on an island in the Pacific' could enjoin the President from enforcing one iteration of the so-called travel ban. But Sessions captured a widespread sentiment about the seeming oddity that one district court judge could declare a federal statute, regulation, or policy invalid and prevent the Executive Branch from enforcing it anywhere or against anyone." Alan M. Trammel, "Demystifying Nationwide Injunctions," 98 *Texas Law Review* 98 (2019): 67.
46. See Texas v. United States, 549 F. Supp. 3d 572 (S.D. Tex. 2021); California v. United States Bureau of Land Management, 277 F. Supp. 3d 1106 (N.D. Cal. 2017); New York v. Wheeler, 2019 U.S. Dist. LEXIS 124339 (S.D.N.Y. 2019).
47. Justice Gorsuch noted that "the increasingly common practice of trial courts ordering relief that transcends the cases before them" is a "real problem" because these orders "direct how the defendant [the agency] must act toward persons who are not parties to the case." Department of Homeland Security v. New York, 140 S. Ct. 599, 600 (2020). As a result, he explained, parties are "forced to rush from one preliminary injunction hearing to another, leaping from one emergency stay application to the next, each with potentially nationwide stakes, and all based on expedited briefing and little opportunity for the adversarial testing of evidence." Ibid. Similarly, Justice Thomas expressed skepticism about nationwide injunctions, stating that their use appears "to be inconsistent with longstanding limits" on the judiciary's equitable relief powers and that "if their popularity continues, this Court must address their legality." Trump v. Hawaii, 138 S. Ct. 2392, 2425 (2018).
48. Paul Fuller, "Is There a Federal Police Power?" *Columbia Law Review* 4, no. 8 (1904): 563–88.
49. Michael A. Foster and Erin H. Ward, *Congress's Authority to Regulate Interstate Commerce*, Congressional Research Service, November 2021, https://crsreports.congress.gov/product/pdf/IF/IF11971.
50. "Commerce," *Webster's Dictionary* 1828, accessed November 29, 2023, https://webstersdictionary1828.com/Dictionary/commerce.
51. Hammer v. Dagenhart, 247 U.S. 251 (1918).
52. United States v. Darby, 312 U.S. 100, 113 (1941).
53. Wickard v. Filburn, 317 U.S. 111 (1942).
54. Ibid., 125.

55. For example, trip- and equipment-related activities by 45 million birders in the United States generate approximately "$96 billion in total industry output, 782,000 jobs, and $16 billion in local, state, and federal tax revenue." US Fish and Wildlife Service, *Birding in the United States: A Demographic and Economic Analysis: Addendum to the 2016 National Survey of Fishing, Hunting, and Wildlife-Associated Recreation*, Report 2016-2, 2019, 13.
56. Gonzales v. Raich, 545 U.S. 1 (2005).
57. Since *Gonzales v. Raich*, many more states have approved the use of marijuana for medical purposes, and some have even decriminalized possession for recreational use to a limited degree. But possession of marijuana products is still illegal at the federal level. The THC gummy bears that one consumes in Colorado remain a violation of the Controlled Substances Act. The executive branch has just chosen to exercise its enforcement discretion and not prosecute. But the states' actions to approve marijuana use and the Department of Justice's forbearance have no effect on Congress's commerce powers.
58. For example, the Court held that Congress exceeded its authority in the Guns-Free School Zones Act when it prohibited the possession of firearms within 1,000 feet of public and private schools. United States v. Lopez, 514 U.S. 549, 551 (1995). Invoking a return to "first principles," that Congress can act only through enumerated powers, the Court thought that "the possession of a gun in a local school zone is in no sense an economic activity that might, through repetition elsewhere, substantially affect any sort of interstate commerce." Ibid., 567. It was up to the states to penalize such conduct. Similarly, the Court concluded that Congress went too far in granting a civil cause of action for victims of gender-based violence. United States v. Morrison, 529 U.S. 598 (2000). The common thread in both cases, according to the Court, was that the regulated activities (gun possession and sexual assault) were criminal and noneconomic.
59. National Federation of Independent Business v. Sebelius, 567 U.S. 519, 558 (2012).
60. James B. Stewart, "How Broccoli Landed on Supreme Court Menu," *New York Times*, June 13, 2012, https://www.nytimes.com/2012/06/14/business/how-broccoli-became-a-symbol-in-the-health-care-debate.html.
61. National Federation of Independent Business v. Sebelius, 567 U.S. at 557.
62. Ibid., 574.
63. Distinctions were even made for alcohol consumers based on sex. See Craig v. Boren, 429 U.S. 190 (1976) (invalidating on equal protection grounds prohibiting males eighteen to twenty years of age from drinking beer with an alcohol content greater than 3.2 percent).
64. Stephen Cucchiaro et al., *The Effect of the 18-Year Old Drinking Age on Auto Accidents*, Massachusetts Institute of Technology Operations Research Center and Laboratory of Architecture and Planning, May 1974, https://dspace.mit.edu/bitstream/handle/1721.1/5242/OR-034-74.pdf?iframe=true&width=900&height=450.
65. Pub. L. 98–363, § 6(a), 98 Stat. 437 (1984).

66. South Dakota v. Dole, 483 U.S. 203, 212 (1987).
67. Ibid., 209.
68. Ibid., 211.
69. National Federation of Independent Business v. Sebelius, 567 U.S. at 541–42.
70. Ibid., 581.
71. Royal C. Gardner, "Exporting American Values: Tenth Amendment Principles and International Environmental Assistance," *Harvard Environmental Law Review* 22 (1998): 10.

Chapter 3

1. "Historian Addresses Wesleyan," *New York Times*, June 4, 1984, https://www.nytimes.com/1984/06/04/nyregion/historian-addresses-wesleyan.html.
2. David McCullough, *The Johnstown Flood* (New York: Simon & Schuster, 1968), 262.
3. Richard L. Madden, "Connecticut Is Drying Out as Swollen Rivers Hit Crest," *New York Times*, June 4, 1984, https://www.nytimes.com/1984/06/02/nyregion/connecticut-is-drying-out-as-swollen-rivers-hit-crest.html.
4. "Historian Addresses Wesleyan."
5. "An Ordinance for the Government of the Territory of the United States North-West of the River Ohio," July 13, 1787, https://www.archives.gov/milestone-documents/northwest-ordinance.
6. Ibid., § 14, article 4.
7. *Act of August 7, 1789*, 1 Stat. 50.
8. Acts of the Fourth Congress of the United States, Statute I. Chap. XXIX(a), § 4 (May 18, 1796), https://tile.loc.gov/storage-services/service/ll/llsl//llsl-c4/llsl-c4.pdf. The provision regarding navigable waters remaining public highways is also found in the act of March 3, 1803, with respect to lands south of Tennessee, as well as the act of March 26, 1804, regarding lands in the Indiana Territory and several acts that admitted states to the Union. Merritt Starr, "Navigable Waters of the United States—State and National Control," *Harvard Law Review* 35 (1921): 169 n.65.
9. Acts of the Fourth Congress of the United States, Statute I. Chap. XXIX(a), § 9.
10. Ibid.
11. Starr, "Navigable Waters," 161 (stating that "rafting is treated as navigation under the Acts of Congress of 1796 and 1804 which dealt with frontier streams and creeks over which rafting, and fur-trading carried on in batteaux, barges, canoes, and similar craft, were the only known forms of navigation").
12. Gibbons v. Ogden, 22 U.S. (9 Wheat.) 1 (1824).
13. S. L. Kotar and J. E. Gessler, *The Steamboat Era: A History of Fulton's Folly on American Rivers, 1807–1860* (Jefferson, NC: McFarland & Co., Inc., 2009), 9.
14. Ibid., 10.
15. Gibbons, 22 U.S. at 71.
16. Ibid.
17. Ibid., 72.
18. U.S. Const. art. I, § 10, cl.2.

19. Gibbons, 22 U.S. at 76.
20. Ibid., 87.
21. Ibid., 94.
22. See James M. McGoldrick, Jr., "The Dormant Commerce Clause: The Origin Story and the 'Considerable Uncertainties'–1824 to 1945," 52 *Creighton L. Rev.* 243, 243, June 2019.
23. Gibbons, 22 U.S. at 94.
24. Willson v. Black Bird Creek Marsh Co., 27 U.S. (2 Pet.) 245 (1829).
25. Ibid., 245–46.
26. Craig Joyce, "The Rise of the Supreme Court Reporter: An Institutional Perspective on Marshall Court Ascendancy," *Michigan Law Review* 83 (1985): 1293.
27. Michael P. Collins, Jr., "*Willson v. Black-Bird Creek Marsh Co.*, 25 U.S. 245 (1829): An Early Test of the Dormant Commerce Clause," 7 n.30 (November 29, 2016), https://digitalcommons.law.umaryland.edu/cgi/viewcontent.cgi?article=1067&context=mlh_pubs.
28. Richard Peters, *Reports of Cases Argued and Adjudged in the Supreme Court of the United States, January Term 1829*, 3rd ed., vol. II, ed. Frederick C. Brightly (New York: The Banks Law Publishing Company, 1903), 153. Richard Peters was the original author or compiler of the opinions, which Brightly later edited and added notes and references.
29. Ibid.
30. Willson, 27 U.S. at 246.
31. Ibid., 248.
32. Ibid., 249.
33. Ibid.
34. Ibid., 252.
35. Ibid.
36. Ibid., 251.
37. Ibid.
38. Louis C. Hunter, *Steamboats on the Western Rivers: An Economic and Technological History* (New York: Dover Publications, 1993): 3–5.
39. See Paul F. Paskoff, *Troubled Waters: Steamboat Disasters, River Improvements, and American Public Policy*, 1821–1860 (Baton Rouge: Louisiana State University Press, 2007).
40. "The Sultana Disaster," American Battlefield Trust, accessed December 3, 2023, https://www.battlefields.org/learn/articles/sultana-disaster.
41. Paskoff, *Troubled Waters*, 20.
42. The Daniel Ball, 77 U.S. (10 Wall.) 557 (1870).
43. Ibid., 563.
44. Ibid.
45. Ibid., 565.
46. Ibid.
47. Jack Sullivan, "Root & Midler's Liquor Floated Their Boats," *Those Pre-Pro Whiskey Men!*, February 14, 2018, http://pre-prowhiskeymen.blogspot.com/2018/02/root-midlers-liquor-floated-their-boats.html.
48. The Daniel Ball, 77 U.S. at 566.

49. "The federal government owns approximately 640 million acres of land within the United States, or about thirty percent of the total land area of the nation." Eric Biber, "The Property Clause, Article IV, and Constitutional Structure," *Emory Law Journal* 71 (2022): 747.
50. Camfield v. United States, 167 U.S. 518, 525 (1897) ("The general government doubtless has a power over its own property analogous to the police power of the several states.").
51. In a 1900 case involving a question of the navigability of a swamp, the US Supreme Court summed up the prevailing attitude: "If there is any fact which may be supposed to be known by everybody, and therefore by courts, it is that swamps and stagnant waters are the cause of malarial and malignant fevers, and that the police power is never more legitimately exercised than in removing such nuisances." Leovy v. United States, 177 U.S. 621, 636 (1900).
52. US Department of Agriculture, *Swamp and Overflowed Lands in the United States: Ownership and Reclamation*, by J. O. Wright, (Washington, DC: US Department of Agriculture, 1907), https://brittlebooks.library.illinois.edu/brittlebooks_open/Books2009-09/wrigjo0001swaove/wrigjo0001swaove.pdf.
53. The General Land Office merged with US Grazing Service in 1946 to become the Bureau of Land Management. See "8 Things You Didn't Know about the Bureau of Land Management," *U.S. Department of Interior*, July 13, 2013, https://www.doi.gov/blog/8-things-you-didnt-know-about-bureau-land-management#:~:text=BLM%20was%20established%20on%20July,of%20present%20and%20future%20generations.
54. Benjamin H. Hibbard, *A History of the Public Land Policies* (New York: Peter Smith, 1939), 269, 275.
55. Ibid., 280.
56. Ibid., 278.
57. Charles Ponzi, of Ponzi scheme fame, was an early adopter. Erika Benson, "Swampland in Florida: 12 Things (2023) You Must Know," Gokce Capital, accessed December 4, 2023, https://gokcecapital.com/swampland-in-florida/.
58. Hibbard, *A History of the Public Land Policies*, 279.
59. Ibid., 281–82.
60. Ibid., 288 ("The Swamp Act provided a means [for the Federal government] of getting rid of land but to a trifling extent of effecting drainage.").
61. Garrett Power, "The Fox in the Chicken Coop: The Regulatory Program of the U.S. Army Corps of Engineers," *Virginia Law Review* 63 (1977): 506.
62. Ibid.
63. Willamette Iron Bridge Co. v. Hatch, 125 U.S. 1 (1888).
64. Tim Askin, "James C. Hawthorne (1819–1881)," *Oregon Encyclopedia*, https://www.oregonencyclopedia.org/articles/hawthorne_j.c/#.Y2EPCezMJR0.
65. Willamette Iron Bridge Co., 125 U.S. at 4.
66. Ibid., 8.
67. Ibid.
68. Ibid., 8–9.

69. Act of August 11, 1888, 25 Stat. 400.
70. Ibid., 425 (section 10).
71. Ibid., 408.
72. Ibid., 425, codified at 33 U.S.C. § 608 (2024).
73. Act of September 19, 1890, 26 Stat. 426, 453 (section 4).
74. Ibid.
75. Ibid. (section 3). The present value of $5,000 in 1890 is approximately $170,000.
76. Ibid.
77. Ibid., 554.
78. Ibid.
79. United States v. Rio Grande Dam & Irrigation Co., 174 U.S. 690 (1899).
80. "Truth or Consequences—What's with That Crazy Name?," *Sierra County New Mexico*, May 14, 2012, https://sierracountynewmexico.info/a-town-named-after-a-game-show/.
81. United States v. Rio Grande Dam & Irrigation Co., 174 U.S. at 708 (emphasis added).
82. Act of March 3, 1899, 30 Stat. 1121.
83. Ibid., 1151.
84. United States v. Keokuk & H. Bridge Co., 45 F. 178, 183 (S.D. Iowa 1891).
85. Act of March 3, 1899, 1151.
86. 33 U.S.C. § 403 (2024).
87. Act of March 3, 1899, 1152 (this section is also known as the Refuse Act of 1899).
88. Cummings v. Chicago, 188 U.S. 410, 428 (1903).
89. Ibid., 415–16.
90. Ibid., 431.
91. Theodore Roosevelt, "Veto Message," *The American Presidency Project*, https://www.presidency.ucsb.edu/node/206160.
92. Pub. L. 59-262, 34 Stat. 386 (1906).
93. Charles K. McFarland, "The Federal Government and Water Power, 1901–1913: A Legislative Study in the Nascence of Regulation," *Land Economics* 42, no. 4 (November 1966): 448 (quoting Letter of Taft to the president of the Merchants' Association of New York, January 27, 1906).
94. Pub. L. 66-280, 41 Stat. 1063 (1920).
95. Ibid., 1064.

Chapter 4

1. Puff Daddy & The Family, "All About the Benjamins," track 10 on *No Way Out*, Bad Boy/Arista (1997).
2. Zack O'Malley Greenberg, "Diddy's Net Worth: $740 Million in 2019," *Forbes*, June 17, 2019, https://www.forbes.com/sites/zackomalleygreenburg/2019/06/17/diddy-net-worth-740-million-in-2019/?sh=520597eb4ef1.
3. Chloe Best, "Mark Wahlberg and P Diddy Join Forces for a Very Surprising Reason," *Hello! Magazine*, February 9, 2018, https://www.hellomagazine.com/cuisine/2018020946172/mark-wahlberg-p-diddy-aquahydrate-uk/.

4. "William Murray Black," Cullum's Register, accessed December 3, 2023, https://penelope.uchicago.edu/Thayer/E/Gazetteer/Places/America/United_States/Army/USMA/Cullums_Register/2641*.html.
5. James H. Hitchman, "Unfinished Business: Public Works in Cuba, 1898–1902," *The Americas* 31, no. 3 (1975): 335–36.
6. Ibid., 347.
7. Ibid.
8. Albert E. Cowdrey, "Pioneering Environmental Law: The Army Corps of Engineers and the Refuse Act," *Pacific Historical Review* 44, no. 3 (1975): 341.
9. "New York's Sewage Problem a Hard One to Handle," *New York Times*, December 25, 1910.
10. War Department, Office of the Judge Advocate General, *A Digest of the Judge Advocates General of the Army, 1912* (Washington, DC: Government Printing Office, 1917), 756.
11. "The United States Public Health Service: Its Evolution and Organization," *Public Health Reports (1896–1970)* 36, no. 21 (1921): 1165.
12. Ibid., 1167.
13. Act of August 14, 1912, 37 Stat. 309 (section 1).
14. Allan J. McLaughlin, "Sewage Pollution of Interstate and International Waters with Special Reference to the Spread of Typhoid Fever," *Hygienic Laboratory Bulletin* no. 89, May 1913.
15. Ibid., 43.
16. Ibid., 44 ("The use of streams for the disposal of sewage is an economic resource and may often be employed without detriment to others.").
17. Ibid. 48–49.
18. Ibid., 49.
19. Pub. Law 68-238, 43 Stat. 604 (1924).
20. Ibid., 605 (section 3). See also Frederick C. Lincoln, "The Menace of Oil Pollution," *The Auk* 47, no. 4 (1930): 546–47.
21. Robert A. Shanley, "Franklin D. Roosevelt and Water Pollution Control Policy," *Presidential Studies Quarterly* 18, no. 2 (1988): 320.
22. Ibid., 321.
23. Ibid.
24. Franklin D. Roosevelt, "Executive Order 6777—Establishing the National Resources Board," June 30, 1934, https://www.presidency.ucsb.edu/documents/executive-order-6777-establishing-the-national-resources-board.
25. James Ridgeway, *The Politics of Ecology* (New York: E.P. Dutton & Co., 1970), 43–44.
26. Shanley, "Franklin D. Roosevelt," 325.
27. Ibid.
28. Ibid., 325–26.
29. "Bills Are Offered to Curb Pollution," *New York Times*, February 9, 1936.
30. John C. Morris, *Clean Water Policy and State Choice: Promise and Performance in the Water Quality Act* (Cambridge, UK: Cambridge University Press, 2022), 58.
31. Ibid.

32. Ibid.
33. H.R. 2711, "To Create a Division of Water Pollution Control in the United States Public Health Service," 75th Cong., 1st Sess., Jan 12, 1937.
34. Ibid.
35. Ibid.
36. "Statement by Roosevelt on His Veto of a Water Pollution Control Bill," June 25, 1938, in Edgar B. Nixon, ed., *Franklin D. Roosevelt and Conservation* (Hyde Park, NY: General Service Administration, 1957), document 799. https://www.nps.gov/parkhistory/online_books/cany/fdr/part3.htm.
37. N. William Hines, "History of the 1972 Clean Water Act: The Story Behind How the 1972 Act Became the Capstone on a Decade of Extraordinary Environmental Reform," *George Washington Journal of Energy and Environmental Law*, 4 (2013): 84.
38. "Statement by Roosevelt on His Veto of a Water Pollution Control Bill."
39. Ibid.
40. Ibid.
41. Ridgeway, *The Politics of Ecology*, 46.
42. H.R. 7971, "To prevent the pollution of the navigable waters of the United States, and for other purposes," 76th Cong., 3d Sess., January 17, 1940 (section 7(b)).
43. Shanley, "Franklin D. Roosevelt," 327.
44. Ibid.
45. "Water Pollution Control Act," Pub. L. 80-845, 62 Stat. 1155 (1948).
46. Ibid., 1161.
47. Ibid., 1156 (section 2(b)), 1160 (section 9(c)).
48. Ibid., 1155.
49. See, e.g., ibid., 1158–59 (section 6(b)).
50. Ibid., 1155–56.
51. Ibid., 1156.
52. Ibid. (section 2(d)(1)).
53. Ibid., 1156–57.
54. Hines, "History of the 1972 Clean Water Act," 85.
55. Ibid., 86.
56. Morris, 60.
57. Hines, "History of the 1972 Clean Water Act," 86.
58. Water Pollution Control Act Amendments of 1956, Pub. L. No. 84-660, 70 Stat. 498 (1956).
59. Ibid., 499–500.
60. Dwight D. Eisenhower, "Veto of Bill to Amend the Federal Water Pollution Control Act," accessed December 5, 2023, https://www.presidency.ucsb.edu/documents/veto-bill-amend-the-federal-water-pollution-control-act.
61. Ibid.
62. Ibid.
63. William L. Andreen, "The Evolution of Water Pollution Control in the United States—State, Local, and Federal Efforts, 1789–1972: Part II," *Stanford Environmental Law Journal* 22 (2003): 285–86.

Chapter 5

1. 33 U.S.C. § 407 (2024).
2. War Department, Office of the Judge Advocate General, *A Digest of the Judge Advocates General of the Army, 1912* (Washington, DC: Government Printing Office, 1917), 756. See also *United States v. Republic Steel Corp.*, 362 U.S. 482 (1960), where industrial waste was found to obstruct the navigable capacity of the Calumet River in violation of section 10 of the Rivers and Harbors Act.
3. United States v. Standard Oil Co., 384 U.S. 224, 225 (1966).
4. Ibid., 230.
5. Ibid., 226–29.
6. Ibid., 229.
7. Ibid.
8. Ibid., 230.
9. Ibid., 234.
10. Antonin Scalia and Bryan A. Garner, "A Note on the Use of Dictionaries," *Green Bag 2d* 16, no. 4 (2013): 422 (referring to *Webster's Third* as "notoriously permissive"). See also "Antonin Scalia v. Merriam-Webster," Merriam-Webster, accessed December 6, 2023, https://www.merriam-webster.com/wordplay/antonin-scalia-v-merriam-webster; Jeff Shesol, "Scalia's Word Games," *The New Yorker*, https://www.newyorker.com/news/news-desk/scalias-word-games.
11. United States v. Standard Oil Co., 384 U.S. at 234.
12. Ibid., 234.
13. Ibid.
14. Ibid., 236–37.
15. Federal Water Pollution Control Act Amendments of 1961, Pub. L. No. 87-88, 75 Stat. 204 (1961).
16. Ibid.
17. Ibid., 208.
18. Water Quality Act of 1965, Pub. L. No. 89-234, 79 Stat. 903 (1965).
19. Ibid., 907–9. N. William Hines, "History of the 1972 Clean Water Act: The Story Behind How the 1972 Act Became the Capstone on a Decade of Extraordinary Environmental Reform," *George Washington Journal of Energy and Environmental Law*, 4 (2013): 88.
20. Water Quality Act of 1965, 908.
21. Ibid., 908–9.
22. Ibid., 909.
23. Ibid.
24. Lyndon B. Johnson, "Remarks at a Ceremony Marking the Transfer of the Water Pollution Control Administration to the Department of the Interior," May 20, 1966, https://www.presidency.ucsb.edu/documents/remarks-ceremony-marking-the-transfer-the-water-pollution-control-administration-the.
25. Nedra Darling, "Transfer of Federal Water Pollution Control Administration to DOI Is Effected," *U.S. Department of Interior Indian Affairs*,

May 10, 1966, https://www.bia.gov/as-ia/opa/online-press-release/transfer-federal-water-pollution-control-administration-doi-effected.

26. Water Quality Improvement Act of 1970, Pub. L. No. 91-224, 84 Stat. 91, 108 (1970).
27. Lance D. Wood, "The Forum's Proposal to Delegate §404 to the States: A Bad Deal for Wetlands," *National Wetlands Newsletter* 11, no. 4 (1989): 4.
28. Richard Nixon, "Annual Message to the Congress on the State of the Union," January 22, 1970, https://www.presidency.ucsb.edu/documents/annual-message-the-congress-the-state-the-union-2.
29. Ibid.
30. Ibid.
31. Richard Nixon, "Special Message to the Congress on Environmental Quality," February 10, 1970, https://www.presidency.ucsb.edu/documents/special-message-the-congress-environmental-quality.
32. Ibid.
33. Richard Nixon, "Reorganization Plan No. 3 of 1970," July 9, 1970, https://www.epa.gov/archive/epa/aboutepa/reorganization-plan-no-3-1970.html.
34. Ibid.
35. Ibid.
36. Act of September 6, 1966, Pub. L. No. 89-554, 80 Stat. 378, 394 (1966) (codified at 5 U.S.C. § 901).
37. Ibid., 395.
38. Ibid.
39. Hines, "History of the 1972 Clean Water Act," 93.
40. Congressional Research Service, "Legislative Vetoes after *Chadha*," by [name redacted], RS22132, (May 2, 2005): 1.
41. Immigration and Naturalization Service v. Chadha, 462 U.S. 919 (1983).
42. 5 U.S.C. § 905 (2024).
43. See "Action Delayed on Elevating EPA's Status," *CQ Almanac 1993*, 49th ed. (Washington, DC: Congressional Quarterly, 1994), 266–68.
44. Olivia B. Waxman, "A Brief History of the State of the Union's Designated Survivor," *Time*, February 7, 2023, https://time.com/6253618/designated-survivor-2023-state-of-the-union/.
45. Jeff Rodriguez, "Another Photo-Op Idea That Was All Washed Up," *Greater Fort Worth Chapter PRSA*, January 21, 2021, https://fortworthprsa.org/shoring-up-the-base/.
46. Hines, "History of the 1972 Clean Water Act," 93.
47. J. S. Ott, "Qui Tam Actions for Citizen Enforcement of the Refuse Act of 1899 against Polluters," *Cleveland State Law Review*, 21 (1972): 184–85.
48. US Department of Justice, Guidelines for Litigation under the Refuse Act (33 U.S.C. 407), reprinted in Bureau of National Affairs, *Environment Reporter* 1, no. 12 (July 17, 1970): 288–90.
49. Ibid., 288.
50. Ibid.
51. Ott, "Qui Tam Actions," 183.
52. Ibid., 182–83.

53. Hines, "History of the 1972 Clean Water Act," 93–94; Charles N. Drennan, "Qui Tam Actions under the 1899 Refuse Act: Possibility of Individual Legal Action to Prevent Water Pollution," *Missouri Law Review* 36 (1971): 499.
54. Ott, "Qui Tam Actions," 185–87.
55. 35 Fed. Reg. 19627 (1970).
56. Ibid.
57. Hines, "History of the 1972 Clean Water Act," 94.
58. Ibid.
59. "The Burns Case," *Time* 97, no. 4 (1971): 43–44.
60. Ibid., 44.
61. Ibid., 43.
62. Kalur v. Resor, 335 F. Supp. 1 (D.D.C. 1971).
63. Ibid., 4–5.
64. Ibid., 12.
65. Ibid.
66. Ibid., 10–11.
67. Ibid., 12.
68. Ibid.
69. Hines, "History of the 1972 Clean Water Act," 98.
70. Richard Nixon, "Veto of the Federal Water Pollution Control Act Amendments of 1972," https://www.presidency.ucsb.edu/documents/veto-the-federal-water-pollution-control-act-amendments-1972.
71. "Clean Water: Congress Overrides Presidential Veto," *CQ Almanac 1972*, 28th ed. (Washington, DC: Congressional Quarterly, 1973).
72. H.R. 11896, 92d Cong., 1st Sess. § 502(8) (1971). Despite the circular definition, the Public Works Committee suggested that the term be given "the broadest possible constitutional interpretation." William W. Sapp, Tracy L. Starr, and M. Allison Burdette, "From the Fields of Runnymede to the Waters of the United States: A Historical Review of the Clean Water Act and the Term 'Navigable Waters,'" *Environmental Law Reporter* 36 (March 2006): 10201.
73. S. 2770, 92d Cong., 1st Sess. § 1 (1971).
74. S. Conf. Rep. No. 92-1236, 92d Cong., 2d Sess., U.S.C.C.A.N. (1972): 3822.
75. 118 Cong. Rec. 33,756–33,757 (1972).
76. 33 U.S.C. § 1251(a) (2024).
77. 33 U.S.C. § 1311 (2024).
78. Hines, "History of the 1972 Clean Water Act," 101.
79. Ibid.; 33 U.S.C. § 1342 (2024).
80. Hines, "History of the 1972 Clean Water Act," 100–1.
81. 33 U.S.C. § 1312 (2024); "Technology-Based Effluent Limitations," in U.S. Environmental Protection Agency, *NPDES Permit Writers' Manual* (Washington, DC: Water Permits Division, 2010): 5-1.
82. 33 U.S.C. § 1251(b) (2024).
83. 33 U.S.C. § 1342(b) (2024).
84. "NPDES State Program Authority," US Environmental Protection Agency, accessed December 7, 2023, https://www.epa.gov/npdes/npdes-state-program-authority.

85. 33 U.S.C. § 1312 (2024); Hines, "History of the 1972 Clean Water Act," 101–2.
86. 33 U.S.C. §§ 1313(b)(1)(A) & 1342 (2024); Hines, "History of the 1972 Clean Water Act," 102.
87. Hines, "History of the 1972 Clean Water Act," 97.
88. Palmer Hough and Morgan Robertson, "Mitigation under Section 404 of the Clean Water: Where It Comes From, What It Means," *Wetlands Ecology and Management* 17, no. 1 (2009): 16.
89. 33 U.S.C. § 1344(b)(1) (2024).
90. Ibid., § 1344(c).
91. Oliver A. Houck, "Hard Choices: The Analysis of Alternatives under Section 404 of the Clean Water Act and Similar Environmental Laws," *University of Colorado Law Review*, 60 (1989): 774–75.
92. 38 Fed. Reg. 1363 (1973). The proposed rule dropped the comma between "United States" and "including" for some reason.
93. 38 Fed. Reg. 13,528 (1973).
94. Ibid.
95. Ibid., 13,529.
96. 39 Fed. Reg. 12,115 (1974).
97. Ibid., 12,119.
98. Natural Resources Defense Council, Inc. v. Callaway, 392 F. Supp. 685 (D.D.C. 1975).
99. Ibid., 686.
100. Ibid.
101. Michael Blumm and D. Bernard Zaleha, "Federal Wetlands Protection under the Clean Water Act: Regulatory Ambivalence, Intergovernmental Tension, and a Call for Reform," *University of Colorado Law Review*, 60 (1989): 705 n. 56 (quoting Dep't of Army, Office of Chief of Engineers, Press Release, May 6, 1975).
102. Congressional Research Service, "Evolution of the Meaning of 'Waters of the United States' in the Clean Water Act," by Stephen P. Mulligan, R44585 (updated March 5, 2019): 10 n.71.
103. Ibid.
104. Ibid.
105. Ibid. See 40 Fed. Reg. 31,324–25 (1975) for the complete definition.
106. Clean Water Act of 1977, Pub. L. No. 95–217, 91 Stat. 1566 (1977).
107. 123 Cong. Rec. 26,710–11 (1977).
108. Ibid., 26,7111.
109. Ibid., 26,721.
110. Ibid., 26,713. Senator Hart offered an organic analogy, suggesting that Senator Bentsen's amendment was akin to saying "that we are only going to treat the cancer if it occurs in the trunk of the body. But not to allow any treatments for the arms and the legs, so that if you have cancer in the hand, the arm, the foot, or the knee, we cannot treat that even though it may spread the rest of the body or cause the loss of the limb." Ibid.
111. Ibid., 23,716.
112. Ibid., 26,728.

113. H.R. 3199, 95th Cong., 1st Sess., § 16 (1977).
114. 123 Cong. Rec. 39,209 (1977).
115. 33 U.S.C. § 1344(f)(1)(A) (2024).
116. Ibid., § 1344(f)(1)(C).
117. Ibid., § 1344(f)(1)(E).
118. Ibid., § 1344(f)(2).
119. Ibid., § 1344(e).
120. "Decision Document Nationwide Permit 40," US Army Corps of Engineers, accessed December 7, 2023, https://usace.contentdm.oclc.org/utils/getfile/collection/p16021coll7/id/16838.
121. 33 U.S.C. § 1344(g) (2024).
122. "U.S. Interactive Map of State and Tribal Assumption under CWA Section 404," US Environmental Protection Agency, accessed December 8, 2023, https://www.epa.gov/cwa404g/us-interactive-map-state-and-tribal-assumption-under-cwa-section-404.
123. 33 U.S.C. § 1344(g)(1).
124. See Susan Roeder Martin and Rachael B. Santana, "State Assumption of the Clean Water Act Section 404 Permitting Program: Part I, an Overview," *Florida Bar Journal* 95, no. 1 (2021): 38.
125. 33 U.S.C. § 1341(a)(1) (2024).
126. Wood, "The Forum's Proposal," 4.
127. 86 Fed. Reg. 16,299 (2021) (explaining when state water quality certifications are required for "a Federal Energy Regulatory Commission hydroelectric project license, or a Natural Gas Act certificate of public convenience and necessity for a natural gas pipeline, or an authorization for an LNG terminal").
128. Pub. L. No. 95-522, 88 Stat. 1660 (1974).
129. 42 U.S.C. § 300g-1 (2024). Every state except for Wyoming (and DC) has been delegated primary SDWA authority. Congressional Research Service, "Safe Drinking Water Act (SDWA): A Summary of the Act and Its Major Requirements," by Elena H. Humphreys and Mary Tiemann, RL31243 (updated July 1, 2021): 1 n.1.
130. For example, even the Clean Water Rule, the broadest WOTUS interpretation, excludes groundwater. 80 Fed. Reg. 37,116 (2015). See also County of Maui v. Hawaii Wildlife Fund, 140 S. Ct. 1462, 1471–72.
131. 42 U.S.C. § 4321 (2024).
132. 40 C.F.R. § 1502.14(c) (2023).
133. Ibid., § 1501.5.
134. Ibid., § 1502.3.
135. 40 C.F.R. § 6.101(a) (2023) (EPA); 33 C.F.R. § 230.7(a) (2023) (Corps).
136. 16 U.S.C. § 1536(a)(2) (2024).
137. Ibid.
138. Congressional Research Service, "Endangered Species Act (ESA) Section 7 Consultation and Infrastructure Projects," by Erin H. Ward and Pervaze A. Sheikh, R46867 (August 4, 2021), 8. A jeopardy opinion may also include reasonable and prudent measures, alternatives that would avoid placing the species in jeopardy. Ibid.

139. The general prohibition on "taking" an endangered species, however, continues to apply, which can create some complications for developers. See Chapter 10 for the unintended consequences of eliminating Clean Water Act jurisdiction for projects that nevertheless may have an endangered or threatened species issue.
140. 33 U.S.C. § 1319(c), (d) & (g) (2024) (criminal, civil, and administrative penalties, respectively).
141. 40 C.F.R. § 19.4, Table 1.
142. 33 U.S.C. § 1319(a).
143. The EPA needs to notify the state, however. Ibid., § 1319(a) & (b).
144. See Congressional Research Service, "Clean Water Act: A Summary of the Law," by Claudia Copeland, RL30030 (October 18, 2016), 7 (noting that "the majority of actions taken to enforce the law are undertaken by states").
145. U.S.C. § 1365 (2024).
146. Ibid., § 1365(b).
147. Ibid., § 1365(d).

Chapter 6

1. Tom Paugh, "Sports Afield and the Candidates," *Sports Afield* 200, no. 4 (1988): 13.
2. "Statement by Press Secretary Fitzwater on Development of Wetlands Conservation Policy," George H.W. Bush Presidential Library & Museum, accessed January 1, 2024, https://bush41library.tamu.edu/archives/public-papers/1439.
3. I attended as the Department of the Army's principal wetland attorney. Upon learning that I was an attorney from Washington, DC, a good-natured farmer pointed to a bale of hay and tried to convince me it was a "cow cocoon"—"where cows come from."
4. Administrative Authority to Construe § 404 of the Federal Water Pollution Control Act," 43 Op. Att'y Gen. 197 (1979).
5. Ibid., 200.
6. Ibid., 200–01.
7. Ibid., 201.
8. Ibid.
9. Ibid., 202.
10. Ibid.
11. Congressional Research Service, "Evolution of the Meaning of 'Waters of the United States' in the Clean Water Act," by Stephen P. Mulligan, R44585 (updated March 5, 2019), 12.
12. 45 Fed. Reg. 33,290, 33424 (1980) (EPA definition); 47 Fed. Reg. 31,7194, 31,811 (1982) (Corps definition).
13. "Lake St. Clair," Wikipedia, accessed January 1, 2024, https://en.wikipedia.org/wiki/Lake_St._Clair.
14. "Lake St. Clair (Lac Sainte Claire)," The Historical Marker Database, accessed January 1, 2024, https://www.hmdb.org/m.asp?m=102458.
15. Christina Hall, "Lake St. Clair, a Destination for Fun and Source of Life, Drives $1.6 Billion in Impact," *Detroit Free Press*, August 6, 2023,

https://www.freep.com/story/news/local/michigan/2023/08/06/lake-st-clair-heart-of-it-all/70407813007/.

16. United States v. Riverside Bayview Homes, Inc., 729 F.2d 391, 393 (6th Cir. 1984).
17. Ibid., 392.
18. Ibid., 393.
19. Ibid.
20. Ibid., 398.
21. Ibid.
22. "United States v. Riverside Bayview Homes, Inc., Oral Argument—October 16, 1985," accessed January 1, 2024, https://www.oyez.org/cases/1985/84-701 (beginning at 5:20).
23. Ibid. (beginning at 7:20).
24. United States v. Riverside Bayview Homes, Inc., 474 U.S. 121 (1985).
25. Ibid., 126–27.
26. Ibid., 129 note 6. Moreover, the proper remedy for a taking is the payment of just compensation, not invalidation of a regulation. The government can almost always take your property; it just has to pay you for it.
27. Ibid., 129.
28. 47 Fed. Reg. 31,7194, 31,811 (1982).
29. "United States v. Riverside Bayview Homes, Inc., Oral Argument—October 16, 1985" (beginning at 16:36).
30. Ibid. (beginning at 48:44).
31. United States v. Riverside Bayview Homes, Inc., 474 U.S. at 131.
32. Ibid.
33. Ibid., 132.
34. Ibid., 133.
35. Ibid., 134.
36. Ibid.
37. Ibid., 131 note 8.
38. "United States v. Riverside Bayview Homes, Inc., Oral Argument—October 16, 1985" (exchanges beginning at 21:50 and 22:38).
39. 51 Fed. Reg. 41,206, 41,210 (1986).
40. Ibid., 41,250.
41. Ibid., 41,217.
42. 53 Fed. Reg. 20,764, 20,765 (1988).
43. Federal Interagency Committee for Delineating Wetlands, *Federal Manual for Identifying and Delineating Jurisdictional Wetlands* (Washington, DC: Government Printing Office, 1989).
44. W. R. Walker and S. C. Richardson, "The Federal Wetlands Manual: Swamped by Controversy," *Virginia Water Resources Research Center*, Special Report No. 24, October 1991.
45. Marianne Lavelle, "Wetlands: The New Battle Cry in Washington," *National Law Journal*, July 23, 1990.
46. Royal C. Gardner, "Public Participation and Wetlands Regulation," *UCLA Journal of Environmental Law & Policy* 10 (1991): 29–31.

47. 56 Fed. Reg. 40,446 (1991).
48. Environmental Defense Fund and World Wildlife Fund, *How Wet Is a Wetland? The Impacts to the Proposed Revisions to the Federal Wetlands Delineation Manual* (Laurel, MD: S & S Graphics, 1992), 70.
49. Congressional Research Service, "Evolution of the Meaning of 'Waters of the United States,'" 16.
50. Energy and Water Development Appropriations Act, 1993, Pub. L. 102-377, 106 Stat. 1315, 1324–25.
51. "Regional Supplements to Corps Delineation Manual," *U.S. Army Corps of Engineers*, accessed January 1, 2024, https://www.usace.army.mil/Missions/Civil-Works/Regulatory-Program-and-Permits/reg_supp/.
52. Solid Waste Agency of Northern Cook County v. U.S. Army Corps of Engineers, 531 U.S. 159, 162-63 (2001).
53. Solid Waste Agency of Northern Cook County v. U.S. Army Corps of Engineers, 191 F3d 845, 848 (7th Cir. 1999).
54. Ibid.
55. Ibid., 847.
56. Ibid., 852.
57. Ibid., 851.
58. Ibid., 850.
59. Ibid.
60. Ibid.
61. Solid Waste Agency of Northern Cook County v. U.S. Army Corps of Engineers, 531 U.S. at 162.
62. Ibid., 172.
63. Ibid., 167 (emphasis added to *significant nexus*).
64. Ibid., 172.
65. Ibid., 173.
66. The method by which Corps promulgated the Migratory Bird Rule may also have contributed to the Court's reluctance to grant *Chevron* deference. The Migratory Bird Rule was not a regulation; as the Court noted in passing, it did not go through the notice and comment rulemaking requirements of the Administrative Procedure Act. Ibid., 164, note 1. Therefore, it was an interpretive rule. There is nothing intrinsically wrong with interpretive rules, but in litigation a court may be less willing to rely on the agency's judgment if it has not been subjected to public scrutiny.
67. Jon Kusler, "The SWANCC Decision: State Regulation of Wetlands to Fill the Gap," Association of State Wetland Managers, 2004.
68. Jan Goldman-Carter, "Isolated Wetland Legislation: Running the Rapids at the State Capitol," *National Wetlands Newsletter* 27, no. 3 (2005): 27–29.
69. 68 Fed. Reg. 1991 (2003).
70. Congressional Research Service, "Evolution of the Meaning of 'Waters of the United States,'" 20; Felicity Barringer, "In Reversal, E.P.A. Won't Narrow Wetlands Protection," *New York Times*, December 17, 2003.
71. Mark C. Rains et al., "Geographically Isolated Wetlands Are Part of the Hydrological Landscape," *Hydrological Processes* 30 (2016): 153–60.

72. Gary Mechanic, "Birds, Bales and Waters of the United States," Friends of the Fox River, accessed January 2, 2024, https://friendsofthefoxriver.org/2017/03/30/birds-bales-waters-united-states/.
73. Rapanos v. United States, 547 U.S. 715, 763 (2006) (Kennedy, J., concurring in the judgment).
74. Ibid, 720 (plurality opinion).
75. United States v. Rapanos, 376 F.3d 629, 632 (6th Cir. 2004).
76. Ibid.
77. Ibid.
78. Ibid. 632–33.
79. Rapanos v. United States, 547 U.S. at 763–64 (Kennedy, J., concurring in the judgment).
80. Ibid., 721 (plurality opinion).
81. Ibid.
82. Ibid.
83. Ibid., 734.
84. Ibid., 727 note 2.
85. Ibid., 732.
86. Ibid.
87. Ariel Wittenberg, "Will Scalia's Dictionary Haunt Trump's Overhaul," *E&E News*, May 15, 2017, https://www.eenews.net/articles/will-scalias-dictionary-haunt-trumps-wotus-overhaul/.
88. Ibid.
89. Ibid.
90. Rapanos v. United States, 547 U.S. at 734 (plurality opinion).
91. Ibid., 742.
92. Ibid., 788 (Stevens, J., dissenting).
93. Ibid.
94. Ibid., 805.
95. Ibid., 788.
96. Ibid., 777 (Kennedy, J., concurring in the judgment).
97. Ibid., 778.
98. Ibid., 780.
99. "John Rapanos Agrees to Pay for Clean Water Act Violations," U.S. Department of Justice, accessed January 2, 2024, https://www.epa.gov/archive/epapages/newsroom_archive/newsreleases/b029ab82bf92cd5f8525752e0072fc60.html.
100. 72 Fed. Reg. 31824 (2007).
101. US Environmental Protection Agency and US Department of the Army, "Clean Water Act Jurisdiction Following the U.S. Supreme Court's Decision in *Rapanos v. United States* & *Carabell v. United States*," June 5, 2007, https://www.epa.gov/sites/default/files/2016-04/documents/rapanosguidance6507.pdf.
102. Ibid.
103. Ibid.
104. Ibid.

105. US Environmental Protection Agency and US Department of the Army, "Clean Water Act Jurisdiction Following the U.S. Supreme Court's Decision in *Rapanos v. United States* & *Carabell v. United States*," December 2, 2008, https://www.epa.gov/sites/default/files/2016-02/documents/cwa_jurisdiction_following_rapanos120208.pdf.

Chapter 7

1. *The Education of Henry Adams* (Boston: Houghton Mifflin Company, 1918).
2. Herbert F. Hahn, "The Education of Henry Adams Reconsidered," *College English* 24 (1963): 447.
3. See John McPhee, *The Control of Nature* (New York: Farrar, Straus and Giroux, 1990); Elizabeth Kolbert, *Under a White Sky* (New York: Crown, 2022).
4. 79 Fed. Reg. 22,187 (2014).
5. "EPA Administrator McCarthy Gives an Overview of EPA's Clean Water Act Rule Proposal," *U.S. Environmental Protection Agency* (March 25, 2014), https://www.youtube.com/watch?v=ow-n8zZuDYc.
6. The proposed change would also effectively respond to an earlier Fourth Circuit decision, *United States v. Wilson*, where the court found the "could affect" interstate commerce language in the 1986/1988 rules to be overly broad. Congressional Research Service, "Evolution of the Meaning of 'Waters of the United States' in the Clean Water Act," by Stephen P. Mulligan, R44585 (updated March 5, 2019): 17–18.
7. 79 Fed. Reg. at 22,217–19.
8. Ibid., 22,189.
9. Ibid., 22,207.
10. Christopher Flavelle et al., "New Data Reveals Hidden Flood Risk across America," *New York Times*, June 29, 2020.
11. 79 Fed. Reg. at 22,236.
12. Ibid., 22,207.
13. Ibid., 22,199.
14. Ibid.
15. US Environmental Protection Agency, "Connectivity of Streams and Wetlands to Downstream Waters: A Review and Synthesis of the Scientific Evidence" (External Review Draft), 2013.
16. 78 Fed. Reg. 58,536 (2013).
17. 79 Fed. Reg. at 22,189.
18. US Environmental Protection Agency, "Connectivity of Streams and Wetlands to Downstream Waters: A Review and Synthesis of the Scientific Evidence" (Final Report), 2015.
19. Ibid., ES-6.
20. Ibid., ES-7 to ES-8; Richard B. Alexander et al., "The Role of Headwater Streams in Downstream Water Quality," *Journal of the American Water Resources Association* 43 (2007): 41–59.
21. US Environmental Protection Agency, Final Report, 6-3.
22. Ibid., 6-3 to 6-4.
23. Ibid., ES-3.

24. Ibid., 2-24.
25. Personal conversation with the author at the National Mitigation and Ecosystem Banking Conference.
26. 79 Fed. Reg. 61,590 (2014).
27. "Mass Comment Campaign Sponsored by Clean Water Action Denver (web)," U.S. Environmental Protection Agency, January 20, 2015, https://www.regulations.gov/comment/EPA-HQ-OW-2011-0880-19244.
28. "Mass Comment Campaign Sponsored by Kentucky Farm Bureau Insurance Companies (paper)," U.S. Environmental Protection Agency, January 26, 2015, https://www.regulations.gov/comment/EPA-HQ-OW-2011-0880-19386.
29. See Richard G. Stoll, "Effective Written Comments in Informal Rulemaking," *Administrative & Regulatory Law News* 32, no. 4 (2007): 15–17.
30. "Comment Submitted by Jannette Brimmer and Jennifer Chavez, Staff Attorneys, Earthjustice," U.S. Environmental Protection Agency, November 13, 2014, https://www.regulations.gov/comment/EPA-HQ-OW-2011-0880-14564.
31. Ibid., 14–16.
32. "Comment Submitted by Deidre G. Duncan et al., Hunton & Williams LLP on Behalf of Waters Advocacy Coalition (WAC)," U.S. Environmental Protection Agency, November 13, 2014, https://www.regulations.gov/comment/EPA-HQ-OW-2011-0880-14568.
33. Ibid., 1.
34. Ibid. The more than 100-page submission called on the agencies to withdraw the proposed rule at least ten times for various perceived deficiencies.
35. 79 Fed. Reg. at 22,216.
36. Ibid., 22,209.
37. Dylan Matthews, "Who Is Saul Alinsky, and Why Does the Right Hate Him So Much?," *Vox* (updated July 19, 2016), https://www.vox.com/2014/10/6/6829675/saul-alinsky-explain-obama-hillary-clinton-rodham-organizing.
38. "'That's Enough' ('Let It Go' Parody)," Missouri Farm Bureau, May 23, 2014, https://www.youtube.com/watch?v=9U0OqJqNbbs.
39. "Clay Family Talks about Their Ditch the Rule Parody Video," American Farm Bureau, June 9, 2014, https://www.youtube.com/watch?v=AGUEsFsfM8k.
40. Susan A. Poling, "Environmental Protection Agency—Application of Publicity or Propaganda and Anti-Lobbying Provisions," U.S. Government Accountability Office, December 14, 2015, https://www.gao.gov/assets/b-326944.pdf.
41. Ibid., 5.
42. Ibid.
43. Jeffrey Kluger, "Senator Throws Snowball! Climate Change Disproven!" *Time*, February 27, 2014, https://time.com/3725994/inhofe-snowball-climate/.
44. Poling, "Environmental Protection Agency," 1.

45. Financial Services and General Government Appropriations Act, Pub. L. No. 113-76, div. E, § 718 (2014); Financial Services and General Government Appropriations Act, Pub. L. No. 113-235, div. E, § 718 (2015).
46. Financial Services and General Government Appropriations Act, Pub. L. No. 113-235, div. E, § 715 (2015); Department of Interior, Environment, and Related Agencies Appropriations Act, Pub. L. No. 113-235, div. F, § 401 (2015).
47. Poling, "Environmental Protection Agency," 12.
48. Ibid., 13.
49. Ibid., 17–18.
50. Ibid., 21–24.
51. Ibid., 24.
52. 80 Fed. Reg. 37,054 (2015).
53. Ibid., 37,058.
54. Ibid.
55. Ibid.
56. Ibid., 37,089.
57. Ibid., 37,105.
58. Ibid.
59. Ibid., 37,090.
60. Charles H. Koch Jr., William S. Jordan III, Richard W. Murphy, and Louis J. Virelli III, *Administrative Law: Cases and Materials*, 8th ed. (Durham, NC: Carolina Academic Press, 2020), 93.
61. 5 U.S.C. § 801 (2024).
62. "Ernst Urges Support of Her Resolution to Eliminate WOTUS Rule," Joni Ernst, U.S. Senator, Iowa, November 5, 2015, https://www.ernst.senate.gov/news/press-releases/ernst-urges-support-of-her-resolution-to-eliminate-wotus-rule.
63. S.J.Res.22, 114th Congress (2015–2016), https://www.congress.gov/bill/114th-congress/senate-joint-resolution/22/actions.
64. Ibid.
65. Barack Obama, "Veto Message from the President—S.J. 22," January 19, 2016, https://obamawhitehouse.archives.gov/the-press-office/2016/01/19/president-obama-vetoes-sj-22.
66. Todd Gaziano, "Congress and Obama Clarify Their Positions on the WOTUS Rule, and It Doesn't Look Good for the President," Pacific Legal Foundation, January 22, 2016, https://pacificlegal.org/congress-and-obama-clarify-their-position-on-the-wotus-rule-and-it-doesnt-look-good-for-the-president/.
67. 33 U.S.C. § 1369(b)(1) (2024).
68. For the cases, based on each state's position, see Table 1 of the Appendix.
69. In re Clean Water Rule, 140 F. Supp. 3d 1340, MDL No. 2663, (Oct. 13, 2015).
70. Ibid.
71. Ohio v. United States Army Corps of Engineers (In re EPA & DOD Final Rule), 803 F.3d 804 (6th Cir. 2015).
72. "Theodore Roosevelt Quotes," Theodore Roosevelt National Park, North Dakota, accessed January 2, 2024, https://www.nps.gov/thro/learn/history-culture/theodore-roosevelt-quotes.htm.

73. "20 Fascinating Things North Dakota Is Known For and Famous For," NomadsUnveiled, https://nomadsunveiled.com/what-is-north-dakota-known-for/.
74. "North Dakota Facts," North Dakota Tourism Division, accessed January 2, 2024, https://www.ndtourism.com/articles/north-dakota-facts.
75. See Thomas C. Winter and Donald O. Rosenberry, "Hydrology of Prairie Pothole Wetlands during Drought and Deluge: A 17-Year Study of the Cottonwood Lake Wetland Complex in North Dakota in the Perspective of Longer Term Measured and Proxy Hydrological Records," *Climatic Change* 40, no. 2 (1998): 189–209.
76. Noah Wicks, "Prairie Pothole Republicans Seek to Eliminate Permanent Federal Easements," *AgriPulse*, November 2, 2022, https://www.agri-pulse.com/articles/18433-prairie-pothole-republicans-seek-to.
77. North Dakota v. United States EPA, 127 F. Supp. 3d 1047 (D.N.D. 2015).
78. Ibid., 1051.
79. Ibid., 1057.
80. Ibid., 1058.
81. Ibid., 1059.
82. Ibid., 1060.
83. "Order Limiting the Scope of Preliminary Injunction to the Plaintiffs," North Dakota v. United States EPA, 127 F. Supp. 3d 1047 (D.N.D. 2015) (order issued Sept. 4, 2015), https://www.agri-pulse.com/ext/resources/pdfs/w/o/t/e/r/WOTUS-Erickson-limiting-order.pdf.
84. "Ralph R. Erikson," *State of North Dakota Courts*, accessed January 2, 2024, https://www.ndcourts.gov/ralph-r-erickson.
85. Ohio (In re EPA & DOD Final Rule), 803 F.3d at 806.
86. Ibid., 807.
87. Ibid., 808.
88. Ibid.
89. Ibid.
90. Ohio v. United States Army Corps of Engineers (In re EPA & DOD Final Rule), 817 F.3d 261 (6th Cir. 2016).
91. Ibid., 274.
92. Ibid., 283 (Keith, J., dissenting).
93. Ibid., 275 (Griffin, J., concurring in the judgment).
94. National Association of Manufacturers v. Department of Defense, 137 S.Ct. 811 (2017).

Chapter 8

1. "Livestock Groups Commend President on Repealing Waters of the US Rule," The Cattle Site, accessed January 4, 2024, https://www.thecattlesite.com/news/51022/livestock-groups-commend-president-on-repealing-waters-of-the-us-rule.
2. Jeff Stein, "Trump's EPA Nominee 'Unsure' if Big Oil Gave Him Hundreds of Thousands of Dollars," *Vox*, January 18, 2017, https://www.vox.com/policy-and-politics/2017/1/18/14311518/trump-epa-nominee.

3. Garrett Haake and Dartunorro Clark, "Winging It: Pruitt Had Top EPA Aide Contact Chick-fil-A CEO about Franchise for His Wife," NBC News, June 5, 2018, https://www.nbcnews.com/politics/white-house/pruitt-had-top-epa-aide-contact-chick-fil-ceo-about-n880301.
4. "Pruitt v. EPA: 14 Challenges of EPA Rules by the Oklahoma Attorney General," *New York Times*, January 14, 2017, https://www.nytimes.com/interactive/2017/01/14/us/politics/document-Pruitt-v-EPA-a-Compilation-of-Oklahoma-14.html.
5. 82 Fed. Reg. 12,497 (2017).
6. Ibid.
7. Administration of Donald J. Trump, "Remarks on Signing an Executive Order on Restoring the Rule of Law, Federalism, and Economic Growth by Reviewing the 'Waters of the United States' Rule," February 28, 2017, https://www.govinfo.gov/content/pkg/DCPD-201700146/pdf/DCPD-201700146.pdf.
8. Ibid.
9. The Administrative Procedure Act defines *rulemaking* to mean the "agency process for formulating, amending, or repealing a rule." 5 U.S.C. § 551(5) (2024).
10. 82 Fed. Reg. 34,899 (2017).
11. Ibid.
12. 583 U.S. 109 (2018).
13. 33 U.S.C. § 1369(b)(1) (2024).
14. Transcript of Oral Argument, National Assn. of Mfrs. v. Department of Defense (16-299), October 11, 2017, at 11, https://www.supremecourt.gov/oral_arguments/argument_transcripts/2017/16-299_3eah.pdf.
15. Ibid.
16. Ibid., 11–12.
17. Ibid., 12.
18. Ibid., 38–39.
19. National Association of Manufacturers v. Department of Defense, 583 U.S. 109 (2018).
20. Ibid., 121–22.
21. Ibid., 122.
22. Ibid., 127.
23. Ibid., 130.
24. Ibid., 133 note 1.
25. See "Press Statements in Response to Media Queries about Presidential Records," National Archives, September 2, 2023, https://www.archives.gov/press/press-releases/2022/nr22-001.
26. "Document Drafting Handbook," *Office of the Federal Register* (August 2018 edition): 3–10, https://www.archives.gov/files/federal-register/write/handbook/ddh.pdf.
27. Natural Resources Defense Council v. National Highway Traffic Safety Administration, 894 F.3d 95, 113 (2d Cir. 2018); Becerra v. U.S. Department of Interior, 276 F.Supp.3d 953, 966 (N.D. Cal. 2017).
28. 82 Fed. Reg. 55,542 (2017).
29. 83 Fed. Reg. 5,200 (2018).

30. New York v. Pruitt, No. 18-CV-1030 (S.D.N.Y. April 5, 2018).
31. Natural Resources Defense Council, v. Environmental Protection Agency, No. 18-cv-1048 (S.D.N.Y. February 6, 2018), https://www.nrdc.org/sites/default/files/complaint-cwr-20180206.pdf.
32. New York v. Pruitt, 2018 WL 2411595, at *2.
33. Ibid., *4.
34. South Carolina Coastal Conservation League v. Pruitt, 318 F. Supp. 3d 959 (D.S.C. 2018).
35. Ibid., 964–67.
36. 83 Fed. Reg. at 5,204–05.
37. South Carolina Coastal Conservation League, 318 F. Supp. 3d at 966.
38. Ibid., 967.
39. Ibid.
40. Ibid., 969.
41. Ibid., 969 note 4 (quoting City of Chicago v. Sessions, 888 F.3d 272, 288 (7th Cir. 2018)).
42. Ibid.
43. Jacqui Fatka, "WOTUS Woes Hit Farmers in 26 States," *FarmProgress*, August 17, 2018, https://www.farmprogress.com/farm-operations/wotus-woes-hit-farmers-in-26-states; "Help NCBA Fight Zombie WOTUS This Halloween!" National Cattlemen's Beef Association, October 31, 2018, https://www.facebook.com/BeefUSA/videos/2150809811904613/.

Chapter 9

1. "About POLITICO," POLITICO, accessed January 5, 2024, https://www.politico.com/about-us.
2. Helena Bottemiller Evich, "WOTUS Is Dead," POLITICO, *Weekly Agriculture*, September 13, 2019, https://www.politico.com/newsletters/morning-agriculture/2019/09/13/wotus-is-dead-741029.
3. 84 Fed. Reg. 56,626 (2019).
4. Ibid., 56,626–27.
5. Ibid., 56,627.
6. Ibid., 56,661.
7. "Groups Sue to Keep Clean Water Protections Intact," Natural Resources Defense Council, accessed January 5, 2024, https://www.nrdc.org/bio/nrdc/groups-sue-keep-clean-water-protections-intact.
8. 84 Fed. Reg. 4,154 (2019).
9. Ibid., 4,203.
10. Ibid., 4,177.
11. Ibid., 4171.
12. Ibid., 4,204.
13. Ibid., 4,189.
14. Ariel Wittenberg and Kevin Bogardus, "EPA Claims 'No Data' on Impact of Weakening Water Rule. But the Numbers Exist," *Science*, December 11, 2018, https://www.science.org/co.ntent/article/epa-claims-no-data-impact-weakening-water-rule-numbers-exist.

15. Ibid.
16. Ibid.
17. "Breakdown of Flow Regimes in NHD Streams Nationwide," *E&E News*, accessed January 6, 2024, https://legacy-assets.eenews.net/open_files/assets/2018/12/11/document_gw_05.pdf (slide 1).
18. "Nationwide Percentage of NWI Potential Wetland Acreage Intersecting NHD-Mapped Streams," *E&E News*, accessed January 6, 2024, https://legacy-assets.eenews.net/open_files/assets/2018/12/11/document_gw_05.pdf (slide 7).
19. "Comment Submitted by American Farm Bureau Federation et al.," US Environmental Protection Agency, May 16, 2019, https://www.regulations.gov/comment/EPA-HQ-OW-2018-0149-11394.
20. "NRDC's Gina McCarthy on President Trump's Dirty Water Rule," Natural Resources Defense Council, accessed January 6, 2024, https://www.nrdc.org/press-releases/nrdcs-gina-mccarthy-president-trumps-dirty-water-rule.
21. "Comment submitted by Jennifer Chavev, Staff Attorney, Earth Justice et al. on behalf of Aaron Isherwood, Phillip S. Berry, Managing Attorney, Sierra Club et al., US Environmental Protection Agency," April 17, 2019, https://www.regulations.gov/comment/EPA-HQ-OW-2018-0149-4343.
22. E.g., "Comment submitted by R. C. Gardner, U.S. Environmental Protection Agency," April 19, 2019, https://www.regulations.gov/comment/EPA-HQ-OW-2018-0149-4782.
23. *Webster's Third New International Dictionary* (Springfield, MA: G.&C. Merriam Co., 1964), 1800.
24. *Webster's New International Dictionary*, 2nd ed. (Springfield, MA: G.&C. Merriam Co., 1954), 1963.
25. *Webster's Third*, 1800.
26. *Webster's Second*, 1963.
27. Intergovernmental Platform on Biodiversity and Ecosystem Services, *Workshop Report on Biodiversity and Pandemics of the Intergovernmental Platform on Biodiversity and Ecosystem Services* (Bonn, Germany: IPBES Secretariat, 2020).
28. 85 Fed. Reg. 22,250 (2020).
29. Ibid., 22,338.
30. "What They Are Saying | EPA and Army Deliver on President Trump's Promise to Issue the Navigable Waters Protection Rule—A New Definition of WOTUS," US Environmental Protection Agency, January 23, 2020, https://www.epa.gov/newsreleases/what-they-are-saying-epa-and-army-deliver-president-trumps-promise-issue-navigable.
31. Ibid.
32. Thomas E. Dahl, *Wetland Losses in the United States 1780's to 1980's* (Washington, DC: US Department of Interior, 1990), 6 (Table 1).
33. Ibid.
34. US Environmental Protection Agency, "What They Are Saying."
35. "What's at Stake with the Dirty Water Rule," *Clean Water Action*, accessed January 5, 2024, https://cleanwater.org/whats-stake-dirty-water-rule.

36. "NRDC's Gina McCarthy on President Trump's Dirty Water Rule," Natural Resources Defense Council, January 23, 2020, https://www.nrdc.org/press-releases/nrdcs-gina-mccarthy-president-trumps-dirty-water-rule.
37. Letter from Dr. Michael Honeycutt, Chair, Science Advisory Board, to Andrew R. Wheeler, Administrator, US EPA, Commentary on the Proposed Rule Defining the Scope of Waters, February 27, 2020, https://legacy-assets.eenews.net/open_files/assets/2020/03/04/document_gw_01.pdf.
38. US Environmental Protection Agency and Department of the Army, "Resource and Programmatic Assessment for the Navigable Waters Protection Rule: Definition of 'Waters of the United States,'" 2020, 20.
39. Ibid., 22.
40. Ibid., 22–23.
41. Ibid., 24.
42. Ibid., 25.
43. Ibid., 26–27.
44. National Research Council, *Models in Environmental Regulatory Decision Making* (Washington, DC: National Academies Press, 2007). See also Save Our Cabinets v. U.S. Department of Agriculture, 254 F. Supp. 3d 1241, 1252–53 (D. Mont. 2017) (stream baseflow model); Greater Yellowstone Coalition v. Larson, 641 F. Supp. 2d 1120, 1139 (D. Idaho 2009) (groundwater model).
45. Roger Meyer and Andrew Robertson, *Clean Water Rule Spatial Analysis: A GIS-Based Scenario Model for Comparative Analysis of the Potential Spatial Extent of Jurisdictional and Non-jurisdictional Wetlands* (Winona: Saint Mary's University of Minnesota, 2019).
46. The rulemaking docket includes references to the model in the following: Comment submitted by Jon Devine, Senior Attorney & Director of Federal Water Policy, Nature Program, Natural Resources Defense Council, 37 & n.91, app. A–pt. 5, April 15, 2019; Comment submitted by Barbara D. Underwood, Attorney General of New York, et al., Attachment A at 21, April 15, 2019) (submission by 15 attorneys general); Comment submitted by Jared Polis, Governor, State of Colorado, and Philip J. Weiser, Attorney General, State of Colorado, 2 n.2, April 15, 2019; Comment submitted by Jan Goldman-Carter, Senior Counsel, Wetlands and Water Resources, National Wildlife Federation, 78 nn.122–123, Attachment 2, April 15, 2019; and Comment submitted by Jennifer Chavez, Staff Attorney, Earthjustice, et al., on behalf of Aaron Isherwood, Phillip S. Berry Managing Attorney, Sierra Club, et al., 26–27 & n.44, 49 & nn.71–72, exhibit G-25, April 15, 2019.
47. Brief of the American Fisheries Society et al. as Amici Curiae in Support of Plaintiffs' Motion for a Preliminary Injunction or Stay, California v. Wheeler, Case 3:20-cv-03005-RS, May 26, 2020, 11.
48. "Judge Says Citizenship Question on Census 'Threatens' Democracy," *PBS News Hour*, March 6, 2019, https://www.pbs.org/newshour/politics/judge-says-citizenship-question-on-census-threatens-democracy.
49. "Trump Water Rule Faces Its First Test," POLITICO, June 18, 2020, https://www.politico.com/newsletters/morning-energy/2020/06/18/trump-water-rule-faces-first-test-788613.

50. Transcript of Videoconference Proceedings, *California v. Wheeler*, Case 3:20-cv-03005-RS, June 18, 2020, 23.
51. Daniel Victor, "'I'm Not a Cat,' Says Lawyer Having Zoom Difficulties," *New York Times*, updated May 6, 2021, https://www.nytimes.com/2021/02/09/style/cat-lawyer-zoom.html.
52. Transcript, 50–51.
53. California v. Wheeler, 467 F. Fupp. 3d 864, 875–76 (N.D. Cal. 2020).
54. Ibid., 874.
55. Ibid., 876.
56. Ibid., 877.
57. Complaint for Declaratory and Injunctive Relief, Colorado v. U.S. Environmental Protection Agency, No. 1:20-cv-01461, May 22, 2020, paragraphs 83–86.
58. Ibid., paragraphs 41 and 85.
59. Ibid., paragraph 85.
60. Colorado v. U.S. Environmental Protection Agency, 445 F. Supp. 3d 1295, 1302–03 (D. Colo. 2020).
61. Ibid., 1307.
62. Ibid., 1311–12.
63. Ibid., 1313.
64. State v. U.S. Environmental Protection Agency, 989 F.3d 874 (10th Cir 2021).

Chapter 10

1. US Environmental Protection Agency, "Connectivity of Streams and Wetlands to Downstream Waters: A Review and Synthesis of the Scientific Evidence (Final Report)," 2015, 6–10.
2. Lainie R. Levick, et al., "The Ecological and Hydrological Significance of Ephemeral and Intermittent Streams in the Arid and Semi-arid American Southwest," US Environmental Protection Agency and USDA/ARS Southwest Watershed Research Center, EPA/600/R-08/134, ARS/233046, November 2008, 5, https://www.epa.gov/sites/default/files/2015-03/documents/ephemeral_streams_report_final_508-kepner.pdf.
3. US Environmental Protection Agency and U.S. Department of the Army, "Review of U.S. Army Corps of Engineers ORM2 Permit and Jurisdictional Determination Data to Assess Effects of the Navigable Waters Protection Rule," June 8, 2021, 3, https://perma.cc/DGR3-4MTS.
4. Ibid.
5. Tony Davis, "Rosemont Mine Wins Big Legal Victory due to Trump Administration Rule Changes," *Arizona Daily Star*, updated July 30, 2021, https://tucson.com/news/local/rosemont-mine-wins-big-legal-victory-due-to-trump-administration-rule-changes/article_f5c838a2-8da5-11eb-bc2b-5b64a5517bc2.html. The portion of the project that would occur on federal land has been delayed because of litigation concerning the US Forest Service's environmental impact statement. Congressional Research Service, "The Proposed Rosemont Cooper Mine," by Brandon S. Tracy, IF12359, March 24, 2023, https://www.everycrsreport.com/

files/2023-03-24_IF12359_e47ea8ff5e6dc19d1199167bd6ce9029338ce7f5.pdf. However, ephemeral streams on private lands have been filled. David Abbott, "Hudbay Ramps Up Excavation for Copper World Complex as Local Resistance Continues and Expands," *Arizona Mirror*, January 6, 2023, https://www.azmirror.com/2023/01/06/hudbay-ramps-up-excavation-for-copper-world-complex-as-local-resistance-continues-and-expands/.

6. "Mining Threatens the Okefenokee Swamp," Georgia Conservancy, accessed January 9, 2024, https://www.georgiaconservancy.org/okefenokee/mining.
7. Ibid.; "Open Letter to the Georgia Community," Science for Georgia, January 6, 2022, https://protectokefenokee.org/wp-content/uploads/2022/01/OKE-Science-Letter.pdf. See also Complaint for Declaratory and Injunctive Relief, National Wildlife Refuge Association v. U.S. Army Corps of Engineers, Case 1:22-cv-03498 (D.D.C., Nov. 15, 2022), https://www.biologicaldiversity.org/programs/public_lands/pdfs/11-15-22--NWRA-v-USACE-Complaint.pdf.
8. See Stanley Dunlap, "Environmentalists Bank on State Regulators to Stop Okefenokee Mine," *The Current*, June 22, 2021, https://thecurrentga.org/2021/06/22/environmentalists-bank-on-state-regulators-to-stop-okefenokee-mine/; see also Hannah Northey, "Georgia Regulators Release Plans for Mine Near Okefenokee," *E&E News*, January 1, 2023, https://www.eenews.net/articles/georgia-regulators-release-plans-for-mine-near-okefenokee/.
9. David Groves, "How the Trump Administration Eased Destruction of the Nation's Wetlands and Streams," *Environmental Law Reporter* 51 (March 2021): 10,195. For other examples of the impact of the Navigable Waters Protection Rule, see Natural Resources Defense Council et al., "Clean Water Act on Trial: The Devastating Potential Consequences of *Sackett v. EPA*," October 2022.
10. Groves, "How the Trump Administration Eased Destruction," 10,196.
11. "Harris County Has Never Seen a Storm Like Harvey," Harris County Flood Control District, accessed January 8, 2024, https://www.hcfcd.org/About/Harris-Countys-Flooding-History/Hurricane-Harvey.
12. "Harris County's Flooding History," Harris County Flood Control District, accessed January 8, 2024, https://www.hcfcd.org/About/Harris-Countys-Flooding-History.
13. Groves, "How the Trump Administration Eased Destruction," 10,196.
14. US Army Corps of Engineers, "Regulatory Guidance Letter (RGL) 05-02," June 14, 2005, https://usace.contentdm.oclc.org/utils/getfile/collection/p16021coll9/id/1246.
15. Amena H. Sayid, "Companies Eager to 'Lock In' Trump-Era Water Rule Exemptions," Bloomberg Law, September 10, 2020, https://news.bloomberglaw.com/environment-and-energy/companies-eager-to-lock-in-trump-era-water-rule-exemptions.
16. 33 U.S.C. § 1329 (2024).
17. Jason Totoiu and Jaclyn Lopez, "Holding States Accountable for Harmful Algal Blooms: Florida's Water Crisis in Focus," *University of Florida Journal of Law & Public Policy* 33 (2022): 7.
18. Ibid., 20, 23–25.

19. "Blue-Green Algae Task Force Recommendations: Implementation Progress Report," Friends of the Everglades, accessed January 10, 2024, https://www.everglades.org/wp-content/uploads/2022/08/FINAL-BGATF-Recs-Implementation-update-progress-report_final-draft.pdf.
20. Fla. Exec. Order No. 19-12, at 3 (January 10, 2019); Rachel A. Brewton, et al., "Septic System–Groundwater–Surface Water Couplings in Waterfront Communities Contribute to Harmful Algal Blooms in Southwest Florida," *Science of The Total Environment* 837 (2022): 155319.
21. Totoiu and Lopez, "Holding States Accountable," 8, 38.
22. Jennifer L. Graham, Neil M. Dubrovsky, and Sandra M. Eberts, "Cyanobacterial Harmful Algal Blooms and U.S. Geological Survey Science Capabilities," US Geological Survey Open-File Report 2016-1174, ver 1.1, December 2017: 12, https://doi.org/10.3133/ofr20161174.
23. "CyanoHABs Newsletters 2022," US Environmental Protection Agency, accessed January 9, 2024, https://www.epa.gov/cyanohabs/cyanohabs-newsletters-2022.
24. Jeanne Christie and Scott Hausmann, "Various State Reactions to the SWANCC Decision," *Wetlands* 23 (2003): 654.
25. Ibid.; Bruce Myers, Catherine McLinn, and James M. McElfish, *State Constraints: State-Imposed Limitations on the Authority of Agencies to Regulate Waters beyond the Scope of the Federal Clean Water Act*, (Washington, DC: Environmental Law Institute, 2013), 33 note 116.
26. Meyers, McLinn, and McElfish, *State Constraints*, 167–68.
27. Ariel Wittenberg, "Calif. Clinches New Regs Just in Time for Federal Rollback," *E&E News*, February 4, 2019, https://www.eenews.net/articles/calif-clinches-new-regs-just-in-time-for-federal-rollback/#:~:text=If%20all%20goes%20to%20schedule%2C%20California%E2%80%99s%20rules%20could,have%20relatively%20permanent%20surface%20water%20connections%20to%20streams.
28. Myers, McLinn, and McElfish, *State Constraints*, 11.
29. Ibid., 12.
30. US Environmental Protection Agency and Department of the Army, "Resource and Programmatic Assessment for the Navigable Waters Protection Rule: Definition of 'Waters of the United States,'" 2020.
31. Ibid., 46.
32. "Deregulate Certain Ephemeral Water Features," Sub. H. B. No. 175, 134th G.A. (effective July 21, 2022), https://www.legislature.ohio.gov/legislation/134/hb175.
33. James McElfish, "State Protection of Nonfederal Waters: Turbidity Continues," *Environmental Law Reporter* 52 (September 2022): 10684.
34. 33 U.S.C. § 1341 (2024).
35. Water Quality Improvement Act of 1970, Public Law No. 91–224, 84 Stat. 91 (1970).
36. 36 Fed. Reg. 22,487 (1971).
37. PUD No. 1 of Jefferson County v. Washington Department of Ecology, 511 U.S. 700 (1994).

38. Ibid., 712.
39. Ibid., 723 (Stevens, J., concurring).
40. S. D. Warren Co. v. Maine Board of Environmental Protection, 547 U.S. 370 (2006).
41. Ibid., 380 (citing S. Rep. No. 92-414, p. 69 (1971)).
42. Steven A. Weiler and Marcia A. Stanford, "New York's Denial of Water Quality Certification for Three FERC-Authorized Pipelines: Flangrant Fiat or Valid Veto?," *Energy Law Journal* 39 (2018): 515.
43. "Millennium Bulk Terminals Longview," State of Washington Department of Ecology, accessed January 10, 2024, https://ecology.wa.gov/Regulations-Permits/SEPA/Environmental-review/SEPA-at-Ecology/Millennium#:~:text=In%20September%202017%2C%20Ecology%20denied,the%20required%20water%20quality%20permit.
44. Chuck Sensiba and Elizabeth McCormick, "Oregon DEQ Denies Jordan Cove Water Quality Certification," *Environmental Law and Policy Monitor*, May 13, 2019, https://www.environmentallawandpolicy.com/2019/05/oregon-deq-denies-jordan-cove-water-quality-certification/; Jes Burns, "Jordan Cove Would Be Oregon's Top Carbon Polluter If Built," *OPB*, May 3, 2019, https://www.opb.org/news/article/jordan-cove-oregon-lng-carbon-pollution/#:~:text=Jordan%20Cove's%20emissions%20would%20represent,proportion%20of%20our%20allowed%20emissions%20%E2%80%A6.
45. Bill Lucia, "Trump Order Puts State Power over Pipeline Approvals in Crosshairs," *Route Fifty*, April 10, 2019, https://www.route-fifty.com/infrastructure/2019/04/trump-executive-order-section-401-certification-clean-water-act/156231/.
46. 84 Fed. Reg. 15,495 (2019).
47. 85 Fed. Reg. 42,210, 42,251 (2020).
48. Ibid., 42,233–34.
49. Ibid., 42,250–63.
50. 42 U.S.C. § 4321 (2024).
51. Stephen M. Johnson, "Individual Permits," in *Wetlands Law and Policy: Understanding Section 404*, eds. Kim Diana Connolly, Stephen M. Johnson, and Douglas R. Williams (Chicago: ABA Publishing, 2005), 197–98.
52. Bringing such a lawsuit does not necessarily portend success, however; see D'Olive Bay Restoration and Preservation Committee, Inc. v. U.S. Army Corps of Engineers, 513 F. Supp. 2d 1261 (S.D. Ala. 2007).
53. 85 Fed. Reg. 43304, 43309 (2020).
54. United States v. South Florida Water Management District, 28 F.3d 1563 (11th Cir. 1994). See also "Big Sugar Strikes Again on Everglades Reservoir, Sues Army Corps of Engineers," Captains for Clean Water, accessed January 9, 2024, https://captainsforcleanwater.org/sugar-sues-army-corps/.
55. Sun Tzu, *The Art of War*, ed. James Clavell (New York: Delacorte Press, 1983), 28.
56. 40 C.F.R. part 6 (2023) (EPA); 33 C.F.R. part 230 (2023) (Corps).
57. 85 Fed. Reg. at 43,357–76.
58. "What They Are Saying | CEQ Issues Final Rule to Modernize Its NEPA Regulations," Executive Office of the President of the United States, July 2020, 18

https://trumpwhitehouse.archives.gov/wp-content/uploads/2020/01/NEPA-FINAL-What-They-Are-Saying-clean.pdf.

59. Ibid., 20.
60. Notices of intent to prepare EISs are published in the *Federal Register*. The database was searched with the terms "Corps," "404," and "environmental impact statement."
61. 16 U.S.C. § 1540 (2024).
62. Babbitt v. Sweet Home Chapter of Communities for a Great Oregon, 515 U.S. 687 (1995).
63. "Endangered Species Case against Farmer Dropped," *Washington Post*, May 3, 1995, https://www.washingtonpost.com/archive/politics/1995/05/03/endangered-species-case-against-farmer-dropped/044c2956-2bc2-439d-ba97-3d7576a46a0e/; Mark Arax, "U.S. Dismisses Charges That Farmer Killed Rare Rats," *Los Angeles Times*, January 18, 1995, https://www.latimes.com/archives/la-xpm-1995-01-18-mn-21314-story.html#:~:text=The%20federal%20government%20has%20dropped,the%20U.S.%20Endangered%20Species%20Act.
64. Arax, "U.S. Dismisses Charges," *Los Angeles Times*.
65. 16 U.S.C. § 1536(a)(2).
66. Ibid., § 1536(b)(4).
67. Royal C. Gardner, "Sackett v. U.S. Environmental Protection Agency: Implications for WOTUS and the Clean Water Act," YouTube video, 45:30, from an April 2023 Society of Wetland Scientists webinar, https://www.youtube.com/watch?v=6RLX_vyEao.
68. See Pamela King, "Supreme Court Water Ruling Could Transform NEPA, ESA," *E&E News*, June 15, 2023, https://www.eenews.net/articles/supreme-court-water-ruling-could-transform-nepa-esa/.
69. See Hannah Northey, "Brewers Urge EPA to Ditch Trump Water Rules," *Greenwire*, April 16, 2021, https://subscriber.politicopro.com/article/eenews/2021/04/16/brewers-urge-epa-to-ditch-trump-water-rules-003023.
70. Ariel Wittenberg, "Trump's Rule Threatens Booming $4B 'Restoration Economy,'" *E&E News*, January 3, 2019, https://www.eenews.net/articles/trumps-rule-threatens-booming-4b-restoration-economy/.
71. National Research Council, *Compensating for Wetland Losses under the Clean Water Act* (Washington, DC: National Academies Press, 2001), 70–73.
72. Royal C. Gardner, *Lawyers, Swamps, and Money: U.S. Wetland Law, Policy, and Politics* (Washington, DC: Island Press, 2011), 105–9.
73. Ibid., 155–56.
74. National Research Council, *Compensating for Wetland Losses*, 9.
75. 60 Fed. Reg. 58,605 (1995).
76. 33 C.F.R. part 332 (2023).
77. Transportation Equity Act for the 21st Century, Pub. L. No. 105-178, § 1106, 112 Stat. 107, 133 (1998).
78. Todd BenDor, T. William Lester, Avery Livengood, Adam Davis, and Logan Yonavjak, "Estimating the Size and Impact of the Ecological Restoration Economy," *PLoS ONE* 10 (2015): e0128339.

79. Wittenberg, "Trump's Rule."
80. Ibid.

Chapter 11

1. County of Maui v. Hawaii Wildlife Fund, 140 S. Ct. 1462 (2020).
2. Warren Cornwall, "'Hydrologists Should Be Happy.' Big Supreme Court Ruling Bolsters Groundwater Science," *Science*, April 23, 2020, https://www.science.org/content/article/scotus-clean-water.
3. "Why *Nature* Supports Joe Biden for US President," *Nature*, October 14, 2020, https://www.nature.com/articles/d41586-020-02852-x.
4. Lurline Wailana McGregor, "How Clean Is Clean?," Sea Grant, University of Hawaii, accessed January 11, 2024, https://seagrant.soest.hawaii.edu/how-clean-is-clean/.
5. Ibid.
6. Hawai'i Wildlife Fund v. County of Maui, 24 F. Supp. 3d. 980, 984 (2014).
7. Ibid.
8. Ibid., 985.
9. See C. R. Glenn et al., "Lahaina Groundwater Tracer Study—Lahaina, Maui, Hawaii, Final Report," 2013 (prepared for the State of Hawaii Department of Health, US Environmental Protection Agency, and US Army Engineer Research and Development Center).
10. Hawai'i Wildlife Fund v. County of Maui, 24 F. Supp. at 998.
11. Ibid., 998 ("An aquifer with a substantial nexus with navigable-in-fact water may itself be protected under the Clean Water Act even if it is not necessarily a conduit for pollutants.").
12. Hawai'i Wildlife Fund v. County of Maui, 886 F.3d 737, 749 (9th Cir. 2018).
13. Ibid, 748.
14. Ibid., 749.
15. 66 Fed. Reg. 2960, 3018 (2001).
16. 83 Fed. Reg. 7,126 (2018).
17. 84 Fed. Reg. 16,810, 16,811 (2019).
18. Ibid., 16,814. The guidance did note that several other federal laws may apply to groundwater contamination (i.e., Safe Drinking Water Act, Resource Conservation and Recovery Act, and Comprehensive Environmental Response, Compensation, and Liability Act). Ibid., 16,824.
19. "Maui Lawmakers Defer Resolution to Settle Clean Water Act Lawsuit," Hawai'i Public Radio, May 20, 2019, https://www.hawaiipublicradio.org/news/2019-05-20/maui-lawmakers-defer-resolution-to-settle-clean-water-act-lawsuit.
20. "Maui Council Committee Votes in Favor of Settling Lahaina Injection Wells Case," Earthjustice, September 9, 2019, https://earthjustice.org/press/2019/maui-council-committee-votes-in-favor-of-settling-lahaina-injection-wells-case.
21. Melissa Tanji, "Mayor Proposes Revised Settlement in Wastewater Case," *Maui News*, August 30, 2019, https://www.mauinews.com/news/local-news/2019/08/mayor-proposes-revised-settlement-in-wastewater-case/.

22. Letter of respondents Hawai'i Wildlife Fund, US Supreme Court docket 18-260, October 3, 2019, https://www.supremecourt.gov/DocketPDF/18/18-260/118784/20191011110231305_Resp%20letter%2018-260.pdf.
23. Letter of petitioner County of Maui, Hawaii, U.S. Supreme Court docket 18-260, October 4, 2019, https://www.supremecourt.gov/DocketPDF/18/18-260/118795/20191011111339958_Petitioner%20letter.pdf.
24. The letter is referenced in Letter of petitioner County of Maui, Hawaii, U.S. Supreme Court docket 18-260, October 10, 2019, https://www.supremecourt.gov/DocketPDF/18/18-260/118796/20191011111745550_Petitioner%20letter%202.pdf.
25. Ibid.
26. Sahr A. M. Brima, "Admission to U.S. Supreme Court Bar," American Bar Association, February 26, 2020, https://www.americanbar.org/groups/litigation/resources/newsletters/minority-trial/admission-us-supreme-court-bar/.
27. Michael Heller and James Salzman, *Mine! How the Hidden Rules of Ownership Control Our Lives* (New York: Doubleday, 2021), 21–23.
28. Brief for Petitioners, County of Maui v. Hawaii Wildlife Fund, No. 18-260 (U.S. May 9, 2019), 28–32.
29. Transcript of Oral Argument, County of Maui v. Hawaii Wildlife Fund, No. 18-260, November 6, 2019, 3.
30. Ibid., 9–11.
31. Ibid., 12.
32. Ibid., 22–24.
33. Ibid., 24.
34. Ibid., 40.
35. Ibid., 36.
36. Ibid. 44–45 (cleaned up).
37. Brief for Aquatic Scientists and Scientific Societies as Amici Curiae in Support of Respondents, County of Maui v. Hawaii Wildlife Fund, No. 18-260 (U.S. July 19, 2019), 13–28.
38. Transcript of Oral Argument, County of Maui v. Hawaii Wildlife Fund, 46.
39. Ibid., 48.
40. County of Maui v. Hawaii Wildlife Fund, 140 S. Ct. 1462 (2020).
41. Ibid., 1471–75.
42. Ibid., 1471–72.
43. Ibid., 1473.
44. Ibid., 1476.
45. Ibid., 1477.
46. Ibid.
47. "History of the Clean Boating Act (CBA)," US Environmental Protection Agency, accessed January 10, 2024, https://www.epa.gov/vessels-marinas-and-ports/history-clean-boating-act-cba.
48. Cornwall, "Hydrologists Should Be Happy."
49. Email to the author.
50. County of Maui v. Hawaii Wildlife Fund, 140 S. Ct. at 1479 (Thomas, J., dissenting).

51. *Glossary of Geology*, 5th ed., ed. Klaus K. E. Neuendorf, James P. Mehl Jr., and Julia A. Jackson (Alexandria, VA: American Geological Institute, 2005), 167.
52. "More on Arizona's Earth Fissures," Arizona Geological Survey, accessed January 11, 2024, https://azgs.arizona.edu/earth-fissures-ground-subsidence/more-arizonas-earth-fissures.
53. County of Maui v. Hawaii Wildlife Fund, 140 S. Ct. at 1483 (Alito, J., dissenting).
54. Ibid., 1490.
55. Ibid. (internal quotation marks omitted).
56. Ibid., 1491.
57. Hawai'i Wildlife Fund v. County of Maui, 550 F. Supp. 3d 871 (D. Haw. 2021).
58. Maya Earls, "Maui Water Case Nets Lawyers $1 Million after Supreme Court Trip," Bloomberg Law, December 30, 2021, https://news.bloomberglaw.com/litigation/maui-clean-water-case-top-court-weighed-nets-1-million-in-fees.
59. Doug Fraser, "Tentative Agreement Reached in Harbor Pollution Case," *Cape Cod Times*, June 1, 2020, https://www.capecodtimes.com/story/news/2020/06/01/tentative-agreement-reached-in-harbor-pollution-case/42650747/.
60. Ibid.
61. Mike Ellis, "Kinder Morgan Gas Pipeline Spill Settlement to Provide $1.5 Million to Upstate SC," *Greenville News*, October 23, 2020, https://www.greenvilleonline.com/story/news/2020/10/23/kinder-morgan-pipeline-spill-settlement-provide-1-5-million-sc/3739456001/.
62. "Kinder Morgan Energy Partners, L.P. v. Upstate Forever," *SCOTUSblog*, accessed January 12, 2024.
63. Nathanial Cary, "First Kinder Morgan Pipeline Spill Grants Awarded in Anderson from $1.5M Settlement," *Post and Courier*, January 13, 2023, https://www.postandcourier.com/greenville/health/first-kinder-morgan-pipeline-spill-grants-awarded-in-anderson-from-1-5m-settlement/article_a4556c00-935d-11ed-827e-c7202c86f164.html.
64. Pamela King and James Marshall, "Clean Water Act Ruling Tees Up Coal Ash Brawl," *Greenwire*, April 28, 2020, https://www.eenews.net/articles/clean-water-act-ruling-tees-up-coal-ash-brawl/; *Vanessa Daza Castillo, "Win or Hidden Hurdle?: A Critical Analysis of County of Maui v. Hawaii Wildlife Fund (2020)," Harvard Environmental Law Review, December 29, 2021, https://journals.law.harvard.edu/elr/2021/12/29/win-or-hidden-hurdle-a-critical-analysis-of-county-of-maui-v-hawaii-wildlife-fund-2020/.*
65. "Mapping the Coal Ash Contamination," Earthjustice, accessed January 11, 2024, https://earthjustice.org/feature/coal-ash-contaminated-sites-map.
66. Congressional Research Service, "Redefining Waters of the United States (WOTUS): Recent Developments," by Laura Gatz and Kate R. Bowers, R46927, updated July 8, 2022, 22.
67. "The Clean Water Case of the Century," Earthjustice, accessed January 10, 2024, https://earthjustice.org/feature/supreme-court-maui-clean-water-case.
68. Ashley Reese, "The 'Notorious,' Insidious Transformation of an Anti-Feminist Judge into a Feminist Superhero," *Jezebel*, September 29, 2020, https://jezebel.com/the-notorious-insidious-transformation-of-an-anti-femi-1845205452.

69. Orchard Hill Building Company v. U.S. Army Corps of Engineers, 893 F.3d 1017 (7th Cir. 2018).
70. United States v. Gerke Excavating, Inc., 464 F.3d 723 (7th Cir. 2006).
71. Orchard Hill Building Company, 893 F.3d at 1025.
72. "Inaugural Address by President Joseph R. Biden, Jr.," The White House, January 21, 2021, https://www.whitehouse.gov/briefing-room/speeches-remarks/2021/01/20/inaugural-address-by-president-joseph-r-biden-jr/.
73. That hot mic incident occurred during the signing of the Affordable Care Act. Richard Adams, "Joe Biden: 'This Is a Big Fucking Deal,'" *The Guardian*, March 23, 2010, https://www.theguardian.com/world/richard-adams-blog/2010/mar/23/joe-biden-obama-big-fucking-deal-overheard.
74. 86 Fed. Reg. 7,037 (2021).
75. Ibid.
76. US Environmental Protection Agency, "EPA, Army Announce Intent to Revise Definition of WOTUS," June 9, 2021, https://www.epa.gov/newsreleases/epa-army-announce-intent-revise-definition-wotus.
77. Ibid.
78. Ibid.
79. "Revised Definition of 'Waters of the United States': History of the Effects of Litigation over Recent Definitions of 'Waters of the United States,'" US Environmental Protection Agency, accessed January 11, 2024, https://www.epa.gov/system/files/documents/2022-12/History%20of%20the%20Effects%20of%20Litigation.pdf.
80. Complaint, Pascua Yaqui Tribe v. U.S. Environmental Protection Agency, Case 4:20-cv-00266-RM (D. Ari. June 22, 2020), 4, https://www.epa.gov/sites/default/files/2020-06/documents/pascua_yaqui_tribe_v._epa_d._ariz._-_complaint_06.22.20.pdf.
81. Ibid., 10.
82. Ibid.
83. Pascua Yaqui Tribe v. U.S. Environmental Protection Agency, 557 F. Supp. 3d 949, 951 (D. Ari. 2021).
84. Ibid., 957.
85. Ibid., 955.
86. "Judge Ditches Trump's Dirty Water Rule," Earthjustice, August 30, 2021, https://earthjustice.org/press/2021/judges-ditches-trumps-dirty-water-rule.
87. Navajo Nation v. Regan, 563 F. Supp. 3d 1164 (D.N.M. 2021).
88. Ibid., 1168.
89. Congressional Research Service, "What's Next for WOTUS: Recent Litigation and Next Steps in Redefining 'Waters of the United States,'" by Kate R. Bowers, LSB10646, (October 7, 2021), 1, https://crsreports.congress.gov/product/pdf/LSB/LSB10646.
90. 86 Fed. Reg. 69,372, 69,384 (2021).
91. Ibid., 69,372.
92. 88 Fed. Reg. 3,004, 3,019 (2023).

93. The agencies stated that "the 2020 NWPR did not properly consider the extensive scientific evidence demonstrating the interconnectedness of waters and their downstream effects, thereby undermining Congress's objective to restore and maintain the chemical, physical, and biological integrity of the nation's waters. The 2020 NWPR's definition of 'waters of the United States' does not adequately consider the way pollution moves through waters or the way filling in a wetland affects downstream water resources." Ibid., 3,017.
94. Ibid., 3,143.
95. Ibid., 3,144.
96. Ibid.
97. "Biden WOTUS Rule in Effect in 48 States," National Association of Home Builders, accessed January 11, 2024, https://www.nahb.org/blog/2023/03/biden-wotus.
98. West Virginia v. U.S. Environmental Protection Agency, No. 3:23-cv-032, 2023 WL 2914389, *19 (D.N.D. April 12, 2023).
99. US Army Corps of Engineers, "Regulatory Guidance Letter 90-07, Clarification of the Phrase 'Normal Circumstances' as It Pertains to Cropped Wetlands," September 26, 1990, https://www.nap.usace.army.mil/Portals/39/docs/regulatory/rgls/rgl90-07.pdf.
100. Ibid., 2.
101. 58 Fed. Reg. 45,008, 45,036 (1993).
102. Ibid., 45,034.
103. "FAQ," Economic Research Service, U.S. Department of Agriculture, accessed January 11, 2024, https://www.ers.usda.gov/faqs/#:~:text=The%2010%20largest%20sources%20of,%2C%20chicken%20eggs%2C%20and%20hay.
104. Joint Guidance from the Natural Resources Conservation Service (NRCS) and the Army Corps of Engineers (COE) Concerning Wetland Determinations for the Clean Water Act and the Food Security Act of 1985, February 25, 2005, 4, https://georgewbush-whitehouse.archives.gov/omb/oira/2000/meetings/763-2.pdf.
105. 746 F. Supp. 2d 1272 (S.D. Fla. 2010).
106. 88 Fed. Reg. 3,004, 3,107 (2023).
107. Ibid.
108. Ibid.
109. Ibid.
110. As noted previously, Iowa has a total area of about 36 million acres, only 4 million of which (11 percent) were even historically wetlands.
111. "House Votes to Overturn Flawed, Overreaching Biden WOTUS Rule," Committee on Transportation and Infrastructure, accessed January 11, 2024, https://transportation.house.gov/news/documentsingle.aspx?DocumentID=406191.
112. Ibid.
113. Carl Hulse, "Congress Votes to Roll Back Biden Administration Rule on Water," *New York Times*, updated April 13, 2023, https://www.nytimes.com/2023/03/29/us/politics/congress-biden-clean-water-rule.html.

114. Jeremy Dillon, "Biden Vetoes Clean Water Act Resolution," *E&E News*, April 6, 2023, https://www.eenews.net/articles/biden-vetoes-clean-water-act-resolution/.
115. Texas v. U.S. Environmental Protection Agency, 662 F. Supp. 3d. 739 (S.D. Tex. 2023).
116. Ibid., 752.
117. Ibid.
118. Ibid., 759.
119. West Virginia v. U.S. Environmental Protection Agency, No. 3:23-cv-032, 2023 WL 2914389 (D.N.D. April 12, 2023).
120. Ibid., *4.
121. Ibid., *14–*15.
122. Ibid., *15.
123. Florida was the one complicated outlier. In light of an injunction, the EPA's position was that the pre-2015 regime should apply. However, Florida had recently assumed the section 404 program and argued that the Navigable Waters Protection Rule should still apply. Hannah Northey, "EPA Clashes with Fla. over Use of Trump WOTUS Rule," Greenwire, February 4, 2022, https://www.eenews.net/articles/epa-clashes-with-fla-over-use-of-trump-wotus-rule/.

Chapter 12

1. Sackett v. U.S. Environmental Protection Agency, No. 2:08-cv-00185-EJL, 2019 WL 13026870, *1, *9 (D. Idaho March 31, 2019).
2. Hugh Hewitt, "They Fought the EPA for 16 Years—Then Received Supreme Court Vindication," *Washington Post*, May 26, 2023, https://www.washingtonpost.com/opinions/2023/05/26/supreme-court-epa-ruling-idaho-couple/.
3. Keith Kinnaird, "Priest Lake Businessman Sentenced in Sex Sting Case," *Coeur d'Alene/Post Falls Press*, September 7, 2015, https://cdapress.com/news/2015/sep/07/priest-lake-businessman-sentenced-in-sex-5/. Judge Hovland, who later enjoined the Biden WOTUS rule, was the sentencing judge.
4. "Idaho's Crown Jewel," Priest Lake Chamber of Commerce, accessed January 19, 2024, https://priestlake.org/.
5. Brief of Amicus Curiae, The National Association of Home Builders of the United States in Support of Petitioners, Sackett v. U.S. Environmental Protection Agency, No. 21-454 (U.S. April 18, 2022), 4.
6. Joint Appendix, Sackett v. U.S. Environmental Protection Agency, No. 21-454 (U.S. April 11, 2022), 32, 41.
7. Sackett v. U.S. Environmental Protection Agency, 566 U.S. 120, 123. Note that the concept of an accumulating fine for a continuing violation has a long history, dating back in the water context to the River and Harbor Act of 1890, when every month that an unapproved bridge remained in place resulted in a fresh $5,000 fine.
8. Ibid., 125–26.
9. Ibid., 126.
10. Ibid., 127.

11. Ibid., 132 (Alito, J., concurring).
12. Ibid.
13. Ibid.
14. Ibid., 133.
15. Sackett v. U.S. Environmental Protection Agency, 2019 WL 13026870, *9.
16. Sackett v. U.S. Environmental Protection Agency, 8 F.4th 1075, 1082 (9th Cir. 2021)
17. Ibid.
18. Ibid., 1083.
19. Ibid.
20. Ibid., 1085–86.
21. Ibid., 1092.
22. Ibid., 1092 note 13.
23. Ibid., 1093.
24. Sackett v. U.S. Environmental Protection Agency, 142 S. Ct. 896 (Mem) (2022).
25. Docket for No. 21-454, US Supreme Court, accessed January 19, 2024, https://www.supremecourt.gov/docket/docketfiles/html/public/21-454.html. It is somewhat absurd for members of Congress to file *amicus* briefs. If they are concerned about the misinterpretation of a law or an abuse of agency discretion, perhaps they should exercise their legislative authority.
26. Brief of Amici Curiae, State of West Virginia and 25 Other States in Support of Petitioners, Sackett v. U.S. Environmental Protection Agency, No. 21-454 (U.S. April 18, 2022), 5–7, 17.
27. Justin Stabley, "What You Need to Know about John Eastman's 2020 Election Charges," *PBS News Hour*, September 21, 2023, https://www.pbs.org/newshour/politics/what-you-need-to-know-about-john-eastmans-2020-election-charges.
28. Brief of Amicus Curiae, The Claremont Institute's Center for Constitutional Jurisprudence in Support of Petitioners, Sackett v. U.S. Environmental Protection Agency, No. 21-454 (U.S. April 18, 2022), 15–16.
29. Brief of the Liberty Justice Center as Amicus Curiae in Support of Petitioners, Sackett v. U.S. Environmental Protection Agency, No. 21-454 (U.S. April 14, 2022), 8–9.
30. Ibid., 9. Americans for Prosperity Foundation also filed an *amicus* brief raising the nondelegation issue. Brief of Amicus Curiae, Americans for Prosperity Foundation in Support of Petitioners, Sackett v. U.S. Environmental Protection Agency, No. 21-454 (U.S. April 14, 2022), 7.
31. Brief of Farm Bureaus of Arkansas, et al., as Amicus Curiae Supporting Petitioners, Sackett v. U.S. Environmental Protection Agency, No. 21-454 (U.S. April 20, 2022), 17.
32. Ibid., 20, 21 note 4.
33. Chris Jones, *The Swine Republic: Struggles with the Truth about Agriculture and Water Quality* (North Liberty, IA: Ice Cube Press, 2023).
34. Brief of Amici Curiae, Congressional Western Caucus Members in Support of Petitioners, Sackett v. U.S. Environmental Protection Agency, No. 21-454 (U.S. April 14, 2022), 8.

35. Ibid., 11.
36. Brief of Scientific Societies as Amici Curiae in Support of Respondents, Sackett v. U.S. Environmental Protection Agency, No. 21-454 (U.S. June 16, 2022), 2.
37. Ibid.
38. Ibid., 33.
39. Ibid., 32–34.
40. Brief for States of New York, et al., as Amici Curiae in Support of Respondents, Sackett v. U.S. Environmental Protection Agency, No. 21-454 (U.S. June 17, 2022).
41. Brief of Menominee Indian Tribe of Wisconsin, et al. as Amicus Curiae in Support of Respondents, Sackett v. U.S. Environmental Protection Agency, No. 21-454 (U.S. June 17, 2022).
42. Brief for American Sustainable Business Network, et al., as Amici Curiae in Support of Respondents, Sackett v. U.S. Environmental Protection Agency, No. 21-454 (U.S. June 16, 2022).
43. Ibid., 9.
44. John Fritze, "Supreme Court Kicks Off a New Term with Controversial Cases—and a New Justice," *USA Today*, October 3, 2022, https://www.usatoday.com/story/news/politics/2022/10/03/supreme-court-ketanji-brown-jackson-new-term/8118090001/.
45. Transcript of Oral Argument, Sackett v. U.S. Environmental Protection Agency, No. 21-454, October 3, 2022, 3–4.
46. Ibid., 4.
47. 33 U.S.C. § 1344(g)(1) (2024).
48. Transcript of Oral Argument, Sackett v. U.S. Environmental Protection Agency, 8.
49. Ibid., 61.
50. Ibid.
51. Ibid., 64.
52. Ibid., 76.
53. Ibid., 86.
54. Ibid., 89.
55. Ibid., 15–17.
56. Ibid., 9.
57. Ibid., 64.
58. It might have been the longest delay ever. Wikipedia provides such information by term but goes back only to 1999. "1999 Term Opinions of the Supreme Court of the United States," *Wikipedia*, accessed January 19, 2024, https://en.wikipedia.org/wiki/1999_term_opinions_of_the_Supreme_Court_of_the_United_States. See also Lawrence Hurley, "This Supreme Court is slow to issue rulings—glacially slow," *NBC News*, April 30, 2023, https://www.nbcnews.com/politics/supreme-court/supreme-court-slow-issue-rulings-glacially-slow-rcna81536.
59. See Brandon Hollingsworth, "In Unanimous Ruling, U.S. Supreme Court Backs North Idaho Couple, Narrows Clean Water Act," Spokane Public Radio, May 26, 2023, https://www.spokanepublicradio.org/

regional-news/2023-05-26/in-unanimous-ruling-u-s-supreme-court-backs-north-idaho-couple-narrows-clean-water-act; Daniel Harris, "A Resounding Victory for Clarity and Limited Government: Analyzing the 9-0 Supreme Court Decision in the Sackett Case," Arizona Farm Bureau, May 26, 2023, https://www.azfb.org/Article/A-Resounding-Victory-for-Clarity-and-Limited-Government-Analyzing-the-90-Supreme-Court-Decision-in-the-Sackett-Case.

60. Sackett v. U.S. Environmental Protection Agency, 598 U.S. 651, 658 (2023).
61. Ibid., 657.
62. Ibid., 658.
63. Ibid., 659.
64. Ibid.
65. Ibid.
66. Ibid., 660.
67. Ibid., 661.
68. Ibid., 660.
69. 48 Fed. Reg. 14,898 (April 6, 1983) (referring to cellar dirt as "excavation dirt and rock, broken concrete, rubble, tile, and other nonfloatable debris").
70. Sackett, 598 U.S. at 670.
71. United States v. Riverside Bayview Homes, Inc., 474 U.S. 121, 127 (1985).
72. Ibid.
73. Sackett, 598 U.S. at 671.
74. Ibid.
75. Ibid. (quoting *Rapanos*, quoting *Webster's Second*) (cleaned up).
76. Ibid., 671–72.
77. Ibid., 672.
78. Ibid.
79. Ibid.
80. Pub. Law No. 106-457, 114 Stat. 1957 (November 7, 2000).
81. Ibid., § 203.
82. "Chesapeake 2000," Chesapeake Bay Program, June 28, 2000, 5, https://d18lev1ok5leia.cloudfront.net/chesapeakebay/documents/cbp_12081.pdf.
83. Ibid.
84. 33 U.S.C. § 1344(g)(1) (2024) (emphasis added).
85. Sackett, 598 US at 675–76.
86. Ibid., 723 (Kavanaugh, J., concurring in the judgment).
87. Ibid., 713 (Kagan, J., concurring in the judgment).
88. Sackett, 598 U.S. at 676. This time, Justice Alito cited the 1976 edition of *Webster's Third*, a 1987 edition of *Random House Dictionary*, and a 2009 edition of the *Oxford American Dictionary & Thesaurus*. Again, he failed to cite a dictionary in use at the time of the enactment of the Clean Water Act, and one is left to wonder whether these happen to be dictionaries in easy reach on his bookcase.
89. Ibid., 678.
90. Ibid., 678–79.
91. Brief of Scientific Societies, 2.

92. Ibid., 32–34.
93. Sackett, 598 U.S. at 683.
94. Sackett, 598 U.S. at 686–87 (Thomas, J., concurring).
95. Ibid., 708–10.
96. Ibid., 685.
97. 77 U.S. (10 Wall.) 557 (1870).
98. Sackett, 598 U.S. at 698–99 (Thomas, J., concurring).
99. Ibid., 698.
100. Ibid., 699 note 5.
101. Ibid., 708.
102. Ibid.
103. Ibid., 711 (Kagan, J., concurring in the judgment).
104. Ibid., 711–12.
105. Ibid., 715.
106. Richard J. Lazarus, "Judicial Destruction of the Clean Water Act: *Sackett v. EPA*," *University of Chicago Law Review Online* (August 11, 2023): *10, https://lawreview.uchicago.edu/sites/default/files/2023-08/Lazarus%20ESSAY%20POST.pdf.
107. Sackett, 598 U.S. at 715–16 (Kavanaugh, J., concurring in the judgment).
108. Ibid., 722.
109. Ibid., 719.
110. Ibid., 716.
111. Ibid., 720–22.
112. "CEQ Chair Brenda Mallory Outlines Biden- Harris Administration's Vision for Clean Water Post-*Sackett v. EPA*," The White House, November 15, 2023, https://www.whitehouse.gov/ceq/news-updates/2023/11/15/ceq-chair-brenda-mallory-outlines-biden-harris-administrations-vision-for-clean-water-post-sackett-v-epa/.
113. Zippy Duvall, "Supreme Court Confirms, EPA Went Out of Bounds on Waters of the U.S.," American Farm Bureau Federation, May 31, 2023, https://www.fb.org/the-zipline/supreme-court-confirms-epa-went-out-of-bounds-on-waters-of-the-u-s.
114. "Geographic Information Systems Analysis of the Surface Drinking Water Provided by Intermittent, Ephemeral, and Headwater Streams in the U.S.," US Environmental Protection Agency, accessed January 19, 2024, https://www.epa.gov/cwa-404/geographic-information-systems-analysis-surface-drinking-water-provided-intermittent.
115. Ibid.
116. US Environmental Protection Agency, "Glossary," accessed January 19, 2024, https://www.epa.gov/sites/default/files/2016-02/documents/realestate_glossary.pdf.
117. Ariel Wittenberg, "Where EPA Saw No Data, Trout Unlimited Crunched the Numbers," *E&E News*, April 1, 2019, https://www.eenews.net/articles/where-epa-saw-no-data-trout-unlimited-crunched-the-numbers/.
118. U.S. Environmental Protection Agency, "Glossary."
119. Rapanos v. United States, 547 U.S. 715, 732 note 5 (2006) (plurality opinion).

120. Ibid.
121. Sackett, 598 U.S. at 726 (Kavanaugh, J., concurring in the judgment).
122. Ibid. As Justice Kavanaugh noted, "Those are just two of many examples of how the Court's overly narrow view of the Clean Water Act will have concrete impact." *Concrete* was an apt word choice, in light of the anticipated filling of now unprotected wetlands.
123. "Unpacking the Revised WOTUS Rule," *Environmental Law Reporter* 53 (2023): 10,890 (remarks of Brian Frazer, Director of the Office of Wetlands, Oceans, and Watersheds, U.S. Environmental Protection Agency).
124. Sackett, 598 U.S. at 678–79, 684.
125. Sackett, 598 U.S. at 727 (Kavanaugh, concurring in the judgment).
126. "CEQ Chair Brenda Mallory Outlines Biden– Harris Administration's Vision for Clean Water Post-*Sackett v. EPA*," The White House.
127. Michael Cain and Tom Bernthal, "Mapping Potential Impacts on WI Wetlands *Post-Sackett*," October 31, 2023, https://www.youtube.com/watch?v=Iv-42AF0AhQ.
128. Ibid.
129. "Protect New Mexico Waters," *Protect New Mexico Waters*, accessed January 20, 2024, https://nmwaters.org/.
130. The analysis was conducted as part of a joint project between Stetson University and the National Parks Conservation Association.
131. "Clean Water Act—"Waters of the United States"—Sackett v. EPA," *Harvard Law Review*, 137 (2023): 397.
132. "Amendments to the 2023 Rule," US Environmental Protection Agency, accessed January 19, 2024, https://www.epa.gov/wotus/amendments-2023-rule.
133. 88 Fed. Reg. 61,964 (2023).
134. Ibid., 61,964–65.
135. Lewis v. United States, 88 F.4th 1073, 1078 (5th Cir. 2023).

Chapter 13

136. Earthea Nance, "U.S. Environmental Protection Agency, Initial Revised Designation Decision and Record of Decision in Response to a Petition by Amigos Bravos for a Determination that Stormwater Discharges in Los Alamos County Contribute to Water Quality Standards Violations and Require Clean Water Act Permit Coverage," Appendix 5, 5–6, November 6, 2023.
137. Jay Austin and Bruce Myers, "Anchoring the Clean Water Act: Congress's Constitutional Sources of Power to Protect the Nation's Waters," Environmental Law Institute, July 2007, https://www.eli.org/sites/default/files/eli-pubs/d17_07.pdf.
138. 88 Fed. Reg. 17,755 (2023).
139. Michael Grunwald, *The Swamp: The Everglades, Florida, and the Politics of Paradise* (New York: Simon & Schuster, 2006): 286–332.
140. Austin and Myers, "Anchoring the Clean Water Act," 12.

141. "Agricultural Conservation Easement Program," Natural Resources Conservation Service, accessed February 5, 2024, https://www.nrcs.usda.gov/programs-initiatives/acep-agricultural-conservation-easement-program.
142. US Government Accountability Office, "Agricultural Conservation: USDA's Environmental Quality Incentives Program Could Be Improved to Optimize Benefits," GAO-17-225, April 2017.
143. Royal C. Gardner, *Lawyers, Swamps, and Money: U.S. Wetland Law, Policy, and Politics* (Washington, DC: Island Press, 2011), 100–1.
144. Rebecca Brooke, Gregory Fogel, Aviva Glaser, Elizabeth Griffin, and Kristen Johnson, "Corn Ethanol and Wildlife," National Wildlife Federation, 2009, https://www.nwf.org/~/media/PDFs/Wildlife/01-13-10-Corn-Ethanol-Wildlife.ashx.
145. Jaclyn Lopez, "From Bail Out to Righting the Course: The Commonsense Action the United States Must Take to Address Its Flood Crisis," *Tulane Environmental Law Journal* 33 (2020): 1–2.
146. James McElfish, "State Protection of Nonfederal Waters: Turbidity Continues," *Environmental Law Reporter* 52 (2022): 10,683–84.
147. Hannah Grover, "Legislature Looks to Address Ramifications of *Sackett* Decision," *New Mexico Political Report*, January 26, 2024, https://www.tricityrecordnm.com/articles/its-time-for-new-mexico-to-protect-its-own-waters-and-wetlands/.
148. Heather Sackett, "Colorado Lawmakers Expected to Consider State Permit Program Protecting Wetlands," *Aspen Journalism*, December 1, 2023, https://aspenjournalism.org/colorado-lawmakers-expected-to-consider-state-permit-program-protecting-wetlands/.
149. "Passed! Historic Wetlands Protections Included in New York State Budget," *Audubon New York*, April 8, 2022, https://ny.audubon.org/about-us/passed-historic-wetlands-protections-included-new-york-state-budget.
150. Jason Totoiu and Jaclyn Lopez, "Holding States Accountable for Harmful Algal Blooms: Florida's Water Crisis in Focus," *University of Florida Journal of Law and Public Policy*, 33 (2022): 1–79.
151. 16 U.S.C. § 1453 (2024). The CZMA applies to the coastal zone, which means "the coastal waters (including the lands therein and thereunder) and the adjacent shorelands (including the waters therein and thereunder), strongly influenced by each other and in proximity to the shorelines of the several coastal states, and includes islands, transitional and intertidal areas, salt marshes, wetlands, and beaches." Ibid., (1). In turn, "coastal waters" includes "estuary-type areas such as bays, shallows, and marshes and . . . in other areas, those waters, adjacent to the shorelines, which contain a measurable quantity or percentage of sea water, including, but not limited to, sounds, bays, lagoons, bayous, ponds, and estuaries." Ibid., (3).
152. "State Coastal Zone Boundaries," National Oceanic and Atmospheric Administration, February 9, 2012, https://coast.noaa.gov/data/czm/media/StateCZBoundaries.pdf.
153. Ibid., 1.
154. Ibid., 4.

155. 33 U.S.C. § 1377 (2024).
156. Jon Kusler, "Common Questions: Local Government Wetland Protection Programs," *Association of State Wetland Managers* (2006): 2.
157. "State, Tribal and Local Initiatives," US Environmental Protection Agency, accessed February 5, 2024, https://archive.epa.gov/water/archive/web/html/initiative_index.html#local.
158. Florida Statutes § 259.1055(3) (2023).
159. Traci Deen, "Florida's Wildlife Corridor Got a Huge Boost in the New Budget," *Tampa Bay Times*, July 12, 2023, https://www.tampabay.com/opinion/2023/07/12/floridas-wildlife-corridor-got-huge-boost-new-budget-column/.
160. Jessica B. Wilkinson, James M. McElfish Jr., Rebecca Kihslinger, Robert Bendick, and Bruce A. McKenney, "The Next Generation of Mitigation: Linking Current and Future Mitigation Programs with State Wildlife Action Plans and Other State and Regional Plans," *Environmental Law Institute and The Nature Conservancy* (2009): 12.
161. "Ballot Initiative," *Ballotpedia*, accessed February 5, 2024, https://ballotpedia.org/Ballot_initiative.
162. "Marijuana Laws and Ballot Measures in the United States," *Ballotpedia*, accessed February 5, 2024, https://ballotpedia.org/Marijuana_laws_and_ballot_measures_in_the_United_States#Marijuana_laws_enacted_by_statewide_ballot_measures.
163. G. T. Davies et al., "Towards a Universal Declaration of the Rights of Wetlands," *Marine and Freshwater Research* 72 (2021): 593–600.
164. Ibid., 597.
165. Ibid.
166. Katie Surma, "Two Lakes, Two Streams and a Marsh Filed a Lawsuit in Florida to Stop a Developer from Filling In Wetlands. A Judge Just Threw It Out of Court," *Inside Climate News*, July 7, 2022, https://insideclimatenews.org/news/07072022/two-lakes-two-streams-and-a-marsh-filed-a-lawsuit-in-florida-to-stop-a-developer-from-filling-in-wetlands-a-judge-just-threw-it-out-of-court/.
167. Ibid.
168. Molly Duerig, "Orange County Is Updating Its Wetlands Protections," WMFE, September 27, 2023, https://www.wmfe.org/environment/2023-09-27/orange-county-updating-wetlands-protections.
169. Julien Bétaille, "Rights of Nature: Why It Might Not Save the Entire World," *Journal for European Environmental & Planning Law* 16 (2019): 35–64.
170. "Legislature Overrides Veto of Bill Cutting Wetland Regulation," CoastalReview.org, June 27, 2023, https://coastalreview.org/2023/06/legislature-overrides-veto-of-bill-cutting-wetland-regulation/.
171. Walker Livingston, "Numerous N.C. Wetlands Lose Protections under Farm Act and SCOTUS Case," *The Daily Tar Heel*, September 5, 2023, https://www.dailytarheel.com/article/2023/09/city-north-carolina-wetlands-farm-bill-environmental-impacts.

172. Nicole Rogers, "Manatee County Strips Wetland Protections, Refers to State Guidelines," News Channel 8, October 6, 2023, https://www.wfla.com/news/local-news/manatee-county/manatee-county-strips-wetland-protections-refers-to-state-guidelines/.
173. Florida Statutes § 373.4592(4)(e)2 (2023).
174. Miccosukee Tribe of Indians of Florida v. United States, 2010 WL 1506267 (S.D. Fla., April 14, 2010).
175. Amy Green, "Climate Change Forces a Rethinking of Mammoth Everglades Restoration Plan," *Inside Climate News*, May 9, 2023, https://insideclimatenews.org/news/09052023/climate-change-florida-everglades-restoration-plan/.
176. Yacob Reyes, "Florida Legislature Moves to Block Fertilizer Bans," *Axios Tampa Bay*, May 3, 2023, https://www.axios.com/local/tampa-bay/2023/05/03/florida-fertilizer-ban-measure.
177. Florida Senate Bill 1240 (2023), https://www.flsenate.gov/Session/Bill/2023/1240/BillText/Filed/PDF.
178. Raphael Warnock, Twitter post. June 16, 2022, 6:48 PM, https://twitter.com/ReverendWarnock/status/1537567707738132495.

Index

Pages indicating figures are in italics. Pages indicating tables are in bold type.

About the Author

Photo by Mary Fahy

Royal C. Gardner is the Hugh F. Culverhouse Professor of Law and Director of the Institute for Biodiversity Law and Policy at Stetson University College of Law in Florida, where he likes to take students on swamp walks in the Western Everglades. He went to Georgetown University on an Army ROTC scholarship, after which the Army was kind enough to permit him to attend Boston College Law School and clerk for a federal judge in Rhode Island before calling him to active duty. He had an odd military career, spent entirely in the Pentagon, where he was the Department of the Army's principal wetland attorney from 1989 to 1993, when he was introduced to WOTUS issues. A member of the National Research Council's Committee on Mitigating Wetland Losses, he co-authored *Compensating for Wetland Losses under the Clean Water Act*, which was an impetus for the US Environmental Protection Agency and US Army Corps of Engineers' compensatory mitigation regulations. He has served as *pro bono* counsel to aquatic scientists and scientific societies, submitting *amicus* briefs on their behalf to federal courts, including the US Supreme Court in *County of Maui v. Hawaii Wildlife Fund* and *Sackett v. U.S. Environmental Protection Agency*.

At the international level, Professor Gardner served two terms (2013–2018) as chair of the Scientific and Technical Review Panel, the scientific advisory body of the Ramsar Convention, a wetland conservation treaty with more than 170 Contracting Parties, including the United States. He was a co-lead coordinating author of the Ramsar Convention's inaugural *Global Wetland Outlook: State of the World's Wetlands and Their Services to People*.

Some of his other works have appeared in *Nature*, *Wetlands*, *Harvard Environmental Law Review*, *Stanford Environmental Law Journal*, *Ecology Law Quarterly*, *Georgetown International Environmental Law Review*, *Virginia Environmental Law Journal*, and *Iowa Law Review*, and includes *Lawyers, Swamps, and Money: U.S. Wetland Law, Policy, and Politics*, published by Island Press.